IMMIGRATION APPEA
[2021] Imm AR 383-678

LONDON: TSO

a Williams Lea company

Published by TSO (The Stationery Office), part of
Williams Lea, and available from:

Online
www.tsoshop.co.uk

Mail, Telephone, Fax & E-mail
TSO
PO Box 29, Norwich, NR3 1GN
Telephone orders/General enquiries: 0333 202 5070
Fax orders: 0333 202 5080
E-mail: customer.services@tso.co.uk
Textphone 0333 202 5077

TSO@Blackwell and other Accredited Agents

First published 2021

ISBN 9780117851405

ISSN 0966-758 X

Printed in the United Kingdom by The Stationery Office

J003788548   c4.75   07/21

Table of Cases

In [2021] Imm AR

Pages 1 – 382 are in the first issue
Pages 383 – 678 are in the second issue

Decisions of the Upper Tribunal, Immigration and Asylum Chamber can be found at https://tribunalsdecisions.service.gov.uk/utiac

Alphabetical Table of Cases

In [2021] Imm AR

Pages 1 – 382 are in the first issue
Pages 383 – 678 are in the second issue

Subject Index of Cases Reported

In [2021] Imm AR

Pages 1 – 382 are in the first issue
Pages 383 – 678 are in the second issue

EVIDENCE

Assessment of Evidence

Credibility of the Claimants

Documentary Evidence

HUMAN RIGHTS

Article 6 of the ECHR

Article 8 of the ECHR

Article 14 of the ECHR

Home Office Policies and Concessions

Proportionality

IMMIGRATION

Entry Clearance

Leave to Remain

PROCEDURE AND PROCESS

Deportation

Grounds of Appeal

Home Office Procedures

Judicial Review

One-stop Appeals

Out-of-country Appeals

Procedure Rules

Review

Rights of Appeal

RISK ON RETURN

Homosexuals

LLD (BY HER MOTHER AND NEXT FRIEND) v SECRETARY OF STATE FOR THE HOME DEPARTMENT

COURT OF APPEAL IN NORTHERN IRELAND

Stephens, Treacy and McCloskey LJJ

[2020] NICA 38
31 July 2020

Immigration – entry clearance – paragraph 320(7A) of the Immigration Rules – false document submitted – dishonesty – Hameed [2019] EWCA Civ 1324 not binding in Northern Ireland – Adedoyin [2010] EWCA Civ 773 followed

The Claimant was a 16-year-old citizen of the Philippines. Her mother, a Filipino national and British citizen, had resided and worked in Northern Ireland during most of the last 17 years. In 2015, the Claimant's mother applied to the Secretary of State for the Home Department for entry clearance for the Claimant, then aged 12, to reside with her in Northern Ireland. In making the application, the Claimant's mother provided a birth certificate in respect of the Claimant. The Entry Clearance Officer ("ECO") refused the application under paragraph 320(7A) of the Immigration Rules HC 395 (as amended) on the ground that the Claimant's birth certificate had been fraudulently obtained. Paragraph 320(7A) provided for the mandatory refusal of entry clearance where, *inter alia*, in relation to the application 'false representations' had been made or 'false documents or information' had been submitted 'whether or not material to the application, and whether or not to the applicant's knowledge'. In March 2018, the First-tier Tribunal ("FtT") dismissed the Claimant's appeal. The Upper Tribunal ("UT") also dismissed the appeal on the ground relating to paragraph 320(7A) of the Immigration Rules, although it set aside the FtT's decision as it related to Article 8 of the ECHR alone and remitted the case for fresh decision-making. It was accepted before the UT that the 'birth certificate' was a false document and the UT held that that alone was sufficient for paragraph 320(7A) to be made out. The UT concluded that, although it was not understood why the Claimant's mother used a false document, that did not take the document out of the category captured by paragraph 320(7A).

On application for permission to appeal against the UT's decision, the Claimant submitted that, interpreted correctly, paragraph 320(7A) of the Immigration Rules was breached in respect of a false document only when there was dishonest promotion of that document for the purpose of obtaining entry clearance. The Claimant further submitted that *Hameed v Secretary of State for the Home Department* [2019] EWCA Civ 1324, in which the Court of Appeal held that a false document was itself dishonest and there was no need to establish dishonesty or deception on the part of an applicant or another, was wrongly decided and conflicted with the approach in *Adedoyin v Secretary of State for the Home Department* (aka *AA (Nigeria) v Secretary of State for the Home Department*) [2010] EWCA Civ 773. The Claimant argued that the application of paragraph 320(7A) to her case breached her rights under Article 8 of the ECHR because, notwithstanding that a refusal to permit a child entry clearance to live with her mother amounted to an obvious interference with family life, paragraph 320(7A) had been treated as mandating a refusal of entry clearance, irrespective of any actual dishonesty on the part of any person being established. It was common ground that the grant of leave to appeal would be appropriate only if the proposed appeal met the 'second appeal test' in that it raised some important point of principle or practice, or there was some other compelling reason to hear the appeal, in accordance with section 13(6) of the Tribunals, Courts and Enforcement Act 2007. The Court considered the correct interpretation of the word 'false' in paragraph 320(7A) of the Immigration Rules, and whether the appeal raised an important point of principle or practice or there was some other compelling reason for the appeal to be heard.

Held, granting the application and allowing the appeal:

(1) In *Adedoyin* the Court of Appeal considered the meaning of the word 'false' in paragraph 322(1A) of the Rules, the language of which replicated precisely that of paragraph 320(7A). It decided that 'false' did not denote 'incorrect' but rather its true meaning was 'dishonest'. It entailed the making of deliberate lies, to be contrasted with statements which did not accord with the true facts. Thus, a representation was to be characterised as false within the compass of paragraph 322(1A), and, by extension, paragraph 320(7A), only if there had been dishonesty or deception on the part of a relevant person. Rix LJ observed that a false document was one which 'tells a lie about itself'. That did not however justify a mandatory refusal decision under the Immigration Rules unless the falsity could be linked to the dishonest state of mind of a relevant person. The Secretary of State's submission that, based on *Adedoyin*, the requirement to establish dishonesty was confined to false representation cases and did not extend to cases of false documents found no support in either the Immigration Rules or the judgment in *Adedoyin*, and was rejected (*paras 28 – 32*).

(2) In *Hameed*, the Court stated that *Adedoyin* established that 'a false document is itself dishonest and that fact avoids the need to establish dishonesty or deception on the part of an applicant or another'. In the instant case, the Court considered that, properly construed and considered in its full context, the passage at paragraph [65] of *Adedoyin* was not intended to suggest that a document was capable of being dishonest, whether in the regime of Part 9 of the Immigration Rules or otherwise. Human beings were capable of being dishonest. Documents, in contrast, were either false or genuine, accurate or inaccurate, correct or incorrect and so forth. The assessment of a document entailed a purely forensic exercise, whereas the assessment of whether a human being had engaged in dishonesty involved exploring the state of mind of the person concerned and the making of findings which would normally be based on appropriate inferences and, sometimes, on direct evidence such as a written or oral statement evincing an intention to deceive. Paragraph [65] of *Adedoyin* was not to be construed narrowly or literally, at the expense of the remainder of the paragraph in question and the ensuing passages. It was important to consider Rix LJ's detailed analysis at paragraphs [65] to [77] of *Adedoyin* as a whole. It was striking that in *Hameed* the later division of the Court of Appeal focused only on paragraph [67] and it misunderstood that discrete passage. The Court of Appeal in *Hameed* purported to

apply *Adedoyin* but fell into error. The decision in *Hameed* was irreconcilable with *Adedoyin* (*paras 33 – 36*).

(3) The Supreme Court's judgment in *Ivey v Genting Casinos (UK) Ltd* [2017] UKSC 67, in which Lord Hughes gave guidance on the issue of dishonesty, was not considered by the Court of Appeal in *Hameed*. Lord Hughes' formulation regarding dishonesty, provided in the context of a civil case, should be accorded broad application. There was no reason in principle or otherwise why it should not apply to the relevant provisions of the Immigration Rules. Coherence and predictability in the legal system were long recognised and essential attributes. The DNA of dishonesty was the same, in whatever legal context it featured. Thus, while the context of the decision in *Hameed* was a specific provision of the Rules it was plainly incompatible with *Ivey*. That reinforced the conclusion that *Hameed* was erroneously decided (*paras 37 – 41*).

(4) The Court was bound by neither of the decisions in *Adedoyin* and *Hameed* because decisions of the English Court of Appeal were of persuasive, and not binding, authority in the instant jurisdiction. Given the conclusion that *Adedoyin* was misunderstood and misapplied in *Hameed* the first step was to choose between the two decisions. The analysis and reasoning in *Adedoyin* were cogent. The more recent decision in *Balajigari and Others v Secretary of State for the Home Department* [2019] EWCA Civ 673, which the Court had endorsed, was harmonious with *Adedoyin* and irreconcilable with *Hameed*. Finally, the decision in *Ivey* was supportive of *Adedoyin* and further undermined *Hameed*. Giving effect to that analysis, the decision in *Adedoyin* would be followed. Thus, the decisions of the FtT and the UT, dismissing the Claimant's appeal against the refusal to grant her entry clearance on the basis that her application had relied upon a birth certificate which had been 'fraudulently obtained', purporting to apply paragraph 320(7A) of the Rules, were erroneous in law. If leave to appeal were granted, the appeal would succeed (*paras 45 – 48 and 51*).

(5) The correct interpretation of the Immigration Rules was certainly a matter of principle. There were two conflicting decisions of the English Court of Appeal on the interpretation of paragraph 320(7A) of the Rules and it was inevitable that uncertainty and debate would have been generated in consequence. The Secretary of State had been making decisions based on an erroneous interpretation of both *Adedoyin* and *Hameed* and would continue to do so indefinitely unless corrected judicially. Allied to that was the consideration that the language of paragraph 320(7A) was mirrored in three further provisions within Part 9 of the Immigration Rules. The appeal raised an important point of principle and it followed that the grant of leave to appeal was appropriate. The ultimate issue to be determined by the FtT upon remittal was whether the refusal decision infringed the Article 8 rights of the Claimant and the other family members concerned. It was for the FtT to explore how and why the contentious birth certificate was generated and provided in support of the Claimant's entry clearance application. If the FtT were to conclude that the Secretary of State's invocation of paragraph 320(7A) was lawful, that would not be determinative of the appeal. Rather, questions such as whose dishonesty, the gravity of the dishonesty, its materiality and the apparent motive would all have a bearing on the Article 8 proportionality balancing exercise (*paras 49 – 57 and 59 – 60*).

Cases referred to:

AA (Nigeria) v Secretary of State for the Home Department [2010] EWCA Civ 773; [2011] 1 WLR 564; [2010] Imm AR 704; [2011] INLR 1

Balajigari and Others v Secretary of State for the Home Department [2019] EWCA Civ 673; [2019] 1 WLR 4647; [2019] 4 All ER 998; [2019] Imm AR 1152; [2019] INLR 619

Baranowski v Rice [2014] NIQB 122; [2016] NI 155

Barton and Booth v R [2020] EWCA Crim 575; [2020] 3 WLR 1333; [2020] 4 All ER 742

Eba v Advocate General for Scotland [2011] UKSC 29; [2011] 3 WLR 149; [2011] STI 1941; [2011] Imm AR 745

Hameed v Secretary of State for the Home Department [2019] EWCA Civ 1324; [2020] Imm AR 154

Ivey v Genting Casinos (UK) Ltd t/a Crockfords [2017] UKSC 67; [2018] AC 391; [2017] 3 WLR 1212; [2018] 2 All ER 406

Khawaja v Secretary of State for the Home Department; Khera v Secretary of State for the Home Department [1984] AC 74; [1983] 2 WLR 321; [1983] 1 All ER 765; [1982] Imm AR 139

LD (Article 8 – best interests of the child) Zimbabwe [2010] UKUT 278 (IAC); [2011] Imm AR 99; [2011] INLR 347

Mostafa (Article 8 in entry clearance) [2015] UKUT 112 (IAC)

PR (Sri Lanka); SS (Bangladesh); TC (Zimbabwe) v Secretary of State for the Home Department [2011] EWCA Civ 988; [2012] 1 WLR 73; [2011] Imm AR 904; [2012] INLR 92

R v Ghosh [1982] QB 1053; [1982] 3 WLR 110; [1982] 2 All ER 689

R v Pabon [2018] EWCA Crim 420

Secretary of State for the Home Department v Pankina and Others [2010] EWCA Civ 719; [2011] QB 376; [2010] 3 WLR 1526; [2011] 1 All ER 1043; [2010] Imm AR 689; [2010] INLR 529

Steponaviciene, In the matter of an application for judicial review v One of the Coroners for Northern Ireland [2018] NIQB 90

Uphill (Widow and Administrator of the Estate of Malcolm Ernest Uphill) v BRB (Residuary) Ltd [2005] EWCA Civ 60; [2005] 1 WLR 2070; [2005] 3 All ER 264

Legislation and international instruments judicially considered:

Civil Procedure Rules, rule 52.13(2)
European Convention on Human Rights, Articles 6 & 8
Human Rights Act 1998, section 6
Immigration Act 1971, sections 1(4) & 3(2)
Tribunals, Courts and Enforcement Act 2007, sections 11, 13 & 14
Tribunal Procedure (Upper Tribunal) Rules 2008, rule 14

Representation

Mr D Scoffield QC and *Mr S McQuitty*, for the Claimant;
Mr P Henry instructed by the Crown Office Solicitor, for the Secretary of State.

Judgment

MCCLOSKEY LJ (delivering the judgment of the court):

Glossary

The Appellant:	LLD
SSHD:	Secretary of State for the Home Department (the Respondent)
FtT:	First-tier Tribunal, Immigration and Asylum Chamber
UT:	Upper Tribunal, Immigration and Asylum Chamber
The Rules:	The Immigration Rules
The 1971 Act:	Immigration Act 1971
The 2007 Act:	Tribunals, Courts and Enforcement Act 2007
The 2008 Rules:	The Tribunal Procedure (Upper Tribunal) Rules 2008

Introduction

[1] This is an application by LLD, whom we shall describe as "the Appellant", for leave to appeal to this court against the decision of the Upper Tribunal, Immigration and Asylum Chamber (the "UT") dated 7 October 2019. The central issue of law raised is the meaning of the word "false" in paragraph 320(7A) of the Immigration Rules.

Relief sought

[2] In the more detailed terms of the formal motion, the Appellant seeks –

"… leave to appeal, pursuant to the provisions of section 13(4) of the Tribunals, Courts and Enforcement Act 2007, against the decision of the Upper Tribunal (Immigration and Asylum Chamber), Upper Tribunal Judge Dawson, promulgated on 07 October 2017 and which affirmed, in part, the decision of the First-tier Tribunal (Immigration and Asylum Chamber), First-tier Tribunal Judge Farrelly, promulgated on 13 March 2018, to the effect that the Appellant's application for entry clearance had breached paragraph 320(7A) of the Immigration Rules by the submission of a false document."

The effect of section 13 of the 2007 Act is that while the Appellant may appeal to this court against the decision of the UT such appeal lies only with the permission of the UT or the leave of this court. In this case the UT has been requested, and has refused, to grant permission to appeal, thus stimulating the present application.

Anonymity

[3] It is appropriate to dwell a little on the issue of anonymity given the *prima facie* incongruity arising out of the differing approaches by the two tribunals in the underlying proceedings. The Appellant, a Filipino national, is aged 16 years. The factual framework is rehearsed in greater detail *infra*. The impetus for every stage of this litigation was the decision of SSHD refusing the Appellant's application for entry clearance to enter and reside in the United Kingdom for family reunification purposes.

[4] In summary:

(a)   The first judicial decision in the litigation history, that of the FtT, did not grant the Appellant anonymity and, indeed, specifically recorded "*NO ANONYMITY DIRECTION MADE*".

(b)   There is no indication that the Appellant sought anonymity in her application for leave to appeal to the UT.

(c)   The Appellant was not anonymised in the decision of the FtT refusing permission to appeal.

(d)   Ditto in the decision of the UT granting leave to appeal.

(e)   In the ensuing decision of the UT the Appellant was anonymised via the acronym of "DL".

(f)   The Appellant is not anonymised in the formal documents constituting the application to this court or in subsequently generated documents such as skeleton arguments. Nor was any application for anonymity made initially.

[5] This court drew to the attention of the parties the apparent incongruity between the substantive decision and order of the UT and everything preceding and following same. In response the parties were unable to provide any enlightenment. In addition the Appellant's representatives initially indicated that they had no specific instructions to apply to this court for the grant of anonymity, adding that nonetheless this protection may be appropriate as the Appellant "… is a minor and the case concerns some sensitive details about her private and family life … [and anonymity] … would effectively limit the Appellant's public exposure by these proceedings". The representatives of SSHD adopted a neutral stance. In response to further specific direction of the court a belated application for anonymity, with accompanying further submissions, materialised.

[6] In summary, the principle of open justice, vouchsafed by both the common law and Art. 6(1) ECHR, falls to be applied in conjunction with the Art. 8 ECHR private life rights of the Appellant and other family members in the context of the duty owed by the court *qua* public authority under s 6 of the Human rights Act 1998. In Article 8 cases, it is incumbent on the court to conduct a balancing exercise, weighing the extent of the interference with the individual's privacy on the one hand against the general interest at issue on the other hand. In cases of the present type, the public interest in play is the imperative for justice to be transacted in public in all respects. Every case in which some degree of anonymity is permitted by the court involves an adjustment of this public interest, with the individual's right prevailing.

[7] The issue of anonymity is the subject of Guidance Notes in both the FtT and the UT. The court invited the parties to address, *inter alia*, these instruments and received further submissions in response. The first of the two relevant instruments is the FtT Presidential Guidance Note No 2 of 2011. This, among other things, provides that where anonymity is granted "brief reasons" for this course should be furnished by the judge.

[8] In the UT the equivalent instrument is Guidance Note No 1 of 2013, made by the Chamber President. The context and rationale of this measure are understood by noting firstly rule 14(1) of the Tribunal Procedure (Upper Tribunal) Rules 2008 (the "2008 Rules") which empowers the UT to make an order prohibiting the disclosure or publication of either "specified documents or information relating to the proceedings" or "any matter likely to lead members of the public to identify any person whom the Upper Tribunal considers should not be identified". Rule 14(2) elaborates on this. Rule 14 of the 2008 Rules features prominently in the aforementioned UT Guidance Note, which contains a section entitled "Principles To Be Applied". In common with its FtT counterpart, the UT Guidance Note also provides (at paragraph 21) that the decision of the tribunal should "explain the reasons for the order and its scope".

[9] The direction to the parties noted in [5] above elicited from the Appellant's legal representatives a formal application for anonymity or, alternatively, a "suitable reporting restriction". This was founded firstly on Article 170(7) of the Children (NI) Order 1995 (the "1995 Order"). It is necessary to consider Article 170(6) and (7) in tandem:

"(6)   This paragraph applies to any proceedings other than criminal proceedings or proceedings to which paragraph (2) applies.

(7)   In relation to any proceedings to which paragraph (6) applies, the court may direct that no person shall publish any material which is intended, or likely, to identify –

(a)   any child as being involved in those proceedings; or

(b)   an address or school as being that of a child involved in any such proceedings,

except insofar (if at all) as may be permitted by the direction of the court."

Any contravention of Article 170 is, per paragraph (9), a summary offence. It is clear from the overall architecture of Article 170 that paragraph (7) is of broad scope. In particular, it is *not* confined to proceedings under the 1995 Order. The scheme of Article 170 is that rules of court are designed to cater for issues of private hearings and the anonymity of children in proceedings under the 1995 Order. But this does not apply to Art. 170(7). We consider that this provision does not modify the common law principles or Art. 6 or Art. 8 ECHR which, in unison, must guide our determination of the anonymity issue.

[10] The Appellant's legal representatives in their further submissions, supported by an affidavit, have highlighted a series of factual matters which they characterised "highly sensitive in nature". We shall refrain from detailing these. It suffices to state that they bear upon the Appellant's true identity, the conduct of and fears relating to her biological father and intimate details of her upbringing and family arrangements.

[11] It was submitted that the protection of anonymity is required in order to avoid an infringement of the Appellant's right to respect for private and family life protected by Article 8 ECHR and section 6 of the Human Rights Act 1998. The application for anonymity also prayed in aid the tribunal instruments and procedural rule noted above. Furthermore, this court was invited to infer that the UT Judge, one of the most experienced members of that chamber (we observe), was clearly satisfied that anonymity was necessary to protect the Article 8 rights of the Appellant and other family members concerned and/or to protect the welfare of the Appellant. It was further contended that this approach is reflected in the content and structure of the UT decision. The court permitted the filing of a belated affidavit sworn by the Appellant's mother provided to establish an evidential foundation for the anonymity application. There was, appropriately, no objection on behalf of SSHD. We admit this further evidence.

[12] There is a further consideration to be reckoned. The UT, acting on its own initiative, specifically made an order under rule 14 of the 2008 Rules –

"... prohibiting disclosure of any matter that may lead to the identification of the Appellant and other parties to these proceedings ... [adding] ... Any breach may lead to contempt proceedings."

In the title of its decision the UT described the Appellant as "DL (Anonymity direction made)". The decision itself was deftly crafted by the UT Judge in a manner which prevents the Appellant from being identified. The anonymity order of the UT Judge benefits from the principle of presumptive validity (or regularity) and has not been challenged from any quarter. It is *prima facie* consonant with the relevant UT instrument and procedural rule.

[13] We determine the issue of the Appellant's anonymity in the following way. In so doing we adopt as our point of departure the overarching principle of open justice. We note further the absence of any mandatory statutory provision or binding judicial authority mandating this court to adopt any particular course. We also take into account the general rule promulgated in the two aforementioned tribunal instruments, in relatively strong terms, that neither the identity of a child nor information which could identify a child should be published. While it is not for this court to question the wisdom of this general rule in the forum of specialised tribunals and we understand it to be one of some longevity, we conceive our primary duty to be to apply the common law principles and Arts 6 and 8 ECHR.

In summary, the principle of open justice, vouchsafed by both the common law and Art. 6(1) ECHR, falls to be applied in conjunction with the Art. 8 ECHR private life rights of the Appellant and other family members in the context of the duty owed by the court *qua* public authority under s 6 of the Human rights Act 1998. In Article 8 cases, it is incumbent on the court to conduct a balancing exercise, weighing the extent of the interference with the individual's privacy on the one hand against the general interest at issue on the other hand. In cases of the present type, the public interest in play is the imperative for justice to be transacted in public in all respects. Every case in which some degree of anonymity is permitted by the court involves an adjustment of this public interest, with the individual's right prevailing.

[14] It follows from the foregoing that the Appellant should have been anonymised in like manner in the application to this court and in all documents generated thereby, with an accompanying application for continuing anonymity. This did not occur. The likely explanation would appear to be human error. We need enquire no further. The question for this court, which must form its own independent view and make a fresh assessment and ruling, is whether there are grounds for differing from the UT. Having considered all of the material evidence and submissions, including the recently provided affidavit, we are satisfied that the Appellant should continue to benefit from anonymity. In a nutshell, the intimate and sensitive details and features of her private and family life and that of other family members outweigh the public interest in open justice in this discrete respect. Accordingly, we replicate the anonymity order of the UT. The principle of open justice will prevail otherwise.

[15] The practical out-workings of this discrete order will impose a series of responsibilities on the parties' legal representatives which must be discharged with the minimum of delay. We draw attention to the Sensitive Schedule devised by the court. Its contents will be read and recorded or stored by the parties and their legal representatives only and will not be published in any way. It will also be available to future courts and tribunals.[1]

Relevant Immigration Rules

[16] The Immigration Rules ("the Rules") are a hybrid species of quasi legislation which, per section 1(4) of the Immigration Act 1971 (the "1971 Act"), specify "... the practice to be followed in the administration of this Act for regulating the entry into and stay in the United Kingdom of persons not having the right of abode...", the latter being the cornerstone of the system of immigration control in the United Kingdom. The Rules, by section 3(2), are laid before Parliament from time to time and may be rejected by negative resolution. Their legal status has been described as that of "quasi-law" (*Secretary of State for the Home Department v Pankina* [2010] EWCA Civ 719, *per* Sedley LJ).

[17] In the present case there is a single provision of the Rules of stand-out importance. Part 9 constitutes a discrete chapter entitled "General Grounds for the Refusal of Entry Clearance, Leave to Enter, Leave to Remain, Variation of Leave to Enter or Remain and Curtailment of Leave in the United Kingdom". The phrases "leave to enter" and "entry clearance" are used interchangeably and are not materially distinct. Within Part 9 is paragraph 320, which provides:

> "In addition to the grounds for refusal of entry clearance or leave to enter set out in Parts 2 – 8 of these Rules, and subject to paragraph 321 below, the following grounds for the refusal of entry clearance or leave to enter apply..."

---

[1] Promulgation of this judgment was deferred pending consideration by and response from the parties, with a view to ensuring that its contents do not undermine the anonymity order. The published judgment reflects the parties' responses and will omit the Sensitive Schedule.

There follows a series of refusal grounds. One of these is paragraph 320(7A). This provides for mandatory refusal:

"… where false representations have been made or false documents (or information) have been submitted (whether or not material to the application, and whether or not to the applicant's knowledge), or material facts have not been disclosed, in relation to the application, or in order to obtain documents from the Secretary of State or a third party required in support of the application."

This is the key provision of the Rules in these proceedings. It proclaims a mandatory – not discretionary – ground of refusal.

[18] In compliance with the court's direction to provide a chronology of material dates and events, the parties have jointly compiled the following, which the court adopts with some linguistic and other minor modifications:

Date	Event
6 November 2015	Application for entry clearance submitted on behalf of the Appellant
28 March 2016	Appellant's half-brother granted entry clearance
9 April 2016	Appellant's entry clearance application refused
9 May 2016	Notice of appeal submitted to the First-tier Tribunal ("FtT")
4 October 2016	Refusal affirmed on review by SSHD
3 November 2017	Hearing of appeal before FtT Judge Farrelly
13 March 2018	Appeal dismissed. Decision of FtT Judge Farrelly promulgated
10 April 2018	Application to FtT, for permission to appeal to the Upper Tribunal ("UT")
18 July 2018	Decision of FtT Judge Harris, dated 6 July 2018, refusing Appellant permission to appeal to the UT promulgated
16 August 2018	Application to UT for permission to appeal.
14 November 2018	Decision by UT Judge Kekić, dated 5 November 2018, granting the Appellant permission to appeal, promulgated
7 August 2019	Hearing before UT Judge Dawson
7 October 2019	Decision and reasons of UT Judge Dawson promulgated: appeal succeeds in part and is remitted to the FtT

7 November 2019	Application to UT for permission to appeal to Court of Appeal
21 November 2019	Decision by UT Judge Blundell, dated 19 November 2019, refusing permission to appeal to the Court of Appeal, promulgated
5 December 2019	Application seeking leave to appeal to the Court of Appeal
4 February 2020	FtT adjourns the re-hearing of the Appellant's appeal (listed 11 February 2020), pending the outcome of this application

[19] The court also directed the provision of a schedule of agreed material facts. This, with certain judicial modifications, is reproduced in the Sensitive Schedule. In brief compass, therefore, the Appellant's mother, a Filipino national and British citizen, residing and working in Northern Ireland during most of the last 17 years, applied to SSHD for entry clearance permitting the Appellant (then aged 12 and now aged 16) to reside with her mother and half-brother in this jurisdiction. In making such application the Appellant's mother provided a birth certificate in respect of the Appellant which contained false information. The entry clearance application was refused on this ground.

The underlying decision

[20] The impugned decision was made by an Entry Clearance Officer on behalf of SSHD and is dated 9 April 2016. It is directed to the Appellant and states in material part:

"You have applied to join your mother [...] who is present and settled in the UK. You have provided a copy of your birth certificate which shows your mother's name only. No father is stated however in your application form you have stated that your father is [...]. It is claimed on your application form that he did not acknowledge your birth. Checks with the Philippines Statistics Authority have revealed that there is no record of your birth. According to records held your mother gave birth to two children, your brother [...] and a daughter [...]. [...] was born on [...] and was the daughter of your mother and [...]. It is further noted on her birth certificate that your mother and [...] married on [...] in [...] ....

Your birth certificate has been fraudulently obtained and I am therefore refusing your application under paragraph 320(7A)."

[We have edited the text in order to give effect to the anonymity order of this court.]

[21] The Appellant exercised her right of "appeal review" to the Entry Clearance Manager who, by his decision dated 4 October 2016, affirmed the initial decision.

The Anterior Tribunal decisions and orders

[22] There are two substantive underlying judicial decisions and three of a procedural nature. The Appellant exercised her right of appeal against the impugned decision. This generated the following series of judicial decisions:

(i)   By its decision promulgated on 13 March 2018 the FtT dismissed the appeal.

(ii)   On 06 July 2018 the FtT refused permission to appeal to the UT.

(iii)   By a decision dated 05 November 2018 a judge of the UT granted permission to appeal.

(iv)   By its decision promulgated on 07 October 2019, the UT (a) dismissed the appeal on the paragraph 320(7a) ground and (b) allowed the appeal on the Article 8 ECHR ground, ordering that the decision of the FtT be set aside on this basis (alone) and remitting the case to a different judge of the FtT for fresh decision making. The paragraph 320(7A) ground of appeal was dismissed.

(v)   On 19 November 2019 a different judge of the UT refused the Appellant's application for leave to appeal to this court.

[23] It is convenient to preface our identification and application of the governing legal principles with the following passage extracted from [21] of the substantive decision of the UT:

"It is accepted in this case that the 'birth certificate' produced by the appellant was a false document *and that alone is sufficient for paragraph 320(7A) to be made out.* Whilst it may not be understandable why the appellant's mother used or caused to be used a false document that does not take the document out of the category captured by the rule. Accordingly, ground 1 of the challenge cannot succeed." [Our emphasis.]

While there is a degree of textual ambiguity in this passage, it is clear that the Appellant's "acceptance" was confined to the false nature of the document in question and did not extend to a concession that paragraph 320(7A) of the Rules was satisfied in consequence.

Procedure

[24] The court received an extensive skeleton argument from each party, supplementing skeleton arguments deployed at earlier stages of these proceedings. Having considered the papers the court, in the context of the Covid-19 pandemic, identified this appeal as a potentially suitable candidate for paper adjudication. Both parties agreed to this course. Given the volume of the skeleton arguments the court then directed the parties to formulate their core propositions.

[25] In response the following was received on behalf of the Appellant:

"1. *Permission to appeal should be granted:*

(i) The proposed appeal raises important points of principle or practice related to: (i) the proper interpretation of paragraph 320(7A) of the Immigration Rules as it applies to false documents; (ii) an actual or apparent conflict between two judgments of the English & Welsh Court of Appeal in *AA* and *Hameed*; and (iii) the correctness, Convention compatibility and/or general legality of the interpretation set down by the English & Welsh Court of Appeal in *Hameed*.

(ii) The proposed appeal raises other compelling reasons for the Court to hear this appeal because: (i) the Court's interpretation of paragraph 320(7A) of the Immigration Rules in *Hameed*, and applied by the UT Judge, was perverse or plainly wrong; (ii) the said interpretation was also inconsistent with the decision of the same court in *AA*; and (iii) this unlawful interpretation has given rise to delay and drastic consequences for the Appellant and her family.

2. *Rule 320(7A) of the Immigration Rules is breached, in respect of a false document, only when there is dishonest promotion of that false document for the purpose of obtaining entry clearance.* This is the correct interpretation of the rule and the one that should be adopted by this Court. This interpretation flows from a proper understanding of the meaning and function of the rule itself; and from a proper reading of what the English & Welsh Court of Appeal said in *AA* at §67. False means dishonest (*AA* at §66). Dishonest promotion in this context means to put forward a document with the intention to deceive the authorities and for the specific purpose of securing entry clearance.

3. *Hameed was wrongly decided by the English & Welsh Court of Appeal.* Their interpretation of the rule at hand (and what had been said in *AA*) at §§25–27 was in error. The court's observations in *Hameed* reveal a clear contrast and, indeed, conflict with the approach taken in *AA* in which the court strove to apply the same meaning to the word 'false' (requiring dishonesty) in respect of both 'representations' and 'documents' (see §72; and see also the reference by the court to the guidance which puts false documents and false representations in pari materia at §44). *Hameed* also creates a perverse or irrational outcome by applying *a stricter test in respect of the provision of a document when compared with other types of representation*. The interpretation of paragraph 320(7A) advanced in *Hameed* (§27) creates a significant (and inconsistent) difference in approach between false representations and the submission of false documents, which does not sit easily with the reasoning in *AA* (at §§67–68) or a fair, correct or Convention-compliant interpretation of the relevant rule.

4.   *The rule, as applied, was in breach of the Appellant's right to respect for her family life under Article 8 ECHR.* Notwithstanding that a refusal to permit a child entry-clearance to live with their mother, a British citizen, amounts to an obvious interference with the family life of that child, the Immigration Rules, as now interpreted by *Hameed*, mandate such a refusal, *irrespective of any actual dishonesty on the part of any person being established.* This is contrary to the child's welfare and best interests. While such a finding may not be determinative of a subsequent human rights appeal, it may amount to a weighty factor against entry-clearance being granted. This approach flies in the face of the 'sins of the parent' principle, which is highly relevant to assessing Convention compatibility, in this context.

5.   *The Supreme Court's judgment in* Ivey v Genting Casinos *strongly supports the Appellant's case on dishonesty.* This important decision was not considered by the court in *Hameed* and has been mostly ignored by the Respondent. It is submitted that the statement in *Hameed* at §27 that there is no need to establish actual dishonesty or deception in cases involving the use of false documents is *wholly inconsistent* with the *dicta* of the Supreme Court on this very issue, summarising the authoritative test 'when dishonesty is in question' at §74 as requiring (a) a factfinding [*sic*] exercise as to the subjective, 'actual state of the [relevant] individual's knowledge or belief'; *and* (b) a determination, in light of that, of 'whether his conduct was honest or dishonest', applying objective standards.

6.   *The Respondent's core argument (§3) is both unattractive and inherently implausible*; (i) as a matter of common sense; (ii) applying conventional canons of interpretation; and (iii) because the English & Welsh Court of Appeal in *AA* sought (consistently with common sense and an ordinary approach to construction) to mandate a uniform, single, interpretation of what the word 'dishonest' means. The Respondent's case would result in two distinct, substantively different meanings of the word 'dishonest', depending on whether one is dealing with a representation or a document. That cannot be correct (nor, indeed, compliant with the Appellant's Convention rights). The Respondent's argument as to alleged futility does not provide a substantive defence."

[26] The core propositions formulated on behalf of SSHD are in the following terms:

"Substantive issue

1.   The Appellant contends that the England and Wales Court of Appeal's (EWCA) decision in *Adedoyin*[2] has been wrongly interpreted by the Upper Tribunal (IAC). In *Adedoyin* the EWCA was concerned with determining the correct meaning of the word 'false' used in Immigration Rule 320(7A), because false can be interpreted to mean two quite different things. Rix LJ's omnibus conclusion was that false in this context meant dishonest, so that dishonesty would result in refusal.

---

[2] [2010] EWCA Civ 773, [2011] 1 WLR 145.

2. Immigration Rule 320(7A) refers to dishonesty in two ways: (1) the submission of a dishonest document along with an application; and (2) the making of a dishonest submission in an application. The Appellant contends that *Adedoyin*, properly interpreted, means that a *false document* case requires *two* separate elements of dishonesty before the application can be refused: (1) submission of a dishonest document; and (2) a dishonest intent (promotion) when submitting that document.

3. The Appellant's interpretation is wrong. Only one episode of dishonesty is required. If a dishonest document is submitted, that is sufficient for refusal. There is dishonesty within the document itself and the grounds for refusal are therefore met. There is no need for additional dishonest intent when it is submitted.

4. The EWCA acknowledged the strong public policy reasons for discouraging all forms of dishonesty in applications for permission to enter the UK.

5. The Appellant has failed to recognise that the dishonesty prohibited by Immigration Rule 320(7A) can manifest in different ways depending on whether it is in a *false document* case or a *false representation* case, but whichever form it takes all that is required is dishonesty (not double dishonesty).

6. There is a single test of dishonesty. The Appellant's reliance on *Ivey*[3] and the suggestion that the Respondent's view results in two tests for dishonesty is misguided. The form the dishonesty takes changes, not the test for dishonesty.

7. The Appellant's interpretation also conflicts with the EWCA later decision in *Hameed* (2019),[4] which again held that submission of a dishonest document was of itself sufficient for refusal under Immigration Rule 320(7A). The Appellant argues *Hameed* conflicts with *Adedoyin*, but that is incorrect – the decisions are the same. The Immigration Rules apply equally throughout the UK and there is no good reason for a different interpretation in Northern Ireland.

Academic case

8. The Appellant's mother obtained two birth certificates: a legitimate one and an illegitimate one. She submitted the illegitimate one along with the application to the Entry Clearance Officer. Knowing that she had a legitimate certificate and an illegitimate certificate, it is difficult to see how there is any prospect of a tribunal deciding that she was not acting dishonestly when submitting the false one.

9. The Appellant's mother has had several opportunities to explain her actions during the various stages of the review and appeal processes. She

---

[3] *Ivey v Genting Casinos (UK) Ltd* [2017] UKSC 67.
[4] [2019] EWCA Civ 1324.

has contributed evidence throughout. Despite the false birth certificate being the central feature of the proceedings, as it was the reason for refusal, she has been unable to provide any explanation capable of grounding a finding that she was not acting dishonestly. Therefore, even if the Appellant secured a favourable outcome to these proceedings, it would be of no benefit to her. Her case is academic.

Second appeal criteria

10. This case has been the subject of multiple considerations during its journey through the specialist immigration appeal tribunal system. For that reason, the Second Appeal Criteria set a high threshold before this Court will consider the case. The Appellant does not satisfy either of the Second Appeal Criteria.

Delay

11. This case involves a child, aged 16 years. The original application was submitted in November 2015 when she was aged 12 years. The impugned decision was reached in April 2016. Since that refusal over 4 years ago, there has been one Home Office review and five separate tribunal decisions touching upon her. The UT has given her a further appeal hearing based on her Article 8 claim, regardless of the outcome of this appeal. The adverse effects of the further delay on the best interests of the child caused by this application for appeal speak loudly against a grant of leave."

The substantive issues of law

[27] We begin by elaborating briefly on paragraph 320(7A) of the Rules. The mandatory refusal of entry clearance on the ground of false representations or false documents was first introduced in 2008 (by HC321, HC607 and HC1113). Paragraph 320(7A) is replicated in three other provisions of this chapter of the Rules. The materiality of the dishonesty or deception is irrelevant. The onus of proof rests on SSHD. While we are mindful of decisions such as *Khawaja v SSHD* (1984) AC 74 and *MH Pakistan* (2010) UKUT 00168 (IAC) it is not necessary for our decision to dilate on the question of standard of proof, which featured in neither party's arguments, and we decline to do so.

[28] We now turn to the relevant jurisprudence. In *Adedoyin v Secretary of State for the Home Department* [2010] EWCA Civ 773 (aka *AA (Nigeria v SSHD)*) the English Court of Appeal considered the meaning of the word "false" in paragraph 322(1A) of the Rules. This decision is central to these proceedings. Paragraph 322(1A) provides that leave to remain in the UK is to be refused –

"... where false representations have been made or false documents or information have been submitted (whether or not material to the application, and whether or not to the applicant's knowledge), or material facts have not been disclosed, in relation to the application."

The language replicates precisely that of paragraph 320(7A): see [15] above.

[29] It is necessary to reproduce the critical passages, [65]–[77], of *Adedoyin* in their entirety:

"65. The essential question is whether 'false' in either paragraph 320(7A) or paragraph 322(1A) is used in the meaning of 'incorrect' or in the meaning of 'dishonest'. Whatever Staughton LJ may have said in *Akhtar* it is quite clear to me that in ordinary English usage 'false' may have either meaning. While 'incorrect' is given as its first meaning in the *Concise English Dictionary*, I am unable to regard its second meaning, which I gloss as 'dishonest', as other than entirely normal: and that is so whether regard is had to the man or woman in the street or to the barrister in the Temple.

66. It seems to me therefore that there is an open choice as to the meaning to be given to 'false' in the relevant rules. In that situation, I would prefer the meaning of 'dishonest', for the following reasons.

67. First, 'false representation' is aligned in the rule with 'false document'. It is plain that a false document is one that tells a lie about itself. Of course it is possible for a person to make use of a false document (for instance a counterfeit currency note, but that example, used for its clarity, is rather distant from the context of this discussion) in total ignorance of its falsity and in perfect honesty. But the document itself is dishonest. It is highly likely therefore that where an applicant uses in all innocence a false document for the purpose of obtaining entry clearance, or leave to enter or to remain, it is because some other party, it might be a parent, or sponsor, or agent, has dishonestly promoted the use of that document. The response of a requirement of mandatory refusal is entirely understandable in such a situation. The mere fact that a dishonest document has been used for such an important application is understandably a sufficient reason for a mandatory refusal. That is why the rule expressly emphasises that it applies 'whether or not to the applicant's knowledge'.

68. Secondly, however, a false representation stated in all innocence may be simply a matter of mistake, or an error short of dishonesty. It does not necessarily tell a lie about itself. In such a case there is little reason for a requirement of mandatory refusal, although a power, even a presumption, of discretionary refusal would be understandable. It is noticeable that paragraphs 320 and 322 also contain grounds on which entry clearance, leave to enter, or leave to remain, as the case may be, 'should normally be refused'. If on the other hand a dishonest representation has been promoted by another party, as happened with the sponsor husband in *Akhtar*, then it is entirely understandable that the rule should require mandatory refusal, irrespective of the personal innocence of the applicant herself. Therefore, the reason of the thing, as well as the natural inference that 'false' in relation to 'representations' should have the same connotation as 'false' in relation to 'documents', together argue for a conclusion that 'false' requires dishonesty – although not necessarily that of the applicant himself.

69. Thirdly, the non-disclosure of material facts is also a mandatory ground of refusal. Such nondisclosure can be entirely honest, or it can be dishonest. If dishonest, the dishonesty may again happen without the knowledge of the

applicant, or the applicant may be personally dishonest. The facts of *Akhtar* again come to mind. In this context, however, the rule says nothing about the knowledge of the applicant, which might suggest that the importance of this aspect of the rule lies in the word 'material'. There has been some uneasy jurisprudence about the effect of that word: see *Akhtar* itself (where the point did not have to be decided) and *Macdonald* at para 3.77. In any event, the rule at this point does not speak in terms of what is 'false'. I say nothing therefore about this part of the rule. In my judgement, it cannot be decisive as to the meaning of 'false'.

70. Fourthly, it seems to me that, in a situation where a word, such as here 'false', has two distinct, and distinctively important, meanings, there is a genuine ambiguity which makes it legitimate, in construing Rules which are expressions of the executive's policy, to consider what the executive has said, publicly, about its rules. Clearly, what a minister says in Parliament, expressed as an assurance, and especially on the occasion of a debate arising out of the tabling of amended rules, is of particular, and may be of decisive, importance (just as the DP 5/96 policy was effectively changed by an announcement in Parliament, see *NF (Ghana)* above). In such a situation of genuine ambiguity, moreover, it seems to me that, perhaps exceptionally, it is even possible to get some assistance from the executive's formally published guidance, such as RFL04 or the relevant IDI. In saying that I do not think I am departing from the observations of Lord Brown in *Mahad*, cited above, about the function and status or probable general unhelpfulness of IDIs.

71. Fifthly, therefore, I consider it necessary in the present case to consider what assurances were given in, and arising out, of the Lords debate of 17 March 2008 when the rule in question was before Parliament. Lord Bassam then made a clear statement, in answer to Baroness Warwick who had noted the ambiguity of the word 'false', that by 'false documents' –

> 'We mean a document that is forged or has been altered to give false information. If people submit such documents, our belief is that they should be refused...'

ILPA then asked for clarity as to whether that answer extended to statements, on the basis that the reference to falsity in the rule 'implies an element of falsehood and not a mere mistake'. Mr Byrne's letter replied to that request for clarification first by saying that the answer was to be found in Entry Clearance Guidelines 'which I believe deals with this point', and secondly by stating in his own words what the new rules were intended to cover, *viz* 'people who tell lies – either on their own behalf or that of someone else – in an application to the UK Borders Agency. They are not intended to catch those who make innocent mistakes in their applications.'

72. For the reasons given above, I consider that that assurance, essentially as to the meaning of the word 'false' in the new rules, was a correct exposition of the true interpretation of those rules. If, however, there were to remain any uncertainty in a situation of genuine ambiguity, then I consider that what the minister said, in answer to ILPA's specific request, was intended to be

definitive of that ambiguity. It will be seen that the minister's answer also confirms my personal understanding of the proper *ratio* of *Akhtar*.

73. Sixthly, in the light of the minister's answer in his letter, it must be legitimate to look at the relevant Entry Clearance Guidelines to which he referred. The current version is RFL04 which I have cited above. It is abundantly clear from that, in my judgement, that 'false' in relation to both 'representations' and 'documents' is being used in the same way and as requiring dishonesty, although not necessarily in the applicant himself: see para 42/43 above. It will be recalled that the whole of the relevant passage in RFL04 is beneath the rubric: 'Deception in an application – paragraph 320(7A)'.

74. Seventhly, especially in the light of the minister's answer, it seems to me legitimate to look at the IDI guidance given as to the rule in paragraph 322(1A) itself. That has been set out above and I refer to my observations upon that guidance (at paras 32/33 above). Although there are to my mind discrepancies here and there, what is striking is that the whole discussion is under the heading of 'Paragraph 322(1A) – Deception used in a current application' and the primary emphasis is on lying.

75. Eighthly, (and this point, although convenient to state last, is rather one of primary importance), it is plain to my mind that paragraph 320(7B) with its reference to 'Deception' is intended to be read together with the rule in paragraphs 320(7A) and 322(1A). Paragraph 320(7B)(d) makes it clear that it applies not only to cases of entry clearance and leave to enter (the subject-matter of paragraph 320) but also to the case of leave to remain (the subject-matter of paragraph 322). 'Deception' picks up the language not itself found in paragraphs 320(7A) and 322(1A) but rather in RFL04 and the IDI on paragraph 322(1A). I accept the submission of Mr Collins which as I understood it was that paragraph 320(7B)(d) was a gloss on paragraphs 320(7A) and paragraph 322(1A) – for otherwise a case within those latter paragraphs would not be dealt with within paragraph 320(7B) at all (see para 28 above), which cannot have been intended – but I reject his submission that 'Deception' does not entail dishonesty. Therefore, once the connection of the rule in paragraph 322(1A) (and in paragraph 320(7A)) with paragraph 320(7B)(d) is made, it is impossible in my judgement to conclude that 'false' in the expression 'false representations' in the rule in question has the morally neutral meaning of 'incorrect'.

76. For these reasons, I conclude that Mr Malik's basic submission is correct. Whether as a matter of the interpretation solely of the relevant rules in paragraphs 320(7A), 320(7B) and 322(1A), but in any event when consideration is also given to the assurances given in the Lords debate as supplemented by the minister's letter to ILPA dated 4 April 2008, and to the public guidance issued on behalf of the executive, the answer becomes plain, and in essence is all of a piece. Dishonesty or deception is needed, albeit not necessarily that of the applicant himself, to render a 'false representation' a ground for mandatory refusal.

77. If it were otherwise, then an applicant whose false representation was in no way dishonest would not only suffer mandatory refusal but would also be barred from re-entry for ten years if he was removed or deported. That might not in itself be so very severe a rule, if only because the applicant always has the option of voluntary departure. If, however, he has to be assisted at the expense of the Secretary of State, then the ban is for five years. Most seriously of all, however, is the possibility, on the Secretary of State's interpretation, that an applicant for entry clearance (not this case) who had made an entirely innocent misrepresentation, innocent not only so far as his personal honesty is concerned but also in its origins, would be barred from re-entry under paragraph 320(7B)(ii) for ten years, even if he left the UK voluntarily."

[30] The Court of Appeal decided, unanimously, that "false" denotes "dishonest". It entails the making of deliberate lies, to be contrasted with statements which do not accord with the true facts. Thus a representation is to be characterised false within the compass of paragraph 322(1A) – and, by extension, paragraph 320(7A) – only if there has been dishonesty or deception on the part of a relevant person. The tribunal had decided that the claimant's state of mind was irrelevant to the question of whether the representation under consideration, which related to previous convictions, was immaterial in determining whether it was "false". The Court of Appeal determined that this was erroneous in law and remitted the case to the tribunal for the main purpose of determining whether the offending representation had been dishonest.

[31] The kernel of what the Court of Appeal decided is encapsulated in pithy terms at [76]:

"Dishonesty or deception is needed, albeit not necessarily that of the applicant himself, to render a 'false representation' a ground for mandatory refusal."

The starting point and cornerstone of the detailed analysis and reasoning of Rix LJ at [65] is that "false" does not denote "incorrect". Rather its true meaning is "dishonest". A false document, he observed, is one which "tells a lie about itself": see [67]. This, however, does not justify a mandatory refusal decision under the provisions of the Rules unless the falsity can be linked to the dishonest state of mind of a relevant person. The court's emphasis was on the state of mind of the applicant or other person (for example the sponsor or an agent), to be contrasted with the falsity in the representation or document under scrutiny. In short, while a representation or document may contain a falsity, the question is whether this is attributable to a relevant person's dishonesty and a mandatory refusal under paragraph 320(7A) of the Rules is lawful only where this question attracts an affirmative answer.

[32] The primary submission of SSHD, based on *Adedoyin*, is that the requirement to establish dishonesty is confined to false representation cases and does not extend to cases of false documents. We consider that this submission finds no support in either the relevant provisions of the Rules or the judgment in *Adedoyin* and reject it.

[33] It is necessary to consider the more recent decision of the English Court of Appeal in *Hameed v Secretary of State for the Home Department* [2019] EWCA Civ 1324. There the Appellant's application for leave to remain in the United Kingdom was refused under paragraph 322(1A) of the Rules – materially

indistinguishable from paragraph 320(7A) as noted above – on the basis that there had been reliance upon a false certificate of sponsorship ("CoS") submitted with his application. The falsity of the document was conceded. The Appellant's case was that the refusal decision was unlawful as he had not been guilty of dishonesty. The court observed at [24] that the "fundamental problem" with the appellant's case was that the Secretary of State had not refused his application on the basis that he had made a false representation but on the ground that he had submitted a false document. The court noted at [23] that while the appellant had made a representation, in completing his application for the relevant student status, he had not acted falsely or dishonestly. The court further observed that the person who had supplied the appellant with the ensuing bogus certificate "may have been acting dishonestly but was not making a representation".

[34] The court stated at [25] – [27]:

"The underlying question in the appeal, namely whether the appellant or another person was responsible for any dishonesty or deception which is implicit in the need for 'falsity', was considered in *Adedoyin v Secretary of State for the Home Department* [2010] EWCA Civ 773, [2011] 1 WLR 564. At [76] Rix LJ held that:

'Dishonesty or deception is needed, albeit not necessarily that of the applicant himself, to render a "false representation" a ground for mandatory refusal.'

That has the effect that where, as in this case, an applicant is not responsible for or aware of the falsity and hence the dishonesty or deception being perpetrated, it is necessary for the Secretary of State to establish dishonesty or deception on the part of another as part of the reasoning for a refusal under paragraph 322(1A) (see, for example *Adedoyin* at [68]).

What *Adedoyin* also established, however, is that a false document is itself dishonest and that fact avoids the need to establish dishonesty or deception on the part of an applicant or another. That was made clear at [67]:

'First, "false representation" is aligned in the rule with "false document". It is plain that a false document is one that tells a lie about itself. Of course it is possible for a person to make use of a false document (for instance a counterfeit currency note, but that example, used for its clarity, is rather distant from the context of this discussion) in total ignorance of its falsity and in perfect honesty. But the document itself is dishonest. It is highly likely therefore that where an applicant uses in all innocence a false document for the purposes of obtaining entry clearance, or leave to enter or to remain, it is because some other party, it might be a parent, or sponsor, or agent, has dishonestly promoted the use of the document. The response of a requirement of mandatory refusal is entirely understandable in such a situation. The mere fact that a dishonest document has been used for such an important application is understandably a sufficient reason for a mandatory refusal. That is why the rule expressly emphasises that it applies "whether or not to the applicant's knowledge".'"

The sentence in bold is, properly analysed, the key part of the judgment. The Court of Appeal upheld the refusal decision of SSHD and its subsequent affirmation by the UT in judicial review proceedings.

[35] At this juncture we draw further attention to the following statement of Rix LJ in *Adedoyin*, at [65]:

> "It is plain that a false document is one that tells a lie about itself. Of course it is possible for a person to make use of a false document (for instance a counterfeit currency note, but that example, used for its clarity, is rather distant from the context of this discussion) in total ignorance of its falsity and in perfect honesty. But the document itself is dishonest."

We consider that, properly construed and considered in its full context, this passage was not intended to suggest that *a document* is capable of being dishonest, whether in the Part 9 regime of the Rules or otherwise. Human beings are capable of being dishonest. Documents, in contrast, are (inexhaustively) either false or genuine, accurate or inaccurate, correct or incorrect – and so forth. The assessment of a document entails a purely forensic exercise. The assessment of whether a human being has engaged in dishonesty is to be contrasted. The latter assessment involves exploring the state of mind of the person concerned and the making of findings which will normally be based on appropriate inferences and sometimes, less typically in practice, on direct evidence such as a written or oral statement evincing an intention to deceive.

[36] We would caution that [65] of *Adedoyin* is not be construed narrowly or literally, at the expense of the remainder of the paragraph in question and the ensuing passages. In *Hameed* a different division of the Court of Appeal purported to apply its earlier decision in *Adedoyin*. In our consideration of *Adedoyin* above we have drawn attention to the detailed analysis of Rix LJ at [65]–[77] and the importance of considering this as a whole. It is striking that in *Hameed* the later division of the Court of Appeal focused only on [67]. Furthermore, we consider with respect that the court misunderstood this discrete passage. In *Hameed* there is no suggestion of any disagreement with *Adedoyin*. Rather the Court of Appeal purported to apply *Adedoyin*. We consider, with deference, that the Court fell into error. In our judgement the decision in *Hameed* is irreconcilable with that in *Adedoyin*. We shall examine the implications of this *infra*.

[37] There is one further element of the juridical equation which falls to be considered. In the clear and focussed skeleton argument of Mr David Scoffield QC and Mr Steven McQuitty (of counsel) on behalf of the Appellant there is a further, free standing submission that *Hameed* is also in conflict with other authority relevant to the question of dishonesty. In *Ivey v Genting Casinos (UK) Ltd* [2017] UKSC 67 the Supreme Court considered an appeal brought by a professional gambler who had been denied £7.7 million in winnings by the respondent casino on the basis that he had cheated during a particular card game (Punto Banco Baccarat). At trial the judge had dismissed his claim against the casino for his winnings on the grounds that, while neither dishonesty nor deception was involved, the appellant's play had amounted to "cheating" in breach of an implied term of his contract with the casino. The Court of Appeal upheld that decision and the appellant appealed to the Supreme Court.

[38] The Supreme Court dismissed his appeal on the basis that the trial judge had been correct to hold that the appellant's conduct amounted, objectively, to cheating and this was sufficient to breach the implied contractual term. The court added some guidance on the issue of dishonesty, at [74], *per* Lord Hughes:

"74. These several considerations provide convincing grounds for holding that the second leg of the test propounded in *R v Ghosh* [1982] QB 1053 does not correctly represent the law and that directions based upon it ought no longer to be given. The test of dishonesty is as set out by Lord Nicholls in *Royal Brunei Airlines Sdn Bhd v Tan* [1995] 2 AC 378 and by Lord Hoffmann in *Barlow Clowes International Ltd v Eurotrust International Ltd* [2006] 1 WLR 1476, para 10: see para 62 above. *When dishonesty is in question the fact-finding tribunal must first ascertain (subjectively) the actual state of the individual's knowledge or belief as to the facts.* The reasonableness or otherwise of his belief is a matter of evidence (often in practice determinative) going to whether he held the belief, but it is not an additional requirement that his belief must be reasonable; the question is whether it is genuinely held. *When once his actual state of mind as to knowledge or belief as to facts is established, the question whether his conduct was honest or dishonest is to be determined by the fact-finder by applying the (objective) standards of ordinary decent people.* There is no requirement that the defendant must appreciate that what he has done is, by those standards, dishonest." [Emphasis added]

[39] While the passage in question was *obiter*, a specially constituted five member panel of the English Court of Appeal has endorsed it unequivocally, concluding that *Ghosh* is no longer to be followed in criminal cases, in *R v Barton and Booth* [2020] EWCA Crim 575. Burnett LCJ expressed the conclusion of the court at [1]:

"For 35 years the approach to dishonesty in the criminal courts was governed by the decision of the Court of Appeal Criminal Division in *R v Ghosh* [1982] QB 1053. In *Ivey v Genting Casinos (UK) (trading as Cockfords Club)* [2017] UKSC 67; [2018] AC 391 the Supreme Court, in a carefully considered lengthy *obiter dictum* delivered by Lord Hughes of Ombersley, explained why the law had taken a wrong turn in *Ghosh* and indicated, for the future, that the approach articulated in *Ivey* should be followed. These appeals provide the opportunity for the uncertainty which has followed the decision in *Ivey* to come to an end. We are satisfied that the decision in *Ivey* is correct, is to be preferred, and that there is no obstacle in the doctrine of *stare decisis* to its being applied as the law of England and Wales."

He added at [104]:

"We conclude that where the Supreme Court itself directs that an otherwise binding decision of the Court of Appeal should no longer be followed and proposes an alternative test that it says must be adopted, the Court of Appeal is bound to follow what amounts to a direction from the Supreme Court even though it is strictly *obiter*. To that limited extent the ordinary rules of precedent (or *stare decisis*) have been modified. We emphasise that this limited modification is confined to cases in which all the judges in the appeal in question in the Supreme Court agree that to be the effect of the decision. Such was a necessary condition before adjusting the rules of precedent accepted by this court in *James* in relation to the Privy Council. Had the minority of the Privy Council in *Holley* not agreed that the effect of the judgment was to state definitively the law in England, it would not have been accepted as such by this court. The same approach is necessary here because it forms the foundation for the conclusion that the result is considered by the Supreme Court to be definitive, with the consequence that a further appeal would be a foregone conclusion, and binding on lower courts."

The precedent status of this decision is considered at [45] – [48] below.

[40] *Ivey* had previously been the subject of strong endorsement from Sir Brian Leveson P in *Patterson v DPP*, the Court of Appeal's approving reference in *R v Pabon* [2018] EWCA Crim 420 and the explicit advice to judges in the *Crown Court Compendium* that it should be followed.

[41] *Ivey* was not considered by the Court of Appeal in *Hameed*. We consider that Lord Hughes' formulation regarding dishonesty, provided as it was in the context of a civil case, should be accorded broad application. We are unable to identify any reason in principle or otherwise why it should not apply to the relevant provisions of the Immigration Rules. Coherence and predictability in the legal system are long recognised and essential attributes. The DNA of dishonesty is the same, in whatever legal context it features. Thus, while the context of the decision in *Hameed* was a specific provision of the Rules it is plainly incompatible with *Ivey*. This reinforces our conclusion that *Hameed* was erroneously decided.

[42] The combined researches of the court and the parties have (perhaps surprisingly) failed to identify any post-*Hameed* reported case in which the decisions in *Hameed* or *Adedoyin* were considered. We have noted that in *R (Balajigari and Others) v Secretary of State for the Home Department* [2019] 1 WLR 4647, decided some weeks before *Hameed*, the Court of Appeal, at [36], cited without demur [76] – [79] of *Adedoyin*. The conjoined appeals in that case were almost exclusively concerned with a different provision of the Rules, namely paragraph 322(5) which provides that SSHD may refuse leave to remain in the United Kingdom or variation of leave to enter or remain in the United Kingdom, on a discretionary basis, on the ground of the applicant's conduct, character or associations. This ground of refusal was invoked in all four cases. In one of the cases only (*Kawos*) the refusal was also based on paragraph 322(2), which contains as a discretionary ground of refusal "the making of false representations or the failure to disclose any material fact …".

[43] In all of the cases under appeal the claimants were required by the Rules to demonstrate a minimum level of earnings in the UK in the previous year and, to this end, made representations and provided evidence which SSHD refused to accept. It was common case that *dishonesty* on the part of the applicant is, in the context of applications of this kind, required: see [35]. This prompted the court's references to *Adedoyin* and *Ivey*. Underhill LJ, delivering the unanimous judgment of the court, stated at [35]:

"The provision of inaccurate earnings figures either to HMRC or to the Home Office in support of an application for leave under Part 6A as a result of mere carelessness or ignorance or poor advice cannot constitute conduct rendering it undesirable for the applicant to remain in the UK. Errors so caused are, however regrettable, 'genuine' or 'innocent' in the sense that they are honest and do not meet the necessary threshold."

It was in this context that reference was made to *Adedoyin*, which the court quoted as providing support for its assessment.

[44] In *Balijigari* the *Ivey* approach to dishonesty was exported, without qualification, to provisions of the Immigration Rules closely comparable to paragraph 320(7A). We consider it immaterial that the other provisions empower discretionary, rather than mandatory, refusal of applications and reject the argument of SSHD to the contrary. This court agrees fully with the foregoing passage in *Balajigari and Others*. The actual outcome of the conjoined appeals – all succeeded on the main ground that SSHD's assessment of dishonesty was the product of a procedurally unfair decision making process – is not directly relevant to the application which we are deciding. However, we shall comment further, and briefly, on this *infra*.

The doctrine of precedent

[45] The foregoing analysis and conclusion are not determinative of the construction of paragraph 320(7A) of the Rules. The reason for this is that this court is bound by neither of the decisions in *Adedoyin* and *Hameed*. By well-established principle decisions of the English Court of Appeal are of persuasive and not binding authority in this jurisdiction: see the summary of the relevant authorities in *Baranowski v Rice* [2014] NIQB 122 at 19. See also, more recently, *Re Steponaviciene's Application* [2018] NIQB 90 at [20]–[24]. The relevant principle was stated by Campbell LJ in *Re Starritt and Cartwright's Applications* [2005] NICA 48 at []:

"It has been long established that while this court is not technically bound by decisions of courts of corresponding jurisdiction in the rest of the United Kingdom, it is customary for it to follow them to make for uniformity where the same statutory provision or rule of common law is to be applied. That is not to say that the court will follow blindly a decision that it considers to be erroneous."

[46] As appears from our analysis above, we consider that the two decisions of the English Court of Appeal under scrutiny, namely *Adedoyin* and *Hameed*, are in conflict with each other. As a matter of principle this court is not strictly bound by either. Given our conclusion that *Adedoyin* was misunderstood and misapplied in *Hameed* the first step for this court is to choose between the two decisions. We have not identified any other option and neither party urged any other course upon us. We consider the analysis and reasoning in *Adedoyin*, as we have expounded them, cogent. We further consider that the more recent decision of the Court of Appeal in *Balajigari and Others*, which we have endorsed, is harmonious with *Adedoyin* and irreconcilable with *Hameed*. The final ingredient in the jurisprudential equation is the decision of the Supreme Court in *Ivey*, noted above, which in our view is supportive of *Adedoyin* and further undermines *Hameed*. Giving effect to this analysis we propose to follow the decision in *Adedoyin*.

[47] In *R v Barton and Booth* (*supra*) the English Court of Appeal devoted much attention to the binding effect of the *obiter* aspect of *Ivey*. Doctrinally, this court's relationship with the UK Supreme Court is the same as that of its English counterpart. As noted above, by well-established principle the Northern Ireland Court of Appeal is not bound by decisions of the English Court of Appeal, which have persuasive, not binding, status. In *Barton and Booth* it was decided that in *Ivey* the Supreme Court had developed and modified the doctrine of *stare decisis*. We are satisfied that *Barton and Booth* was correctly decided (the contrary not having been contended) and propose to follow it accordingly.

[48] From the foregoing follows inexorably the conclusion that the successive decisions of the FtT and the UT dismissing the Appellant's appeal against the refusal of SSHD to grant her entry clearance on the basis that her application had relied upon *inter alia* a birth certificate which had been "fraudulently obtained", purporting to apply paragraph 320(7A) of the Rules, were erroneous in law.

The second appeal test

[49] As noted in [1] above, this is not an appeal against the decision of the UT. It is, rather, an application for leave (permission) to appeal to this court under section 13(4) of the 2007 Act. Section 13(5) provides that an application of this nature must first be made to, and refused by, the UT. By section 13(6):

> "The Lord Chancellor may, as respects an application under subsection (4) that falls within subsection (7) and for which the relevant appellate court is the Court of Appeal in England and Wales or the Court of Appeal in Northern Ireland, by order make provision for permission (or leave) not to be granted on the application unless the Upper Tribunal or (as the case may be) the relevant appellate court considers –
>
> (a)   That the proposed appeal would raise some important point of principle or practice; or
>
> (b)   That there is some other compelling reason for the relevant appellate court to hear the appeal."

The present application falls within the scope of section 13(7) as "… the application is for permission (or leave) to appeal from any decision of the Upper Tribunal on an appeal under section 11".

[50] The Lord Chancellor has exercised the power conferred on him by section 13(6) in the Appeals from the Upper Tribunal to the Court of Appeal Order 2008 (SI 2008/2834). Accordingly, the grant of leave to appeal to this court will be appropriate only if we consider that the proposed appeal would raise some important point of principle or practice or that there is some other compelling reason to hear the appeal.

[51] In applying these tests we acknowledge firstly that while the inevitable effect of our primary conclusion above is that if leave to appeal is granted the appeal will succeed this of itself does not satisfy either of the statutory tests. Furthermore, success for the Appellant in this court will not achieve finality as this is clearly a case for the exercise of this court's power of remittal to the FtT for the purpose of conducting a fresh appeal hearing which will *in particular* examine whether there was dishonesty on the part of the Appellant or her mother or any other person in the provision and reliance upon the false birth certificate in making the entry clearance application and make appropriate findings.

[52] It is convenient to consider whether either of the statutory tests is satisfied by reference to the submissions advanced in the clear and comprehensive skeleton argument of Mr Philip Henry (of counsel) on behalf of SSHD.

(i) Mr Henry's first submission has the merit of clarifying beyond peradventure that the only person alleged to have acted with "dishonest intent" is the Appellant's mother. Investigation and determination of this purely factual issue would, therefore, be the main task to be performed by the FtT in the event of this appeal succeeding and a remittal order following. Given the erroneous assessment of the FtT (endorsed by the UT) of the decision in *AA (Nigeria)* this court cannot be satisfied that this factual issue has been adequately considered. Furthermore, as the decision of the UT makes particularly clear, the appeal to the FtT was based on Art. 8 ECHR and the UT set aside the first instance decision on the ground that the Art. 8 analysis was inadequate. The "dishonesty" ground of appeal failed. This *per se* operates to defeat the first of Mr Henry's submissions.

(ii) Mr Henry's second submission, linked to his first, is that as matters stand the FtT will have to conduct a "full analysis" of the Appellant's Article 8 case consequent upon the remittal order of the UT. This could result in the Appellant succeeding. While all of this is correct it does not sound on the question of whether either of the statutory tests is satisfied and, further, does not engage with our analysis in (i) above.

(iii) Mr Henry's third submission is predicated entirely on an interpretation of the decision in *Adedoyin* which we have rejected above. At the beginning of his analysis, in [67], Rix LJ states unequivocally that the mandatory refusal enshrined in paragraph 320(7A) of the Rules is appropriate where there has been dishonest promotion of the use of the false document by any person, whether it be the applicant, a parent, a sponsor, an agent or someone else. At the conclusion of his analysis, in [76], Rix LJ states equally unambiguously that dishonesty or deception on the part of some person is an essential pre-requisite to mandatory refusal. The central submission on behalf of SSHD entails a distortion and misconception of the key passages in *Adedoyin*.

(iv) This court has also rejected Mr Henry's fourth submission which is that there is no conflict between the decisions in *Adedoyin* and *Hameed*.

[53] In determining whether either of the statutory tests is satisfied what is required of this court is an evaluative judgement. Focusing on the terms of section 14(6), we consider the specific question in this case to be whether the appeal raises an important point of principle. The correct interpretation of the Immigration Rules is a matter of principle. Thus the question becomes whether the specific point of interpretation raised by this appeal *is important*. It is implicit in the submissions of both parties, and we accept, that *Adedoyin* is the leading decision in the discrete sphere to which it belongs. Being a decision of the Court of Appeal it is binding on all lower courts and tribunals and, subject to the *Young v Bristol Aeroplanes* principles, binding on the Court of Appeal itself. A later division of that court has made a decision, in *Hameed*, which in our judgement misunderstands and misapplies *Adedoyin*. It is inevitable that uncertainty and debate will have been generated in consequence and will continue to arise. In short, there are two conflicting decisions of the English Court of Appeal on the interpretation of paragraph 320(7A) of the Rules. This is the first factor to be weighed.

[54] The second relevant factor is that SSHD, the public authority concerned, has been making – and doubtless continues to make – decisions based on an erroneous interpretation of both *Adedoyin* and *Hameed*. SSHD's misinterpretation and misapplication of the decision in *Adedoyin* is likely to have affected all decisions based on paragraph 320(7A) of the Rules since 2010 and, given the submissions made to this court, will clearly continue to do so indefinitely unless corrected judicially. Allied to this is the consideration that the language of paragraph 320(7A) is mirrored in three further provisions within Part 9 of the Rules.

[55] The three factors identified above all have a bearing on the first of the two statutory tests. To these we would add the following. It is a notorious fact that the admission of non-British nationals to the United Kingdom is a matter of significant public interest, one which generates acute controversy and polarised debate among members of society. One discrete facet of this topic is the trustworthiness, honesty and motives of persons seeking such admission and those belonging to their circle, such as family members, sponsors and agents. This consideration sounds on the second of the statutory tests.

[56] We have considered the inexhaustive guidance formulated by the English Court of Appeal in *Uphill v BRB (Residuary) Limited* [2005] 1 WLR 2070 in the kindred context of the second appeal test enshrined in CPR 52.13(2). We have also been assisted by the erudite analysis of Carnwath LJ in *PR (Sri Lanka) v SSHD* [2011] EWCA Civ 988. In addition we have been mindful of the statement of Lord Hope in *Eba v Advocate General for Scotland* [2012] 1 AC 710, at [48], that in order to satisfy the first of the statutory tests the issue "... would require to be one of general importance, not one confined to the petitioner's own fact and circumstances".

[57] Drawing these several threads together we conclude that the first of the statutory tests is satisfied. This conclusion requires no added weight. However, insofar as necessary such is found in our consideration of the second statutory tests above. For the reasons given we consider that the appeal which the Appellant seeks to bring to this court raises an important point of principle. It follows that the grant of leave to appeal is appropriate. Given our resolution of the substantive issues raised, it further follows that the appeal must succeed substantively.

Conclusion and order

[58] Giving effect to the foregoing the court concludes and orders:

(i) Leave to appeal is granted.

(ii) The appeal is allowed.

(iii) The case is remitted to the FtT for *de novo* consideration and determination, guided by the judgment of this court.

Post-remittal

[59] It is instructive to recall that the ultimate issue to be determined by the FtT upon remittal will be whether the refusal decision of SSHD infringes the right to respect for family life conferred on the Appellant and the other family members concerned by Article 8 ECHR under section 6 of the Human Rights Act 1998. As explained in decisions such as *LD Zimbabwe* [2010] UKUT 278 (IAC) and *Mostafa (Article 8 in entry clearance)* [2015] UKUT 112 (IAC) any demonstrated breach of a material provision of the Rules is not *per se* determinative of the Article 8 issue. Rather, it ranks as something which is "… capable of being a weighty, though not determinative, factor in deciding whether [a refusal of entry clearance] is proportionate to the legitimate aim of enforcing immigration control" (drawn from the headnote in *Mostafa*). Of course, if following further enquiry the FtT is not satisfied that SSHD has established dishonesty on the part of some person or persons, as explained in this judgment, the sole ground of the refusal decision will be extinguished and, taking into account *inter alia* the positive decision in the entry clearance application of the Appellant's older brother, the breach of Article 8 ECHR may not be contentious.

[60] In its fresh consideration and determination of the Article 8 appeal it will be for the FtT to explore in particular how and why the contentious birth certificate was generated and provided in support of the Appellant's entry clearance application. If the FtT were to conclude that SSHD's invocation of paragraph 320 (7A) was lawful this would not be determinative of the appeal. Rather, questions such as whose dishonesty, the gravity of the dishonesty, its materiality and the apparent motive will all have a bearing on the Article 8 ECHR proportionality balancing exercise. Foolishness or naivety, for example, are not on a par with a deliberate intention to deceive entailing elaborate cunning and mischievous plotting and scheming. Furthermore, there is no sustainable extant finding of any tribunal adverse to *the Appellant*, who will be entitled to a fresh judicial determination based on an entirely clean sheet.

[61] We would add one final observation. The central conclusion of the Court of Appeal in *Balijigari* was that the refusal decisions of SSHD, all based on the asserted dishonesty of the applicants, were vitiated by procedural unfairness. This has not featured as a ground of appeal in the present case thus far. It appears to this court that the *ratio* of *Balijigari* is *prima facie* indistinguishable from refusal decisions under paragraph 320 (7A) of the Rules (*viz* the present case). This issue will predictably arise for future judicial determination.

Postscript [1]: costs

[62] Having considered the parties' submissions, the court orders that SSHD will pay the Appellant's costs, to be taxed in default of agreement. There will also be a legal aid taxation order in the usual terms.

Postscript [2]: appeal to the Supreme Court

[63] Following distribution of this judgment in draft, the possibility of an application by SSHD for leave to appeal to the Supreme Court was raised. The court was subsequently notified that no such application would be pursued.

SECRETARY OF STATE FOR THE HOME DEPARTMENT v ADIUKWU

COURT OF SESSION

Lady Dorrian (Lord Justice-Clerk), Lord Glennie and Lord Woolman

[2020] CSIH 47
14 August 2020

Immigration – leave to remain – delay in granting leave to remain – exercise of statutory functions – no common law duty of care – procedure and process – grounds of appeal – absence of pleading

The Claimant applied for leave to remain in the United Kingdom in March 2010. The Secretary of State for the Home Department refused the application. The First-tier Tribunal ("FtT") allowed the Claimant's appeal, finding that removal would be incompatible with her rights under Article 8 of the ECHR. The Upper Tribunal ("UT") dismissed the Secretary of State's appeal against the FtT's decision in March 2015. The Secretary of State did not seek to challenge the UT's decision and she issued the Claimant with a 'leave to remain' status letter, in November 2016. No explanation for the delay between March 2015 and November 2016 was provided. The Claimant sought damages in respect of loss and damage allegedly suffered by her because of the failure to issue her with the appropriate status letter for some 20 months between March 2015 and November 2016. She contended in her pleadings that this failure prevented her from obtaining employment as a lawyer within the United Kingdom; that it prevented her from accessing benefits of any kind for herself and her children; and that it made it impossible for her to pay her rent, as a result of which she was evicted from her home and forced to seek refuge in emergency accommodation.

The case went before the Sheriff of Grampian for debate on the Secretary of State's preliminary plea that the Claimant's pleadings were irrelevant or lacking in specification. The Claimant's written case was that the Secretary of State owed her a duty of care in the administrative implementation of immigration decisions in her favour. It was averred that, as a consequence of the Secretary of State's 'maladministration', the Claimant suffered 'reasonably foreseeable, and predictable, financial loss and damage'. The Secretary of State relied on *Home Office v Mohammed and Others* [2011] EWCA Civ 351 in her submission that no duty of care was owed to the Claimant in circumstances where the Secretary of State was simply fulfilling her statutory function. On the basis of oral submissions, the Sheriff held that at the relevant time, Home Office policy guidance stated that persons in the Claimant's position should be granted discretionary leave to remain for up to 30 months. The Claimant's written pleadings contained no averments of any policy allegedly operated by the Secretary of State. In making his decision in the Claimant's favour, the Sheriff relied on *R (on the application of A and Kanidagli) v Secretary of State for the Home Department* [2004] EWHC 1585 (Admin), in which the judge concluded that it was fair, just and reasonable that an administrative error of this kind, involving no judgement but simple administration and with a predictable financial effect, for which there was no other remedy, should be regarded as arising out of a sufficiently proximate relationship to found a claim for damages.

On appeal, the Secretary of State relied on the judgment in *Poole Borough Council v GN (through his litigation friend "The Official Solicitor") and Another* [2019] UKSC 25 in support of her argument that, although she could confer a benefit on the Claimant in the exercise of her statutory functions, she did not owe a duty of care to do so. The Court considered whether the Secretary of State owed a duty of care to grant the Claimant discretionary leave to remain and to issue a letter confirming that status within a reasonable time of her decision not to seek to challenge the UT's decision.

Held, allowing the appeal:

(1) The respective tribunals did not make any order in their decisions that the Secretary of State should issue a status letter. They determined that the Claimant's removal would be a disproportionate interference with her rights pursuant to Article 8 of the ECHR. How to address that remained a matter for the Secretary of State. As far as predicated on assertions that the tribunals ordered the Secretary of State to grant leave to remain, the case was irrelevant. It was unsatisfactory and inappropriate that the Sheriff proceeded on the basis of submissions made 'on the hoof'. If the Claimant's case was said to rest on the existence and operation of a policy, those matters should have been clearly made the subject of averment so that an informed and reliable understanding of the policy and its operation might be achieved. The Claimant now said, orally, that there was 'a systemic failure' to ensure that policies were applied. That, rather than foreseeability, was said to be the source from which a duty on the Secretary of State might be deduced. There was no valid issue for inquiry on that matter in the absence of averments. Equally there were no averments which would establish of a duty of care on the Secretary of State for failing to confer a benefit. Whilst the case should not be determined purely on the basis of an absence of pleading, if the absence caused difficulty in reaching a conclusion on any matter, the benefit should be given to the Secretary of State (*paras 3 – 5*).

(2) The decision in *Mohammed* was that the Secretary of State did not owe a common law duty of care to applicants for leave to remain in the United Kingdom to avoid maladministration in the exercise of her statutory power to grant leave to remain. *Mohammed* disapproved the rationale of *A and Kanidagli* and the Sheriff's reasoning in the instant case could not stand. Neither *A and Kanidagli* nor *Mohammed* assisted in determining the correct approach, given the extent to which understanding of the law in this area had been clarified and developed by *Michael v Chief Constable of South Wales Police* [2015] UKSC 2; *Robinson v Chief Constable of West Yorkshire Police* [2018] UKSC 4 and *GN*. In *GN*, Lord Reed explained, *inter alia*, that public authorities could come under a common law duty to protect from harm in circumstances where the principles applicable to private individuals or bodies would impose such a duty, as for example where the authority had created the source of danger or had assumed a responsibility to protect the claimant from harm, unless the imposition of such a duty would be inconsistent with the relevant legislation. It was common ground in the instant case that no duty of care arose directly from statute. The Claimant suggested that a failure to grant leave to remain was alone sufficient to create liability by

reclassifying it as the creation of a danger. Her case was not one of causing harm, but rather one of failing to confer a benefit. It thus fell within the established principle that a duty of care did not arise save in very limited exceptions. The Claimant was in no worse position as a result of the Secretary of State's actions. A failure to act to put the Claimant in a better position could not truly be equated with creating a source of danger (*paras 9 – 11*).

(3) The basis upon which the Secretary of State might be said to have assumed responsibility towards the Claimant was very difficult to identify. In *GN*, Lord Reed stated that the operation of a statutory scheme did not automatically generate an assumption of responsibility, but it might have that effect if a defendant's conduct pursuant to the scheme met the criteria set out in such cases as *Hedley Byrne & Company Limited v Heller & Partners Limited* [1964] AC 465 and *Spring v Guardian Assurance Plc* [1995] 2 AC 296. Such a situation was sometimes described as being where the relationship between the parties was equivalent to a contractual one: *Hedley Byrne* applied. That categorisation was not valid in the instant case. In *Gorringe v Calderdale Metropolitan Borough Council* [2004] UKHL 15, Lord Hoffman referred to circumstances where public authorities had done acts or entered into relationships or undertaken responsibilities which gave rise to a common law duty of care. In the instant case, the Secretary of State did nothing and established no relationship that would bring her within the scope of a duty of care. In reality, nothing was relied on save the nature of the statutory functions and those did not suggest that there was any assumption of responsibility to the Claimant to perform those functions with reasonable care (*paras 12 – 16*).

(4) (*Per* Lord Glennie) The Claimant had two possible means of redress. First, she could have petitioned for judicial review based on the principle of legitimate expectation. Secondly, she could have made a complaint to the Parliamentary Ombudsman (*para 67*).

Cases referred to:

Caparo Industries Plc v Dickman [1990] 2 AC 605; [1990] 2 WLR 358; [1990] 1 All ER 568

Customs and Excise Commissioners v Barclays Bank Plc [2006] UKHL 28; [2007] 1 AC 181; [2006] 3 WLR 1; [2006] 4 All ER 256

Gorringe v Calderdale Metropolitan Borough Council [2004] UKHL 15; [2004] 1 WLR 1057; [2004] 2 All ER 326

Hedley Byrne & Company Limited v Heller & Partners Limited [1964] AC 465; [1963] 3 WLR 101; [1963] 2 All ER 575

Henderson v Merrett Syndicates Ltd (No.1) [1995] 2 AC 145; [1994] 3 WLR 761; [1994] 3 All ER 506

Home Office v Mohammed and Others [2011] EWCA Civ 351; [2011] 1 WLR 2862

Kiani v Secretary of State for Business, Innovation and Skills [2013] CSOH 121

M (Algeria), In a petition for judicial review [2013] CSOH 114

McCreaner v Ministry of Justice [2014] EWHC 569 (QB); [2015] 1 WLR 354

Michael v Chief Constable of South Wales Police [2015] UKSC 2; [2015] AC 1732; [2015] 2 WLR 343; [2015] 2 All ER 635

Micosta SA v Shetland Islands Council [1984] 2 Lloyd's Rep 525; 1986 SLT 193

Philp v Highland Council [2018] CSIH 53

Poole Borough Council v GN (through his litigation friend "The Official Solicitor") and Another [2019] UKSC 25; [2019] 2 WLR 1478; [2019] 4 All ER 581

R (on the application of A and Kanidagli) v Secretary of State for the Home Department [2004] EWHC 1585 (Admin)

Robinson v Chief Constable of West Yorkshire Police [2018] UKSC 4; [2018] 2 WLR 595; [2018] 2 All ER 1041

Rowley v Secretary of State for Work and Pensions [2007] EWCA Civ 598; [2007] 1 WLR 2861

Royal Bank of Scotland Plc v Holmes 1999 SLT 563; 1999 SCLR 297

Sebry v Companies House [2015] EWHC 115 (QB); [2016] 1 WLR 2499; [2015] 4 All ER 681

Shetland Line (1984) Ltd v Secretary of State for Scotland 1996 SLT 653

Spring v Guardian Assurance Plc [1995] 2 AC 296; [1994] 3 WLR 354; [1994] 3 All ER 129

Stovin v Wise [1996] AC 923; [1996] 3 WLR 388; [1996] 3 All ER 801

W v Home Office [1997] Imm AR 302

White v Jones [1995] 2 AC 207; [1995] 2 WLR 187; [1995] 1 All ER 691

X v Hounslow London Borough Council [2009] EWCA Civ 286

Legislation and international instruments judicially considered:

Courts Reform (Scotland) Act 2014, section 112
Crown Suits (Scotland) Act 1857, section 4A
European Convention on Human Rights, Article 8
Immigration Act 1971, sections 3 & 4

Representation

Mr *McIlvride* QC and Mr *Pugh* instructed by Morton Fraser LLP, for the Advocate General for Scotland;
Ms *Crawford* QC and Mr *Dewar* instructed by Drummond Miller LLP, for the Claimant.

Opinion

LADY DORRIAN:

The nature of the respondent's case

[1] I am grateful to Lord Glennie for setting out the detail of the factual background of this case, and the pleadings, in his own opinion with which I am in agreement.

[2] This is a case which went to the sheriff for debate on the reclaimer's preliminary plea that the respondent's pleadings were irrelevant *et separatim* lacking in specification. The focus of such a debate is, or should be, the averments made by the respondent, with such relevant averments by the reclaimer which may bear on the issue which is essentially whether the respondent has averred a relevant case from which it may be established that the Home Secretary was under a duty of care to her. The foundation of that alleged duty of care should be clearly

specified in the pleadings. It is, I think worth taking a moment to examine what the respondent's written case is before turning to see how differently the case was eventually argued before the sheriff; and how differently again it was argued in this court. The written case is that:

(a)   The Home Secretary owed the respondent a duty to take care in the administrative implementation of the immigration decisions in her favour; more specifically she had a duty to ensure that the respondent received a status letter which she could use to obtain paid employment and/or access state benefits for herself and her children.

(b)   The Home Secretary was under a duty to obtemper both orders of the immigration tribunals and, ultimately, to issue the respondent with a status letter in implementation thereof.

(c)   The claim appears to be based entirely on foreseeability, although it is very baldly stated. The central averment is simply that the respondent knew or ought to have known that the respondent was entitled to be granted leave to remain in the United Kingdom as early as 15 December 2014. It is then averred that "as a consequence of the maladministration committed by the Home Secretary, or those acting on her behalf, the [respondent] suffered reasonably foreseeable, and predictable, financial loss and damage".

[3] It is hardly necessary to point out that these averments follow a false premise, as specified at paragraphs (a) and (b): the decisions of the respective tribunals did not involve making any order that the Home Secretary should issue a status letter. They determined that her removal would be a disproportionate interference with her Article 8 rights. How to address that remained a matter for the Home Secretary. It may well be that in reality there was little doubt that these decisions would be followed by the issuing of a status letter but the matter was nevertheless still one for the exercise by the Home Secretary of her section 4 discretion. None of this is the matter of any averment. I agree with Lord Glennie's observation that as far as predicated on assertions that the tribunals ordered the Home Secretary to grant leave to remain the case is irrelevant.

[4] It is striking that the pleadings contain no averments of any policy allegedly operated by the Home Secretary, the details of any policy, when and how it was put in place, the extent to which it was implemented in practice, how it might affect the respondent or any other matters of that kind. Notwithstanding this, the sheriff felt able to proceed on the basis that there was a policy that would have operated favourably towards the respondent on the basis of oral submissions made at the bar, and to base his decision to a degree on this. In my view that is an unsatisfactory way of proceeding. If a case is said to rest on the existence and operation of a policy those matters should be clearly made the subject of averment so that an informed and reliable understanding of the policy and its operation may be achieved. Proceeding on the basis of submissions made "on the hoof" is not appropriate. It is now said, orally, that there was "a systemic failure to ensure that policies are applied". This, rather than foreseeability, is now said to be the source from which a duty on the respondent may be deduced. How on earth this court

could consider there to be a valid issue for inquiry on that matter in the absence of averments I cannot see.

[5] In the second place there are equally no averments of any kind such as would bring the case within the classification of the creation of a danger or the assumption of responsibility which may be relevant to the establishment of a duty of care for failing to confer a benefit, which at heart is what the respondent's case is. When the case has proceeded this far, I share your Lordships' reluctance to decide the issue on a mere pleading point, but we should remind ourselves of the observations made by Lord Reed in *N and another v Poole Borough Council* [2019] 2 WLR 1478, para 82:

> "Since such an inference depends on the facts of the individual case, there may well be cases in which the existence or absence of an assumption of responsibility cannot be determined on a strikeout application. Nevertheless, the particulars of claim must provide some basis for the leading of evidence at trial from which an assumption of responsibility could be inferred."

[6] In short, whilst I do not suggest that the case should be determined purely on the basis of an absence of pleading, I do consider that if the absence of pleadings causes a difficulty in reaching a conclusion on any matter the benefit should be given to the appellant in the absence of any, let alone clear and detailed, pleadings. I also agree with the observations made by Lord Glennie about these matters at paragraph 11 of his opinion.

The legal issues

[7] The shifting sands which have bedevilled this area of the law over many years have been converted into firm terrain during a series of important decisions of the UKSC, notably *Michael v Chief Constable of South Wales Police* 2015 AC 1732; *Robinson v Chief Constable of West Yorkshire Police* [2018] AC 736 and *N and another v Poole Borough Council*. The first significant area of clarification relates to the effect of *Caparo Industries plc v Dickman* [1990] 2 AC 605. These recent decisions have made it clear that *Caparo* should not be taken as establishing a universal tripartite test for the existence of a duty of care. On the contrary, in the ordinary case the court should continue to apply established principles of law. The *Caparo* test was appropriate when considering novel situations, where an incremental approach by analogy with established categories of liability was to be adopted. In such situations the question of whether it was fair, just and reasonable to impose a duty would be part of the assessment whether such an incremental step required to be taken.

[8] The sheriff did not rely on *Caparo*, having reached the conclusion that the matter was covered by the decision in *R (Kanidagli) v Secretary of State for the Home Department* [2004] EWHC 1585 (Admin), where the judge concluded that it was fair, just and reasonable that an administrative error of this kind, involving no judgement but simple administration and with a predictable financial effect, for which there was no other remedy, should be regarded as arising out of a sufficiently proximate relationship to found a claim for damages. Somewhat mystifyingly, the sheriff **concluded** that nevertheless, had he been required to go through a *Caparo* exercise himself he would have adopted the same general approach, notwithstanding that he tells us he "was not addressed in any detail in

relation to the factors to be taken into account in applying the fair, just and reasonable test set out in *Caparo*". The sole basis for the sheriff's decision was that (a) *Kanidagli* applied; (b) the *ratio* of that case, namely that there was a sound basis for distinguishing *W v Home Office* [1997] Imm AR 302, was correct; and (c) the *ratio* had not been impliedly overturned by the appeal court in the case of *Mohammed & Ors v Home Office* [2011] 1 WLR 2862.

[9] I disagree. The decision in *Mohammed* was that the Home Secretary did not owe a common law duty of care to applicants for leave to remain in the United Kingdom to avoid maladministration in the exercise of her power to grant leave to remain under section 4(1) of the Immigration Act 1971. The argument which had been advanced was put solely on the basis that the court should follow *Kanidagli*. At paragraph 15 the Appeal Court made it clear that it did not think that the reasons given in *Kanidagli* for distinguishing W – the basis upon which the case had effectively succeeded – were valid. In W, the claimant had been held in immigration detention because of a crass administrative mistake, which could not be dignified as an error of judgement, yet the court held that no claim lay in negligence. I cannot read *Mohammed* as doing other than disapprove of the rationale of *Kanidagli*. In addition the facts of this case are much closer to those of *Mohammed* itself. I do not therefore think the sheriff's reasoning can stand. However, in any event, I am not convinced that any of the three cases, *W*, *Kanidagli*, or *Mohammed*, assist in determining the correct approach to this case, given the extent to which understanding of the law in this area has been clarified and developed by *Michael*, *Robinson* and *N*.

[10] I turn then to examine the matter from the basis of the "established principles of law" referred to in *N*, further guidance about which was given succinctly by Lord Reed in para 65:

"It follows (1) that public authorities may owe a duty of care in circumstances where the principles applicable to private individuals would impose such a duty, unless such a duty would be inconsistent with, and is therefore excluded by, the legislation from which their powers or duties are derived; (2) that public authorities do not owe a duty of care at common law merely because they have statutory powers or duties, even if, by exercising their statutory functions, they could prevent a person from suffering harm; and (3) that public authorities can come under a common law duty to protect from harm in circumstances where the principles applicable to private individuals or bodies would impose such a duty, as for example where the authority has created the source of danger or has assumed a responsibility to protect the claimant from harm, unless the imposition of such a duty would be inconsistent with the relevant legislation."

It was accepted in submissions in this appeal that no duty of care arose directly from the relevant statute. Rather than focus on the way the case had originally been argued under reliance on *Kanidagli*, senior counsel accepted that the respondent's case had to come within paragraphs (1) or (3) of paragraph 65 of *N*. The respondent's argument was that the failure complained of did not arise in the course of the exercise of a statutory function or power by the Secretary of State; rather the failure arose in the course of the simple administration of something that required to be done by the Secretary of State. I confess that I have difficulty in understanding the distinction in the circumstances of this case. It seems to me that there is an essential circularity in the approach adopted for the respondent; it is accepted that there is generally no liability for failing to confer a benefit, yet it is argued that that very failure is alone sufficient to create liability by reclassifying it as the creation of a danger. As with the arguments on assumption of responsibility it essentially rests on the proposition that a duty of care exists merely because there existed a statutory power the exercise of which could have conferred a benefit on the respondent.

[11] The respondent's case is in my view not one of causing harm to the claimant but is one of failing to confer a benefit on the respondent. It is thus a case falling within the established principle that a duty of care does not arise save in very limited exceptions, *viz*: where the defender has created the source of the danger or where there has been a voluntary assumption of responsibility. I have little difficulty in rejecting the suggestion that the Home Secretary created a source of danger for the respondent or that the situation may be equiparated with such a circumstance. The respondent was in no worse position following the decision of the First-tier Tribunal as a result of the Home Secretary's actions; the point of her claim is that the Home Secretary did not take action to put her in a better position. I find it very difficult to see how this can truly be equiparated with creating a source of danger for the respondent.

Assumption of responsibility

[12] The same applies to the question of assumption of responsibility. The basis upon which the Home Secretary may be said to have assumed responsibility towards the respondent is very difficult to identify. It was not identified in the pleadings and I remain unclear as to the basis of the current assertion.

[13] The principles underlying the circumstances in which a duty of care may be said to arise from an assumption of responsibility were examined by Lord Reed in *N* in paras 66 – 73. The development was traced from early cases through *Hedley Byrne & Co Ltd v Heller & Partners Ltd* [1964] AC465 to *Henderson v Merrett Syndicates Ltd* [1995] 2 AC 145 and *Spring v Guardian Assurance plc* [1995] 2 AC 296. Lord Reed quoted the words of Lord Goff in the latter:

"Accordingly where the plaintiff entrusts the defendant with the conduct of his affairs, in general or in particular, the defendant may be held to have assumed responsibility to the plaintiff, and the plaintiff to have relied on the defendant to exercise due skill and care, in respect of such conduct."

[14] The argument that a public authority cannot assume responsibility merely by operating a statutory scheme, on the basis that the responsibility must be "voluntarily accepted or undertaken", was also examined specifically under reference to *Rowley v Secretary of State for Work and Pensions* [2007] 1 WLR 2861 and *X v Hounslow London Borough Council* [2009] EWCA Civ 286. At para 72 of *N*, Lord Reed noted:

"The correctness of these decisions is not in question, but the dicta should not be understood as meaning that an assumption of responsibility can never arise out of the performance of statutory functions."

He went on:

"the operation of a statutory scheme does not automatically generate an assumption of responsibility, but it may have that effect if the defendant's conduct pursuant to the scheme meets the criteria set out in such cases as *Hedley Byrne* and *Spring v Guardian Assurance plc*."

[15] These criteria essentially relate to circumstances of the kind described in *Hedley Byrne* in the speech of Lord Morris of Borth-y-Gest, pp502–503:

"… if someone possessed of a special skill undertakes, quite irrespective of contract, to apply that skill for the assistance of another person who relies upon such skill, a duty of care will arise. … Furthermore, if in a sphere in which a person is so placed that others could reasonably rely upon his judgement or his skill or upon his ability to make careful inquiry, a person takes it upon himself to give information or advice to, or allows his information or advice to be passed on to, another person who, as he knows or should know, will place reliance upon it, then a duty of care will arise".

[16] The situation is sometimes described (see the speech of Lord Devlin in *Hedley Byrne*) as being where the relationship between the parties is equivalent to a contractual one. I do not see that categorisation as valid in the present case. In *Gorringe v Calderdale Metropolitan Borough Council* [2004] 1 WLR 1057 Lord Hoffman (para 38) referred to circumstances where public authorities have actually done acts or entered into relationships or undertaken responsibilities which give rise to a common law duty of care. If we ask what has the Home Secretary done here or what relationship has she established to bring her within the scope of a duty of care? The answer is nothing: it is in reality purely based on a statutory power under section 4. In short, in my view nothing is relied on save the nature of the statutory functions and these do not suggest that there was any assumption of responsibility to the respondent to perform those functions with reasonable care.

[17] Accordingly, it is my view that the appeal must succeed.

LORD GLENNIE:

Introduction

[18] This is an appeal from an interlocutor of the sheriff of Grampian, Highland and Islands sitting at Aberdeen dated 12 June 2019 repelling the defender's plea to the relevancy of the pursuer's case and allowing parties a proof of their averments.

[19] The appeal raises an important and, on one view, novel point of law as to whether, in circumstances where both the First-tier Tribunal and the Upper Tribunal (the "FtT" and the "UT") have held that her refusal of an application for leave to remain was unlawful, and she has not sought to appeal the decision of the UT, the Secretary of State for the Home Department (the "Home Secretary") owes a duty of care to grant the applicant discretionary leave to remain and issue to the applicant a "status letter" confirming that she has such leave, thereby enabling the applicant to obtain employment and access welfare benefits, and to do that within a reasonable time of the decision not to seek to challenge the UT's decision.

[20] The pursuer and respondent is the applicant for leave to remain. I shall generally call her "the pursuer", but given her status at certain material times it is convenient sometimes to refer to her as "the applicant". She claims damages in the amount of £56,000 in respect of loss and damage allegedly suffered by her as a result of the Home Secretary's failure to issue her with the appropriate status letter for some 20 months between March 2015, when the UT found in her favour, and November 2016, when the letter was eventually issued. She contends in her pleadings that this failure prevented her from obtaining employment as a lawyer within the United Kingdom, she having obtained a law degree in Nigeria and a Masters in Oil and Gas Law at Robert Gordon University in Aberdeen; that it prevented her from accessing benefits of any kind for herself and her children to which she would otherwise have been entitled if unable to obtain employment; and that it made it impossible for her to pay her rent, as a result of which she was evicted from her accommodation and forced to seek refuge in emergency accommodation.

[21] The defender and appellant is the Advocate General for Scotland. He is sued as the appropriate Law Officer in respect of these proceedings in terms of s.4A of the Crown Suits (Scotland) Act 1875. For all practical purposes, the defender and appellant is the Home Secretary. I shall refer to them as "the defender".

[22] Recognising that the appeal raised both complex and possibly novel points of law, the Sheriff Appeal Court on 29 October 2019 remitted the appeal to the Court of Session under section 112 of the Courts Reform (Scotland) Act 2014.

Outline facts

[23] The assumed facts relevant to this appeal fall within a narrow compass. Sections 3 and 4 of the Immigration Act 1971 entitle the Home Secretary to grant a person leave to remain in the United Kingdom for a limited or an indefinite period. On 16 March 2010 the applicant applied for leave to remain, her application being based on Article 8 ECHR, the right to respect for private and family life. Her application was refused in December 2010. In December 2013[*] the applicant appealed to the FtT (Immigration and Asylum Chamber) against that refusal. On 31 July 2014, the FtT allowed the applicant's appeal. The Home Secretary appealed to the UT. On 16 March 2015 that appeal was refused. The Home Secretary did not seek to challenge the decision of the UT refusing her appeal. She became, to use the jargon, "appeal rights exhausted". We were not taken specifically to the reasoned decisions of either the FtT or the UT, but those decisions were included in the productions in this case and we have read them as part of the background to our consideration of the issues. The sheriff records in paragraph 2 of his Note that it was a matter of agreement that those decisions were to the effect that removal of the applicant from the UK was incompatible with her rights under Article 8 ECHR.

[24] It appears to have been a matter of agreement before the sheriff – though the matter is not referred to at all in the pursuer's pleadings and no such agreement was recorded in a joint minute or any other written document – that there was in

---

[*] Some explanation of the delay of three years between the Home Secretary's decision and the appeal to the FtT is contained within the decisions of the FtT and the UT, but the delay is of no importance for present purposes.

existence at the time relevant Home Office policy guidance stating that persons in the class of the pursuer should be granted discretionary leave to remain for up to 30 months. The sheriff records it in this way in paragraph 2 of his Note:

"The Secretary of State has published policy guidance that provided between 2010 and 8 July 2012 a person whose removal from the UK would be incompatible with Article 8 of the ECHR should be given discretionary leave to remain for up to three years. From 9 July 2012, the policy changed so that, subject to certain exceptions, the maximum period of discretionary leave which would be granted at any one time was thirty months. The grant of leave to remain is dealt with by issuing a 'status letter'."

The full text of the relevant guidance is set out by Lord Doherty at para [15] of his Opinion in *DM Ptr* [2013] CSOH 114. It is convenient to quote it in full:

"15. At the material times the Secretary of State's published policy guidance was as follows:

Discretionary leave to remain – Immigration Rule 395C

Chapter 53 of the EIG provided guidance on the 'relevant factors' to which UKBA officials should have regard in terms of rule 395C before making a decision on removal under section 10 of the Immigration Act 1999. The version of Chapter 53 which was extant immediately before April 2008 provided:

'Should the decision maker conclude that removal is not appropriate then leave outside the Rules should be granted. Such leave should generally be Indefinite Leave to Remain unless limited leave or deferred removal is the appropriate course of action to take. However, each case must be considered on its own individual merits.'

Between April 2008 and 19 July 2011 Chapter 53 did not prescribe the length of time for which leave to remain should be granted in the event of a decision not to remove on Rule 395C grounds. From 20 July 2011 until rule 395C was revoked on 13 February 2012 Chapter 53 provided that in such circumstances discretionary leave to remain for a period of up to three years should be granted.

Discretionary leave to remain – Article 8

Between 2010 and 8 July 2012 a person whose removal would be incompatible with Article 8 ECHR should be given discretionary leave to remain for up to three years.

Discretionary leave to remain – change in policy

From 9 July 2012 the policy changed so that, subject to certain exceptions, the maximum period of discretionary leave which would be granted at any one time was 30 months."

The present case concerns events after July 2012, so the policy with which we are concerned was that, subject to certain exceptions (which neither party has suggested are relevant here), once it had been determined that an applicant's removal from the United Kingdom would be incompatible with Article 8 ECHR, that applicant should be given discretionary leave to remain for up to 30 months.

[25] It is contended by the pursuer, and I did not understand it to be disputed, that without the grant of a status letter a person will find it impossible to obtain employment and access welfare benefits.

[26] The Home Secretary did not issue the pursuer with a "leave to remain" status letter, until November 2016. No explanation for the delay between March 2015 and November 2016 has been provided. It is not said that the delay was due to any requirement on the part of the Home Secretary to make further enquiries or to exercise a discretion as to whether or not to issue a status letter in light of the UT's determination of her appeal, or to any need to resolve some question as to the applicability of her policy to the case of the pursuer. At paragraph 9 of his Note, the sheriff records the position adopted by Mr Pugh on behalf of the Home Secretary:

> "He summarised the factual basis of the case categorising the failure on the part of the defender as a delay in granting the pursuer leave to remain. No explanation is given in the defender's pleadings for the delay in issuing a status letter. Mr Pugh explained that there was no dispute but that there was a delay. The Secretary of State accepts that. From the date of the Upper Tribunal's decision the natural consequence was that leave to remain should have been granted to the pursuer. No explanation was offered in submissions. It was accepted that the defender simply failed to do something which should have happened, namely the issuing of the status letter."

That position taken before the sheriff reflects the position adopted by Mr McIlvride QC on behalf of the Home Secretary before this court.

The pursuer's pleadings

[27] Since the matter comes before this court on the question of relevancy, it is of some importance to examine the pleadings. Article 2 of Condescendence sets out in narrative form the decisions made leading to the point where the Home Secretary became appeal rights exhausted. Article 3 avers that in those circumstances the Home Secretary came under certain duties:

> "3. The Defenders knew or ought to have known that the Pursuer was entitled to be granted leave to remain in the United Kingdom as early as 15th December 2014. That entitlement was expressly recorded in writing on 16th March 2015. It is explained and averred that the Home Secretary owed the Pursuer a duty to take care in the administrative implementation of the immigration decisions in her favour. More particularly, the Home Secretary owed the Pursuer a duty to ensure that she received a status letter which she could use to obtain paid employment and/or access state benefits for herself and her children. ..."

The relevance of 15 December 2014 appears to be that this was the date of the hearing at which the UT indicated that it was minded to refuse the appeal from the FtT. We are not concerned with that in this appeal. The UT's formal decision is dated 16 March 2015. The nub of the pursuer's case on breach of duty is set out in Article 4 of Condescendence. This reads as follows:

> "4.   Despite repeated requests by the Pursuer, the Secretary of State for the Home Department refused or at least delayed to issue the Defender with leave to remain until in or around November 2016. The Home Secretary was under a duty to obtemper both orders of the immigration tribunals and, ultimately, to issue the Pursuer with a status letter in implementation thereof. It is averred that the Home Secretary, or those acting on her behalf, ought to have done so within a reasonable time; and the Secretary of State was under a duty to issue the leave to remain to the Pursuer within a reasonable period. By not so doing the Secretary of State for the Home Department failed in their (*sic*) duties and were wilfully negligent. As a consequence of the maladministration committed by the Home Secretary, or those acting on her behalf, the Pursuer suffered reasonably foreseeable, and predictable, financial loss and damage. But for the Home Secretary's failure(s) (or the failure(s) of those acting on her behalf) to obtemper and implement the orders of the immigration tribunals, at all or within a reasonable time, the loss and damage would not have occurred. ..."

The alleged duty is encapsulated in the pursuer's first plea-in-law as follows:

> "1.   The Pursuer having suffered loss and damage through fault on the part of the Secretary of State for the Home Department, is entitled to reparation from them therefor."

The reference in Article 4 to "maladministration" is not supported by averments of malice or want of probable cause, a matter to which I return briefly below, nor is it followed through to any appropriate plea-in-law. All that is focused in the plea-in-law is "fault", which, in light of what has gone before, presumably refers to alleged breaches of the duties identified in Article 3, namely the duty "to take care in the administrative implementation of the immigration decisions in [the pursuer's] favour", and Article 4, namely the duty "to obtemper [within a reasonable time] both orders of the immigration tribunals and, ultimately, to issue the Pursuer with a status letter in implementation thereof".

[28] I shall refer in due course to the submissions before this court, but it should be noticed at this stage that Ms Crawford QC, who appeared for the pursuer before us (though she did not appear in the sheriff court), focused her arguments not on the alleged duties set out in the passages quoted but on an assumption of responsibility by the Home Secretary. That was said to arise to a significant extent from the existence of the policy guidance referred to above. This line of argument does not feature in the pursuer's pleadings. Legal arguments do not require to be set out in terms. However, in so far as the assumption of responsibility is based upon anything said or done by the Home Secretary, or the Home Office, those facts should be averred. It is a matter of some concern that, in a procedure focused on the relevance of the pursuer's pleadings, those pleadings do not even mention the key elements of her case. For my part I would not wish to decide this case in the absence of averments on this critical point, but it seems to me that if this

matter is to proceed further in the sheriff court, whether by way of proof or proof before answer, the pursuer should be required to amend so as to make relevant averments of all matters relied upon in support of her argument, including in particular the terms of the relevant guidance, its statutory or other basis, and the impact of that guidance on the arguments anent the existence or otherwise of the duty of care contended for, as well as any actions of the Home Secretary or those acting on her behalf upon which the pursuer relies to justify the assumption of responsibility argument. This is not an insistence on procedural niceties for their own sake. These key matters will be of direct relevance to the success or otherwise of the pursuer's case; and the question of whether the policy applied to the pursuer's case, or whether the Home Secretary was entitled to disapply it, may also be of relevance. That latter point is hinted at in the pursuer's Note of Argument where she says that the Home Secretary "has not argued that the policy did not, or should not, apply to the pursuer", a statement of fact which may well be correct, though it is difficult to see where such an argument would be made by the Home Secretary, in the pleadings at least, when the policy itself is not mentioned by the pursuer. Other points of importance are similarly not mentioned in the pleadings. It is said by the pursuer in her Note of Argument that the status letter entitles the person to whom it is issued to obtain employment and access welfare benefits. That, too, does not appear to be in dispute, but it is not apparent from the pursuer's pleadings in the sheriff court action whether this is said to be the legal effect of the issue of a status letter or, conversely, whether the position is simply that the practical consequence of not having such a letter is that one is prevented from obtaining employment and accessing such benefits. This too would benefit from elaboration.

[29] I do not suggest, however, that we decide the case on the basis of the deficiencies in the pursuer's pleadings. The point of law raised in this case is capable of being decided on the pleadings as they stand as amplified in the course of submissions.

The debate in the sheriff court and the sheriff's decision

[30] Before the sheriff, it was argued on behalf of the Home Secretary that no duty of care was owed to the pursuer in circumstances where the Home Secretary was simply fulfilling her statutory function. There was authority against there being any such duty of care (*W v Home Office* [1997] Imm AR 302 and *Mohammed v Home Office* [2011] 1 WLR 2862). *Esto* those cases were not decisive, the court should proceed incrementally from the existing authorities. There was no basis upon which it could be held that there was a relationship of proximity between the defender and the pursuer or that it was fair, just and reasonable to impose a duty of care (*Caparo Industries plc v Dickman* [1990] 2 AC 605). On behalf of the pursuer, reliance was placed upon the decision of Keith J in *R (Kanidagli) v Secretary of State for the Home Department* [2004] EWHC 1585 (Admin). It was submitted that that case was clear authority for the proposition that a duty of care was owed by the Home Secretary in a case such as this. Esto that case was not on all fours with the present, it provided the basis for the court in this case, proceeding incrementally, to hold that a duty of care was owed to the pursuer.

[31] It is apparent from the sheriff's Note that the argument before him came to be focused almost exclusively on the question whether the judge in *Kanidagli* had

correctly distinguished the reasoning of the Court of Appeal in *W*; and whether the reasoning in *Kanidagli* had in its turn been disapproved by the Court of Appeal in *Mohammed*. The sheriff accepted the arguments advanced on behalf of the pursuer, held that *Kanidagli* had correctly distinguished *W* and had not been disapproved in *Mohammed*, and concluded that *Kanidagli* determined the issue in the pursuer's favour. In any event, the decision in *Kanidagli* provided a sound basis for holding, on an incremental basis, that the relationship between the pursuer and the Home Secretary was sufficiently proximate and that it was fair, just and reasonable to impose such a duty.

[32] Accordingly, he repelled the first plea in law for the defender (a plea to the relevancy of the action) and appointed the case to a proof. For my part, if we had otherwise been in favour of the pursuer, I would have thought that the appropriate disposal was to order a proof before answer, rather than a proof simpliciter.

Submissions before this court

[33] For the Home Secretary, Mr McIlvride invited the court to allow the appeal, sustain the first plea in law for the defender and dismiss the action.

[34] He submitted that, in Scots law, a public official will be liable in damages for maladministration in exercising his or her public functions only if proved to have been acting with malice or want of probable cause: *Micosta SA v Shetland Islands Council* 1986 SLT 193, Lord Justice-Clerk Ross at 198G-I, *Shetland Line (1984) Ltd v Secretary of State for Scotland* 1996 SLT 653, Lord Johnson at 658 sub-para.(5); and see also *Kiani v Secretary of State for Business, Innovation and Skills* [2013] CSOH 121, Lord Hodge at para [17] and *Philp v Highland Council* [2018] CSIH 53, Lord President Carloway, giving the judgment of the court, at paras [34]–[35]. The pursuer made no averments of malice or want of probable cause. It was not enough for the pursuer to say, as she did say in her written submissions, that malice could be inferred from the conduct of the Home Secretary in failing to issue a status letter without any attempt to explain how that failure occurred. The only question for determination was whether the pursuer's pleadings were relevant for enquiry. As already observed, those pleadings made no mention of malice or want of probable cause, either expressly or by inference. Accordingly, in so far as the case was based upon maladministration, it was irrelevant.

[35] Mr McIlvride submitted that the Home Secretary owed no duty of care to the pursuer to issue a status letter within a reasonable time. In so far as the pursuer's case was based in negligence, it was bound to fail and was irrelevant. *Kanidagli*, upon which the sheriff had based his decision, was wrongly decided and had been disapproved by the Court of Appeal in *Mohammed*. The 1971 Act conferred a power on the Home Secretary to grant leave to remain but did not impose any duty on her in that respect. Even if the effect of the FtT and UT decisions was to leave the Home Secretary with no alternative but to issue the pursuer with a status document, so that her failure to do so within a reasonable time or at all might be susceptible to judicial review, it did not follow that that public law duty, to use that shorthand, transposed into a duty of care at common law. Mr McIlvride referred us to the decision of the House of Lords in *Gorringe v Calderdale MBC* [2004] 1 WLR 1057 for the statement by Lord Hoffmann that where a statute did not create a private right of action, "it would be, to say the least, unusual if the mere existence of the statutory duty could generate a common

law duty of care" (para 23); and he found it "difficult to imagine a case" in which a common law duty could be founded simply upon the failure, however irrational, to provide some benefit which a public authority has power, or even a public law duty, to provide (para 32). Those observations were reflected in the judgment of Sedley LJ in *Mohammed* at para 14: "As a general rule the proximity created by a statutory relationship does not by itself create a duty of care". Particular reliance was placed on two recent Supreme Court decisions (*Robinson v Chief Constable of West Yorkshire* [2018] AC 736 and *N v Poole Borough Council* [2019] 2 WLR 1478) which both explained the development of the common law in this area up to and including the decision in *Caparo*, and sought to establish a coherent framework for the assessment of whether a duty of care is owed by a public body in any particular case. In *Robinson* at para 29 Lord Reed explained that, properly understood, *Caparo* achieved a balance between legal certainty and justice. He pointed out that in the ordinary case the courts generally consider what has been decided previously and follow those precedents. In other cases, where the question of the existence of a duty of care has not previously been decided, the courts consider the closest analogy in the existing law with a view to maintaining legal coherence and the avoidance of inappropriate distinctions; and they also weigh up the reasons for and against imposing liability in order to decide whether the existence of a duty of care would be fair, just and reasonable. Mr McIlvride submitted that the previously decided cases of *W* and *Mohammed* already established that no duty of care existed in a case such as this. In so far as those cases did not provide a complete answer to the question whether a duty arose in the present case, they were the cases most closely analogous to the present. No incremental development of the common law starting from those cases would permit a finding that the Home Secretary owed a duty of care in the present case. In *N*, a case about whether certain provisions of the Children Act 1989 gave rise to a duty of care, Lord Reed took the opportunity of clarifying what he called the "shifting approaches by the highest court" on the issue of the liability of public authorities for their conduct of their statutory powers and duties: see para 25. At para 28, Lord Reed pointed out that, like private individuals, "public bodies did not generally owe a duty of care to confer benefits on individuals", but that, as in the case of private individuals, "a duty to protect from harm, or to confer some other benefit, might arise in particular circumstances, as for example where the public body had created the source of danger or have assumed responsibility to protect the claimant from harm". He deliberately drew the distinction between "causing harm (making things worse) and failing to confer a benefit (not making things better)" rather than the more traditional distinction between acts and omissions, and Mr McIlvride submitted that the present case was one in which it was being asserted that the Home Secretary owed a duty to confer a benefit. At para 65 Lord Reed gave the following summary of the relevant principles concerning the potential liability of public authorities (I quote it in full because it assumed centre stage in the argument before us):

"65. It follows (1) that public authorities may owe a duty of care in circumstances where the principles applicable to private individuals would impose such a duty, unless such a duty would be inconsistent with, and is therefore excluded by, the legislation from which their powers or duties are derived; (2) that public authorities do not owe a duty of care at common law merely because they have statutory powers or duties, even if, by exercising their statutory functions, they could prevent a person from suffering harm; and (3) that public authorities can come under a common law duty to protect from harm in circumstances where the principles applicable to private individuals or bodies would impose such a duty, as for example where the authority has created the source of danger or has assumed a responsibility to protect the claimant from harm, unless the imposition of such a duty would be inconsistent with the relevant legislation."

Mr McIlvride submitted that the present case effectively fell within that second category. The Home Secretary could confer a benefit on the respondent in the exercise of her statutory functions, but did not owe a duty of care to do so. The pursuer's argument depended entirely upon the statutory relationship of the Home Secretary towards the pursuer. The pursuer's attempt to translate that statutory relationship into an assumption of responsibility by the Home Secretary was bound to fail. There was no basis upon which to hold that the Home Secretary had assumed the responsibility to the pursuer. The only relevant facts were that the tribunals refused the Home Secretary's appeal and that, in light of that refusal, the matter went back to the Home Secretary to operate the statutory scheme.

[36] Mr McIlvride submitted that, even if the relationship of proximity was established, it was neither fair, just nor reasonable to impose a duty of care in a case such as this. The losses sought to be recovered were pure economic losses, in respect of which the courts are slow to create duties of care. And in any event the pursuer had other remedies, whether by judicial review, or a claim under Article 8 ECHR, or, as noted in *Mohammed* at paras [25][26], by seeking assistance from the Parliamentary Ombudsman.

[37] For the pursuer, Ms Crawford QC invited the court to refuse the appeal, alternatively to allow it only to the extent of appointing the matter to a proof before answer, leaving all pleas standing, rather than a proof simpliciter.

[38] Ms Crawford made it clear that she was not advancing a case of "maladministration" in support of which it would be necessary to show malice or want of probable cause: *Micosta*. However, if malice or want of probable cause were necessary in order to instruct a case that the Home Secretary was in breach of a common law duty of care, then it could be established from the fact of the unexplained delay and the absence of any attempt to argue that consideration was being given to departing from the policy – in other words it was a case where there was no real exercise by the Home Secretary of her statutory function.

[39] Ms Crawford's primary submission was that the duty of care incumbent on the Home Secretary was based on orthodox principles of negligence. It arose in respect of her failure to take reasonable care in the exercise of a purely administrative or operational act. She contrasted this with what she described as the Home Secretary's erroneous contention that the pursuer sought to impose a common law duty of care in respect of the discharge of a statutory power. The distinction was well illustrated by comparing the cases of *W* and *Mohammed* with the decision of Keith J in *Kanidagli*. In *W* and *Mohammed* the Home Secretary still had something to investigate and determine. Whatever the nature of the failure, it occurred in the course of exercising the statutory discretion. By contrast, in *Kanidagli*, once the tribunals had made their decisions and it had been resolved that there was to be no further appeal, all that remained for the Home Secretary was to issue the status letter in accordance with the then existing policy. That was

a critical distinction which the Court of Appeal in *Mohammed* had failed to recognise.

[40] Ms Crawford submitted that the Home Secretary had assumed responsibility to take care to grant the pursuer leave to remain and to issue a status letter within a reasonable time. A number of factors were relied upon in support of the assumption of responsibility argument. They were: (i) the decision of the UT; (ii) the lack of challenge to that decision; (iii) the Home Secretary's policy designed to regulate dealings with, and to ensure continuity of decision-making in respect of, a defined class of persons, i.e. granting discretionary leave of up to 30 months to those whose enforced removal from the United Kingdom would contravene ECHR; (iv) the absence of a departure from that policy; (v) the fact that leave to remain was required to access welfare benefits and employment; (vi) the 20 month delay in granting leave to remain. Ms Crawford also relied on: (vii) the fact that the pursuer forms part of a limited and identifiable class; and (viii) the absence of any suggestion that a duty of care would not impose any undue burden on the Home Secretary timeously to carry out her administrative functions. Put compendiously, this was a case where it could be said that the Home Secretary had created the source of danger, *viz* the inability of a person in the position of the pursuer to access benefits or obtain work without a status letter, or at least had control over it; she had set up a system for the issuing of a status letter to an applicant who, in light of decisions by the FtT and the UT could not lawfully be removed on ECHR grounds; and she was aware of the need to issue such a letter within a reasonable time, since without it the applicant would be likely to suffer hardship. In light of all that it could properly be said that she had assumed responsibility for the issuing of such a letter within a reasonable time.

[41] Thus understood, the case fell within classic common law principles instructing a case of negligence. Public authorities are generally subject to the same general principles of the law of negligence as private individuals and bodies, except to the extent that legislation requires a departure from those principles: see *N*, Lord Reed at paras 64 and 65. Lord Reed makes it clear in *N*, at para 65, that public authorities do not owe a duty of care at common law merely because they have statutory powers or duties the exercise of which might prevent a person from suffering harm; but he emphasises, at para 72, that previous cases should not be understood as meaning that an assumption of responsibility can never arise out of performance of statutory functions; it may do if the conduct of the authority pursuant to its statutory duties meets the criteria set out in cases such as *Hedley Byrne & Co Ltd v Heller & Partners Ltd* [1964] AC 465 and *Spring v Guardian Assurance plc* [1995] 2 AC 296. Each case requires attention to be directed to the detailed circumstances of the particular case and the particular relationship between the parties: *Gorringe*, *per* Lord Steyn at para 2; *Customs & Excise Commissioners v Barclays Bank plc.* [2007] 1 AC 181, *per* Lord Bingham of Cornhill at para 8 and *per* Lord Mance at para 93. The pursuer does not seek to impose on the Home Secretary a common law duty based solely on the existence of a public law duty.

[42] *Esto* the case was properly classed as "novel", Ms Crawford submitted that it met the incremental approach. She relied on a number of cases – *Kanidagli*, *McCreaner v Ministry of Justice* [2015] 1 WLR 354 and *Sebry v Companies House* [2016] 1 WLR 2499 – as illustrating situations in which a public body was found to be under a duty of care at common law for actions taken, not at the stage where a discretion was being exercised and a judgement made about what action to take, but at the later stage where all that was left was implementation of the decision which had been arrived at. The headnote in the law report of *Mohammed*, she submitted, accurately stated the *ratio* in the case and, far from being against her, in fact supported this distinction. *W* was a case where the wrongful action, the "crass administrative mistake" as Sedley LJ called it in *Mohammed*, did not of itself involve the exercise of any decision making judgement, but it occurred during the stage where the Secretary of State still had a decision to make on the merits of the application for leave to remain. *W* was correctly distinguished on that basis in *Kanidagli*. For the same reasons, both *W* and *Mohammed* were correctly distinguished in *McCreaner*. These cases suggested that there was a sound basis for proceeding by analogy and holding there to be a common law duty of care in the present case.

Analysis and decision

[43] Before turning to consider the critical arguments in this case, it is useful to clear away some of the incidental issues which have raised their heads.

Maladministration

[44] It is important to remind oneself that this is not a case where the pursuer advances a case of maladministration in the *Micosta* sense, in support of which it is necessary to prove malice or want of probable cause. Ms Crawford expressly disclaimed any such contention and the pursuer has, in any event, no pleadings to support such a case. Although there is a reference to "maladministration" in Article 4 of Condescendence, that stands alone and can be disregarded in light of Ms Crawford's disclaimer.

[45] Ms Crawford rather faintly suggested that if it were necessary to show malice, that could be found in the Home Secretary's failure to put forward any explanation for failing to issue the status document for some 20 months. I do not understand how this point arises. If, as Ms Crawford concedes, the pursuer's case is based upon there being a duty of care owed to her by the Home Secretary, breach of such duty is established by proof that due care was not in fact taken. In those circumstances it is not contended on behalf of the Home Secretary that the pursuer would have to go further and prove malice or want of probable cause. However, in any event, it simply will not do to raise the question of malice without there being any averment of malice in the pleadings. If malice is to be part of the pursuer's case it must be pleaded with full particularisation, even if it focuses mainly or even exclusively upon an inference sought to be drawn from the absence of any explanation by the Home Secretary for her failure to issue the document. In this respect it is akin to an allegation of fraud, as to which see *Royal Bank of Scotland plc v Holmes* 1999 SLT 563, Lord Macfadyen at 569–570.

Applying the tribunals' decisions

[46] A substantial part of the pursuer's case is based on the assertion that the Home Secretary had a duty "to obtemper both orders of the immigration tribunals and, ultimately, to issue [the applicant] with a status letter in implementation thereof". Ms Crawford did not support this line of argument in her submissions. And rightly so, because neither the FtT nor the UT made any order directing the Home Secretary to grant leave to remain or to issue a status letter in accordance

with her policy. They had no power to do so. Those tribunals found only that the applicant's removal from the United Kingdom would amount to a disproportionate interference with her and her family's Article 8 rights. It was then for the Home Secretary to decide whether to seek to challenge those decisions or, if there was to be no further challenge, to determine how to act consistently with them. In so far as the case for the pursuer is premised upon an assertion that the tribunals ordered the Home Secretary to grant leave to remain, and that the Home Secretary was bound to obtemper such orders, the action is plainly irrelevant.

[47] The averment in Article 3 of Condescendence, that the Home Secretary owed the pursuer duties "to take care in the administrative implementation of the immigration decisions in her favour" and "to ensure that she received a status letter which she could use to obtain paid employment and/or access state benefits for herself and her children.", deserves more attention. It is in support of these averments that the pursuer advances her argument that the Home Secretary owed the pursuer a duty of care to protect her from harm (or to confer a benefit on her) by issuing, within a reasonable time of the promulgation of the UT decision (and the expiry of the time for appealing against it), a status document enabling her to obtain employment and/or to access benefits.

A public law duty?

[48] In her written and oral submissions, Ms Crawford emphasised that the pursuer does not argue that the Home Secretary owed her any duty of care to exercise reasonable care to protect her from harm, or to confer a benefit on her, when discharging statutory functions and duties under the 1971 Act. But she argues that after the decision had been taken not to challenge the decision of the UT, the only option available to the Home Secretary in terms of her own guidance was to grant the pursuer discretionary leave to remain for a period of up to 30 months and to issue the pursuer with a status document enabling her to obtain work and/or access benefits. By that stage there were no other alternatives open to the Home Secretary (I leave out of account that there was in theory at least still a decision to be made as to the length of the period in respect of which discretionary leave to remain would be granted). She was under a public law duty to act in this way. That public law duty to act, and to act in a particular way, was an important plank in the argument that the Home Secretary also owed the pursuer a common law duty to take reasonable care to do these things within a reasonable time. It was not clear to me, in listening to his submissions, whether Mr McIlvride accepted that the Home Secretary was under a public law duty to act in this way during that period and that her failure to do so put her in breach of that public law duty.

[49] On this limited aspect of the case I consider that Ms Crawford is correct. Once the UT had upheld the decision of the FtT to the effect that the removal of the pursuer from the United Kingdom would amount to a disproportionate interference with her and her family's Article 8 rights, and once the Home Secretary had determined not to challenge that decision and had become appeal rights exhausted, then in terms of her own policy the Home Secretary was required to grant the pursuer discretionary leave to remain for a period of up to 30 months. It is, to my mind, axiomatic that she should do so within a reasonable time. If she did not do so, she would have been susceptible to an order made by the court on a petition for judicial review. Standing the terms of her own policy, it is difficult to see what answer there could have been. That is what I refer to when I say that the Home Secretary was under a public law duty to act in this way. But I need not

decide that finally for present purposes. It would be sufficient for the pursuer, in an argument anent the relevance of her pleadings, to maintain that it is at least arguable that the Home Secretary would have been compelled by judicial review to issue her with discretionary leave to remain in accordance with her policy and issue her with a status document. I consider that that is indeed highly arguable; and for the purpose of the discussion that follows I proceed upon the basis that the Home Secretary did indeed owe the pursuer a public law duty to grant discretionary leave to remain and issue her with the status document.

[50] Having said all that, however, I am not persuaded that this point takes the pursuer very far. In *Gorringe v Calderdale MBC* [2004] 1 WLR 1057, a case concerned with the extent of the public law duty of a highway authority to maintain the highway and whether that public law duty translated into a duty of care at common law, the House of Lords appears not to have considered that its analysis would have been any different depending upon whether the failure by the public authority was a failure to exercise a power or a failure to act in accordance with a public law duty: see, for example, Lord Hoffmann at para 32. One can see the logic in saying it is more difficult to fashion a common law duty of care out of a public law power, since the decision by the authority as to whether or not to exercise a power involves a measure of policy, judgement and discretion on their part; but it does not follow from this that a common law duty of care will readily be implied in the case of the authority being under a public law duty.

[51] The difference between a power and a duty overlaps to a large extent with the distinction, relied on by the pursuer, between policy (i.e. exercising discretion or judgement) and operations (implementation of whatever policy decision has been reached). This distinction was addressed by Lord Hoffmann in *Stovin v Wise* [1996] AC 923, where he said (at page 951):

"There are at least two reasons why the distinction [i.e. between policy and operations] is inadequate. The first is that … the distinction is often elusive. … But another reason is that even if the distinction is clear cut, leaving no element of discretion in the sense that it would be irrational (in the public law meaning of that word) for the public authority not to exercise its power, it does not follow that the law should superimpose a common law duty of care."

He went on, at page 953, as follows:

"In summary, therefore, I think that the minimum preconditions for basing a duty of care upon the existence of a statutory power, if it can be done at all, are, first, that it would in the circumstances have been irrational not to have exercised the power, so that there was in effect a public law duty to act, and secondly, that there are exceptional grounds for holding that the policy of the statute requires compensation to be paid to persons who suffer loss because the power was not exercised."

In *N*, at para 31, under reference to these passages, Lord Reed spoke of the distinction between policy and operations having been "rejected" in *Stovin v Wise*. Accordingly, the common law will not impose a duty of care to run alongside a public law duty, save for very good reason.

Development of the law of negligence

[52] The law of negligence, particularly as applied to public authorities, has now to be understood in light of the seminal decisions of the Supreme Court in a trilogy of recent cases, *viz Michael v Chief Constable of South Wales Police* [2015] AC 1732, *Robinson v Chief Constable of West Yorkshire* [2018] A.C. 736 and *N v Poole BC* [2019] 2 WLR 1478.

[53] In *Michael*, the Supreme Court made it clear that it was a mistake to regard *Caparo Industries plc v Dickman* [1990] 2 AC 605 as establishing a tripartite test for the determination of whether and in what circumstances a duty of care may be owed by one person to another. Lord Reed returned to this theme in *Robinson*:

"29. Properly understood, the *Caparo* case thus achieves a balance between legal certainty and justice. In the ordinary run of cases, courts consider what has been decided previously and follow the precedents (unless it is necessary to consider whether the precedents should be departed from). In cases where the question whether a duty of care arises has not previously been decided, the courts will consider the closest analogies in the existing law, with a view to maintaining the coherence of the law and the avoidance of inappropriate distinctions. They will also weigh up the reasons for and against imposing liability, in order to decide whether the existence of a duty of care would be just and reasonable. In the present case, however, the court is not required to consider an extension of the law of negligence. All that is required is the application to particular circumstances of established principles governing liability for personal injuries."

Duty of care – public bodies

[54] So far as concerns the position of public bodies, our attention was drawn to passages in the judgment of Lord Reed in *N*, where he referred with approval to the earlier decisions of the House of Lords in *Stovin v Wise* [1996] AC 923 and *Gorringe v Calderdale MBC* [2004] 1 WLR 1057, the significance of which, he said, "took time … to be fully appreciated": *N* para 34. A number of points can be taken from these cases which are of direct applicability to the present case:

(1)   Public authorities may owe a duty of care in circumstances where private individuals would owe such a duty, unless that duty is inconsistent with or excluded by the terms of any legislation imposing or regulating the duty: *Stovin v Wise, per* Lord Hoffmann at 947, *Robinson, per* Lord Reed at paras 32–40, *N* at paras 31 and 65. Neither private individuals nor public bodies generally owe a duty of care to confer benefits on others: *N* at para 28. The distinction is drawn between causing harm, as in making things worse, and failing to confer a benefit, as in not making things better. This terminology conveys the rationale better than the traditional distinction between acts and omissions: and see also *Robinson per* Lord Reed at para 69 points 4 and 5. In the present case the duty allegedly owed by the Home Secretary is, in this terminology, a duty to confer a benefit by granting discretionary leave to remain and providing a status letter enabling the pursuer to access employment and/or benefits.

(2)   In considering whether a public body is liable in damages to an individual claiming to have been harmed by its conduct, the first step is

to ascertain whether the relevant legislation under which it is acting itself creates a private right of action. If the answer to that is in the negative, "it would be, to say the least, unusual if the mere existence of the statutory duty could generate a common law duty of care": *Gorringe*, Lord Hoffmann para 23 (and see also para 32). The same point is made by Lord Hoffmann in *Stovin v Wise* at page 952, cited with approval in *N* at para 31.

(3)   It follows that except in a case where the relevant statute expressly or by implication itself creates a private right of action to run alongside the statutory duties incumbent on the public body, the mere existence of a statutory duty is not sufficient to give rise to a common law duty of care. There must be something more.

[55] Lord Reed provided a summary of the position in *N* at para 65:

"65. It follows (1) that public authorities may owe a duty of care in circumstances where the principles applicable to private individuals would impose such a duty, unless such a duty would be inconsistent with, and is therefore excluded by, the legislation from which their powers or duties are derived; (2) that public authorities do not owe a duty of care at common law merely because they have statutory powers or duties, even if, by exercising their statutory functions, they could prevent a person from suffering harm; and (3) that public authorities can come under a common law duty to protect from harm in circumstances where the principles applicable to private individuals or bodies would impose such a duty, as for example where the authority has created the source of danger or has assumed a responsibility to protect the claimant from harm, unless the imposition of such a duty would be inconsistent with the relevant legislation."

[56] It was Mr McIlvride's submission that the present case fell into the second category. In other words, the pursuer's case was based solely upon the existence of the statutory power or duty to grant discretionary leave to remain for a limited period and to issue a status document to that effect. As such it was bound to fail for the reasons set out by Lord Reed. Ms Crawford's response was that this was a case falling within both the first and third categories. There was no question here of such a duty being excluded by, or by implication from, the terms of the legislation. The "danger", *viz* the precarious situation in which an applicant for leave to remain in the United Kingdom finds herself, being unable to access work or benefits, was created by the Home Secretary. Her acceptance of the tribunal's ruling that removal from the United Kingdom would disproportionately interfere with the applicant's Article 8 rights, coupled with her policy setting out what was to happen in such circumstances, meant that she had assumed responsibility for ensuring that the applicant was protected from that danger. If that meant imposing on the Home Secretary a common law duty of care to confer a benefit on the pursuer, so be it; the circumstances of the case justified that result.

[57] In *N*, at paras 66–73, Lord Reed discussed what is meant by an assumption of responsibility in this context. He emphasised that that did not mean that an assumption of responsibility could never arise from the performance of statutory functions. The distinction is between the statutory duty itself, which cannot give

rise to a common law duty of care, and things undertaken in the performance of that duty, which might. Lord Reed concluded his review of the relevant authorities at para 73 in this way:

"There are indeed several leading authorities in which an assumption of responsibility arose out of conduct undertaken in the performance of an obligation, or the operation of a statutory scheme. An example mentioned by Lord Hoffmann is *Phelps v Hillingdon*, where the teachers' and educational psychologists' assumption of responsibility arose as a consequence of their conduct in the performance of the contractual duties which they owed to their employers. Another example is *Barrett v Enfield*, where the assumption of responsibility arose out of the local authority's performance of its functions under child care legislation. The point is also illustrated by the assumption of responsibility arising from the provision of medical or educational services, or the custody of prisoners, under statutory schemes. Clearly the operation of a statutory scheme does not automatically generate an assumption of responsibility, but it may have that effect if the defendant's conduct pursuant to the scheme meets the criteria set out in such cases as *Hedley Byrne* and *Spring v Guardian Assurance plc*."

[58] The question therefore comes to this: what has the Home Secretary done in the performance of her statutory obligations to justify the inference that she has assumed responsibility to the pursuer to take reasonable care to grant her discretionary leave to remain for a limited period and to issue her with a status document enabling her to access work and/or benefits? To my mind we have been shown nothing that would come anywhere near answering this question in favour of the pursuer. Ms Crawford was at pains to point out, under reference to remarks of Lord Bingham in *Customs and Excise Comrs. v Barclays Bank plc* [2007] 1 AC 181 at para 8 and of Lord Steyn in *Gorringe* at para 2, that in each case the court must focus its enquiry on the particular facts and particular statutory background. I accept this, but, as already pointed out, we have been shown nothing which goes beyond a bare reliance on the Home Secretary's policy document. In my opinion the pursuer has failed to put forward any cogent basis for suggesting that the Home Secretary has assumed responsibility to individuals in the position of the pursuer to act in accordance with that policy document and to do so within a reasonable time. Put short she owes no common law duty of care. The argument seems to me to be just another way of saying that because the Home Secretary has a statutory duty to grant discretionary leave to remain for a limited period and to issue the appropriate status document, then she has a common law duty of care running alongside that statutory duty.

Other analogous cases?

[59] Before the sheriff, it was argued for the pursuer that the imposition of a common law duty of care could be justified on the basis that it was consistent with a number of analogous cases. Much attention was paid to *Kanidagli* and whether it should be regarded as disapproved by the Court of Appeal in *Mohammed*. Ms Crawford did not spend much time on this point. But she did not abandon it, and as well as *Kanidagli* referred to the first instance decisions in *McCreaner v Ministry of Justice* [2015] 1 WLR 354 and *Sebry v Companies House* [2016] 1

WLR 2499. It is necessary to consider those cases. I propose to do so chronologically.

[60] In *Kanidagli*,* the Home Office had allowed the wife of a refugee into the United Kingdom but had mistakenly marked her status letter in such a way as to bar her from claiming benefits. Keith J concluded that it was fair, just and reasonable that an administrative error of this kind, involving no judgement but simple administration and with a predictable financial effect for which there was no other remedy, should be regarded as arising out of a sufficiently proximate relationship to found a claim for damages. Key to his reasoning was the fact that the error in that case occurred after any policy decisions had been reached; it was purely a matter of implementation of what had already been decided. In reaching his decision, the judge distinguished the decision of the Court of Appeal in *W v Home Office* [1997] Imm AR 302 on the ground that the error in that case had occurred during the policy or decision-making stage.

[61] Some or all of the reasoning in *Kanidagli* was disapproved by the Court of Appeal in *Mohammed & Ors v Home Office* [2011] 1 WLR 2862. In that case a number of individuals sued the Home Office, alleging breaches of a duty of care at common law. Home Office officials had failed properly to implement Home Office policy with resulting detriment to the individuals concerned and to their applications (ultimately successful) for leave to remain. The leading judgment in that case was delivered by Sedley LJ. He rejected the idea that any common law duty of care was owed by the Home Office in respect of things that had occurred in the actual discharge of their functions. He rejected as "a distinction without a difference" the distinction drawn by Keith J in *Kanidagli* when seeking to distinguish between that case and the earlier decision of the Court of Appeal in *W*, essentially because the crass error shown to have occurred in *W* itself had little to do with the decision-making process in that case. It is arguable that that is not quite the distinction sought to be made by Keith J – he was focussing on the different stages of the process, decision-making on the one hand and implementation on the other, rather than on the nature of the error. However, it is unnecessary to resolve that question. The distinction between policy and operations, between decision making and implementation of the decision, is no longer regarded as critical: see *N* at para 31, under reference to the opinion of Lord Hoffman in *Stovin v Wise*. To label something as mere operation or implementation does not, without more, mean that that activity is subject to a common law duty of care. More than that is needed, as discussed above.

[62] *McCreaner v Ministry of Justice* [2015] 1 WLR 354 was a case involving early release of prisoners. Cranston J held that after the Home Office policy had been established, the prison authorities owed the prisoner a common law duty of care to implement that policy. In the course of reaching the decision, the judge distinguished the cases of *W* and *Mohammed* on the grounds that those cases had concerned acts or omissions during and forming part of the policy or decision-making process, whereas in the case before him the failure was at the implementation stage: see in particular para 44. That is the same distinction as was made by Keith J in *Kanidagli*. It is not clear whether *Kanidagli* was cited, but clearly the judge was referred to *Mohammed* which in turn contained a critical

---

* As noted in a footnote to the judgment of the Court of Appeal in *Mohammed*, the appeal in *Kanidagli* was allowed of consent, the Home Office having agreed to pay the claim in full.

reference to *Kanidagli*. Without meaning to cast doubt upon the decision on that aspect of the case, it seems to me that the judge there paid rather more respect to the distinction between policy and operations than would now be given to it in light of the recent Supreme Court authorities.

[63] The case of *Sebry v Companies House* [2016] 1 WLR 2499 arose out of an incorrect entry in the companies register to the effect that a particular company had gone into liquidation, when in fact the information which was received by Companies House and which ought to have been recorded on the register related to a different company. As a result the company wrongly shown to have gone into liquidation went out of business. The error was due to a systemic failure to ensure that policies were correctly applied and/or to an individual act of carelessness. Edis J held that that the registrar owed a common law duty, to take reasonable care to ensure that a winding up order was not registered against the wrong company. He so held on three separate but overlapping grounds: (i) assumption of responsibility; (ii) the *Caparo* three-stage test; and (iii) the incremental approach.

[64] So far as concerned assumption of responsibility, the judge referred to a number of cases in which it had been said that any assumption of responsibility must be "voluntary". Having referred to a passage in the speech of Lord Nolan in *White v Jones* [1995] 2 AC 207 at 294, the judge said this (at para 109):

> "I understand this to mean that if a person does an act which is capable of causing harm to a particular person if done carelessly he will be held to have assumed responsibility to that person in respect of that task unless (where the act is done further to a contractual duty or statutory function) the terms of the contract or the statute negate or limit that responsibility."

As I read this passage, the judge is saying that performance by a public body of a statutory duty may without more give rise to a common law duty of care unless such a duty is excluded by the terms of the relevant legislation. This does not sit easily with the remarks of Lord Hoffman in *Gorringe* and in *Stovin v Wise* cited above and quoted with approval by Lord Reed in *N* (see in particular at paras 31 and 65).

[65] The judge's analysis in terms of the *Caparo* three-stage test was given before the decisions in *Robinson* and *N* and the greater understanding of *Caparo* which emerges from the judgments in those cases. I need say nothing about the judge's approach to the incremental test. Each case will fall to be decided on its own facts and the judge in that case went into the relevant facts in great detail before arriving at the conclusion that a duty of care was owed to a very limited class of persons in respect of a limited class of acts. I do not consider that this decision assists the pursuer in the present case.

[66] For these reasons I do not consider that these first instance decisions provide any assistance to the pursuer. They do not support the assumption of responsibility argument in this case. Nor do they provide a basis for proceeding to find a common law duty of care here by analogy with other cases.

[67] It is impossible not to feel some sympathy for the pursuer in the circumstances of this case. She did, however, have two possible means of redress. First, she could have petitioned for judicial review based on the principle of legitimate expectation. Second, she could have made a complaint to the Parliamentary Ombudsman.

Disposal

[68] I would hold that the pursuer's case is irrelevant and should not be admitted to proof. I would allow the appeal, sustain the first plea in law for the defender (the Home Secretary), and dismiss the action. I would reserve all questions of expenses.

LORD WOOLMAN:

[69] I have had the benefit of reading the opinions of the Lord Justice Clerk and Lord Glennie. I agree with their reasoning and conclusions. I wish to add a few brief observations.

[70] It is just and appropriate for this court to address the merits of the pursuer's argument, despite it having no sure foundation in her pleadings. That is subject to one qualification. There is no basis for a claim based on maladministration. That would require specific averments of malice or want of probable cause.

[71] The sheriff held that the Home Secretary could owe a duty of care to the pursuer. In reaching his decision he wrongly relied on *R (Kanidagli) v SSHD* [2004] EWHC 1585 (Admin). The decision of the Court of Appeal in *Mohammed & Ors v Home Office* [2011] 1 WLR 2862 pointed to the opposite conclusion.

[72] Matters have, however, moved on since then. The Supreme Court has revisited this branch of the law. It has set out the relevant principles in *Michael v Chief Constable of South Wales Police* [2015] AC 1732, *Robinson v Chief Constable of West Yorkshire Police* [2018] AC 736, and *N & Anor v Poole Borough Council* [2019] 2 WLR 1478.

[73] In *N* Lord Reed advanced three propositions (at para 65), the second being that: "public authorities do not owe a duty of care at common law merely because they have statutory powers or duties, even if, by exercising their statutory functions, they could prevent a person from suffering harm"

[74] This case falls four-square into that category. The Home Secretary could have prevented the pursuer from suffering harm by expeditiously issuing a status letter. But that does not justify the imposition of a duty of care.

ZULFIQAR ('FOREIGN CRIMINAL'; BRITISH CITIZEN)

UPPER TRIBUNAL (IMMIGRATION AND ASYLUM CHAMBER)

O'Callaghan and Mandalia UTJJ

[2020] UKUT 312 (IAC)
11 September 2020

Human rights – Article 8 of the ECHR – private and family life – proportionality – public interest – risk of re-offending – rehabilitation – procedure and process – deportation – meaning of 'foreign criminal' – Part 5A of the 2002 Act and Part 13 of the Immigration Rules – former British citizen

The Claimant was born in the United Kingdom in 1979 as a British citizen. He was also a citizen of Pakistan by descent. He had resided in the United Kingdom since birth. In November 2005, he was convicted of murder and sentenced to a mandatory term of life imprisonment with a minimum term of 15 years. He was further sentenced to concurrent sentences of two years for violent disorder and two years for assault occasioning actual bodily harm. The offences were committed in November 2004 when the Claimant and two other men randomly attacked the victim after a night of heavy drinking. All three men were arrested after planning to leave the country and travel to Pakistan to avoid arrest and prosecution. The Claimant had remained in custody and latterly immigration detention since November 2004. In January 2007, the Secretary of State for the Home Department decided not to pursue deportation because the Claimant was a British citizen.

In October 2008, the Claimant applied to be repatriated to Pakistan under the terms of the Prisoner Transfer Agreement. The Ministry of Justice refused the application as, upon release from a prison in Pakistan, the Claimant would not be subject to the supervision requirements necessary for his life licence in the United Kingdom. In August 2011, the Claimant applied to renounce his British citizenship. He stated that he was motivated to do so because he wanted to transfer to Pakistan and serve his sentence in that country, enabling him to be close to his parents who were in poor health. The Secretary of State approved the renunciation in October 2011 being satisfied that the Claimant also held Pakistani citizenship. In June 2015, the Claimant married Z, a British citizen, with whom he had been friends since 2003. Consequent to the Claimant's arrest and imprisonment the couple enjoyed limited contact until Z visited the Claimant in prison in January 2013 and they commenced their relationship in April of the same year. Z had two children from her first marriage, both of whom were minors and British citizens.

In October 2017, the Claimant applied to resume his British citizenship under section 13 of the British Nationality Act 1981. The Secretary of State rejected the application on the grounds that the Claimant could not satisfy the good character requirement given his convictions. The Secretary of State concluded that, as the Claimant was a British citizen at the time of the offence, he could not be considered a foreign criminal for deportation purposes under the definition set out by section 32 of the UK Borders Act 2007 ("the 2007 Act"). Accordingly, she issued a notice of intention to make a deportation order under section 3(5)(a) of the Immigration Act 1971 ("the 1971 Act") in January 2018. The Claimant asserted that deportation would breach his right to family and private life under Article 8 of the ECHR. The Secretary of State refused his human rights claim in October 2018.

The First-tier Tribunal ("FtT") dismissed the Claimant's appeal against that decision in November 2019. In considering the relevant legal framework regarding deportation, the FtT Judge mistakenly understood that the Secretary of State had conceded that the Claimant was not a foreign criminal for the purposes of Part 13 of the Immigration Rules HC 395 (as amended). The Judge undertook a 'very compelling circumstances' consideration of the Claimant's Article 8 rights outside the Rules, though erroneously reducing the weight to be given to the public interest consequent to her misunderstanding as to the Secretary of State's concession. The Judge concluded that deportation would not be a disproportionate interference with the Claimant's right to respect for his family and private life.

Before the Upper Tribunal, the Claimant relied upon four grounds of appeal, which were advanced as rationality challenges. First, the FtT Judge gave unsustainable and/or inadequate reasons for rejecting his assertion that he was induced by the Secretary of State to renounce his British citizenship and further that his citizenship would resume if he were not repatriated to Pakistan. Secondly, the Judge had raised a doubt as to him having been informed as to the possibility of being repatriated when that was not a fact in issue. Thirdly, the Judge 'downgraded' the weight to be attributed to his family life on the basis that it was formed at a time when he had renounced his citizenship. Fourthly, the Judge failed lawfully to consider the factors favourable to him when considering his private life rights, such as his having lived his entire life in the United Kingdom, his extensive rehabilitation and his not being a continuing risk of perpetrating criminal behaviour.

Held, dismissing the appeal:

(1) In ground one, the Claimant submitted that the FtT Judge had erred in not accepting both his evidence and the evidence of Z and other family members as to his having been induced to renounce his British citizenship, and so 'wrongly discounted' a highly material factor mitigating the public interest in his deportation. That submission was, however, simply a disagreement with the Judge's factual findings. It was implicit that the hearsay evidence presented by family and friends could carry no positive weight in circumstances where it relied solely upon information provided by the Claimant. The Claimant had erred in fact by mistakenly asserting that he was advised to renounce his British citizenship by 'immigration officers'. The named individuals were employed by the Ministry of Justice but were not agents or servants of the Secretary of State at the relevant time and were clearly not immigration officers. The documentary evidence was not capable of evidencing the Claimant's contention that he was induced to renounce his citizenship upon being informed that it would resume if he were not transferred within a specified period. On the evidence presented it was lawfully open to the FtT Judge to conclude that the Claimant had not met the burden placed upon him to establish that he was materially influenced by the purported representations when deciding to renounce his British citizenship and that the sole material influence upon his decision was his desire to act in a manner he

considered best for his parents. In all the circumstances, the rationality challenges advanced by grounds one and two could not succeed (*paras 56 – 63*).

(2) In addressing the Article 8 issues it was necessary to determine whether the Claimant was a foreign criminal for the purposes of Part 5A of the Nationality, Immigration and Asylum Act 2002 ("the 2002 Act") and Part 13 of the Immigration Rules. The meaning of 'foreign criminal' was not consistent over the 2002 Act and the 2007 Act. Section 32 of the 2007 Act created a designated class of offender that was a foreign criminal and established the consequences of such designation. That was, for the purposes of section 3(5)(a) of the 1971 Act, the deportation of that person was conducive to the public good and the Secretary of State must make a deportation order in respect of that person. A temporal link was established by section 32(1) requiring the foreign offender not to be a British citizen at the date of conviction. Part 5A of the 2002 Act prescribed a domestically refined approach to the public interest considerations which the Tribunal was required to take into account when considering Article 8 in a deportation appeal. Unlike the 2007 Act it was not a statutory change to the power to deport, rather it was a domestic refinement as to the consideration of the public interest question. Part 5A established no temporal link to the date of conviction, rather the relevant date for establishing whether an offender was a foreign criminal was the date of the decision subject to the exercise of an appeal on human rights grounds under section 82(1)(b) of the 2002 Act. Paragraph A398 of the Rules governed each of the rules in Part 13 that followed it. The expression 'foreign criminal' in paragraph A398 was to be construed by reference to the definition of that expression in section 117D of the 2002 Act: *SC (paras A398–339D: 'foreign criminal': procedure) Albania* [2020] UKUT 187 (IAC) applied (*paras 64 – 79(6)*).

(3) At the date of the Secretary of State's decision in October 2018 the Claimant was a foreign criminal as defined in section 117D(2) of the 2002 Act, as he was 'not a British citizen', had 'been convicted in the United Kingdom of an offence' and had 'been sentenced to a period of imprisonment of at least 12 months.' He was therefore a foreign criminal for the purposes of section 117A(2)(b) and section 117C. Consequently, Part 13 of the Rules was applicable. The Judge's error as to the Claimant being a foreign criminal was not material because the nature of his sentence meant that he could not rely upon the statutory Exceptions to the public interest and the Judge proceeded to consider whether very compelling circumstances arose. Though she applied a lesser weight to the public interest than should have been applied under section 117C(6) of the 2002 Act and paragraph 398 of the Rules, that was to the benefit of the Claimant who was still unsuccessful before her. Consequently, the error of law was not material (*paras 79(7) – 80*).

(4) The FtT Judge did not downgrade the weight to be attributed to the Claimant's family life with Z on the basis that it was formed at a time when he had renounced his citizenship. The Judge did not state that the weight to be attached to the relationship was in any way reduced because of the Claimant's status at any point. To the contrary, insofar as the Claimant's status was concerned, the Judge expressly stated that she had borne in mind that the Claimant was formerly a British citizen and that did carry 'substantial weight'. The Claimant's challenge on the issue simply amounted to a disagreement with the Judge's conclusion (*paras 82 – 90*).

(5) The claim that the Judge failed lawfully to consider the factors favourable to the Claimant when considering his private life rights was rejected. The Judge

had proper regard, *inter alia*, to the Claimant's length of residence in the United Kingdom, the ties that he retained with his family in this country, his immigration and offending history, and his family circumstances. In adopting the balance sheet approach, the Judge carefully considered the matters that weighed in favour of, and against, the Claimant. In addition to his only having ever lived in this country, she noted that the Claimant was remorseful, had accepted responsibility for his previous convictions and that there was extensive evidence as to rehabilitation. The Judge gave substantial weight to the personal ties the Claimant enjoyed in this country through his long enjoyment of British citizenship. She also gave appropriate weight to his ability to establish his life in Pakistan and to integrate into the community (*paras 92 – 105*).

(6) Contrary to the Claimant's submission, the FtT Judge made no express finding of fact that he was a very low risk of re-offending in the future. She identified that the Claimant had shown positive evidence of rehabilitation, and thus a reduced risk of re-offending, and included it as a positive factor within the overall proportionality exercise. She was not, however, required to give it great weight because the public interest in the deportation of criminals was not based only on the need to protect the public from further offending by the foreign criminal but also on wider policy considerations of deterrence and public concern. Though the Judge erred in the weight that she gave to the public interest, such error was in the Claimant's favour and he was unsuccessful. The challenge to the Judge's consideration of the Article 8 appeal on rationality grounds could not succeed. The Claimant could not succeed under section 117C(6) of the 2002 Act or paragraph 398 of the Rules as no very compelling circumstances arose to lessen the public interest in his deportation (*paras 106 – 117*).

Cases referred to:

AK (Sierra Leone) v Secretary of State for the Home Department [2016] EWCA Civ 999; [2017] Imm AR 319; [2017] INLR 681

AT (Pakistan) and JT (Pakistan) v Secretary of State for the Home Department [2010] EWCA Civ 567; [2010] Imm AR 675; [2011] INLR 277

Akinyemi v Secretary of State for the Home Department (No. 2) [2019] EWCA Civ 2098; [2020] 1 WLR 1843; [2020] 3 All ER 857; [2020] INLR 175

*Bah (*EO (Turkey) – *liability to deport)* [2012] UKUT 196 (IAC); [2013] INLR 115

CI (Nigeria) v Secretary of State for the Home Department [2019] EWCA Civ 2027; [2020] Imm AR 503; [2020] INLR 191

CL v Secretary of State for the Home Department [2019] EWCA Civ 1925; [2020] 1 WLR 858

Danso v Secretary of State for the Home Department [2015] EWCA Civ 596

EG and NG (UT rule 17: withdrawal; rule 24: scope) Ethiopia [2013] UKUT 143 (IAC); [2013] Imm AR 670; [2013] INLR 700

Guardian News and Media Ltd and Others, Re [2010] UKSC 1; [2010] 2 AC 697; [2010] 2 WLR 325; [2010] 2 All ER 799

HA (Iraq) v Secretary of State for the Home Department; RA (Iraq) v Secretary of State for the Home Department [2020] EWCA Civ 1176; [2021] 1 WLR 1327; [2020] INLR 639

Herrera v Secretary of State for the Home Department [2018] EWCA Civ 412; [2018] Imm AR 1033

Hesham Ali (Iraq) v Secretary of State for the Home Department [2016] UKSC 60; [2016] 1 WLR 4799; [2017] 3 All ER 20; [2017] Imm AR 484; [2017] INLR 109
Hussein v Secretary of State for the Home Department [2009] EWHC 2492 (Admin); [2010] Imm AR 320
Khuja v Times Newspapers Ltd and Others [2017] UKSC 49; [2019] AC 161; [2017] 3 WLR 351
OH (Serbia) v Secretary of State for the Home Department [2008] EWCA Civ 694; [2009] INLR 109
OLO and Others (para 398 – "foreign criminal") [2016] UKUT 56 (IAC)
RU (Bangladesh) v Secretary of State for the Home Department [2011] EWCA Civ 651; [2011] Imm AR 662
SC (paras A398–339D: 'foreign criminal': procedure) Albania [2020] UKUT 187 (IAC); [2020] Imm AR 1121
Secretary of State for the Home Department v Devani [2020] EWCA Civ 612; [2020] 1 WLR 2613; [2020] Imm AR 1183
Yussuf (meaning of "liable to deportation") [2018] UKUT 117 (IAC); [2018] INLR 678

Legislation and international instruments judicially considered:

British Nationality Act 1981, section 13
Crime (Sentences) Act 1997, sections 28(5) & 31(3)
European Convention on Human Rights, Article 8
Human Rights Act 1998, section 6
Immigration Act 1971, sections 3(5)-(6) & 5
Immigration Rules HC 395 (as amended), Part 13; paragraphs A398, 398(a), 399 & 399A
Nationality, Immigration and Asylum Act 2002, Part 5A; sections 82, 84 & 117A–D
Tribunals, Courts and Enforcement Act 2007, section 11(2)
Tribunal Procedure (Upper Tribunal) Rules 2008, rule 24
UK Borders Act 2007, sections 32, 34(1) & 59(4)(d)
UK Borders Act 2007 (Commencement No. 3 and Transitional Provisions) Order 2008, Articles 2 & 3

Representation

Mr S Muquit instructed by Turpin & Miller LLP, for the Claimant;
Mr T Lindsay, Senior Home Office Presenting Officer, for the Secretary of State.

DECISION AND REASONS

UPPER TRIBUNAL JUDGE O'CALLAGHAN:

A. INTRODUCTION

[1] Both members of the panel have contributed to this decision.

[2] This is an appeal against a decision of Judge of the First-tier Tribunal Feeney ('the Judge') sent to the parties on 13 November 2019 dismissing the appellant's appeal against a decision of the respondent to refuse an application for leave to remain on human rights (Article 8 ECHR) grounds and to deport him to Pakistan.

[3] Designated Judge of the First-tier Tribunal McClure granted permission to appeal on all grounds advanced by the appellant by a decision sent to the parties on 11 December 2019.

B. REMOTE HEARING

[4] The hearing before us was a Skype for Business video conference hearing held during the Covid-19 pandemic. On the first day, 5 August 2020, we were present in a hearing room situated in the Birmingham Civil Justice Centre. The hearing was not concluded on the day and resumed with us sitting at Field House on 27 August 2020. On both occasions the hearing rooms and the buildings were open to the public. Both hearings and their starting time were publicly listed. We were addressed by the representatives in exactly the same way as if we were together in the hearing room. We are satisfied: that this constituted a hearing in open court; that the open justice principle has been secured; that no party has been prejudiced; and that, insofar as there has been any restriction on a right or interest, it is justified as necessary and proportionate.

[5] The parties agreed that all relevant documents were before us. The video and audio link were connected between the representatives and the Tribunal throughout the hearing. At the conclusion of the hearing both parties confirmed that the hearing had been completed fairly.

[6] No member of the public attended the hearing either remotely or in person. Mr. Muquit confirmed at a preliminary hearing in March 2020 that there was no request for the appellant to be produced from HMP Norwich to attend the hearing. We accept that the appellant was content to rely upon his representative's attendance before us on his behalf and further accept that the appellant has remained thoroughly engaged in his appeal.

C. ANONYMITY

[7] The Judge was not requested to issue an anonymity direction. The applicant requested such direction before this Tribunal relying upon the media coverage of the index offence, murder, at the time of his trial and thereafter, particularly on what are identified by the applicant to be far-right anti-immigrant websites. He further relied upon the impact of publication upon his wife and her two children.

[8] We are mindful of Guidance Note 2013 No 1 concerned with the issuing of an anonymity direction and we observe that the starting point for consideration of such a direction in this Chamber of the Upper Tribunal, as in all courts and

tribunals, is open justice. The principle of open justice is fundamental to the common law. The rationale for this is to protect the rights of the parties and to maintain public confidence in the administration of justice. Revelation of the identity of the parties is an important part of open justice: *Re: Guardian News & Media Ltd* [2010] UKSC 1, [2010] 2 AC 697. Such revelation has an important practical benefit in ensuring public scrutiny of and confidence in the justice system.

[9] In the present case the appellant's private and family life are interests which must be respected. On the other side, publication of our decision and the accompanying identification of the appellant is a matter of general public interest as it accords with the principle of open justice.

[10] At the hearing on 5 August 2020 we refused the appellant's application for anonymity, concluding that the appellant's concern as to the identification of his wife and her children to the wider public could properly be addressed by the less draconian use of referring to them in this decision by initials. In reaching our decision we observe that paragraph 18 of the Guidance Note confirms that the identity of children whether they are appellants or the children of an appellant (or otherwise concerned with the proceedings), will not normally be disclosed nor will their school, the names of their teacher or any social worker or health professional with whom they are concerned, unless there are good reasons in the interests of justice to do so. We are satisfied that there is no requirement to name either the appellant's wife or her children and we have ensured that no reference is made to where they reside, the ages of the children or what school they attend.

[11] As for the appellant's concern that publication of his name will present a future risk to him from active members of the far-right, he has failed to demonstrate risks to his life and safety such as to require the principle of open justice and the right to freedom of expression protected by Article 10 of the ECHR to be outweighed by his Article 8 private life rights. In reaching our conclusion on this issue we are mindful that there is a consistent line of authority emphasising the importance of open justice and the permitting of media reporting of judicial proceedings: *Khuja v Times Newspapers Ltd* [2017] UKSC 49, [2019] AC 161.

D. THE APPELLANT

[12] The appellant is a national of Pakistan and is aged 40. His father was naturalised as a British citizen in 1973 and his mother in 1981. At the time of the index offence the appellant was a dual national. He held British nationality having been born in this country in 1979 and is a citizen of Pakistan by descent.

[13] He has resided in the United Kingdom since birth and attended primary and secondary school in this country. Upon leaving school he initially worked with Royal Mail and was then self-employed, operating a car dealership in east London.

[14] Prior to the index offence, the appellant had accumulated 5 previous convictions for 8 offences involving taking a motor vehicle without consent, driving a vehicle with no insurance, driving a motor vehicle with excess alcohol, obtaining property by deception and possession of drugs.

Index offence

[15] The index offence, murder, was committed in the company of two other men during the early hours of Sunday 7 November 2004. Following the incident, all three men travelled from east London to a hotel in Pontefract, West Yorkshire, where they were arrested. The appellant admitted to the police that all three men were planning to leave the country and travel to Pakistan to avoid arrest and prosecution. He further admitted to having been binge-drinking over the weekend of the index offence.

[16] The appellant was convicted by a jury of murder, having previously pleaded guilty to violent disorder and assault occasioning actual bodily harm. He was sentenced to a mandatory term of life imprisonment with a minimum term of 15 years by HHJ Stephens QC at the Old Bailey on 24 November 2005. He was further sentenced to concurrent sentences of 2 years for violent disorder and 2 years for assault occasioning actual bodily harm. By means of his sentencing remarks, HHJ Stephens QC observed, *inter alia*:

'[The victim] had the misfortune to come across the three of you at 4.30 in the morning when he had had a good drink, perfectly legitimately, but was in no position to defend himself. Between you, you punched and kicked him to the ground. Between you, you then stamped on his face as he lay helpless on the ground. You stamped on his face so viciously and violently that the front part of his face became detached from his head. Witnesses who were not able to see the incident in full thought from what they saw and heard that you were playing football with something.

Quite who did what cannot be established with any certainty, but I am perfectly satisfied that you were all in on this attack together as a team. One witness saw three people kicking and I am sure that all three of you were actively physically participating in the attack. Not content with what you did, you left Mr. Y dead or dying on the ground.

You then went, as a team, to streets nearby where you damaged cars and other property and brought fear to the neighbourhood. You then went on to an Asian curry house where you assaulted a waiter and did more wilful damage to property. Then you, Zulfiqar, assaulted a gentleman who just happened to be passing by.'

[17] HHJ Stephens QC accepted that the murder of Mr. Y was not racially aggravated and observed that there were attacks on people of several races:

'Between you that morning you attacked people of all races: white, black and Asian. These, in my judgement, were random attacks carried out on people and property who had the misfortune to come across you in your drink-fuelled rampage.'

[18] In imposing the minimum term, HHJ Stephens QC concluded:

'I consider that it can readily be inferred from what you did to that unfortunate man that you intended to kill him. I accept there was no great premeditation, however all in all I consider that I should look at all that you did on that morning, including events after the murder of Mr. Y, and I have concluded that the appropriate minimum sentence in your case, the minimum term, is 15 years …'

[19] The appellant was arrested for the index offence in November 2004, He has remained in custody and latterly immigration detention since this date.

Application for a prison transfer to Pakistan

[20] The appellant applied in October 2008 to be repatriated to Pakistan under the terms of the Prisoner Transfer Agreement ('the Agreement') signed by the United Kingdom and Pakistan in August 2007 and in force from August 2008, save for three periods of suspension. The Agreement does not confer on an applicant an automatic right to transfer and the consent of both States is required before transfer can take place. The Ministry of Justice refused the application by a decision authored by Jason Ruffy, Cross Border Transfers, and dated 24 June 2010, which details, *inter alia*:

'The Secretary of State has considered your application and has determined that it should be refused. The Secretary of State has taken into account that you are a dual national that has both British and Pakistani nationality.

The Pakistani authorities confirmed that under the Pakistani Penal Code 1860 they will enforce a sentence of life imprisonment for murder and you would serve a minimum period of 15 years imprisonment following transfer, after which time your automatic release will be directed by the competent authority in Islamabad. However, the Secretary of State has determined that as a British national you could return to the United Kingdom following your release in Pakistan without sanction or supervision, which in view of the serious nature of your offence is not in the public interest …'

[21] We understand the core of the Ministry of Justice's concern to be that upon release from a prison in Pakistan, the appellant would not have been subject to the supervision requirements necessary for his life licence in this country as required by section 28(5) of the Crime (Sentences) Act 1997 ('the 1997 Act'). Although licences for indeterminate sentence prisoners are prepared by the relevant public protection section of the Ministry of Justice, conditions can only be imposed, varied or cancelled in accordance with the recommendations of the Parole Board: section 31(3) of the 1997 Act. In this matter, we understand the Ministry of Justice to be concerned that as a British citizen the appellant could return to this country upon his release from a prison in Pakistan and in so doing would not be subject to life licence conditions imposed in accordance with recommendations of the Parole Board.

Renunciation of British citizenship

[22] On 3 August 2011 the appellant applied to renounce his British citizenship. The respondent approved the renunciation of 21 October 2011 being satisfied that the appellant also held Pakistani citizenship.

[23] The appellant pursued repatriation but was ultimately unsuccessful. During such time the Agreement was suspended on several occasions: by the United Kingdom in 2010* and 2019 and by Pakistan in 2015.

Family life

[24] The appellant's first marriage took place in Pakistan and ended in divorce. The appellant married his second wife, Z, a British citizen, by means of an Islamic ceremony on 5 June 2015. They had first met in 2003 prior to Z's first marriage in 2004. Consequent to the appellant's arrest and imprisonment the couple enjoyed limited contact until Z visited the appellant in prison in January 2013 and they commenced their relationship in April of the same year.

[25] Z has two children from her first marriage, both of whom are minors and British citizens. At the time of the hearing before the Judge Z's first husband had secured a Prohibited Steps Order preventing the children visiting the appellant in prison. We were orally informed by Mr. Muquit that this order has now been set aside consequent to an application made by Z, though he accepted that this was a post-decision event and not a matter relevant to our error of law consideration.

Applications to resume British citizenship following renunciation

[26] In October 2017, the appellant applied to register to resume British citizenship under section 13 of the British Nationality Act 1981 ('the 1981 Act'). The respondent rejected the application by a decision dated 16 October 2017 detailing, *inter alia*:

'As your client is unable to register his biometrics at this time his application must be considered invalid and therefore rejected in line with current policy.

I should inform you that even had your client's application been valid, it would have still fallen for refusal as your client is unable to satisfy the Good Character requirement.

"Good Character" is not defined in the British Nationality Act 1981, but applicants are expected to have shown due regard for the laws of this country. In exceptional circumstances, we would disregard a recent conviction for a single, minor offence but normally we would not grant citizenship to a person who has been:

1. Sentenced to a period of imprisonment of four years or more …

However, as your client is currently serving a lengthy custodial sentence having been convicted of murder, violent disorder and assault occasioning actual bodily harm, it would not be appropriate to allow discretion in your client's favour.'

[27] The appellant did not challenge the decision rejecting his application.

---

* Question for Ministry of Justice UIN 159578, tabled on 2 July 2018.

Deportation proceedings

[28] The appellant initially came to the attention of the respondent following his conviction and on 8 January 2007 a decision was made not to pursue deportation because he was a British citizen. Following his renunciation of British citizenship, the appellant was issued with a notice of decision to make a deportation order under section 32(5) of the UK Borders Act 2007 ('the 2007 Act') in October 2016. The appellant submitted human rights (Article 8) representations in November 2016. In October 2017 the appellant applied to resume British citizenship which was refused by the respondent later that month.

[29] The respondent concluded that as the appellant was a British citizen at the time of the offence he could not be considered a foreign criminal under the definition set out by section 32 of the 2007 Act and so deportation was to be pursued under the Immigration Act 1971 ('the 1971 Act'). The appellant was therefore issued with a notice of intention to make a deportation order under section 3(5)(a) of the 1971 Act on 16 January 2018 and he served human rights (Article 8) representations upon the respondent on 14 February 2018. The respondent issued her reasons for refusing the appellant's human rights claim by her decision of 3 October 2018, which is subject to this appeal.

[30] Following a decision of the Parole Board the appellant was released on life licence in July 2020, post the hearing before the Judge, and presently remains in immigration detention.

E. RELEVANT STATUTORY PROVISIONS

[31] Section 3(5) and (6) of the 1971 Act establishes the grounds upon which the respondent may order that a person is to be deported under the Act:

'(5)   A person who is not a British citizen is liable to deportation from the United Kingdom if –

(a)   the Secretary of State deems his deportation to be conducive to the public good; or

(b)   another person to whose family he belongs is or has been ordered to be deported.

(6)   Without prejudice to the operation of subsection (5) above, a person who is not a British citizen shall also be liable to deportation from the United Kingdom if, after he has attained the age of seventeen, he is convicted of an offence for which he is punishable with imprisonment and on his conviction is recommended for deportation by a court empowered by this Act to do so.'

[32] Section 5 of the 1971 Act is concerned with the procedure for, and further provisions as to, deportation. Section 5(1) provides:

'(1)   Where a person is under section 3(5) or (6) above liable to deportation, then subject to the following provisions of this Act the Secretary of State may make a deportation order against him, that is to say an order requiring him to leave and prohibiting him from entering the United Kingdom; and a deportation order against a person shall invalidate any leave to enter or remain in the United Kingdom given him before the order is made or while it is in force.'

[33] Section 32(1), (2) and (5) of the 2007 Act confirm:

'(1)   In this section "foreign criminal" means a person –

(a)   who is not a British citizen,

(b)   who is convicted in the United Kingdom of an offence, and

(c)   to whom Condition 1 or 2 applies

(2)   Condition 1 is that the person is sentenced to a period of imprisonment of at least 12 months.

…

(5)   The Secretary of State must make a deportation order in respect of a foreign criminal (subject to section 33).'

[34] As to timing of an automatic deportation order, section 34(1) confirms:

'(1)   Section 32(5) requires a deportation order to be made at a time chosen by the Secretary of State.'

[35] Section 59(4)(d) provides a mechanism as to commencement in relation to section 32:

'(4)   In particular, transitional provision –

…

(d)   in the case of an order commencing section 32 –

(i)   may provide for the section to apply to persons convicted before the passing of this Act who are in custody at the time of commencement or whose sentences are suspended at the time of commencement …'

[36] In so far as is relevant to our considerations as to section 32, the UK Borders Act 2007 (Commencement No. 3 and Transitional Provisions) Order 2008 SI 2008 No 1818 was made on 8 July 2008 and provides at articles 2 and 3:

'**2. Commencement**

The following provisions of the UK Borders Act 2007 shall come into force on 1 August 2008

    (a)   the provisions set out in the Schedule to this Order [i.e. sections 32 to 38 inclusive] in respect of a person to whom Condition 1 (within the meaning of section 32 of that Act) applies; and

    (b)   section 39 (consequential amendments)

3. Transitional Provision

(1)   Subject to paragraph (2), section 32 applies to the extent to which it is commenced in article 2(a), to persons convicted before the passing of that Act who are in custody at the time of commencement or whose sentences are suspended at the time of commencement.

(2)   Paragraph (1) does not apply to a person who has been served with a notice of decision to make a deportation order under s.5 of the Immigration Act 1971 before 1 August 2008.'

[37] From 28 July 2014 section 19 of the Immigration Act 2014 ('the 2014 Act') was brought into force, amending the Nationality, Immigration and Asylum Act 2002 ('the 2002 Act') by introducing a new Part 5A which applies where the Tribunal considers Article 8(2). By virtue of section 117A, which addresses the application of Part 5A:

'(1)   This Part applies where a court or tribunal is required to determine whether a decision made under the Immigration Acts –

    (a)   breaches a person's right to respect for private and family life under Article 8, and

    (b)   as a result would be unlawful under section 6 of the Human Rights Act 1998.

(2)   In considering the public interest question, the court or tribunal must (in particular) have regard –

    (a)   in all cases, to the considerations listed in section 117B, and

    (b)   in cases concerning the deportation of foreign criminals, to the considerations listed in section 117C.

(3)   In subsection (2), "the public interest question" means the question of whether an interference with a person's right to respect for private and family life is justified under Article 8(2).'

[38] Section 117B is concerned with the application of the public interest consideration in all Article 8 cases:

'(1)   The maintenance of effective immigration controls is in the public interest.

(2)   It is in the public interest, and in particular in the interests of the economic well-being of the United Kingdom, that persons who seek to enter or remain in the United Kingdom are able to speak English, because persons who can speak English –

    (a)   are less of a burden on taxpayers, and

    (b)   are better able to integrate into society.

(3)   It is in the public interest, and in particular in the interests of the economic well-being of the United Kingdom, that persons who seek to enter or remain in the United Kingdom are financially independent, because such persons –

    (a)   are not a burden on taxpayers, and

    (b)   are better able to integrate into society.

(4)   Little weight should be given to –

    (a)   a private life, or

    (b)   a relationship formed with a qualifying partner, that is established by a person at a time when the person is in the United Kingdom unlawfully.

(5)   Little weight should be given to a private life established by a person at a time when the person's immigration status is precarious.

(6)   In the case of a person who is not liable to deportation, the public interest does not require the person's removal where –

    (a)   the person has a genuine and subsisting parental relationship with a qualifying child, and

    (b)   it would not be reasonable to expect the child to leave the United Kingdom.'

[39] Section 117C details additional considerations applicable to cases involving foreign criminals:

'(1)   The deportation of foreign criminals is in the public interest.

(2)   The more serious the offence committed by a foreign criminal, the greater is the public interest in deportation of the criminal.

(3)   In the case of a foreign criminal ("C") who has not been sentenced to a period of imprisonment of four years or more, the public interest requires C's deportation unless Exception 1 or Exception 2 applies.

(4)　Exception 1 applies where –

    (a)　C has been lawfully resident in the United Kingdom for most of C's life,

    (b)　C is socially and culturally integrated in the United Kingdom, and

    (c)　there would be very significant obstacles to C's integration into the country to which C is proposed to be deported.

(5)　Exception 2 applies where C has a genuine and subsisting relationship with a qualifying partner, or a genuine and subsisting parental relationship with a qualifying child, and the effect of C's deportation on the partner or child would be unduly harsh.

(6)　In the case of a foreign criminal who has been sentenced to a period of imprisonment of at least four years, the public interest requires deportation unless there are very compelling circumstances, over and above those described in Exceptions 1 and 2.

(7)　The considerations in subsections (1) to (6) are to be taken into account where a court or tribunal is considering a decision to deport a foreign criminal only to the extent that the reason for the decision was the offence or offences for which the criminal has been convicted.'

[40] Section 117D provides the interpretation to Part 5A. Relevant to our considerations are:

'(1)　In this Part –

"Article 8" means Article 8 of the European Convention on Human Rights;

…

(2)　In this Part, "foreign criminal" means a person –

    (a)　who is not a British citizen,

    (b)　who has been convicted in the United Kingdom of an offence, and

    (c)　who –

        (i)　has been sentenced to a period of imprisonment of at least 12 months,

        (ii)　has been convicted of an offence that has caused serious harm, or

        (iii)　is a persistent offender.'

[41] Section 82 of the 2002 Act establishes the statutory basis for a right of appeal to the First-tier Tribunal. Relevant to this appeal is section 82(1)(b):

'(1)　A person ("P") may appeal to the Tribunal where –

...

(b)   the Secretary of State has decided to refuse a human rights claim made by P, ...'

[42] Section 84 of the 2002 Act establishes permitted grounds of appeal, including:

'(2)   An appeal under section 82(1)(b) (refusal of human rights claim) must be brought on the ground that the decision is unlawful under section 6 of the Human Rights Act 1998.'

[43] Section 13 of the 1981 Act provides the mechanism by which a person can resume British citizenship where the renouncing of such citizenship took place on or after 1 January 1983:

'(1)   Subject to subsection (2), a person who has ceased to be a British citizen as a result of a declaration of renunciation shall be entitled, on an application for his registration as a British citizen, to be registered as such a citizen if –

(a)   he is of full capacity; and

(b)   his renunciation of British citizenship was necessary to enable him to retain or acquire some other citizenship or nationality.

(2)   A person shall not be entitled to registration under subsection (1) on more than one occasion.

(3)   If a person of full capacity who has ceased to be a British citizen as a result of a declaration of renunciation (for whatever reason made) makes an application for his registration as such a citizen, the Secretary of State may, if he thinks fit, cause him to be registered as such a citizen.'

F. DECISION OF THE FTT

[44] The hearing came before the Judge sitting at Hendon Magistrates' Court on 1 October 2019. The appellant attended in custody and was represented by Mr. Muquit. The appellant and Z gave oral evidence and were cross-examined.

[45] The appellant contended that in 2008 he was advised that he could be repatriated to a prison in Pakistan to serve the remainder of his custodial sentence under the Arrangement. He stated that his only wish for doing so was because his father had returned to live in Pakistan and his health was deteriorating. He hoped that his father would visit him in prison in Pakistan and this would aid his father's mental health. He detailed that in March 2010 the Pakistani authorities had agreed to his transfer, but the United Kingdom authorities subsequently refused the application because he held dual nationality. By his witness statement dated 10 September 2019 the appellant asserted, *inter alia*:

'24. On the 18 March 2010 I received confirmation that the Pakistan authorities had agreed for me to be repatriated to Pakistan. I thereafter received correspondence on the 24 June 2010 advising me that the Secretary of State [for Justice] had noted that I had dual nationality and I would need to renounce my British Nationality before the request could be authorised. My priority was my parents, their health was deteriorating and to this day I feel responsible for this, with the stress I had placed upon them. I was informed by Immigration Officers that if I renounced my nationality it would increase the chances of the application being processed successfully. I asked for this to be confirmed to me in writing, however, this request was not forthcoming.

...

26. I can confirm that I would regularly speak with Jason Ruffy at Cross Borders Transfers in respect of my position in relation to repatriation. I was clearly advised by him that in the event that I was not repatriated within a period of three years, then I would be able to regain my British nationality. I was informed by him that if I was not moved by 2013 then I would not be going anywhere. I was told this in 2011. Jason Ruffy stated that my British citizenship would accordingly be reinstated if I was not sent back. We had a direct number for Jason and would speak to him regularly, however in around 2014 he was no longer contactable, and it is my understanding that he left his employment at Cross Border Agency.

...

30. I confirm that I was also of the view that my Pakistani citizenship would expire in 2013 and therefore I would not have any form of nationality and would be stateless. I recall a conversation with an Immigration Officer, it was either Jason Ruffy or Christopher Binns, that informed me that I would not be left stateless and in any event I would revert back to being a British citizen by default.'

[46] It was not asserted before the Judge that the appellant has lost his Pakistani citizenship leaving him stateless.

[47] The Judge concluded, applying the correct burden and standard of proof, that the appellant was motivated to renounce his British citizenship because he wanted to transfer to Pakistan and serve his sentence in that country, enabling him to be close to his father. Further, she was not satisfied that the respondent had misrepresented the position as to registering to resume British citizenship or induced the appellant to believe that his British citizenship would be reinstated.

[48] As to the relevant legal framework, the Judge understood that the respondent had conceded that the appellant was not a foreign criminal for the purposes of Part 13 of the Immigration Rules, at [12] and [16]:

'12. There are detailed provisions within the Immigration Rules Part 13 as to when the respondent will consider that a person's circumstances are such that the public interest is outweighed. The Rules provide a specific framework as to how applicants with criminal convictions should be dealt with. However, the Rules do not remove the respondent's discretionary power under the 1971 Act. Part 13 of the Immigration Rules only apply to cases involving a foreign criminal and as conceded by the respondent this does not apply to the appellant.

However, in accordance with the guidance in *NA (Pakistan) v. SSHD and ors* [2016] EWCA Civ 662 it is sensible to examine whether the appellant could have succeeded under the Exceptions and then go on to consider whether any compelling circumstances exist as this provides a basis upon which to further consider the proportionality of the respondent's decision. Section 117B of the 2002 Act provides a list of considerations mandatory in all appeals concerning Article 8 proportionality.

...

16. ... I do however bear in mind that the appellant does not come within the framework of the deportation rules and so he does not need to provide evidence of a very strong Article 8 claim over and above the circumstances described in the exceptions to deportation. In fact, the appellant can potentially succeed in a freestanding proportionality assessment in circumstances where his claim may be weaker than the exceptions as only Section 117B applies and not Section 117C.'

[49] As to family life, the Judge found that the appellant enjoyed no parental responsibility for Z's children and that it was in the best interests of the children to remain in the United Kingdom and reside with their mother. She further found that the appellant enjoyed a genuine and subsisting relationship with Z, though it was formed after the appellant renounced his British citizenship. She concluded that it would be unduly harsh for Z to relocate to Pakistan but that it would not in the circumstances of this case be unduly harsh for her to remain in this country after the appellant's deportation to Pakistan. The Judge observed that Z is in good health and has been able to live her life and raise her children in the absence of the appellant.

[50] The Judge undertook a 'very compelling circumstances' consideration of the appellant's Article 8 rights outside of the Immigration Rules, though erroneously reducing the weight to be given to the public interest consequent to her misunderstanding as to the respondent's concession. She adopted the balance sheet approach recommended by Lord Thomas in *Hesham Ali v Secretary of State for the Home Department* [2016] UKSC 60; [2016] 1 WLR 4799. She concluded that such circumstances did not arise, and so the appellant's deportation would not be a disproportionate interference with his right to respect for his family and private life.

G. ISSUES

[51] The appellant relies upon four grounds of appeal, which are advanced as rationality challenges:

I.   The Judge gave unsustainable and/or inadequate reasons for rejecting the appellant's assertion that he was induced by the respondent to renounce his British citizenship and further that his citizenship would resume if he were not repatriated to Pakistan.

II.   The Judge raised a doubt as to the appellant having been informed as to the possibility of being repatriated when this was not a fact in issue.

III.   The Judge 'downgraded' the weight to be attributed to the appellant's family life on the basis that it was formed at a time when he had renounced his citizenship.

IV.   The Judge failed to lawfully consider the factors favourable to the appellant when considering his private life rights, such as his having lived his entire life in this country, his extensive rehabilitation and his not being a continuing risk of perpetrating criminal behaviour.

[52] The respondent filed a rule 24 response and grounds of cross-appeal on 21 February 2020. By means of the document the respondent submitted that the Judge materially misdirected herself in concluding that the appellant is not a foreign criminal as defined in Part 5A of the 2002 Act. As the successful party before the First-tier Tribunal, Mr. Lindsay submitted that the document constituted a rule 24 response, with a cross-appeal in the alternative, placing reliance upon para. 46 of *EG and NG (UT rule 17: withdrawal; rule 24: scope) Ethiopia* [2013] UKUT 00143 (IAC), the material part of which confirms:

'46. ... Rule 24 does not create a right of appeal to a party who has not asked for permission to appeal. Rule 24 is not in any way to do with seeking permission to appeal and it is not an alternative to seeking permission where permission is needed. It is to do with giving notice about how the respondent intends to respond to the appeal that the appellant has permission to pursue. If a respondent wants to argue that the First-tier Tribunal should have reached a materially different conclusion then the respondent needs permission to appeal.'

[53] On behalf of the appellant Mr. Muquit accepted that the respondent did not require permission from the Tribunal to advance the contention as to misdirection in this matter, in circumstances where the core of the respondent's argument advanced by the rule 24 response is that consequent to the findings of fact made the Judge was correct to refuse the appeal, but on an issue which she lost before the Judge. Such approach is consistent with section 11(2) of the Tribunals, Courts and Enforcement Act 2007 where a right of appeal is enjoyed by any party only against some aspect of the actual order of the First-tier Tribunal: *Secretary of State for the Home Department v Devani* [2020] EWCA Civ 612; [2020] 1 WLR 2613.

[54] The Tribunal orally confirmed to the parties at a preliminary hearing held at Field House on 10 March 2020 that the respondent did not require permission to advance her argument as to misdirection by means of her rule 24 response. It was noted that neither party asserted that if there was an error of law as to the Judge's self-direction concerning the status of 'foreign criminal' that it was material. We confirmed that there was no cross-appeal before us.

H. DECISION ON ERROR OF LAW

[55] From the outset we are grateful to Mr. Muquit and Mr. Lindsay for their helpful and thorough written and oral submissions.

Renunciation of British citizenship.

[56] We proceed by considering grounds 1 and 2 together. In a passage of her decision that was subject to considerable forensic examination before us by both parties, the Judge concluded as to the appellant's contention that he had been induced to renounce his British citizenship, at [15]:

'15. It may be helpful at this stage to consider the information I have been given regarding the appellant's decision to renounce his British citizenship. The appellant explains that he was advised in 2008 that he could apply to be repatriated to a prison in Pakistan. He does not explain who advised him. In 2010 the Pakistani authorities agreed to the repatriation. However, the Secretary of State explained that as the appellant was a British citizen he could not be repatriated. The appellant explained that he was told by Immigration Officers that if he renounced his nationality then it would increase the chances of a successful application. I have not been told who he spoke to or when. The appellant states that he had conversations with Jason Ruffy at Cross Border Transfers in respect of his position and was assured that his citizenship would revert in the event that he was not transferred. He tells me that Jason Ruffy has since left the department and that SAR's [subject access requests] have not been replied to. I have seen limited documentary evidence regarding the discussions the appellant is said to have had regarding the renunciation of his British citizenship. Given the significance of such an event, it is not unreasonable to suppose that he would have taken formal advice from a solicitor about the potential consequences. It is not unreasonable that he would have obtained written confirmation from the Home Office that his citizenship would be reinstated in the event that he was not transferred. He is not someone who is unfamiliar with the importance of obtaining and following legal advice having been involved in legal proceedings, albeit in a different context. It was argued that I should consider proportionality against the backdrop that he was told by officials that his citizenship would be reinstated if he was not transferred to Pakistan. However, on the basis of the evidence available to me I am not satisfied that I can reach that conclusion. I find the appellant made the decision to renounce his citizenship as he wanted to be transferred to Pakistan. I find his decision was motivated by the reasons he set out at paragraph 24 of his witness statement. Based on the information before me I am not satisfied that the respondent misrepresented the position to the appellant or that the respondent led him to believe that his citizenship would be reinstated.'

[57] She incorporated this finding into her Article 8 assessment:

'27. I do bear in mind he was formerly a British citizen and that does carry substantial weight. Although I reject the claim that he renounced his citizenship on the basis of a misrepresentation, or an inducement made by the respondent as there is insufficient evidence before me to make that finding. I note the Home Office letter dated June 2010 but all this states is that as the appellant is a dual national, he will not be transferred to Pakistan to serve the remainder of his sentence as a result.'

[58] We asked the representatives to identify the Home Office letter of June 2010 referred to by the Judge, which we could not locate in the respondent's bundle, nor in the two bundles relied upon by the appellant. We were informed that it was the letter from Mr. Ruffy dated 24 June 2010 referred to at [20] above. That is a letter from the Ministry of Justice and not from the Home Office, as erroneously identified in para. [8(i)] of the Judge's decision. We note that although the appellant claims at para. 24 of his statement dated 10 September 2019 that the letter he received dated 24 June 2010 advised him that he would need to renounce his British citizenship before the transfer request could be authorised, the letter does not set out any such advice or suggestion.

[59] Mr. Muquit accepted before us that his challenge to these paragraphs of the Judge's decision was on rationality grounds.

[60] The appellant complains by means of ground 1 that the Judge erred in not accepting both his evidence and the evidence of Z and other family members as to his having been induced to renounce his British citizenship, and so 'wrongly discounted' a highly material factor mitigating the public interest in the appellant's deportation.

[61] Having considered Mr. Muquit's submissions with care we are satisfied that this challenge is simply a disagreement with the Judge's factual findings. At the outset, we observe that the appellant and Z had little, if any, communication with each other at the time the appellant applied to renounce his British citizenship in August 2011. Z's evidence as to such events is reliant upon information provided to her by the appellant. The appellant further relied upon witness statements from eight family members and two friends at his hearing, of whom eight refer to the appellant having informed them as to events surrounding his renunciation of his citizenship and to his having being informed that he would regain his citizenship after a period of time. We again observe that the witnesses, though well-meaning, are simply repeating information provided by the appellant to them. Save for the appellant, the sole direct evidence on this issue is from Z who details that she maintained regular contact with Mr. Ruffy, said in her witness statement to be 'for [the appellant's] British Nationality to be reinstated' and that during a conversation in August 2013 she was advised that the appellant should apply for his British citizenship to be reinstated. She further detailed that Mr. Ruffy informed her that the Agreement between the United Kingdom and Pakistan had been suspended. We observe that Z does not provide explicit evidence that she was informed by an official that the appellant was entitled to resume his British citizenship if he were not transferred within 3 years, i.e. by 2014. Whilst not expressly addressed within the Judge's decision, we are satisfied that it is implicit that the hearsay evidence presented by family and friends could carry no positive weight in circumstances where it relied solely upon information provided by the appellant and his evidence as having been induced to renounce his British citizenship was not accepted.

[62] In considering ground 2 we observe from the outset that the appellant has erred in fact by mistakenly referring to Mr. Ruffy and Mr. Binns as being immigration officers. Following discussion between the representatives before us we understand Mr. Ruffy to be have been employed at the relevant time in the Offender Safety, Rights and Responsibilities Group, Cross Border Transfers, Ministry of Justice and Mr. Binns to have been employed in the Equality, Rights and Decency Group, National Offender Management Service, Ministry of Justice. Neither of these men were agents or servants of the respondent at the relevant time

and were clearly not immigration officers. We note that this mistake as to fact is further identifiable within Mr. Muquit's grounds of appeal where, we accept on instruction, Mr. Ruffy is expressly identified as one of the 'immigration officers' to whom the appellant spoke. The Judge was reasonably entitled to conclude that the documentary evidence said no more than that the appellant would not be transferred to Pakistan because he was a dual national. We are satisfied that the Ministry of Justice letter of 24 June 2010 is not capable of evidencing the appellant's contention that he was induced to renounce his citizenship upon being informed that it would resume if he were not transferred within a specified period.

[63] The burden was upon the appellant to establish that he was materially influenced by the purported representations when deciding to renounce his British citizenship. Upon carefully considering the Judge's reasoning and the evidence before her we conclude that she adopted an exemplary approach and gave cogent, lawful reasons for her conclusion that the appellant had not been induced by the respondent, or the United Kingdom authorities, to renounce his British citizenship. On the evidence presented it was lawfully open to her to conclude that the appellant had not met the burden placed upon him and that the sole material influence upon his decision was his desire to act in a manner he considered best for his parents. In all the circumstances, the rationality challenges advanced by grounds 1 and 2 cannot succeed and are dismissed.

Is the appellant a 'foreign criminal' for the purposes of Part 5A of the 2002 Act and Part 13 of the Immigration Rules?

[64] There is a threefold framework to deportation in domestic law. By means of section 5 of the 1971 Act, the respondent enjoys a discretionary power to make a deportation order, and such order may only be on the alternative grounds specified in section 3(5) and (6) of the 1971 Act. Section 32 of the 2007 Act designates a particular class of offender as a foreign criminal and sets out the consequences of such designation. The implicit amendment to section 3(5)(a) of the 1971 Act by section 32 of the 2007 Act solely relates to the removal of the respondent's function of deeming a person's deportation to be conducive to the public good, in the case of a foreign criminal within the meaning of the 2007 Act, and substituting an automatic deeming provision in such a case: *Yussuf (meaning of "liable to deportation")* [2018] UKUT 00117 (IAC). The final strand to the framework is the expulsion of persons exercising EU Treaty rights or their family members.

[65] The respondent decided that the appellant's deportation would not breach the United Kingdom's obligations under Article 8. The appellant's right of appeal against that decision was exercised under section 82(1)(b) of the 2002 Act in relation to a decision to refuse a human rights claim and the ground of appeal advanced was that the decision was unlawful under section 6 of the Human Rights Act 1998 ('the 1998 Act'): section 84(2) of the 2002 Act.

[66] We initially find that the Judge erred in her understanding that the respondent had made a concession that the appellant was not a 'foreign criminal' and that Part 13 of the Rules did not apply in the appeal before her. Consequent to such misunderstanding she did not place the considerations in section 117C into her proportionality assessment. In terms, the decision letter of 3 October 2018 conceded only that as the appellant was a British citizen at the time of his offence, he could not be considered to be a foreign criminal under the definition set out at

section 32 of the 2007 Act. It was for this reason that deportation was pursued under section 3(5)(a) of the 1971 Act. We note that in her decision letter the respondent proceeded to expressly rely upon Part 13 of the Rules as well as sections 117A–D of the 2002 Act.

[67] Mr. Muquit sought to persuade us that the Judge was ultimately correct to find that the appellant was not a foreign criminal and so Part 5A of the 2002 Act did not apply to him and that Part 13 of the Rules was to be applied as in the case of those who are not foreign criminals in the way adumbrated in *Bah (*EO (Turkey*) – liability to deport)* [2012] UKUT 00196 (IAC). He submitted that the temporal quality of a criminal conviction in the definition of foreign criminal under the 2002 Act was the same as under the 2007 Act thereby establishing that both statutory provisions should be read as being consistent with each other. At our direction, the parties addressed the automatic deportation provisions under section 32 of the 2007 Act, though we recognise that the decision to deport in this matter was under the 1971 Act.

[68] Before us Mr. Lindsay sought to withdraw the concession made in the decision letter as to the automatic deportation provisions under the 2007 Act not being applicable to the appellant on the basis that he did not meet the requirements of being a foreign criminal. As the decision to deport was under the 1971 Act the fact that there was a concession as to automatic deportation is ultimately not relevant to our decision and so it was not a concession that determines the appeal before us. We find that the principles established in *AK (Sierra Leone) v Secretary of State for the Home Department* [2016] EWCA Civ 999 are not met and consequently the application to withdraw the concession contained in the respondent's decision is refused.

[69] We are satisfied that the respondent's initial concession as to the 2007 Act was correctly made in her decision letter. The provisions introduced by the 2007 Act were a statutory change in deportation powers by which an element of the respondent's discretion was replaced by an automatic requirement as to deportation. The implied amendment to section 3(5)(a) of the 1971 Act by the 2007 Act established that where someone meets the requirements to be considered a foreign criminal for the purposes of the Act they are so designated, and their deportation deemed conducive to the public good so that they are subject to automatic deportation, save for the ability to rely upon statutory exceptions to deportation. As confirmed by Aikens LJ in *RU (Bangladesh) v Secretary of State for the Home Department* [2011] EWCA Civ 651; [2011] Imm AR 662, at [34]:

'34. The effect of sections 32(1)-(3) of the UKBA must be that if a person meets the conditions which bring him within the definition "foreign criminal", then his deportation is deemed by statute to be conducive to the public good. I therefore agree with Sedley LJ's statement (when sitting in the Upper Tribunal) in *SSHD v MK* [[2010] UKUT 281, at 23] that what was in the field of "executive policy" (because it was for the SSHD to decide whether it was conducive to the public good to deport a foreign criminal) has now become "legislative policy". Parliament has stated that it is conducive to the public good to deport "foreign criminals". I also agree with Sedley LJ's statement, at [24] in the same Determination, that where a "foreign criminal" challenges a deportation order made by the SSHD under section 32(5) of the UKBA, on the basis that his removal would infringe his ECHR rights and it would be disproportionate to deport him, it is not open to that person to argue that his deportation is not conducive to the public good, nor is it necessary for the SSHD to prove that it is. In such cases it will be so: see the proviso to section 33(7) of the UKBA.'

[70] Mr. Muquit placed reliance upon the judgment of Nicol J in *R (Hussein) v Secretary of State for the Home Department* [2009] EWHC 2492 (Admin), [2010] Imm AR 320 and his conclusion that section 32 of the 2007 Act, read in the light of the commencement provision at section 59(4)(d), must have been intended to cover individuals who had been convicted in the past as well as those who were convicted after commencement. We note para. [20] of Nicol J's judgment:

'20. The statute does use the present tense in the sections to which Mr Husain drew attention, but in my judgement this will not bear the significance which he attributes to it. Section 59(4)(d) uses the past tense – 'persons convicted before the passing of this Act.' I infer from this that the drafter contemplated that s.32 embraced those who had been convicted at the time of the passing of the Act. Section 59(4)(d) expressly allowed the Secretary of State to make a transitional provision in their case so as to confine the application of s.32 to those who were also in custody on the date of commencement, but section 59 is dealing with the mechanics of commencement. It empowered (but did not oblige) the Secretary of State to make certain transitional provisions. It did not itself set the parameters of automatic deportation. That was done by s.32. Thus section 32, read in the light of s.59(4)(d), must have been intended to cover those who had in the past been convicted as well as those who were convicted after commencement.'

[71] Section 32 applies prospectively. Importantly, Nicol J observes the qualification of section 59(4)(d) as being confined to a limited temporal exception applied in a manner consistent with the general automatic deportation regime. Such qualification does not dislocate the temporal link of the section to the conviction as established by section 32(1). We cannot read the contrary into the Court of Appeal's approval of Nicol J's judgment in *AT (Pakistan) v Secretary of State for the Home Department* [2010] EWCA Civ 567, [2010] Imm AR 675, at [9]–[11].

[72] In this matter, as the appellant was convicted before the passing of the Act, was in custody at the time of the commencement of section 32 and was not subject to deportation proceedings made under section 5 of the 1971 Act before 1 August 2008 his is a conviction that falls within section 32(1)(b) of the 2007 Act consequent to the relevant Commencement Order. However, neither section 59(4) nor the relevant Commencement Orders establish a limited temporal exception to the requirement that the appellant not be a British citizen at the time of conviction, and so we are in agreement that the respondent was correct to concede that the appellant is not a foreign criminal for the purpose of the 2007 Act consequent to section 32(1)(a).

[73] We turn to Mr. Muquit's submission that the temporal quality of a criminal conviction in the definition of foreign criminal under the 2002 Act is the same as under the 2007 Act.

[74] Sections 117A to 117D in Part 5A of the 2002 Act set out the correct approach to considering Article 8 claims. Section 117A(1) of the 2002 Act sets out how the Article 8 provisions are to be applied and is clear in terms. In respect of

this appeal the Tribunal is to determine whether the respondent's decision made under the Immigration Acts breaches a person's right to respect for private and family life under Article 8, and as a result would be unlawful under section 6 of the 1998 Act.

[75] Section 117A(2) is equally clear in terms: in considering the public interest question, the Tribunal must (in particular) have regard in all cases to the considerations listed in section 117B, and in cases concerning the deportation of foreign criminals, to the considerations listed in section 117C.

[76] Section 117D sets out the interpretation of sections 117A to 117C. The focus of the parties' submissions upon us were directed to section 117D(2) where the definition of a 'foreign criminal' is set out.

[77] Part 5A prescribes a domestically refined approach to the public interest considerations which the Tribunal is required to take into account when considering Article 8 in a deportation appeal. Unlike the 2007 Act it is not a statutory change as to the exercise of power to deport, rather it is a domestic refinement as to the consideration of the public interest. The listed considerations are intended to be applied to a 'decision' made under both the 1971 Act, which applies no temporal link to the date of conviction, and the 2007 Act which does. There is no express confirmation as to the relevant time for the consideration of whether an offender is a foreign criminal, though we observe that the present tense is used at section 117D(2)(a) – 'who is not a British citizen' – and the past tense is used in relation to conviction and sentence at section 117D(2)(b),(c) save for in relation to 'persistent offender' at section 117D(2)(c)(iii) which is in the present tense. We observe at section 117D(2)(b) the phrase '... who has been convicted ...' is used. That is a different tense to that concerned with the same issue at section 32(1)(a) of the 2007 Act. We are satisfied that Parliament intended to use different tenses in the two statutes and did so because the provisions are for different purposes. The relevant provisions of the 2007 Act are concerned with the automatic deportation of foreign criminals that have been convicted and sentenced to a period of imprisonment of at least 12 months or convicted of a specified offence and sentenced to a period of imprisonment. The relevant provisions of the 2002 Act are concerned with the public interest question that arise when a Court or Tribunal is required to determine whether a decision made under the Immigration Acts breaches a person's right to respect for private and family life. We further observe that there is no express confirmation within the definition at section 117D(2) that the offender was not to be British at the date of conviction. We therefore conclude that the Judge erred in not considering the appellant to be a foreign criminal under Part 5A of the 2002 Act.

[78] In *SC (paras A398–339D: 'foreign criminal': procedure) Albania* [2020] UKUT 187 (IAC) the Tribunal confirmed that paragraph A398 of the Rules governs each of the rules in Part 13 that follows it. The expression 'foreign criminal' in paragraph A398 is to be construed by reference to the definition of that expression in section 117D of the 2002 Act. The Tribunal affirmed the approach in *OLO and Others (para 398 – 'foreign criminal')* [2016] UKUT 00056. Consequently, as a foreign criminal sentenced to a mandatory term of life imprisonment the appellant fell to be considered under paragraph 398(a) of the Rules and could not be considered under either paragraphs 399 or 399A. He is therefore required to establish very compelling circumstances over and above those described in paragraphs 399 and 399A to establish that the public interest in deportation is outweighed. We conclude that the Judge erred in not considering the appeal under Part 13 of the Rules.

[79] In summary we find as to whether the appellant is a 'foreign criminal' for the purposes of Part 5A of the 2002 Act and Part 13 of the Immigration Rules:

(1) The meaning of 'foreign criminal' is not consistent over the 2002 Act and the 2007 Act.

(2) Section 32 of the 2007 Act creates a designated class of offender that is a foreign criminal and establishes the consequences of such designation. That is, for the purposes of section 3(5)(a) of the 1971 Act, the deportation of that person is conducive to the public good and the respondent must make a deportation order in respect of that person.

(3) A temporal link is established by section 32(1) requiring the foreign offender not to be a British citizen at the date of conviction.

(4) Part 5A of the 2002 Act prescribes a domestically refined approach to the public interest considerations which the Tribunal is required to take into account when considering Article 8 in a deportation appeal. Unlike the 2007 Act it is not a statutory change to the power to deport, rather it is a domestic refinement as to the consideration of the public interest question.

(5) Part 5A establishes no temporal link to the date of conviction, rather the relevant date for establishing whether an offender is a foreign criminal is the date of the decision subject to the exercise of an appeal on human rights grounds under section 82(1)(b) of the 2002 Act.

(6) Paragraph A398 of the Rules governs each of the rules in Part 13 that follows it. The expression 'foreign criminal' in paragraph A398 is to be construed by reference to the definition of that expression in section 117D of the 2002 Act: *SC (paras A398–339D: 'foreign criminal': procedure) Albania.*

(7) At the date of the respondent's decision in October 2018 the appellant was a foreign criminal as defined in section 117D(2) of the 2002 Act, namely that he 'is not a British citizen', 'has been convicted in the United Kingdom of an offence' and 'has been sentenced to a period of imprisonment of at least 12 months.' He is therefore a foreign criminal for the purposes of section 117A(2)(b) and section 117C. Consequently, Part 13 of the Rules was applicable.

[80] However, as accepted by both parties, the Judge's error as to the appellant being a foreign criminal was not material because the nature of his sentence means that he cannot rely upon the statutory Exceptions to the public interest and the Judge proceeded to consider whether very compelling circumstances arose. Though she applied a lesser weight to the public interest than should have been applied under section 117C(6) of the 2002 Act and para. 398 of the Rules, this was to the benefit of the appellant who was still unsuccessful before her. Consequently, we find that the error of law was not material.

Article 8

[81] There are three strands to the appellant's claim that the Judge erred in her assessment of the Article 8 claim before her. First, the appellant claims the Judge 'downgraded' the weight to be attributed to the appellant's family life on the basis that it was formed at a time when he had renounced his British citizenship. Second, the appellant claims that the Judge failed to consider the factors favourable to the appellant when considering his private life rights, such as his having lived his entire life in this country, his extensive rehabilitation and his not being a continuing risk of perpetrating criminal behaviour. Finally, connected to that second strand, although not immediately apparent from the grounds of appeal, Mr Muquit submits that at para. [28] of her decision, the Judge noted the appellant 'is a very low risk of reoffending in the future ...', but concluded, at para [34], that the removal of the appellant is proportionate to the legitimate end sought to be achieved, namely the prevention of crime. We deal with each in turn.

Did the Judge downgrade the weight to be attributed to the appellant's family life?
[82] The Judge accepted the appellant to be in a genuine and subsisting relationship with Z. At para. [22], she observed that the relationship was formed at a time after the appellant had renounced his citizenship and was a citizen of Pakistan with no status in the United Kingdom.
[83] Mr. Muquit submits the appellant was not to be regarded as being in the United Kingdom 'unlawfully' at the time his relationship with his partner began because his residence throughout was either as of right through British citizenship or because he was made to stay by the respondent's direction, having not been permitted to transfer his custodial sentence to Pakistan. Further, Mr. Muquit seeks to pin the commencement of the relationship to the time they became friends, submitting that at the time the appellant and his wife first met, '... their relationship began in general they were both in the UK as British citizens.' It is said in the appellant's skeleton argument that at the time the appellant and his partner elevated their relationship, a time when the appellant was no longer a British citizen, his presence in the United Kingdom was consequent to the respondent '... not seeking to repatriate him and he was not then liable to deportation ...'
[84] The development of the relationship between the appellant and Z is set out in their respective witness statements and as addressed above generally accepted by the Judge. We observe that they were, on *their* own account, friends from the end of 2003 to 2013, with contact over time by means of letter and telephone call. The appellant was married when they first met. Z married in 2004 and became a mother to her two children. Following the appellant's arrest in November 2004, having known each other for approximately one year, they did not meet until Z undertook a prison visit to the appellant in January 2013. The appellant had by this time renounced his British citizenship.
[85] The appellant claims that there was no justification in law for the Judge diluting the weight to be attached to the family life established by him with Z. We note that the Judge's consideration was undertaken through the mistaken understanding that the respondent had conceded that the appellant was not a foreign criminal, but nevertheless she noted that it was sensible to examine whether the appellant could have succeeded under the Exceptions set out in the

statutory framework and to then consider whether there were any compelling circumstances, as a basis upon which to consider whether deportation of the appellant was proportionate.

[86] The Judge found that it would be unduly harsh for Z to relocate to Pakistan, at para. [23] of her decision. The Judge further concluded that it would not be unduly harsh for Z to remain in this country in the absence of the appellant, in circumstances where she has been the primary carer of her children, raising them in the absence of the appellant, and there are no concerns as to her ability to do so. She further noted that Z has financial and emotional support to rely upon when the appellant is in Pakistan and whilst weight was to be placed upon the lack of face to face contact, having weighed all factors no undue harshness arose.

[87] In his grounds of appeal the appellant refers to the decision of the Court of Appeal in *CL v Secretary of State for the Home Department* [2019] EWCA Civ 1925; [2020] 1 WLR 858 with reference to paras. [50] to [66]. The Court in CL held that a judge was wrong to say that section 117B(4) of the 2002 Act required him to attach little weight to a couple's relationship when that relationship has been entered into at a time when the applicant's immigration status is precarious. There is no rational basis for requiring family life established with a partner who is a British citizen by a person whose immigration status is precarious to be given less weight when there is no such requirement where the partner is not a British citizen. Furthermore, the Court held that the Strasbourg Court has made it clear that in striking the balance between the right to respect for family life and the State's interest in controlling immigration, it is necessary to consider the particular circumstances of the individuals concerned including their immigration status and history.

[88] We reject the claim that the Judge diluted the weight to be attached to the family life established by the appellant. Broadly stated, although the appellant and Z had known each other since 2003 and had remained in contact with each other despite each of them being married to another person at various times over the years, their relationship developed from a friendship, which had grown closer over time, following the visit by Z to the appellant in prison in January 2013. Both the appellant and Z confirm in their respective witness statements that it was in April 2013 that they discussed their feelings for each other for the first time, each being previously unaware of the other's personal thoughts on the issue. It is clear that the observation made by the Judge at para. [22] of her decision that the relationship between the appellant and Z was formed at a time after the appellant had renounced his citizenship, a time when he was a citizen of Pakistan who enjoyed no status in the United Kingdom, is properly rooted in the evidence.

[89] Properly read the Judge does not say at paras. [22] to [34] of her decision that she attaches little weight to the relationship between the appellant and Z because that relationship was entered into at a time when the immigration status of the appellant was in anyway precarious. Neither does the Judge say that the appellant is to be regarded as being in the United Kingdom 'unlawfully' at the time his relationship with his partner began. We were not directed to any paragraph within the findings and conclusions in which the Judge stated that the weight to be attached to the relationship was in any way reduced because of the appellant's status at any point. To the contrary, insofar as the appellant's status is concerned the Judge expressly states at para. [27] that she has borne in mind that the appellant was formerly a British citizen and 'that does carry substantial weight'.

[90] We conclude that the appellant's challenge on this issue simply amounts to a disagreement with the Judge's conclusion.

[91] Before turning to the remaining grounds of appeal, we have considered the submission made by Mr. Lindsay that the Judge appeared to have taken an overly generous approach in para. [27] of her decision that 'substantial weight' should be attached to the fact the appellant was formerly a British citizen. He submits that the Judge provides no reasons or authority to support the claim that the appellant's status as a former British citizen carries 'substantial weight'. The status of an individual as a British citizen prevents their deportation and so the question regarding the weight to be attached to their status as a British citizen will rarely arise. Where the question does arise because the status as a British citizen has come to an end, in our judgement the weight to be attached to such a factor is entirely fact specific. At one end of the spectrum are those who have British nationality, as here, by birth, and who have spent all of their life in the United Kingdom. The fact that they have lived in the United Kingdom as a British citizen for the majority of their life is a factor to which a Tribunal is entitled to attach 'substantial' or 'significant' weight, but that is not to say it is a factor that will be determinative of the proportionality assessment. At the other end of the spectrum are those who secured British citizenship after arrival in the United Kingdom, lived in this country as a British citizen but it subsequently transpires that the status was obtained, for example, by deception. Undoubtedly, such an individual could not rationally contend that 'substantial' or 'significant' weight attaches to their former status as a British citizen. On the facts here, it was in our judgement open to the Judge to proceed on the basis that the appellant was formerly a British citizen and had been for over thirty years since birth, and that does carry substantial weight.

Did the Judge fail to consider the factors favourable to the appellant when considering his private life rights?

[92] We reject the claim made by the appellant that the Judge failed to lawfully consider the factors favourable to him when considering his private life rights. The Judge noted, at para. [17], that the appellant was a British citizen at birth. The Judge was satisfied that there was evidence before her of the appellant's social and cultural integration in this country, notwithstanding his offending behaviour. In considering whether there are very significant obstacles to the appellant's integration in Pakistan the Judge also noted, at para. [20], that the appellant has spent very little time in that country.

[93] The Judge further noted at para. [20] that the appellant is likely to be familiar with Pakistani culture and traditions. He has possessed a Pakistani passport and was prepared to be repatriated to Pakistan to serve out the rest of his sentence in a Pakistani prison. She observed that the appellant is of working age, of good health and from his experience of working in this country has acquired transferable skills. She noted that the appellant can speak basic Urdu and would be able to acquire greater fluency in Pakistan together with attendant reading and writing skills. The Judge found that the appellant would be able to secure employment within a reasonable timeframe and it is likely that he does have extended family in Pakistan. The Judge accepted that although it may be disruptive at first, the appellant would be able to integrate in Pakistan at a practical level. She acknowledged there would be a period of adjustment, but for reasons set out in paras. [20] and [21] concluded that there are no very significant obstacles to the appellant's integration in Pakistan.

[94] We observe that in her assessment the Judge did not place into the balance the fact that the appellant's intention consequent to having committed murder was to flee to Pakistan and reside there to avoid arrest and prosecution. It would have been reasonable for her to place adverse reliance upon this fact, but she did not do so.

[95] The Judge assessed whether there were exceptional circumstances which made refusing the appellant leave to remain in this country disproportionate and hence incompatible with Article 8. We again observe that at para. [27] the Judge confirmed that the appellant having been a former British citizen was a factor that carried substantial weight in the proportionality assessment.

[96] In support of the submission that the appellant's previous status as a British citizen weighs heavily in his favour, Mr. Muquit refers to the decision of the Court of Appeal in *CI (Nigeria) v Secretary of State for the Home Department* [2019] EWCA Civ 2027; [2020] Imm AR 503. We observe the factual circumstances that arose in that appeal and the confirmation by the Court that in deportation appeals judges are to be mindful as to the importance of the particular facts surrounding an individual's presence and length of residence in the United Kingdom and features such as whether the appellant is a settled migrant who has spent almost his whole life in the United Kingdom and grown up with a British social and cultural identity. Leggatt LJ addressed the issue of weight to be given to such history, at [113]:

'113. ... although little weight should generally be given to a private life established when a person was present in the UK unlawfully or without a right of permanent residence, it would not (as the Upper Tribunal judge recognised) be fair to adopt this approach on the particular facts of this case, where the grant of indefinite leave to remain was delayed for many years when CI was a child no good reason and through no fault of his. In determining whether it is compatible with Article 8 to deport him from the UK, CI should not in the circumstances have less weight according to the fact that he has spent his childhood and youth in the UK than would be the case if he had had a vested right of residence for most of that period.'

[97] Mr. Muquit further relied upon the decision of the Court of Appeal in *Akinyemi v Secretary of State for the Home Department (No. 2)* [2019] EWCA Civ 2098; [2020] 1 WLR 1843, in which the Court of Appeal held that the correct approach to the balancing exercise is to recognise that the public interest in the deportation of foreign criminals is a flexible one, and that there will be a small number of cases where the individual circumstances reduce the legitimate and strong public interest in removal. In *Akinyemi (No. 2)* the Court held that the Upper Tribunal attached insufficient weight to the fact that the appellant had been lawfully in the United Kingdom for his whole life. At para. [39] of his judgment Sir Ernest Ryder set out the correct approach as to a flexible consideration of the public interest:

'39. ... The correct approach to be taken to the 'public interest' in the balance to be undertaken by a tribunal is to recognise that the public interest in the deportation of foreign criminals has a movable rather than fixed quality. It is necessary to approach the public interest flexibly, recognising that there will be cases where the person's circumstances in the individual case reduce the legitimate and strong public interest in removal. The number of these cases will necessarily be very few i.e. they will be exceptional having regard to the legislation and the Rules ...'

[98] At para. [40], he observed:

'40. In support of that general proposition, it is necessary to go back to the facts of this case and the court's reasoning in the first appeal. First, one has to be careful to identify as a relevant fact that the appellant was in the UK lawfully for the whole of his life. It was a feature of the first appeal to this court that the UT had wrongly factored into the balance that his residence was unlawful or at least that it had the character of "the absence of any lawful leave" (see *Akinyemi* at [30] and [31]). The conclusion of this court was unequivocal: subject to the deportation provisions of the 1971 Act, the appellant was "irremovable" because 'he was in breach of no legal obligation by being here' (see Underhill LJ at [35]).

[99] At paras. [50] and [51]:

'50. In my judgement there can be no doubt, consistent with the Strasbourg jurisprudence, that the Supreme Court has clearly identified that the strength of the public interest will be affected by factors in the individual case, i.e. it is a flexible or moveable interest not a fixed interest. Lord Reed provides the example at [26] of a person who was born in this country as a relevant factor. Applying this approach to the weight to be given to the public interest in deportation on the facts of this case could lead to a lower weight being attached to the public interest.

51. I am strengthened in my view by the conclusion of the ECtHR in *Maslov v Austria* (*supra*), one of the cases relied upon by the Supreme Court in *Hesham Ali*. In that case, the court said at [74]:

> "Although Article 8 provides no absolute protection against expulsion for any category of aliens (see *Üner* cited above, #55), including those who were born in the host country or moved there in early childhood, the Court has already found that regard is to be had to the special situation of aliens who have spent most, if not all, of their childhood in the host country, were brought up there and received their education there (see *Üner*, #58 *in fine*)."'

[100] We observe that on several occasions during his submissions Mr. Muquit referred to the appellant as being 'super-*Akinyemi*' consequent to his having enjoyed British citizenship from birth to the renunciation of his citizenship in 2011, a period of a little over 32 years. In *Akinyemi (No. 2)* the appellant was born in this country but had not acquired British nationality automatically due to legislative changes that occurred just before his birth. Despite for many years being entitled to British citizenship, he had never taken steps to acquire it and so remained a Nigerian national by virtue of his birth. Mr. Muquit's submissions were based upon the previous enjoyment of British citizenship being of significant weight in the proportionality assessment, though he correctly did not seek to go so far as to say that it was determinative of the issue.

[101] We remind ourselves that the appellant advances this challenge on a rationality basis. As required the Judge was careful to identify as a relevant factor that the appellant was born British and has lived in the United Kingdom for most of his life as a British citizen. The Judge expressly referred to the appellant being a British citizen at birth when she was considering a private life claim at para. [17] of her decision and at para. [27] she expressly stated that his having been formerly a British citizen carried substantial weight in her proportionality assessment. We are satisfied that she lawfully adopted the approach endorsed by the Court of Appeal in *CI (Nigeria)* as to the weight to be given to his long enjoyment of British citizenship, and her assessment was in accordance with that subsequently confirmed in *Akinyemi (No. 2)* which post-dates her decision.

[102] The substance of the complaint advanced, both in the appellant's skeleton argument and orally before us, is that the Judge erred in not treating the appellant's personal history of British citizenship as a stronger, special situation beyond that enjoyed by the appellants in *CI (Nigeria)* and *Akinyemi (No. 2)*. The Judge's purported failure was to fail to allocate a 'special' weight to the depth of the appellant's social and cultural integration, secured through his enjoyment of British citizenship, relative to the public interest. We are satisfied that the Judge did consider such integration when placing as a positive fact for the appellant in the balance sheet approach that he had only ever lived in this country. She did not underestimate the importance of the appellant having enjoyed British citizenship for many years, including his formative ones. There is no requirement to forensically detail each individual inherent factor flowing from the long-term enjoyment of British citizenship in the balance sheet when they are reasonably identified by reference to the appellant having enjoyed such citizenship.

[103] The assessment of an Article 8 claim such as this is inevitably fact sensitive, as noted by Leggatt LJ when considering the personal circumstances arising in *CI (Nigeria)*, at [117]:

'117. The first is the severity of the difficulties and suffering that CI would potentially face if sent to Nigeria. There was a material difference between returning an immigrant to a country with which he retains some social and cultural ties and deporting him to a country to which he has none and which, in the words of CI's sister in this case, 'is as foreign to us as China'. The harshness of such deportation is magnified in the present case to the extent that it could be cruel by the evidence of the devastating impact that it would have upon CI's mental health.'

[104] In this matter, the Judge acknowledged that though the appellant has spent very little time in Pakistan, it is not a country that is entirely unfamiliar to him. She found that the appellant was desirous of being transferred to a prison in Pakistan to enjoy greater contact with his father and this motivated his decision to renounce his citizenship. Unlike the appellants in *CI (Nigeria)* and *Akinyemi (No. 2)*, the appellant has sought over time to relocate to Pakistan.

[105] In our judgement the Judge undoubtedly considered all relevant matters in the round. The public interest in the deportation of a foreign criminal is not set in stone and must be approached flexibly. The Judge had proper regard, *inter alia*, to the appellant's length of residence in the United Kingdom, the ties that he retains

with his family in this country, his immigration and offending history, and his family circumstances. In adopting the balance sheet approach, at paras [32] and [33], the Judge carefully considered the matters that weighed in favour of, and against, the appellant. In addition to his only having ever lived in this country she noted that the appellant is remorseful, has accepted responsibility for his previous convictions and that there is extensive evidence in the appeal bundle as to rehabilitation. The Judge gave substantial weight to the personal ties the appellant enjoys in this country through his long enjoyment of British citizenship. She also gave appropriate weight to the appellant's ability to establish his life in Pakistan and to integrate into the community. The appellant does not challenge the weight the Judge gave to the murder conviction.

The risk of re-offending

[106] In a paragraph subjected to considerable analysis by the parties before us, the Judge detailed, at [28]:

'28.   I do note that the appellant has committed, using the terminology in the skeleton argument, a 'historic' offence. I appreciate that he has been recommended for parole which suggests that he is a very low risk of reoffending in the future. I accept there is no evidence of any pro-criminal attitudes or that the appellant associates with people involved in criminal activities. I also take note of the extensive evidence of rehabilitation in the appellant's bundle.'

[107] Mr. Muquit informed us that he had not sought to downplay the seriousness of the offence when referring to it as a 'historic' offence in his skeleton argument. It was simply a term used to identify that the conviction had occurred several years before and was not meant to imply that such fact alone diminished the public interest in deportation. We understand that the Judge used the term as meant by Mr. Muquit and nothing more is to be read into it.

[108] Mr. Muquit contended before us that the Judge had accepted, at para. [28], that the appellant is a very low risk of re-offending in the future and sought to place reliance upon it as evidencing a difficulty in reconciling such finding of fact with her conclusion that the appellant's deportation is proportionate to the legitimate end sought to be achieved, namely the prevention of crime.

[109] We reject this submission. Upon a natural reading of the paragraph, the Judge is careful to identify when she is making observations as to the evidence before her – 'note' and 'appreciate' – and when she is making a finding of fact – 'accept'. Our conclusion is reinforced by the Judge not placing a finding that the appellant is a very low risk of reoffending into her structured balance sheet at paras. [32] to [33]. The appellant erroneously seeks to elevate a simple observation made upon the evidence into a finding of fact. We are satisfied that the Judge accepted that there is no evidence of any criminal attitudes or that the appellant associates with people involved in criminal activities.

[110] During his oral submissions, in which he relied upon the Judge having made a finding of fact as to the appellant being a 'very low risk' of future reoffending, Mr. Muquit asserted in the alternative that if the Judge had not made such finding, she had erred in not doing so because it was a weighty matter in favour of the appellant. Whilst permission to appeal had not been granted on this ground, we heard submissions from Mr. Muquit and Mr. Lindsay on the issue.

[111] We firstly observe that the risk of reoffending is one facet of the public interest but, in the case of very serious crimes, it is not the most important facet: *OH (Serbia) v Secretary of State for the Home Department* [2008] EWCA Civ 694, [2009] INLR 109, at [15(a)].

[112] Before the Judge were several documents prepared by the Ministry of Justice concerned with the appellant's sentence management, including a parole assessment report, National Offender Management Service (NOMS) report and OASys, all dated October 2016. The appellant further relied upon a psychologist's report dated June 2008, a psychological risk assessment dated 2012, a summary of a sentence planning and review meeting held in 2016 and a considerable number of documents attesting to the completion of offender behaviour work, educational study and good behaviour in prison. Evidence was also filed as to the appellant working in the community on day release from prison. We note the Judge's observation that there was extensive evidence of rehabilitation before her.

[113] We observe that nowhere in the documentation before us was the appellant identified as being a 'very low risk' of future offending. The Offender Manager's report identified the risk of reoffending as low, which was consistent with that identified at the time of the sentence, and the risk of serious harm if the appellant reoffended as medium, which also was consistent with the situation at the time of sentence. Such risk assessment was consistent with OASys. Both the Offender Manager's report and the OASys are dated 2016.

[114] The Judge was entitled to observe that there was evidence before her that was suggestive as to risk, but to implicitly conclude that there was insufficient evidence upon which she could make a finding of fact. Such approach was lawful in circumstances where the evidence as to risk relied upon by the appellant dated from between 2008 and 2016 and when the Parole Board had not yet considered this evidence as well as the evidence prepared for its expert assessment in 2020. We note the observation of Underhill LJ in *HA (Iraq) v Secretary of State for the Home Department* [2020] EWCA Civ 1176, at [141] that '... tribunals will properly be cautious about their ability to make findings on the risk of re-offending, and will usually be unable to do so with any confidence based on no more than the undertaking of prison courses or mere assertions of reform by the offender ...'

[115] Further, we are satisfied that by placing the extensive evidence of rehabilitation in the 'pro' column in the structured balance sheet, at para. [33(3)] the Judge was mindful as to a body of evidence before her concerned with the appellant's risk. By its nature, rehabilitation, or desisting from crime and behaviour leading to crime, is indicative of a reduced risk of re-offending and so such evidence could properly considered as relevant to rehabilitation, rather than requiring an express finding of fact to be made as to 'risk' in the community, or future risk, and for such finding to be placed in the balance sheet exercise. To that end, we are satisfied that the Judge adopted the approach confirmed by the Court of Appeal in *Danso v Secretary of State for the Home Department* [2015] EWCA Civ 596, at [20].

[116] We are fortified in our decision by the recent consideration of rehabilitation in deportation matters by Underhill LJ in *HA (Iraq)*, at [134] to [142] and agree that the Judge adopted the approach identified by the Court of Appeal. She identified that the appellant has shown positive evidence of rehabilitation, and thus a reduced risk of re-offending, and included it as a positive factor within the overall proportionality exercise. However, she was not required to give it great weight because the public interest in the deportation of criminals is not based only on the need to protect the public from further offending by the foreign criminal but also on wider policy considerations of deterrence and public concern, which in this matter are rooted in the index offence of murder.

[117] Though the Judge erred in the weight that she gave to the public interest, such error was in the appellant's favour and he was unsuccessful. The challenge to the Judge's consideration of the Article 8 appeal on rationality grounds cannot succeed. We are satisfied that in the circumstances arising in this appeal the appellant could not succeed under section 117C(6) of the 2002 Act or para. 398 of the Rules as no very compelling circumstances arise to lessen the public interest in his deportation.

I. CONCLUSION

[118] It is in our judgement clear from her assessment of the appellant's Article 8 claim that the Judge considered the matter very carefully and had regard to all relevant matters. Having done so, she concluded at para. [34] that the decision to deport the appellant on conducive grounds struck a fair balance against the appellant's rights and interests and those of his wife when weighed against the wider interests of society. She found that deportation was proportionate to the legitimate end sought to be achieved, namely the prevention of crime, and therefore the appellant's removal in pursuance of a deportation order did not constitute a disproportionate interference with his right to respect for his family and private life. We find that it is clear such decision was properly open to the Judge on the evidence before her and was made following a careful assessment of the appellant's Article 8 claim.

[119] As the Court of Appeal said in *Herrera v Secretary of State for the Home Department* [2018] EWCA Civ 412; [2018] Imm AR 1033, at [18], it is necessary to guard against the temptation to characterise as errors of law what are in truth no more than disagreements about the weight to be given to different factors. The assessment of such a claim is always a highly fact-sensitive task. The Judge was required to consider the evidence as a whole and she plainly did so, giving adequate reasons for her decision. The findings and conclusions reached were neither irrational, as asserted by the appellant, or unreasonable in the *Wednesbury* sense and it follows that our judgement is that there is no material error of law identifiable in the decision of the First-tier Tribunal and the appeal is dismissed.

J. NOTICE OF DECISION

[120] The decision of the First-tier Tribunal did not involve the making of a material error on a point of law.

[121] The decision of the First-tier Tribunal, dated 13 November 2019, is upheld and the appeal is dismissed.

MAHMOOD (PARAS. S-LTR.1.6. & S-LTR.4.2.; SCOPE)

UPPER TRIBUNAL (IMMIGRATION AND ASYLUM CHAMBER)

Blum and O'Callaghan UTJJ

[2020] UKUT 376 (IAC)
7 October 2020

Immigration – leave to remain – suitability requirements – paragraphs S-LTR.1.6. & S-LTR.4.2. of Appendix FM – scope – false representations

The Claimant, a citizen of Bangladesh, asserted that he arrived in the United Kingdom as a visitor in 1994. He was encountered by immigration officers in 1996 and subsequently claimed asylum. The Secretary of State for the Home Department refused his application. The Claimant's appeal was dismissed, and he became appeal rights exhausted. He remained in the United Kingdom and secured employment by falsely adopting the identity and national insurance number of a British citizen. In July 2009, he made an unsuccessful application for indefinite leave to remain ("ILR"). In 2014, he applied for leave to remain ("LTR") on human rights grounds relying on Article 8 of the ECHR. The Secretary of State refused the application on the ground that the Claimant did not meet the eligibility requirements of paragraph 276ADE(1)(iii)-(vi) of the Immigration Rules HC 395 (as amended), but expressly accepted that he met the relevant suitability requirements under Appendix FM. The First-tier Tribunal ("FtT") dismissed the Claimant's appeal in January 2016.

By way of further submissions in September 2016, the Claimant sought LTR on private life grounds under Article 8 of the ECHR, relying on his having been present in the United Kingdom for over 20 years. He provided documentation showing his false identity to establish that he had been employed in the United Kingdom since 1997. The Secretary of State observed that, when the Claimant applied for ILR in July 2009, he submitted documents which were not genuine, namely eleven P60 forms dated from 1998 to 2009. Consequently, she refused the application in December 2017, concluding that the Claimant failed to meet the suitability requirements for LTR under paragraphs S-LTR.1.6. and S-LTR.4.2. of Appendix FM. Paragraph S-LTR.1.6 applied when the presence of the applicant in the United Kingdom was not conducive to the public good because his conduct, character, associations, or other reasons, made it undesirable to allow him to remain. Paragraph S-LTR.4.2. applied where the applicant had "made false representations or failed to disclose any material fact in a previous application for entry clearance, leave to enter, leave to remain or a variation of leave, or in a previous human rights claim; or did so in order to obtain from the Secretary of State or a third party a document required to support such an application or claim".

The FtT dismissed the Claimant's appeal against the Secretary of State's decision in December 2018. The FtT Judge found that the Claimant had engaged in sustained deceit over the course of more than a decade and concluded that the documents relied upon arising from employment possessed an innate character as documents containing false representations. She also determined that the

Claimant's personal history made it undesirable to allow him to remain in this country and so his application fell for refusal under both the mandatory suitability ground established by paragraph S-LTR.1.6. and the discretionary ground of paragraph S-LTR.4.2.

Before the Upper Tribunal, the Claimant submitted first, that the Secretary of State had accepted that he met the relevant suitability requirements in 2014 and before the FtT in 2016, and that previous stance and concession should have been a strong factor in the instant appeal. Secondly, he submitted that both paragraph S-LTR.1.6. and paragraph S-LTR.4.2. were discretionary in nature and so required a balancing assessment, which was not undertaken by the FtT, and that the FtT Judge failed properly to engage with the fact that there had been no deception in respect of the application. The Claimant asserted that he had been forthcoming about the fact that he had relied on documents in someone else's name to obtain employment and had not therefore made a false representation to the Secretary of State.

Held, allowing the appeal:

(1) Paragraph S-LTR.1.6. of Appendix FM to the Immigration Rules was mandatory in nature. It was the clear stricture of paragraph S-LTR.1.1. that a mandatory refusal would result if one or more of seven discrete factual circumstances were established and paragraph S-LTR.1.6. identified one such circumstance. The wording of the provision was general in its terms, confirming that an applicant's presence in this country was 'not conducive to the public good' because his 'conduct', 'character', 'associations' or 'other reasons' made it 'undesirable' to allow him to remain in this country. The explanatory memorandum to the Statement of Changes to the Immigration Rules HC 877 was an aid to construction and provided that the context of the introduction of paragraph S-LTR.4.2. was to give authority to the Secretary of State to refuse an application on grounds of suitability if false representations had been submitted, or there had been a failure to disclose material facts, in a previous immigration application. That authority was given because such power did not previously exist within the suitability requirements established by section S-LTR, including paragraph S-LTR.1.6., in respect of an application for LTR. Upon considering the Immigration Rules, and in particular Appendix FM, in the round, the scope of paragraph S-LTR.1.6. of Appendix FM was not sufficiently wide to cover the use of false representations or a failure to disclose material facts in an application for LTR or in a previous application for immigration status (*paras 50 – 51 and 63 – 75*).

(2) The exercise of refusal on suitability grounds under paragraph S-LTR.4.2 of Appendix FM was discretionary in nature by application of paragraph S-LTR.4.1. Paragraph S-LTR.4.2. was specific as to its scope of application and was disjunctive with two independent clauses. The Secretary of State was obliged to plead and reason her exercise of discretion to refuse an application for LTR based on one or both of those clauses. In relation to the first clause, the suggestion that any false representation arising in an earlier application was sufficient to enable refusal, regardless of whether it was made in support of the application and whether the falsity was drawn to the Secretary of State's attention, clearly went beyond the meaning of the words used. The FtT erred in adopting that broad

interpretation. The natural meaning of the first clause of paragraph S-LTR.4.2 required that the false representation or the failure to disclose any material fact must have been made in support of a previous application and not be peripheral to that application. In the instant case, the Claimant's reliance upon employment and tax documents, openly confirmed to have been secured through the long-time use of a false identity, was peripheral to the previous application for LTR on private life grounds under paragraph 276ADE(1)(iii) and also peripheral to the earlier application for ILR on long residence grounds. The Claimant relied on P60 forms, genuinely issued but the product of dishonesty, to establish his long residence, a task they were capable of satisfying, and not to establish that he was the person named upon them. Nor did the documents establish that the Claimant enjoyed a right to work lawfully in this country or meet any financial requirement established by the Rules. The FtT Judge materially erred in finding that the suitability requirement established by the first clause of paragraph S-LTR.4.2. was applicable to the Claimant (*paras 77 – 84*).

(3) Whilst the Secretary of State did not rely upon the second clause of paragraph S-LTR.4.2. in her 2017 decision or before the FtT in 2018, she indicated that she wished to rely upon it at the remaking stage. The use of the words 'required to support' in the second clause in paragraph S-LTR.4.2 confirmed a compulsory element to the use of the document(s) within the application or claim process, and the obtaining of the document(s) must be for the purposes of the immigration application or claim. Upon a natural reading of the second clause, the employment documents relied upon by the Claimant were not secured through false representations to support an application for LTR. The false representation was to his employer(s) and the documents were solely generated consequent to the Claimant having secured employment. In any event such employment and tax documents were not required for an application for LTR under paragraph 276ADE(1)(iii). Consequently, even taking the Secretary of State's case at its highest, she could not succeed under the second clause of paragraph S-LTR.4.2. The Claimant did not fall to be refused under the suitability requirements detailed at paragraph 276ADE(1)(i). On the evidence, he had been continuously present in the United Kingdom for over 20 years. He therefore met the requirements of paragraph 276ADE(1)(iii) of the Immigration Rules (*paras 85 – 90*).

Cases referred to:

AA (Nigeria) v Secretary of State for the Home Department [2010] EWCA Civ 773; [2011] 1 WLR 564; [2010] Imm AR 704; [2011] INLR 1
Aspinalls Club Ltd v Commissioners for Her Majesty's Revenue & Customs [2013] EWCA Civ 1464; [2014] 2 WLR 1574
Devaseelan (Second Appeals – ECHR – Extra-Territorial Effect) Sri Lanka * [2002] UKIAT 702; [2003] Imm AR 1
Flora v Wakom (Heathrow) Ltd [2006] EWCA Civ 1103; [2007] WLR 482
Mahad (previously referred to as AM) (Ethiopia) and Others v Entry Clearance Officer; Muhumed (previously referred to as AM (No. 2)) (Somalia) v Entry Clearance Officer [2009] UKSC 16; [2010] 1 WLR 48; [2010] 2 All ER 535; [2010] Imm AR 203; [2010] INLR 268

R (on the application of D & M) v Secretary of State for Work & Pensions; R (on the application of EM & Others) v Secretary of State for Work and Pensions [2010] EWCA Civ 18; [2010] 1 WLR 1782
Westminster City Council v National Asylum Support Service [2002] UKHL 38; [2002] WLR 2956; [2002] 4 All ER 654
ZH (Bangladesh) v Secretary of State for the Home Department [2009] EWCA Civ 8; [2009] Imm AR 450; [2009] INLR 434

Legislation and international instruments judicially considered:

European Convention on Human Rights, Article 8
Immigration Rules HC 395 (as amended), paragraphs 276ADE, 276B, A320, 320(7B), 322(1), 322(1A), 322(2) & 322(5); paragraphs S-LTR 1.1, S-LTR 1.6, S-LTR 2.1, S-LTR 2.2, S-LTR 4.1, S-LTR 4.2, S-EC 1.1, S-EC 1.5, S-EC 2.1, S-EC 2.2 and S-ILR 1.1, S-ILR 1.8 S-ILR 2.1 & S-ILR 2.2 of Appendix FM
Tribunals, Courts and Enforcement Act 2007, section 12(2)(a)

Representation

Mr M K Mustafa instructed by Kalam Solicitors, for the Claimant;
Mr I Jarvis, Senior Home Office Presenting Officer, for the Secretary of State.

DECISION AND REASONS

UPPER TRIBUNAL JUDGE O'CALLAGHAN:

A. INTRODUCTION

[1] Both members of the panel have contributed to this decision.
[2] This is an appeal against a decision of Judge of the First-tier Tribunal Courtney ('the Judge') sent to the parties on 14 December 2018 by which the appellant's appeal against a decision of the respondent to refuse him leave to remain in this country on human rights (Article 8) grounds was refused.
[3] Upper Tribunal Judge McWilliam granted the appellant permission to appeal by means of a decision dated 11 March 2019.
[4] The Judge did not issue an anonymity direction and the parties did not seek one before us.

B. THE APPELLANT

[5] The appellant is a national of Bangladesh who was born in 1979 and is presently aged 41. He asserts that he arrived in this country as a visitor in 1994. He was encountered by immigration officers at his place of work in 1996 and subsequently claimed asylum. The respondent refused the application by way of a decision dated 11 June 1996. The appellant's appeal against the respondent's decision was dismissed and he became appeal rights exhausted in February 1997.
[6] Whilst in this country the appellant contends that he worked in various restaurants having falsely adopted the identity of a British citizen, 'Rezaul Karim', who was born in 1976. In securing employment, he used Mr. Karim's National Insurance number ('NI number').

[7] On 29 July 2009 the appellant applied for indefinite leave to remain ('ILR'). The respondent refused the application by a decision dated 4 February 2010 and the appellant enjoyed no attendant right of appeal.

[8] The appellant applied for leave to remain on human rights (Article 8) grounds on 19 June 2014 and the respondent refused the application by means of a decision dated 26 June 2014, detailing the appellant's failure to meet the eligibility requirements of paragraph 276ADE(1)(iii)-(vi) of the Immigration Rules ('the Rules'). The respondent observed that previously submitted tax documents were not in the appellant's name and that the NI number relied upon belonged to another person but expressly accepted at para. 7 of the decision that the appellant met the relevant suitability requirements to be considered under Appendix FM.

[9] The appellant exercised his right of appeal to the First-tier Tribunal and his appeal was dismissed by Judge of the First-tier Tribunal Macdonald. By his decision of 14 January 2016, the Judge noted, at [52]:

'52. It is accepted by the respondent that the requirements of S-LTR in Appendix FM are met …'

[10] JFtT Macdonald found at [49] of his decision that the earliest date the appellant could establish his presence in the United Kingdom was 19 January 1996 and in the same paragraph accepted that it was unlikely that the appellant had left this country since his entry.

[11] By means of further submissions prepared by his current legal representatives, dated 8 September 2016, the appellant sought leave to remain on human rights (Article 8) grounds, relying upon his having been present in this country for over 20 years. Under cover of a letter from his legal representatives dated 5 December 2017, the appellant confirmed that he had been residing with his uncle in Wales since 1995 and relied upon documentation in his false identity to establish that he had been employed since 1997 and thereafter secured access to the NHS.

[12] The respondent accepted that the further representations constituted a fresh human rights claim under paragraph 353 of the Rules but refused the application by a decision dated 14 December 2017. She accepted that the appellant entered the United Kingdom on 18 December 1994 and that he remained in this country until 1997. However, she noted that no satisfactory evidence had been provided confirming that the appellant had resided in this country after the conclusion of his appeal in 1997 and his application for settlement in 2009. She decided that the appellant was unable to provide evidence of continuous residence between those years and concluded that he failed to meet the requirements of paragraph 276ADE(1)(iii) of the Rules.

[13] Further, the respondent observed as to suitability that when the appellant applied for ILR on 29 July 2009, he submitted documents which were verified as not being genuine, namely eleven P60 forms dated from 1998 to 2009. The respondent detailed HM Revenue & Customs' confirmation that the documents submitted did not match their records and that the NI number used was not issued in the appellant's name. Consequently, the appellant was found to have failed to meet the suitability requirements for leave to remain under paragraphs S-LTR.1.6. and S-LTR.4.2. of Appendix FM applied.

C. RELEVANT LEGISLATIVE PROVISIONS

[14] The following paragraphs of the Rules are relevant to our consideration:

a. Paragraph 276ADE

[15] Paragraph 276ADE was inserted into the Rules from 9 July 2014: Statement of Changes in Immigration Rules (HC 194). It incorporates protected Article 8 private life rights considerations into the Rules. Paragraph 276ADE(1) details requirements to be met by an applicant for leave to remain on the grounds of private life:

'(1)   The requirements to be met by an applicant for leave to remain on the grounds of private life in the UK are that at the date of application, the applicant:

(i)   does not fall for refusal under any of the grounds in Section S-LTR 1.1 to S-LTR 2.2. and S-LTR.3.1. to S-LTR.4.5. in Appendix FM; and

(ii)   has made a valid application for leave to remain on the grounds of private life in the UK; and

(iii)   has lived continuously in the UK for at least 20 years (discounting any period of imprisonment); or

(iv)   is under the age of 18 years and has lived continuously in the UK for at least 7 years (discounting any period of imprisonment) and it would not be reasonable to expect the applicant to leave the UK; or

(v)   is aged 18 years or above and under 25 years and has spent at least half of his life living continuously in the UK (discounting any period of imprisonment); or

(vi)   subject to sub-paragraph (2), is aged 18 years or above, has lived continuously in the UK for less than 20 years (discounting any period of imprisonment) but there would be very significant obstacles to the applicant's integration into the country to which he would have to go if required to leave the UK.'

b. Section S-LTR

[16] Section S-LTR of Appendix FM details the suitability requirements to be met in a leave to remain application made by those seeking to remain in the United Kingdom.

[17] Paragraph S-LTR.1.1. details:

'S-LTR.1.1.   The applicant will be refused limited leave to remain on grounds of suitability if any of paragraphs S-LTR.1.2. to 1.8. apply.'

[18] Paragraph S-LTR.1.6.:

'S-LTR.1.6.   The presence of the applicant in the UK is not conducive to the public good because their conduct (including convictions which do not fall within paragraphs S-LTR.1.3. to 1.5.), character, associations, or other reasons, make it undesirable to allow them to remain in the UK.'

[19] Both provisions apply to applications made on or after 9 July 2012 (HC 194). Paragraph S-LTR.1.6. has not been amended since its introduction to the Rules, whilst paragraph S-LTR.1.1. has been amended to bring into its scope the insertion of paragraph S-LTR.1.8. into the Rules on 24 November 2016. Such amendment is not relevant to the Tribunal's considerations in this matter.

[20] Paragraph S-LTR.2.1.:

'S-LTR.2.1.   The applicant will normally be refused on grounds of suitability if any of paragraphs S-LTR.2.2. to 2.5. apply.'

[21] Paragraph S-LTR.2.2.:

'S-LTR.2.2.   Whether or not to the appellant's knowledge –

    a)   false information, representation or documents have been submitted in relation to the application (including false information submitted to any person to obtain a document used in support of the application); or

    b)   there has been a failure to disclose material facts in relation to the application.'

[22] Paragraph S-LTR.4.1.:

'S-LTR.4.1.   The applicant may be refused on grounds of suitability if any of paragraphs S-LTR.4.2. to S-LTR.4.5. apply.'

[23] Paragraph S-LTR.4.2.:

'S-LTR.4.2.   The applicant has made false representations or failed to disclose any material fact in a previous application for entry clearance, leave to enter, leave to remain or a variation of leave, or in a previous human rights claim; or did so in order to obtain from the Secretary of State or a third party a document required to support such an application or claim (whether or not the application or claim was successful).'

[24] Paragraph S-LTR.4.2. was inserted into Section S-LTR from 6 April 2016 (HC 877) and substituted in its present form from 24 November 2016 for applications decided on or after that date (HC 667).

c. Paragraph S-EC

[25] Section S-EC of Appendix FM details the suitability requirements to be met for entry clearance.

[26] Paragraph S-EC.1.1. details:

'S-EC.1.1.   The applicant will be refused entry clearance on grounds of suitability if any of paragraphs S-EC.1.2. to 1.9. apply.'

[27] Paragraph S-EC.1.5.:

'S-EC.1.5.   The exclusion of the applicant from the UK is conducive to the public good because, for example, the applicant's conduct (including convictions which do not fall within paragraph S-EC.1.4.), character, associations, or other reasons, make it undesirable to grant them entry clearance.'

[28] Paragraph S-EC.2.1.:

'S-EC.2.1.   The applicant will normally be refused on grounds of suitability if any of paragraphs S-EC.2.2. to 2.5. apply.'

[29] Paragraph S-EC.2.2.:

'S-EC.2.2.   Whether or not to the applicant's knowledge –

    a)   false information, representations or documents have been submitted in relation to the application (including false information submitted to any person to obtain a document used in support of the application); or

    b)   there has been a failure to disclose material facts in relation to the application.'

d. Paragraph S-ILR

[30] Section S-ILR of Appendix FM details the suitability requirements for indefinite leave to remain.

[31] Paragraph S-ILR.1.1. details:

'S-ILR.1.1.   The applicant will be refused indefinite leave to remain on grounds of suitability if any of paragraphs S-ILR.1.2. to 1.10. apply.'

[32] Paragraph S-ILR.1.8.:

'S-ILR.1.8.   The presence of the applicant in the UK is not conducive to the public good because their conduct (including convictions which do not fall within paragraphs S-ILR.1.3. to 1.6.) character, associations, or other reasons, make it undesirable to allow them to remain in the UK.'

[33] Paragraph S-ILR.2.1.:

'S-ILR.2.1.   The applicant will normally be refused on grounds of suitability if any of paragraphs S-ILR.2.2. to 2.4. apply.'

[34] Paragraph S-ILR.2.2.:

'S-ILR.2.2.   Whether or not to the applicant's knowledge –

　　c)　　false information, representations or documents have been submitted in relation to the application (including false information submitted to any person to obtain a document used in support of the application); or

　　d)　　there has been a failure to disclose material facts in relation to the application.'

e. Paragraph A320

[35] Paragraph A320 was inserted into the Rules from 9 July 2012 (HC 194) and amended from 6 September 2012 (HC 565). It includes, *inter alia*, a specific restriction upon the application of paragraph 322 to private life claims:

'A320　Paragraphs 320 (except subparagraphs (3), (10) and (11)) and 322 do not apply to an application for entry clearance, leave to enter or leave to remain as a Family Member under Appendix FM, and Part 9 (except for paragraph 322(1)) does not apply to an application for leave to remain on the grounds of private life under paragraphs 276ADE–276DH.'

f. Paragraph 320(7B)

[36] Paragraph 320(7B) of the Rules:

'*Grounds on which entry clearance or leave to enter the United Kingdom is to be refused.*

320(7B)　where the applicant has previously breached the UK's immigration laws (and was 18 or over at the time of his most recent breach) by:

　　(d)　　using deception in an application for entry clearance, leave to enter or remain, or in order to obtain documents from the Secretary of State or a third party required in support of the application (whether successful or not)

g. Paragraph 322(1), (1A)

[37] Paragraph 322(1) of the Rules:

'*Grounds on which leave to remain and variations of leave to enter or remain in the United Kingdom are to be refused.*

322(1)   the fact that variation of leave to enter or remain is being sought for a purpose not covered by these Rules.'

[38] Paragraph 322(1A) was inserted into the Rules from 27 November 2008 (HC 1113), with amendment from 6 April 2012 (HC 1888):

322(1A) where false representations have been made or false documents or information have been submitted (whether or not material to the application, and whether or not to the applicant's knowledge), or material facts have not been disclosed, in relation to the application or in order to obtain documents from the Secretary of State or a third party required in support of the application.'

h. Paragraph 322(2) and (5)

[39] Paragraph 322 of the Rules:

'*Grounds on which leave to remain and variations of leave to enter or remain in the United Kingdom should normally be refused.*

(2)   the making of false representations or the failure to disclose any material facts for the purpose of obtaining leave to enter or a previous variation of leave or in order to obtain documents from the Secretary of State or a third party required in support of the application for leave to enter or a previous variation of leave.

(5)   the undesirability of permitting the person concerned to remain in the United Kingdom in the light of his conduct (including convictions which do not fall within paragraph 322(1C)), character or associations or the fact that he represents a threat to national security.'

D. THE DECISION OF THE FIRST-TIER TRIBUNAL

[40] The appellant's appeal was heard by the Judge sitting at Hatton Cross on 26 November 2018. The appellant attended and gave oral evidence. By her decision dated 14 December 2018 the Judge noted, at [14] of her decision, the appellant's acknowledgment that he had used Mr. Karim's identity in order to obtain employment and medical services and that during the course of an earlier application for settlement he had produced P60s in Mr. Karim's name.

[41] As to the deception, the Judge found that the respondent had discharged the evidential burden of proving that the appellant practised dishonesty or deception in his application for ILR in July 2009 and so the burden shifted to the appellant to provide a plausible innocent explanation. The Judge proceeded to conclude, at

[16], that the use of Mr. Karim's NI number, said by the appellant to be solely to secure 'work to survive, pay the tax and insurance only' did not constitute an innocent explanation and so, on balance, the appellant had not dispelled the *prima facie* case of deception established against him.

[42] Upon considering the appellant's explanation that the appellant had not attempted to deceive the respondent in his settlement application, having openly declared that he had been using Mr. Karim's name and NI number in order to work, the Judge found, at [17]:

> 17. … The fact that the appellant made his 2009 application in the name of Sultan Mahmood and openly admitted that the P60s were in a false identity, relying upon them not as evidence of identity but as proof of residence, does not in my judgement deprive them of their innate character as documents containing false representations (even assuming that they are genuine P60s, which is unclear). Falsity carries the meaning of deliberately dishonest: see *A v SSHD* [2010] EWCA Civ 773. The P60s contain a statement made to HMRC which Mr. Mahmood knew to be untrue, namely that he was a man named Rezaul Karim who was entitled to work in the UK.'

[43] The Judge's reasoning as to the application of the suitability requirements is addressed at [20]–[22] of her decision. She concluded that the appellant had not simply used the alias of Rezaul Karim in order to obtain work but also to access NHS services, visiting his GP on a regular basis since 2001 and having been referred on several occasions for hospital investigations. She therefore found that the appellant had engaged in sustained deceit over the course of more than a decade. The Judge concluded that the documents relied upon arising from employment, such as the P60s, possessed an innate character as documents containing false representations. She determined that the appellant's personal history including character, conduct and employment history made it undesirable to allow him to remain in this country and so his application fell for refusal under both the mandatory suitability ground established paragraph S-LTR.1.6. and the discretionary ground of paragraph S-LTR.4.2.

[44] Consequently, the Judge found that the appellant did not meet the suitability requirements of the Rules and so could not meet the requirements for leave to remain on the grounds of private life in the UK set out in paragraph 276ADE.

E. GROUNDS OF APPEAL

[45] The appellant raised six grounds of complaint by way of his grounds of appeal to this Tribunal. The grounds were drafted by counsel, but the Tribunal acknowledges that they were not drafted by Mr. Mustafa nor by the appellant's representative at the hearing before the Judge, Mr. Hasan. In granting permission to appeal, the focus of UTJ McWilliam's reasoning was directed at grounds 1 and 3.

[46] At the hearing before us on 20 June 2019 Mr. Mustafa accepted that ground 2 was not arguable and, on instruction, he withdrew grounds 4 to 6. The Tribunal is therefore only required to consider grounds 1 and 3.

[47] Ground 1 is rooted in the principle that when approaching the findings of fact made by a Tribunal in earlier proceedings, the earlier determination stands as an assessment of the claim the appellant made at the time of the first decision and so is a 'starting point' for the purposes of the later fact-finding exercise: *Devaseelan (Second Appeals – ECHR – Extra-Territorial Effect) Sri Lanka* * [2002] UKIAT 00702; [2003] Imm AR 1. The appellant relies upon the respondent having accepted that he met the relevant suitability requirements in 2014, and before JFtT Macdonald in 2016, submitting '[t]hat previous stance and concession/acceptance ... should have been a strong factor in the instant appeal'.

[48] Ground 3 contains two separate challenges. The first contends that both paragraph S-LTR.1.6. and paragraph S-LTR.4.2. are discretionary in nature and so require a balancing assessment, which was not undertaken by the Judge. The second contention is the Judge failed to lawfully engage with there being no deception in respect of the present application. Paragraph 6 of the grounds of appeal details:

> 6. The FTJ does not engage with what the apparent false representation is made [*sic*] in the previous application (i.e. the present or previous application). Indeed, reliance on documents in someone else's name to obtain employment is not a false representation made to the respondent in an application, especially given that the appellant accepted he had done this (see [32] of Judge Macdonald's determination) and had been forthcoming about it. The FTJ has not assessed whether the representations were false within the meaning of *AA (Nigeria) v Secretary of State for the Home Department* [2010] EWCA Civ 773.

[49] At the conclusion of the hearing on 20 June 2019, following a request by the parties, the Tribunal permitted the filing of further written submissions, which were subsequently received from Mr. Jarvis, dated 25 June 2019, and from Mr. Mustafa, dated 26 June 2019. Upon considering the written submissions, the Tribunal concluded that it would be aided by further oral argument and a further hearing took place on 4 December 2019. At the conclusion of the hearing the parties were directed to file and serve further written submissions and we received them from Mr. Jarvis, dated 17 January 2020, and Mr. Mustafa, dated 5 February 2020.

F. DECISION

a. Paragraph S-LTR.1.6

i. Mandatory requirement

[50] At the outset and observing that it was not pursued by Mr. Mustafa with vigour before us, the Tribunal rejects the contention advanced by the grounds of appeal that paragraph S-LTR.1.6. is discretionary in nature. The appellant's submission places misconceived reliance upon the requirement as to the establishment of conduct making presence in this country 'undesirable' as being capable, by itself, of introducing a balancing exercise into the assessment. However, we are satisfied that this submission fails to engage with the clear stricture of paragraph S-LTR.1.1. that a mandatory refusal will result if one or more of seven discrete factual circumstances are established and paragraph S-LTR.1.6. identifies one such circumstance.

ii. Scope

[51] The wording of the provision is general in its terms, confirming that an applicant's presence in this country is 'not conducive to the public good' because their 'conduct', 'character', 'associations' or 'other reasons' make it 'undesirable' to allow them to remain in this country.

[52] We have reminded ourselves that the Rules should be read sensibly and are mindful of the function which they serve in the administration of immigration policy. We observe Lord Brown's confirmation in *Mahad v Entry Clearance Officer* [2009] UKSC 16, [2010] 1 W.L.R. 48, at [10], in a judgment approved by the other members of the Court, that '[t]he Rules are not to be construed with all the strictness applicable to the construction of a statute or a statutory instrument but, instead, sensibly according to the natural and ordinary meaning of the words used, recognising that they are statements of the Secretary of State's administrative policy.'

[53] It is appropriate at this juncture to identify the approach adopted by the respondent over time as to the employment and tax documents secured through the appellant's adoption of Mr. Karim's identity. By means of the decision of 4 February 2010 the respondent detailed, *inter alia*:

'HM Revenue & Customs have confirmed that the eleven P60 forms dated 1998, 1999, 2000, 2001, 2002, 2003, 2004, 2005, 2006, 2008 and 2009 submitted with your application do not match their records and that the National Insurance number used was not issued to anyone by your name, the Secretary of State is satisfied that false representations have been made or false documents or information have been submitted (whether or not material to the application, and whether or not to the applicant's knowledge), or material facts have not been disclosed, in relation to the application.'

[54] We note that the decision of February 2010 was a consideration of the requirements under paragraph 276B(i)(b) of the Rules as they then stood, to which the mandatory ground of refusal under paragraph 322(1A) was applicable where false representations have been made or false documents have been submitted, whether or not material to the application, and whether or not to the applicant's knowledge, in relation to the application.

[55] In respect of the appellant's employment and tax documents the respondent's decision of 26 June 2014 details:

'14. ... The earliest record of your client in the United Kingdom is when he was encountered working without authority and claimed asylum on 19 January 1996, however, satisfactory evidence has not yet been provided to show that he has lived continuously in the United Kingdom since that date. Tax documents have previously been provided, however, as stated in previous refusal letters, the P60s are not in your client's name and HMRC confirmed that the National Insurance number is that of a British citizen born in 1976.'

[56] By her decision of 14 December 2017, the respondent considered suitability under Appendix FM and as to paragraph S-LTR.1.6. reasoned:

'For the reasons given below, your application falls for refusal on the grounds of suitability in Section S-LTR under paragraphs 276ADE(1)(I) of the Immigration Rules because:

When you applied for indefinite leave to remain on 29 July 2009 you submitted a number of documents which were verified as not being genuine. HM Revenue & Customs confirmed that the eleven P60 forms dated 1998, 1999, 2000, 2001, 2002, 2003, 2004, 2005, 2006, 2008 and 2009 submitted with that application did not match their records and that the National Insurance number used was not issued to anyone by your name.

Given the above your presence in the UK is not conducive to the public good as your conduct and character make it undesirable to grant leave to remain. You therefore fail to meet the requirements for leave to remain because paragraph S-LTR.1.6. of Appendix FM of the Immigration Rules applies.'

[57] Initially before us the respondent's position was that she was permitted to rely upon paragraph S-LTR.1.6. and the hearing in June 2019 therefore focused, in part, upon whether the respondent had made a concession as to suitability by her June 2014 decision. The respondent contended that as the decision in 2014 did not expressly establish that there had been a material investigation as to the use of the P60 documents in a different name it was not possible to justify a conclusion that she had, in substance, conceded her position as to deception.

[58] At the resumed hearing in December 2019 the focus of discussion before the Tribunal concerned paragraph S-LTR.4.2. We observe that as this matter progressed over the two hearings Mr. Jarvis placed greater reliance upon paragraph S-LTR.4.2. and after the second hearing he very helpfully clarified by means of his further written submissions the respondent's position as being that it was not open to her to rely upon paragraph S-LTR.1.6 either when making her decision in 2014 or in the present matter. This is so, according to the respondent, because the provision was not intended to cover the use of deception/dishonesty in a previous application for immigration status. He relied upon several strands in seeking to establish that such interpretation was consistent with the Rule.

[59] Firstly, he relied upon the respondent's guidance detailed in '*General grounds for refusal – section 1 of 5: about this guidance, general grounds for refusal and checks*' (version 16.0) 30 April 2014, and in particular drew our attention to the section entitled 'What the rules require'.

'The Immigration rules define fraud and forgery as a form of deception.

If a person submits a document or information with an application which is independently verified as being forged or not genuine, you may consider refusing entry or leave to remain. When you have evidence that a person has done this, either as part of their current or previous application, the Immigration Rules state that you should refuse the application unless the particular paragraph of the rules allows you to use discretion.

A false document includes:

- genuine document which has been altered or tampered with

- counterfeit document (one that is completely false)

- genuine document that is being used by an imposter

- genuine document which had been fraudulently obtained or issued, and/or

- genuine document which contains a falsified or counterfeit visa or endorsement.

For entry clearance

- When you refuse because fraud and forgery has been used in a current application, paragraph 320(7A) of the rules apply. Where there is evidence they have contrived in a significant way to frustrate the intentions of the rules, paragraph 320(11) applies.

- When you refuse on fraud and forgery grounds in a previous application, paragraph 320(7B) applies.

- When you refuse because forged counterfeit passport has been used, paragraphs 320(3) and 320(19) apply.

- When you refuse for false employment documentation, paragraph 320(15) and 320(19) apply

- When you refuse for other deceptive documents, paragraph 320(19) applies.

For leave to remain

- When you refuse because of fraud and forgery in the current application, paragraph 322(1A) of the rules applies.

- When you refuse because of fraud and forgery in a previous application, paragraph 322(2) of the rules applies.

- If an applicant has used fraud and forgery in a current or previous application to get a document from the Secretary of State to show that they have a right to reside in the UK, you must refuse the application under paragraph 322(2A) of the Immigration Rules.'

[60] As to this document Mr. Jarvis relied upon there being no reference to false representations also being considered under paragraph S-LTR.1.6. We observe the Court of Appeal's confirmation in *ZH (Bangladesh) v Secretary of State for the Home Department* [2009] EWCA Civ 8, [2009] Imm. A.R. 450, at [32], that the respondent's instructions, and by analogy her guidance, are not an aid to the construction of the Rules notwithstanding that their author is in law the author of the Rules. They do not have, and cannot be treated as if possessing, the force of law. This is consistent with Lord Brown's observation in *Mahad*, at [11], that instructions issued by the respondent have on occasion been issued inconsistently with the Rules as interpreted by the courts. Further, we agree that having considered the document we are not aided by it because it expressly confirms on page 2 that it 'explains each part of paragraph 322 and identifies which are mandatory refusals and which are discretionary'. Its limited scope precludes consideration of the suitability requirements under Appendix FM.

[61] Mr. Jarvis next submitted that paragraph A320, which was inserted into the Rules on 9 July 2012, was relevant as to the decision of June 2014 because it establishes that paragraph 322, save for paragraph 322(1), does not apply to applications for leave to remain under paragraph 276ADE and Appendix FM. Paragraph 322(1A), which is concerned with, *inter alia*, utilising false representations and false documents in an application and paragraph 322(2) which addresses their use in a previous application for leave to remain are thereby excluded from consideration and application.

[62] We are satisfied that whilst the introduction of paragraph A320 expressly precludes the respondent from utilising paragraphs 322(1A) and 322(2) in identified circumstances, it does not by itself aid us in establishing the scope of paragraph S-LTR.1.6. We note that the latter was introduced as part of the structured approach to Article 8 established by Appendix FM in July 2012, such approach setting out in detail the requirements to be met in securing leave to enter or remain on Article 8 grounds under the Rules and the requirement to meet this suitability requirement was incorporated from the outset within paragraph 276ADE(1)(i).

[63] Mr. Jarvis further relied upon the Explanatory Memorandum to Statement of Changes to the Immigration Rules (HC 877) which introduced paragraph S-LTR.4.2. into the Rules from 6 April 2016. He submitted before us that such introduction was predicated upon an express policy decision to allow for the previous use of false representation grounds to be deployed in decision-making on Appendix FM and paragraph 276ADE applications or claims where previously there had been no available ground of refusal. He drew our attention to paragraph 7.41 of the Explanatory Memorandum:

'7.41. The following changes and clarifications are being made to the Immigration Rules relating to family and private life:

• To enable an application to be refused on grounds of suitability if false representations have been submitted, or there has been a failure to disclose materials facts, in a previous immigration application; or where the applicant has failed to pay litigation costs awarded to the Home Office ...'

[64] From June 2004 onwards explanatory memoranda must be provided by the relevant government department with all instruments subject to Parliamentary procedure. Their purpose is to provide the public with an easy-to-understand explanation of the delegated, or secondary, legislation's intent and purpose in a manner akin to explanatory notes which are documents which explain the purpose of all Government Bills and some Private Members' Bills. They provide a clear explanation of what part of the law the delegated legislation is changing and why. However, they do not form part of the delegated legislation, are not endorsed by Parliament and cannot be amended by Parliament. They are intended to be neutral in political tone and their aim is to explain the effect of the text, not to justify it. We observe that the Explanatory Memorandum was presented to Parliament with Statement of Changes (HC 877) on 11 March 2016.

[65] Lord Steyn confirmed in *R (Westminster City Council) v National Asylum Support Service* [2002] UKHL 38, [2002] 4 All ER 654, at [5], that explanatory notes may be a useful aid to construction in so far as they 'cast light on the objective setting or contextual scene of the statute and the mischief at which it is aimed, such materials are therefore always admissible aids to construction'.

[66] Brook LJ held in *Flora v Wakom (Heathrow) Ltd* [2006] EWCA Civ 1103; [2007] 1 WLR 482, at [16], that 'the text of an Act does not have to be ambiguous before a court may be permitted to take into account an explanatory note in order to understand the contextual scene in which the Act is set.' This is subject to the caveat that if the statutory language is unambiguous a court or tribunal is not free to rewrite it by reference to the explanatory notes: *R (RD) v Secretary of State for Justice* [2010] EWCA Civ 18, [2010] 1 WLR 1782, *per* Carnwath LJ, at [45].

[67] We observe Brook LJ's confirmation in *Flora*, at [16], that 'the value of … explanatory notes as an aid to construction … is that [they identify] the contextual scene … That is all.' A court or tribunal must therefore resist attempts to elevate explanatory notes to a status where they supplant the language of the legislation itself: *Aspinalls Club Ltd v Revenue and Customs* [2013] EWCA Civ 1464, [2015] Ch. 79, *per* Moses LJ, at [22].

[68] We agree that the strong similarity between explanatory notes and explanatory memoranda as to their provenance and their purpose is such that the same interpretative principles apply to explanatory memoranda.

[69] In this matter, we are satisfied that the use of the word 'enable' at paragraph 7.41 of the explanatory memorandum identifies the mischief that paragraph S-LTR.4.2. was intended to address. Giving the word its usual and ordinary meaning, to give the authority or means to do something, we are satisfied that the context of the introduction of paragraph S-LTR.4.2. was to give authority to the respondent to refuse an application on grounds of suitability if false representations have been submitted, or there has been a failure to disclose materials facts, in a previous immigration application. We are satisfied that this authority was given because such power did not previously exist within the suitability requirements established by Section S-LTR, including paragraph S-LTR.1.6., in respect of an application for leave to remain.

[70] Our decision is reinforced upon considering the Rules, and in particular Appendix FM, in the round. Under Part 9 of the Rules there is a mandatory requirement under paragraph 322(1A) to refuse where false representations or false documents or information have been submitted in relation to the application. The respondent enjoys a discretionary power under paragraph 322(2) to refuse leave to remain consequent to the making of false representations, or the failure to disclose any material fact for the purpose of obtaining leave to enter or a previous variation of leave. From 6 April 2012 the power to refuse was extended to the making of false representations in order to obtain documents from the respondent or a third party required in support of the application for leave to enter or a previous variation of leave: (HC 1888). Thus, by means of paragraph 322(2) the respondent enjoys power to refuse an application where there has been fraud or forgery in a previous application.

[71] We note that in entry clearance and leave to enter matters refusal is mandatory, not discretionary, where an applicant has previously breached the United Kingdom's immigration laws, when aged 18 or over at the time of their most recent breach, by using deception in an application for entry clearance, leave to enter or remain or in order to obtain documents from the respondent or a third party required in support of the application, whether successful or not, unless they meet an identified exception: paragraph 320(7B)(d).

[72] As observed above, paragraph A320 of the Rules was inserted into the Rules on 9 July 2012 and prohibits the application of both paragraphs 322(1A) and 322(2) to considerations of applications for leave to remain made under Appendix FM. The suitability requirements in Appendix FM mirror, to a certain extent, the general grounds for refusal which are set out in the Rules. However, it was Parliament's intention that the suitability requirements in Appendix FM did not adopt all of the requirements established by Part 9 of the Rules.

[73] Instead, paragraphs S-EC.1.5, S-LTR.1.6 and S-ILR.1.8. adopt a similar approach in entry clearance, leave to remain and indefinite leave to remain applications as to conduct, character and association. Separate discretionary power to refuse applications where false information, representations or documents have been submitted in relation to the present application, whether or not the applicant had knowledge of their submission is established by paragraphs S-EC.2.2., S-LTR.2.2. and S-ILR.2.2.

[74] We agree that the absence of a suitability requirement addressing the previous use of false representations or a failure to disclose any material fact, as provided for by paragraph 322(2) of the Rules, when Appendix FM was inserted into the Rules was consistent with Parliament's then intention. We therefore agree that the insertion of paragraph S-LTR.4.2. which mirrors, in part, paragraph 322(2) was to address a failure of the suitability requirements previously established under Section S-LTR in not permitting the respondent to adversely rely upon the previous use of false representations and related concerns. In such circumstances, we are satisfied that the scope of paragraph S-LTR.1.6. is not sufficiently wide to capture the use of false representations in an application for leave to remain before the respondent or in a previous application for leave to enter or remain.

[75] We conclude the paragraph S-LTR.1.6., a mandatory ground of refusal, does not cover the use of false representations or a failure to disclose material facts in an application for leave to remain or in a previous application for immigration status.

[76] Consequently, the Judge materially erred in law in finding that the respondent could refuse the appellant's application on suitability grounds under paragraph S-LTR.1.6. of Appendix FM.

b. Paragraph S-LTR.4.2

i) Disjunctive nature

[77] The exercise of refusal on suitability grounds under this paragraph is discretionary in nature by application of paragraph S-LTR.4.1.

[78] Paragraph S-LTR.4.2. is specific as to its scope of application and the combination of a semicolon with 'or' establishes an exclusive sense to the rule by which two independent clauses are joined, so establishing the paragraph's disjunctive nature. Mr. Jarvis accepted on behalf of the respondent that consequent to such disjunctive nature, the respondent is obliged to explain why the applicable discretion has or has not been exercised in respect to this Rule.

[79] The two separate basis upon which the respondent may exercise discretion to refuse an application for leave to remain can be summarised as i) the use of false representations or a failure to disclose any material fact in a previous

application and ii) the use of false representations in order to obtain a document required to support such an application. Consequent to their independent nature, the Tribunal is satisfied that reliance upon one or both of the elements must be specifically pleaded and reasoned by the respondent in her decision letter, or if upon becoming aware of further information the respondent seeks to exercise her discretion during the course of the subsequent appeal process it should be by means of an addendum decision providing reasons with an appellant being given sufficient time to counter the serious nature of the underlying allegation as to conduct.

ii) 'The applicant has made false representations or failed to disclose any material fact in a previous application for entry clearance, leave to enter, leave to remain or a variation of leave, or in a previous human rights claim'

[80] By her decision of 14 December 2017, the respondent relied upon the first independent clause of paragraph S-LTR.4.2. concerned with the applicant having made false representations in a previous application for leave to remain or a variation of leave, or in a previous human rights claim.

[81] Mr. Jarvis did not seek to persuade us that a broad reading should properly be applied to this clause so as to permit any false representation arising in an earlier application, regardless of whether it was made in support of the application and regardless of whether the falsity was drawn to the respondent's attention, as being sufficient to enable the refusal of an application. We agree that Mr. Jarvis was correct not to because such approach would clearly go beyond the natural meaning of the words used in this clause of the paragraph. The use of the first 'or' in the sentence is inclusive, bringing together two separate elements namely the making of false representations and the failure to disclose any material fact, which relate to a 'previous application'. If the intention had been to adopt the broader approach, the word 'any' would have been used in the first element, concerned with false representations, as well as in the second, concerned with failure to disclose material. Further, the plain meaning of 'has made false representations ... in a previous application ...' is that the false representation is made in relation to a previous application. There is no counter-indication that any false representation not made in support of the application, should be read into this clause.

[82] In this matter the appellant has consistently informed the respondent that whilst he dishonestly assumed an identity and a NI number to secure employment, and used the identity as a British citizen to secure access to the NHS, he was open and honest to the respondent as to the employment and tax documents accompanying the application having been secured through the use of the false identity. We consider it important that the P60 forms, genuinely issued but the product of dishonesty as to identity, were peripheral to the application for leave to remain on long residence grounds. Their purpose was to demonstrate long residence, but it was not a requirement of the relevant rule that the appellant provide P60s. They were relied upon by the appellant to establish his long residence, a task they were capable of satisfying, and not to establish that the appellant was the person named upon them. Nor did the documents establish that the appellant enjoyed a right to work lawfully in this country or to meet any financial requirement established by any relevant paragraph of the Rules. The false representation in this matter was in providing various employers with a dishonesty assumed identity and NI number to secure employment. The employment and tax documents were produced consequent to the appellant having

secured employment in his false identity. Having openly informed the respondent from the outset as to his actions, there were no false representations made on the appellant's behalf in his application that he was a British citizen called Rezaul Karim who was born in 1976, possessed a particular NI number, was lawfully entitled to work and through the course of lawful employment had earned the sums detailed by the eleven P60 forms.

[83] Upon considering [17] of the decision we are satisfied that the Judge materially erred in adopting the broader interpretation of the first independent clause of paragraph S-LTR.4.2. Whilst observing that the appellant had openly declared that he assumed the identity of Mr. Karim to secure employment, the Judge considered the innate characteristic of the documents are containing 'false representations' through the deliberate dishonesty employed to secure them. Such an approach uncoupled the requirement that the false representation be made 'in a previous application' and instead broadened the use of a false representation to the securing of any document used in the previous application, even if there were clear and adequate admissions to the respondent from the outset as to the circumstances in which the documents were obtained.

[84] We conclude that paragraph S-LTR.4.2. is disjunctive with two independent clauses. The respondent is consequently obliged to plead and reason her exercise of discretion to refuse an application for leave to remain based on one or both of those clauses. By her decision of 14 December 2017, the respondent only relied upon the first clause. The natural meaning of the first clause requires that the false representation or the failure to disclose any material fact must have been made in support of a previous application and not be peripheral to that application. The reliance upon employment and tax documents, openly confirmed to have been secured through the long-time use of a false identity, was peripheral to the previous application for leave to remain on private life grounds under paragraph 276ADE(1)(iii) and also peripheral to the earlier application for ILR on long residence grounds. The Judge therefore materially erred in finding that the suitability requirement established by the first clause of paragraph S-LTR.4.2. was applicable to the appellant.

G. REMAKING THE DECISION

[85] Mr. Jarvis informed us at the hearing that though the respondent did not rely upon the second clause of paragraph S-LTR.4.2., namely the use of false representations in order to obtain a document required to support such an application, either in her 2017 decision or before the Judge in 2018, and so it could not be considered at the error of law hearing, she would now wish to rely upon it at the remaking stage. He accepted that the reasons for the exercise of discretion would have to be conveyed to the appellant in writing.

[86] When considering whether to permit the respondent time to issue an addendum decision we have considered her case under the second clause of paragraph S-LTR.4.2 at its highest and we conclude that she could not, on any view, meet the requirements of the second clause on the facts of this case.

[87] The use of false representations is clearly linked to the obtaining 'from the Secretary of State or a third party a document required to support such an application or claim'. Mr. Jarvis accepted before us that, in principle, the deception should relate to the act of obtaining the document for the purposes of supporting an application or claim to remain in the United Kingdom. This is consistent with the use of the words 'required to support' which confirms a compulsory element to the use of the document(s) within the application or claim process. Such compulsion is identified by the relevant Rules or guidance.

[88] We therefore conclude that the use of the words 'required to support' in the second clause of paragraph S-LTR.4.2. confirms a compulsory element to the use of document(s) within the application or claim process, and the obtaining of the document(s) must be for the purposes of the immigration application or claim.

[89] We observe that the appellant has relied upon documents arising from his employment, such as the P60s, in long residence and Article 8 (private life) applications alone and not, for example, in an application where he was required to establish his earnings. He always confirmed by means of his applications that the documents were secured with the adoption of another person's identity. The false representation was to his employer(s), namely that he was a British citizen called Rezaul Karim who was born in 1976, possessed a certain NI number and was lawfully permitted to work. Such false representations were not made to obtain a document for the purpose of supporting an application for leave to remain in the United Kingdom. The documents were solely generated consequent to the appellant having secured employment. We are satisfied that upon a natural reading of the second clause the securing of the employment documents relied upon by the appellant in this matter were not secured through false representations to support an application for leave to remain. In any event we observe that such employment and tax documents are not required for an application for leave to remain under paragraph 276ADE(1)(iii). Consequently, even taking the respondent's case at her highest under the second clause of paragraph S-LTR.4.2. she could not succeed.

[90] We find that the appellant does not fall to be refused under the suitability requirements detailed at paragraph 276ADE(1)(i). Noting the unchallenged finding of JFtT Macdonald that the appellant has been present in this country since 19 January 1996 and upon considering the evidence before us we are satisfied that the appellant has been continuously present in this country since that date, a period of over 20 years. We therefore find that the appellant meets the requirements of paragraph 276ADE(1)(iii) and allow his appeal on Article 8 private life grounds.

H. NOTICE OF DECISION

[91] The decision of the First-tier Tribunal involved the making of an error on a point of law and we set aside the Judge's decision promulgated on 14 December 2018 pursuant to section 12(2)(a) of the Tribunals, Courts and Enforcement Act 2007.

[92] Upon remaking the decision, the appeal is allowed on human rights (Article 8) grounds.

R (ON THE APPLICATION OF TOPADAR) v SECRETARY OF STATE FOR THE HOME DEPARTMENT

COURT OF APPEAL

Floyd, Males and Lewis LJJ

[2020] EWCA Civ 1525
13 November 2020

Immigration – leave to remain – variation of leave – Tier 2 (General) Migrant – certificate of sponsorship – request for further information from the sponsor – procedure and process – review – administrative review was separate from decision-making process – requirements of procedural fairness

The Claimant, a citizen of Bangladesh, entered the United Kingdom as a Tier 4 (General) Student in 2009. In 2016, he applied to vary his existing leave and be granted leave to remain ("LTR") as a Tier 2 (General) Migrant. He had a certificate of sponsorship ("CAS") from his proposed employer ("the sponsor") to work as an account manager with a salary of £21,000 a year. On 7 August 2018, the Secretary of State for the Home Department wrote to the sponsor requesting various information, including a full job description and an explanation as to why it required an accounts manager. The letter stated that the information was required by 14 September 2018 and that failure to send it by that date might result in the refusal of the application. The Secretary of State did not notify the Claimant that she had sought further information from the sponsor. The sponsor made no reply to the Secretary of State's request. On 27 September 2018, the Secretary of State refused the Claimant's application for LTR by reference to paragraph 245HD(f) of the Immigration Rules HC 395 (as amended) and paragraphs 77H and 77J of Appendix A. She stated that there were reasonable grounds to believe that the job vacancy described on the Claimant's CAS was not a genuine vacancy. On 9 October 2018, the Claimant requested an administrative review of the refusal decision. On 18 October 2018, the Claimant's solicitors wrote to the Secretary of State submitting that the Claimant had established a private life in the United Kingdom, and he should be granted leave to remain under Article 8 of the ECHR. On 31 October 2018, the Claimant was informed that his request for administrative review had been unsuccessful.

On application for judicial review, the Claimant submitted that the Secretary of State had acted in a way that was procedurally unfair by seeking further information from the sponsor without also notifying him that further information was required and that if it were not provided the application might be refused. The grounds further contended that the Claimant's application for LTR as a Tier 2 (General) Migrant was not finally determined until the conclusion of the administrative review on 31 October 2018 and that, before that date had been reached, he had varied the application by making a human rights claim on 18 October 2018. He argued that, as a result, he continued to have leave to remain by virtue of section 3C of the Immigration Act 1971 ("the 1971 Act") until the application, as varied by the human rights claim, was determined. In refusing the application, the Upper Tribunal ("UT") held that the Claimant's application had been determined on 27 September 2018 and it was not therefore open to him to seek to vary the application on 18 October 2018. The UT further held that there was no procedural unfairness in the way in which the Secretary of State dealt with the application. The Claimant appealed against the UT's decision.

Held, dismissing the appeal:

(1) Under section 3C of the 1971 Act, where a person, such as the Claimant, had LTR as a Tier 4 (General) Student and applied to vary that leave and be granted leave as a Tier 2 (General) Migrant, he continued to have LTR in the United Kingdom until the application was determined. An application was decided, as a matter of ordinary language, when a decision was reached granting or refusing the application. It was clear from the provisions of the Immigration Rules dealing with administrative review, that the review was separate from the process of deciding. There was a difference between 'the decision', which was the refusal of the application, and the 'administrative review', which checked whether that decision was wrong. Section 3(2) of the 1971 Act conferred a power to provide for such a system of administrative review and expressly contemplated that the system might draw a distinction between the decision refusing the application and a review of that decision. Section 3C(2)(a) provided for leave to be continued while the application seeking to vary an existing leave remained undecided. Section 3C(2)(d) also expressly provided for leave to continue when 'an administrative review of the decision on the application' could be sought or was pending. If the process of administrative review were an extension of the decision-making process, it would not have been necessary to include section 3C(2)(d) in the 1971 Act because LTR would continue under section 3C(2)(a). In the light of those considerations, it was clear that an application seeking to vary existing leave was decided within the meaning of section 3C(2)(a) of the 1971 Act when the application was refused. Any further variation of that application must be made before the decision refusing the application was made and notified to the claimant, because once the application was determined there was nothing to vary. The system of administrative review operated as a review of the decision and was not an extension of that decision-making process (*paras 38 – 44*).

(2) The position above was not altered by the UT's decision in *R (on the application of Sukhwinder Singh) v Secretary of State for the Home Department* JR/1361/2015. That case was concerned with identifying when the time limit for bringing a claim began to run and to reconcile that with the requirement that alternative remedies should generally be used before resorting to judicial review. The reference in *Sukhwinder Singh* to the review decision as the 'final decision' was to be understood in that context. The UT was not seeking to interpret and apply the provisions of section 3C of the 1971 Act. It followed that any variation in the instant case had to be made before 27 September 2018 when the decision refusing the Claimant's application was made. No such variation was made by that date. The Claimant continued to have LTR whilst the administrative review of the decision was pending by virtue of section 3C(2)(d) of the 1971 Act. Once the outcome of that review was notified to the Claimant on 31 October 2018, his leave ceased to continue in force (*paras 46 – 49*).

(3) The requirements of procedural fairness depended upon the facts and the context in which a decision was taken, including the nature of the legal and

administrative system. In the instant case, the context was the operation of the points-based system for determining applications for LTR. The system was intended to enable high volumes of applications to be processed in a fair and efficient manner and operated by specifying what evidence must be submitted. Paragraph 77J of Appendix A to the Immigration Rules specifically provided that, in order to consider whether a job vacancy specified on a CAS was a genuine one, the Secretary of State 'could request additional information and evidence from the applicant or the sponsor' and could refuse the application if the information or evidence was not provided. In that context, there was nothing procedurally unfair in the Secretary of State asking the sponsor for additional information and evidence. The information she sought was about why the organisation required an accounts manager and what the duties would be, and the additional evidence related to the sponsor's bank accounts, staff list, company accounts and tax details. Those were matters that the sponsor was able to provide, not the Claimant. Procedural fairness did not require the Secretary of State to give the Claimant the opportunity to chase the sponsor for information. It was incumbent on the sponsor to provide any additional information sought. Requiring the Secretary of State to notify the Claimant would not be consistent with the operation of the points-based system (*paras 52 – 57*).

(4) The purpose of a request for information was to enable the Secretary of State to assess whether the requirements for a grant of LTR as a Tier 2 (General) Migrant had been satisfied. The purpose was not to give the Claimant time to find an alternative employer, or a different basis for seeking leave if the employer failed to provide the information requested: *R (on the application of Pathan) v Secretary of State for the Home Department* [2020] UKSC 41 distinguished. The Supreme Court in *Pathan* did not intend to establish an absolute or universal requirement that the Secretary of State must give a claimant prior notice of something that might affect the consideration of an application, with a view to him being able to take steps to address that matter. Rather it was recognised that the requirements of procedural fairness were flexible and were not set in stone. Furthermore, this was not a case where the Secretary of State was making adverse findings against an individual such that fairness required that he was told and given the opportunity to respond. This was a case where the Immigration Rules stated that information could be required to enable the Secretary of State to assess whether a job vacancy was genuine. In the absence of that information, she could not make the assessment and could not be satisfied that the vacancy was genuine. There was nothing unfair in that process. There was no allegation or issue that needed, in fairness, to be put to the Claimant for comment before his application for LTR was refused. The UT was right to hold that the claim of procedural unfairness was not made out on the facts of the case (*paras 58 – 63*).

Cases referred to:

Balajigari and Others v Secretary of State for the Home Department [2019] EWCA Civ 673; [2019] 1 WLR 4647; [2019] 4 All ER 998; [2019] Imm AR 1152; [2019] INLR 619
EK (Ivory Coast) v Secretary of State for the Home Department [2014] EWCA Civ 1517; [2015] Imm AR 367; [2015] INLR 287
HK (An Infant), Re [1967] 2 QB 617; [1967] 2 WLR 962; [1967] 1 All ER 226

JH (Zimbabwe) v Secretary of State for the Home Department; R (on the application of JH (Zimbabwe)) v Asylum and Immigration Tribunal and Secretary of State for the Home Department [2009] EWCA Civ 78; [2009] Imm AR 499; [2009] INLR 385
R v London Borough of Hackney ex parte Decordova (1995) 27 HLR 108
R v Secretary of State for the Home Department ex parte Doody [1993] UKHL 8; [1994] AC 531; [1993] 3 WLR 154
R (on the application of Pathan) v Secretary of State for the Home Department [2020] UKSC 41; [2020] 1 WLR 4506; [2021] Imm AR 235; [2021] INLR 91
R (on the application of Shrestha) v Secretary of State for the Home Department [2018] EWCA Civ 2810
R (on the application of Sukhwinder Singh) v Secretary of State for the Home Department JR/1361/2015

Legislation and international instruments judicially considered:

European Convention on Human Rights, Article 8
Immigration Act 1971, sections 3, 3C & 4
Immigration Rules HC 395 (as amended), paragraph 245HD; paragraphs 76 to 79D, 77H & 77J of Appendix A; paragraphs AR2.1, AR.2.2, AR2.9 & AR3.2(b) of Appendix AR
Nationality, Immigration and Asylum Act 2002, section 113

Representation

Mr M Biggs instructed by Hubers Law, for the Claimant;
Ms L Giovannetti QC and *Mr W Hansen* instructed by the Government Legal Department, for the Secretary of State.

Judgment

Covid-19 Protocol: This judgment was handed down remotely by circulation to the parties' representatives by email, release to BAILII and publication on the Courts and Tribunals Judiciary website. The date and time for hand-down is deemed to be at 10:30am on Friday, 13 November 2020.

LORD JUSTICE LEWIS:

Introduction

[1] This is an appeal against a decision of the Upper Tribunal (Immigration and Asylum Chamber) dated 18 July 2019 dismissing the Appellant's claim for judicial review of a decision of the respondent refusing to grant the appellant leave to remain in the United Kingdom as a Tier 2 (General) Migrant.
[2] In summary, the appellant came to the United Kingdom with leave to enter as a Tier 4 (General) Student. He made an application seeking to vary his existing leave and be granted leave to remain as a Tier 2 (General) Migrant. That application was refused on 27 September 2018. An administrative review of that decision was concluded on 31 October 2018 and the decision upheld. The appellant submitted that the application was not finally determined until the

administrative review was complete. He contended that he was entitled to vary the application at any time until it was finally determined and had done so on 18 October 2018 by making a human rights claim. In those circumstances, he submitted that he continued to have leave to remain by virtue of section 3C of the Immigration Act 1971 ("the 1971 Act") until the application (as varied to include the human rights claim) was decided.

[3] Secondly, the appellant submitted that the respondent determined his application in a way that was procedurally unfair. The respondent had sought further information from the sponsor of his Tier 2 application without also notifying the appellant that further information was required and telling him that if it were not provided the application might be refused.

[4] The respondent submitted first that the application was decided on 27 September 2018 when it was refused. Any variation of that application had to be made before it was decided, i.e. before 27 September 2018. The appellant could not vary that application by making a human rights claim on 18 October 2018. Further, the respondent submits that the human rights claim was not in any event a valid variation as it was not in the prescribed form, no fee was paid and mandatory requirements were not satisfied. Secondly, the respondent submitted that there was no unfairness in the way that she dealt with the application and, in particular, procedural fairness did not require her to notify the appellant that she had made a request to the appellant's sponsor for further information.

The factual background

[5] The appellant is a national of Bangladesh born on 9 December 1987. He was granted leave to enter the United Kingdom as a Tier 4 (General) Student on 19 November 2009. That leave was valid until 31 August 2011. He was subsequently granted further periods of leave to remain up to 6 July 2016.

The application for leave to remain as a Tier 2 (General) Migrant
[6] On 6 July 2016, the appellant applied using form FLR (O) to vary his existing leave. On 22 August 2016, he applied for leave to remain as a Tier 2 (General) Migrant. On 24 August 2016, he submitted a letter to the respondent varying his FLR (O) application to an application seeking further leave to remain as a Tier 2 (General) Migrant.

[7] Applicants for Tier 2 (General) Migrant leave are required to score 50 points for certain attributes. This in effect required the applicant to submit a certificate of sponsorship showing that he had been offered a job which met certain criteria and paid a certain level of salary.

[8] The appellant's application recorded that he had a certificate of sponsorship from his proposed employer, Orchid Money Transfer Ltd. It stated that the job was as an accounts manager with a salary of £21,000 a year. The sponsor provided a letter dated 22 August 2016 indicating that it was pleased to sponsor the appellant conditionally upon him being granted a successful extension of his leave to remain. It confirmed that it had a certificate of sponsorship for the appellant. A further document provided (in two paragraphs) a summary of the role and the skills required.

[9] On 7 August 2018, the respondent wrote to the sponsor indicating that she had received applications from the appellant and a second person for Tier 2 (General) Migrant leave to remain in the United Kingdom in order to work for the

sponsor as an accounts manager and sales manager respectively. The letter explained that specified information was required before the respondent could proceed further with the applications. The letter then requested the sponsor to provide information about the jobs including full job descriptions listing the duties of the proposed employees and an explanation as to why the sponsor required an accounts manager and a sales manager. The letter also requested other information including the sponsor's business bank account statements for the last 12 months, a full staff list, the latest company accounts, HMRC reference numbers, a chart of all employees, CVs for the appellant and the other applicant and marketing material and website details. It requested the sponsor to answer various questions. It stated that the information was required by 14 September 2018 and that:

"Failure to send in the information by the required date may result in the refusal of all the applications."

[10] The respondent did not notify the appellant that it had sought further information from the sponsor nor that failure to provide the information might lead to his application being refused.

[11] The sponsor did not send in the information requested by 14 September 2018. It did not seek an extension of time for doing so. It made no reply to the e-mail request of 7 August 2018.

[12] On 27 September 2018, the respondent refused the application for leave to remain as a Tier 2 (General) Migrant and notified the appellant in writing of the decision and the reasons. The decision noted that the respondent had considered whether the vacancy was a genuine vacancy within the meaning of the Immigration Rules. It noted that the sponsor had been asked to provide further information. It continued:

"We were unable to complete the above assessment because to date we have not received any of the information requested.

Based on the evidence we have and the job description provided on your Certificate of Sponsorship and the fact that the sponsor has failed to respond to a request for information; we are not satisfied that your Sponsor would require an Accounts Manager on £21,000 per annum and we are satisfied that it is an inappropriate vacancy.

The Secretary of State is therefore refusing your application because there are reasonable grounds to believe that the job described on your Certificate of Sponsorship is not a genuine vacancy, when assessing, on the balance of probabilities, paragraph 245HD(f) with reference to Appendix A paragraph 77H and the additional information or evidence requested under paragraph 245HD(f) with reference to Appendix A paragraph 77J of the Immigration Rules."

The administrative review

[13] On 9 October 2015, the appellant requested an administrative review of the refusal. He said that the refusal was unfair as, if the respondent had contacted him, "he could have definitely pursued his employer to get the issues being sorted".

[14] On 11 October 2018, the director of the sponsor company wrote to the respondent saying it had been informed that the appellant's Tier 2 application had

been refused because the sponsor, as employer, had failed to provide some additional documents requested by the respondent. The letter said that the information covered various areas of the sponsor's business and as a result more time was needed to prepare them. It said that:

"I would like to confirm you that the job offered to Mr Topadar is completely genuine and we will send all the relevant document request by your office as soon as they are available as support of this claim."

The letter of 18 October 2018

[15] On 18 October 2018, solicitors for the appellant wrote to the respondent. The letter said, amongst other things, that it was a human rights claim within the meaning of section 113 of the Nationality, Immigration and Asylum Act 2002 ("the 2002 Act") and that there was no requirement to make the claim by way of a fee paid application. It stated that the appellant had established a private life in the United Kingdom and that leave to remain should be granted under Article 8 of the Convention for the Protection of Human Rights and Fundamental Freedoms ("the Convention").

The decision on administrative review

[16] On 31 October 2018, the appellant was informed that his request for administrative review had been unsuccessful and reasons were given for that decision.

The claim for judicial review

[17] By a claim form issued on 4 December 2018, the appellant sought judicial review of what the claim form described as the decision of the respondent dated 27 September 2018 that refused to grant the appellant leave to remain under the Tier 2 (General) rules, upheld on administrative review on 31 October 2018. The remedies sought were an order quashing the decision of 27 September 2018 and the administrative review and a declaration that the appellant had leave to remain under section 3C of the 1971 Act.

[18] The grounds of claim were that the respondent had acted in a way that was procedurally unfair by not warning the sponsor that unless it provided the information by a specified date the application would be rejected and by not warning the appellant of those matters.

[19] The grounds further contended that the appellant had made an application for leave to remain as a Tier 2 (General) Migrant which was not finally determined until the conclusion of the administrative review on 31 October 2018. Before that date had been reached, the appellant had varied the application by making a human rights claim on 18 October 2018. Leave to remain would continue in force by virtue of section 3C of the 1971 Act until the application for leave (as varied by the human rights claim) was determined.

The decision of the Upper Tribunal

[20] The Upper Tribunal held that the appellant could only apply to vary an application before it had been determined. In the present case, the application had been determined on 27 September 2018. The process of administrative review was

not an extension of the decision-making process. It was a review of the decision. Consequently, it was not open to the appellant to seek to vary the application on 18 October 2018 as the application had been determined by that time. Further, the Upper Tribunal did not consider that, on the facts, the letter of 18 October 2018 did amount to an application to vary the earlier application.

[21] The Upper Tribunal further held that there was no procedural unfairness in the way in which the respondent dealt with the application. The Immigration Rules provided that the respondent may request additional information and evidence from the sponsor and may refuse the application if the information or evidence is not provided. The sponsor was asked to provide information and was given a period of 25 business days to do so (longer than the ten business days referred to in the Immigration Rules). The Upper Tribunal concluded that the primary onus was on the appellant to provide all the necessary information. There was no obligation on the respondent to inform the appellant that information had been sought from the sponsor or to remind the sponsor of what was clearly set out in the letter of 7 August 2018 that the consequence of a failure to provide the information might be the refusal of the application.

The legislative framework

The 1971 Act

[22] The 1971 Act sets out a framework governing immigration control for those seeking to enter and remain in the United Kingdom. Section 3 of the 1971 Act provides so far as material that:

"(1) Except as otherwise provided by or under this Act, where a person is not a British citizen

> (a) he shall not enter the United Kingdom unless given leave to do so in accordance with the provisions of, or made under this Act;
>
> (b) he may be given leave to enter the United Kingdom (or, when already there, leave to remain in the United Kingdom) either for a limited or for an indefinite period;
>
> (c) if he is given leave to enter or remain in the United Kingdom, it may be given subject to all or any of the following conditions, namely….

(2) The Secretary of State shall from time to time (and as soon as may be) lay before Parliament statements of the rules, or any changes in the rules, laid down by him as to the practice to be following in the administration of this Act for regulating the entry into and stay in the United Kingdom of persons required by this Act to have leave to enter, including any rules as to the period in which leave is to be given and the conditions to be attached in different circumstances…".

[23] Section 3C of the 1971 Act deals with the circumstances in which a person who has leave to enter or remain, and applies to vary that leave (for example by seeking a further period of leave on the same or a different basis) continues to

have leave to remain until that application is determined. The section provides that:

"3C Continuation of leave pending variation decision

(1) This section applies if –

  (a) a person who has limited leave to enter or remain in the United Kingdom applies to the Secretary of State for variation of the leave,

  (b) the application for variation is made before the leave expires, and

  (c) the leave expires without the application for variation having been decided.

(2) The leave is extended by virtue of this section during any period when –

  (a) the application for variation is neither decided nor withdrawn,

  (b) an appeal under section 82(1) of the Nationality, Asylum and Immigration Act 2002 could be brought, while the appellant is in the United Kingdom against the decision on the application for variation (ignoring any possibility of an appeal out of time with permission),

  (c) an appeal under that section against that decision [, brought while the appellant is in the United Kingdom,]4 is pending (within the meaning of section 104 of that Act),

  (ca) an appeal could be brought under the Immigration (Citizens' Rights Appeals) (EU Exit) Regulations 2020 ('the 2020 Regulations'), while the appellant is in the United Kingdom, against the decision on the application for variation (ignoring any possibility of an appeal out of time with permission),

  (cb) an appeal under the 2020 Regulations against that decision, brought while the appellant is in the United Kingdom, is pending (within the meaning of those Regulations), or

  (d) an administrative review of the decision on the application for variation –

    (i) could be sought, or

    (ii) is pending.

(3) Leave extended by virtue of this section shall lapse if the applicant leaves the United Kingdom.

(3A)   Leave extended by virtue of this section may be cancelled if the applicant —

(a)   has failed to comply with a condition attached to the leave, or

(b)   has used or uses deception in seeking leave to remain (whether successfully or not).

(4)   A person may not make an application for variation of his leave to enter or remain in the United Kingdom while that leave is extended by virtue of this section.

(5)   But subsection (4) does not prevent the variation of the application mentioned in subsection (1)(a).

(6)   The Secretary of State may make regulations determining when an application is decided for the purposes of this section; and the regulations–

(a)   may make provision by reference to receipt of a notice,

(b)   may provide for a notice to be treated as having been received in specified circumstances,

(c)   may make different provision for different purposes or circumstances,

(d)   shall be made by statutory instrument, and

(e)   shall be subject to annulment in pursuance of a resolution of either House of Parliament.

(7)   In this section – 'administrative review' means a review conducted under the immigration rules; the question of whether an administrative review is pending is to be determined in accordance with the immigration rules."

[24] Section 4 of the 1971 Act is headed "Administration of control" and makes further provision for the way in which the power to grant or vary leave to remain in the United Kingdom conferred by section 3 may be exercised.

The Immigration Rules

[25] The Immigration Rules provide for a points based system for the grant of leave to remain for certain categories of persons including those seeking leave to remain as a Tier 2 (General) Migrant. Paragraph 245HD of the Immigration Rules sets out the requirements that an application must meet. Paragraph 245HD(f) provides that:

"if applying as a Tier 2 (General) Migrant, the applicant must have a minimum of 50 points under paragraphs 76 to 79D of Appendix A."

[26] Those paragraphs in Appendix A require applicants to provide a certificate of sponsorship and for points to be scored in respect of that certificate. Paragraph 76A of Appendix A provides that the points available are shown in Table 11A the material parts of which provide as follows:

Certificate of Sponsorship	Points	Appropriate Salary	Points
Job offer passes Resident Labour Market Test	30	Appropriate Salary	20

[27] Paragraph 77H and 77J of Appendix A provide, so far as material, as follows:

"77H. No points will be awarded for a Certificate of Sponsorship if the Entry Clearance Officer or the Secretary of State has reasonable grounds to believe, notwithstanding that the applicant has provided the evidence required under the relevant provisions of Appendix A, that:

> (a)   the job as recorded by the Certificate of Sponsorship Checking Service is not a genuine vacancy...

77J. To support the assessment in paragraph 77H(a)-(c), the Entry Clearance Officer or the Secretary of State may request additional information and evidence from the applicant or the Sponsor, and refuse the application if the information or evidence is not provided. Any requested documents must be received by the Entry Clearance Officer or the Secretary of State at the address specified in the request within 10 business days of the date the request is sent."

[28] Applications for leave to remain, and for variations of such applications, must be in the prescribed form, the relevant fee must be paid and satisfy the mandatory requirements. Applications in either case are invalid and will not be considered if they fail to meet the prescribed requirements. See paragraph 34, 35A and 34E of the Immigration Rules.

Administrative review
[29] The provisions governing administrative review are contained in an appendix to the Immigration Rules. AR2.1 and AR.2.2 provide:

"AR2.1 Administrative review is the review of an eligible decision to decide whether the decision is wrong due to a case working error.

AR2.2 The outcome of an administrative review will be:

> (a)   Administrative review succeeds and the eligible decision is withdrawn; or

(b)   Administrative review does not succeed and the eligible decision remains in force and all of the reasons given or the decision are maintained; or

(c)   Administrative review does not succeed and the eligible decision remains in force but one or more of the reasons given for the decision are withdrawn; or

(d)   Administrative review does not succeed and the eligible decision remains in force but with different or additional reasons to those specified in the decision under review."

[30] The decisions eligible for administrative review are defined in section AR3. They include at A3.2(b):

"A decision on an application where the application is made on or after 2nd March 2015 for leave to remain, as:

(1)   a Tier 1, 2 or 5 Migrant under the Points Based System …"

[31] AR2.9 defines when an administrative review is pending for the purposes of section 3C2(d) of the 1971 Act. It includes a period:

"When an application for administrative review has been made until:

…

(iii)   the notice of outcome at AR2.2(a), (b), or (c) is served in accordance with Appendix SN of these Rules."

The appeal and the issues

[32] There are four grounds of appeal. As appears from the grounds, the skeleton arguments and the oral submissions, the following issues arise:

(1)   May an application falling within section 3C(1) be varied at any time up to the conclusion of an administrative review of the decision refusing the application and, if so, did the letter of 18 October 2018 amount to a valid variation of the appellant's application? (Grounds 1 to 3 of the Grounds of Appeal)

(2)   Did the respondent act in a way which was procedurally unfair by not informing the appellant that she had requested further information from the sponsor and that the application might be refused if that information was not provided? (Ground 4 of the Grounds of Appeal).

The first issue – when an application for leave to remain is determined

Submissions

[33] Mr Biggs for the appellant submitted that, where a person makes an application to vary existing leave to remain, he may make a further variation of the application at any time until the application is determined. The application is only finally determined when the process of administrative review is completed. A decision refusing the application is an initial, inchoate, or provisional decision and the final determination is only made on the outcome of the administrative review. He submitted that the provisions governing the process of administrative review must necessarily be read as an extension of the process of deciding the application. There would otherwise be no legal basis for a formal system of administrative review leading to a fundamentally different decision from the decision refusing the application. He submitted that that was consistent with the approach of the Vice President of the Upper Tribunal (Immigration and Asylum Chamber) refusing permission to apply for judicial review in *R (Sukhwinder Singh) v Secretary of State for the Home Department* JR/1361/2015. In considering whether the claim was brought out of time, the Vice-President considered that the process of administrative review was different in character from the informal process of reconsideration of decisions previously undertaken. The final decision was the decision reached on the administrative review.

[34] Mr Biggs submitted, therefore, that in this case the application seeking to vary the appellant's existing leave and to be granted leave to remain as a Tier 2 (General) Migrant was not determined until the administrative review process of the refusal of that application was complete. The application was refused on 27 September 2018 but the administrative review was not completed until 31 October 2018. Consequently, the appellant could vary that application at any time before 31 October 2018. The appellant continued to have leave to remain by virtue of section 3C of the 1971 Act until the application, as varied to include the human rights claim, is determined.

[35] Mr Biggs submitted it was open to the appellant to vary an application by including a human rights claim without complying with any particular formality. It was not necessary for such a variation to be made on any prescribed form or to require payment of a fee or the provision of mandatory information. He submitted that that was consistent with paragraph 99 of the judgment of Underhill LJ in *R (Balajigari) v Secretary of State for the Home Department* [2019] 1 WLR 4647.

[36] Ms Giovannetti QC, for the respondent, submitted that variations of an application could only be made before the application was determined. That occurred when a decision was taken granting or refusing the application and the applicant was notified of the decision. The process of administrative review was a review of a decision that had been taken and was not an extension of the decision-making process. Consequently where, as here, the application had been refused by a particular date, 27 September 2018, the application had been determined and there was nothing left to vary.

[37] Further, Ms Giovannetti submitted that the letter of 18 October 2018 did not amount to a valid variation in any event. A distinction needed to be drawn between an application for leave to remain on the basis that refusal would be incompatible with the right to family or private life under Article 8 of the Convention and a decision to remove a person who did not have leave to remain. The former was required to be made on a prescribed form, with payment of a fee, and the provision of relevant information as required by paragraph 34E of the

Immigration Rules. In relation to the latter, the respondent would be unable to remove a person without leave where he or she claimed that to do so would be incompatible with his or her rights under the Convention and such a claim could be made without any prescribed formality. That, Ms Giovannetii submitted, was what was decided by the Court of Appeal in *R (Balajigari) v Secretary of State for the Home Department* [2019] 1 W.L.R. 4647, having regard to paragraphs 97 to 102; and in *R (Shrestha) v Secretary of State for the Home Department* [2018] EWCA Civ 2810. In so far as the letter of 18 October 2018 was said to be a variation of an application, it was invalid as it did not comply with the requirements of the Immigration Rules.

Discussion

[38] The starting point is the wording of section 3C of the 1971 Act. The section applies if a person has limited leave to enter or remain in the United Kingdom and applies for variation of that leave before the leave expires and the leave expires without the application having been decided: see section 3C(1)(a)–(c). In those circumstances the existing leave is extended for the periods permitted by section 3C(2) of the 1971 Act. Thus, where a person such as the appellant has leave to remain as a Tier 4 (General) Student and applies to vary that leave and be granted leave as a Tier 2 (General) Migrant, he continues to have leave to remain in the United Kingdom until the application is determined. Furthermore, the applicant may vary the application by substituting a different basis for seeking to vary the existing leave: see section 3C(5) of the 1971 Act. A variation may only made before the application is determined. Once the application is determined there is nothing to vary. That is recognised by the Court of Appeal in *JH (Zimbabwe) v Secretary of State for the Home Department* [2009] Imm AR 499 Richards LJ, with whom Wall and Laws LJJ agreed, held at paragraph 35 of his judgment that:

> "35. The key to the matter is an understanding of how s.3C operates.... The section applies, by subs.(1), where an application for variation of an existing leave is made before that leave expires (and provided that there has been no decision on that application before the leave expires). In that event there is, by subs.(2), a statutory extension of the original leave until (a) the application is decided or withdrawn, or (b), if the application has been decided and there is a right of appeal against that decision, the time for appealing has expired, or (c), if an appeal has been brought, that appeal is pending: I paraphrase the statutory language, but that seems to me to be the effect of it. During the period of the statutory extension of the original leave, by subs.(4) no further application for variation of that leave can be made. Thus, there can be only one application for variation of the original leave, and there can be only one decision (and, where applicable, one appeal). The possibility of a series of further applications leading to an indefinite extension of the original leave is excluded. However, by subs.(5) it is possible to vary the one permitted application. If it is varied, any decision (and any further appeal) will relate to the application as varied. But once a decision has been made, no variation to the application is possible since there is nothing left to vary."

[39] An application is decided, as a matter of ordinary language, when a decision is reached granting or refusing the application. The question in the present case is whether the process of administrative review is intended, or must as a matter of law be understood, to be part of the process of deciding the application so that the application is only decided when the administrative review is concluded.

[40] First, as a matter of interpretation of the provisions dealing with administrative review, it is clear that the review is separate from, not part of, the process of deciding an application. Administrative review is defined in AR2.1 as "the review" of an eligible decision (here a decision refusing leave to remain as a Tier 2 (General) Migrant). The purpose is to decide whether "the decision is wrong due to a case working error". It is clear that the process envisages a difference between "the decision" which is the refusal of the application and the "administrative review" which checks whether that decision was wrong. That is further reflected in the provisions at AR2.2 which sets out the possible outcome of the administrative review. The decision to refuse the application is either withdrawn or "remains in force" either for the same or different reasons. The same distinction between the decision to refuse the application and an administrative review of that decision, is reflected throughout the provisions governing an administrative review.

[41] Secondly, section 3(2) of the 1971 does confer power to provide for such a system of administrative review. Section 3(2) provides power to make rules "as to the practice to be followed in the administration of this Act for regulating the entry into and stay in the United Kingdom". Rules providing for an administrative review to determine whether decisions refusing applications to vary an existing leave to remain should be withdrawn or remain in force are rules as to the practice to be followed in the administration of the 1971 Act for regulating stay in the United Kingdom.

[42] Thirdly, the provisions of section 3C(2) of the 1971 Act expressly contemplate that a system of administrative review may have that effect and may draw a distinction between the decision refusing the application and a review of that decision. Section 3C(2)(a) provides for leave to be continued while the application seeking to vary an existing leave remains undecided. Section 3C(2)(d) also expressly provides for leave to continue when "an administrative review of the decision on the application" could be sought or is pending. In other words, the provisions of section 3C themselves draw a distinction between a decision on the application and an administrative review of that decision.

[43] Further, if the appellant were correct, and if the process of administrative review were an extension of the process for deciding the application, it would not be necessary to include section 3C(2)(d) in the 1971 Act to allow for leave to continue pending the administrative review. On the appellant's hypothesis, leave to remain would continue under section 3C(2)(a) because the application is not decided until the process of administrative review is complete.

[44] In the light of those considerations, it is clear that an application seeking to vary an existing leave is decided within the meaning of section 3C(2)(a) of the 1971 Act when the application is refused. Any further variation of that application must be made before the decision refusing the application is made and notified to the applicant. The system of administrative review operates as a review of that decision. It is not an extension of that decision-making process.

[45] I do not, therefore, accept Mr Biggs' submission that section 3(2) of the 1971 Act does not provide power to make rules providing for administrative review of that nature and that the provisions must therefore be interpreted differently in order to avoid them being *ultra vires*.

[46] Nor do I consider that the position is altered by the decision of the Vice-President of the Upper Tribunal in the *Sukhwinder Singh* case. The Tribunal Procedure Rules, like the provisions of CPR 54.5, provide a time limit for bringing claims for judicial review. In the case of the Upper Tribunal, the rules provide that a claim must be received by the Upper Tribunal no later than "3 months after the decision, action or omission to which the application relates" (see rule 28 of the Tribunal Procedure (Upper Tribunal) Rules 2008). CPR 54 requires that a claim for judicial review issued in the Administrative Court must be brought promptly and, in any event, no later than 3 months after the date when the grounds of claim first arose. In addition, judicial review is a remedy of last resort and should not be generally be pursued where there is an adequate alternative remedy available.

[47] The courts have considered the relationship between the rules on time limits for bringing claims and the emphasis on the use of alternative remedies. In that context, the courts have held that the time for bringing a claim is to be understood as beginning when the alternative remedy had been exhausted, or the courts have treated the use of an alternative remedy as a reason for extending the time limit for bringing a claim, or have permitted a claim to be brought against the decision on appeal or review on the grounds that it failed to correct the error in the initial decision. The decision in *Sukhwinder Singh* was concerned with identifying when the time limit began to run and to reconcile that with the requirement that alternative remedies should generally be used before resorting to judicial review. Its reference to the review decision as the final decision is to be understood in that context. The review decision was the final decision for those purposes as "that is the decision from the date of which the passage of time for judicial review is to be measured". It was not seeking to interpret and apply the provisions of section 3C of the 1971 Act.

[48] For those reasons, any variation in the present case had to be made before the 27 September 2018 when the decision refusing the application was made. No such variation was made by that date. The appellant continued to have leave to remain whilst the administrative review of the decision was pending by virtue of section 3C(2)(d) of the 1971 Act. Once the outcome of that review was notified to the appellant on 31 October 2018, his leave ceased to continue in force as the administrative review was no longer pending as defined in AR2.9.

[49] In the light of that conclusion, it is not necessary to address the question of whether the letter of 18 October 2018 was a valid variation of the application. Grounds 1 to 3 of the Grounds of Appeal are not made out.

The second issue – procedural fairness

Submissions

[50] Mr Biggs submitted that procedural fairness in the present case required the respondent to notify the appellant that she had requested the sponsor to provide further information and, if that information was not provided, the application might be refused. Mr Biggs submitted that the situation was analogous to that in *R (Pathan) v Secretary of State for the Home Department* [2020] UKSC 41. There, at least four members of the Supreme Court held that procedural fairness required the respondent to notify the applicant of a fact which was fatal to the application and which was known to the respondent but not the applicant. If the appellant had been informed of the request in this case, he might have supplied the relevant information, or taken steps to encourage the sponsor to do so, or taken steps to find other employment or make an application for leave to remain on a different basis. Further, the respondent here was treating the failure by the sponsor to provide information as a basis for inferring that the accounts manager post was not a genuine vacancy. Procedural fairness required that an individual adversely affected by adverse inferences of that nature be given the opportunity to respond before a decision was taken based on those inferences. In that regard, Mr Biggs relied upon *In re HK (An Infant)* [1967] 2 QB 617, *Gaima v Secretary of State for the Home Department* [1989] Imm AR 527 and *R v London Borough of Hackney ex p. Decordova* (1994) 27 HLR 108.

[51] Ms Giovannetti submitted that the requirements of procedural fairness depended upon the context and the facts. In the context of a points based system intended to ensure the efficient processing of a high volume of applications for leave to remain, there was nothing unfair in placing the obligation on an applicant to demonstrate that he or she satisfied the requirements for the grant of leave to remain. In that context, the respondent had requested the sponsor, in accordance with the rules, to provide specific information and said that failure to do so might result in the application being refused. Procedural fairness did not impose any obligation on the respondent to notify the appellant of the request to the sponsor for information. The situation in *Pathan* was different and involved a specific act by the respondent, the revocation of the sponsor's sponsorship licence, which meant that the application for leave would inevitably fail. Here the situation involved a failure by a sponsor to provide the information requested and which led to the refusal of the application.

Discussion

[52] The requirements of procedural fairness depend upon the facts and the context in which a decision is taken including the nature of the legal and administrative system within which the decision is taken. See generally the observations of Lord Mustill in *R v Secretary of State for the Home Department ex p. Doody* [1994] A.C. 531 at 560d–g.

[53] In the present case, the context is the operation of the points based system for determining applications for leave to remain. That is recognised as a system which is intended to simplify the procedure for applying for leave to enter and remain in the cases of students and certain classes of economic migrants. The system is intended to enable high volumes of applications to be processed in a fair and efficient manner. The system operates by specifying what evidence must be submitted by applicants. The requirements of procedural fairness are to be understood in that context. See generally, the observations of Sales L.J., as he then was, with whom Briggs L.J., as he then was, agreed at paragraphs 28 to 30 of his judgment in *EK (Ivory Coast) v Secretary of State for the Home Department* [2015] Imm AR 367.

[54] The specific context in this case was an application by the appellant to vary his existing leave and be granted leave to remain as a Tier 2 (General) Migrant. He was required to supply a certificate of sponsorship from his prospective employer in order to obtain sufficient points to be eligible for that leave. That certificate was intended to demonstrate that the job vacancy was a genuine one and the respondent could effectively refuse the application if she had reasonable grounds for believing that it was not a genuine vacancy. Paragraph 77J of the Immigration Rules specifically provided that, in order to consider that matter, the respondent "could request additional information and evidence from the applicant or the

Sponsor" and could refuse the application if the information or evidence was not provided.

[55] In that context, there was nothing procedurally unfair in the respondent asking the sponsor for additional information and evidence. That was inherent in the system and specifically provided for in the Immigration Rules. The sponsor was told that failure to provide the additional information and evidence might result in the application being refused. In the event, the sponsor did not provide the additional information or evidence requested and, in those circumstances, the respondent could not be satisfied on the evidence available that the job vacancy was genuine. There was nothing procedurally unfair in the way in which the respondent acted.

[56] Further, none of the matters referred to by the appellant demonstrate that any procedural unfairness had occurred. The information sought was information from the sponsor about, for example, why the organisation required an accounts manager and what the duties would be. The additional evidence related to the sponsor's bank accounts, staff list, company accounts, tax details and the like. Those were matters that the sponsor was in a position to provide not the appellant and there was nothing unfair in asking the sponsor to provide the information.

[57] The appellant suggests that if he had known that a request for information had been made, he could have chased the sponsor to provide the information and evidence. But the system operates on the basis that the applicant will obtain a certificate of sponsorship from a sponsor for a genuine job vacancy and the respondent can request further information from either the applicant for leave or the sponsor to assess that. Procedural fairness in this context does not require the respondent to give the appellant the opportunity to chase the sponsor for information. If the employer intends to employ the appellant, and has provided a certificate of sponsorship, it is incumbent on the employer to provide any additional information sought by the respondent. Furthermore, requiring the respondent to notify the appellant so that the appellant can chase the sponsor would not be consistent with the operation of the points based system in general, or the rules in respect of applications for leave as a Tier 2 (General) Migrant in particular. Procedural fairness does not require the respondent "to have to distort the ordinary operation of the [points based system] to protect an applicant" (adapting the words of Sales LJ at paragraph 35 of his judgment in *EK (Ivory Coast)* against the possibility that a sponsor may not respond to requests for information. Nor is the purpose of a request for information to give the appellant time to find an alternative employer, or a different basis for seeking leave, in the event that the employer cannot, or fails for whatever reason to, provide the information requested. It is to enable the respondent, as paragraph 77J of the Immigration Rules provides, to assess whether the requirements for grant of leave as a Tier 2 (General) Migrant have been satisfied.

[58] The situation here is different from the situation in *Pathan*. There the applicant was a person who was already employed by the sponsor and applied to renew his leave to remain on the basis of an apparently valid certificate of sponsorship. The respondent revoked the sponsor's licence and, as a consequence, the certificate was no longer valid and the application for leave was bound to fail. The applicant knew nothing about the revocation of the sponsor's licence. Three months passed before a decision was taken to refuse the application for leave. It was in that context that Lord Kerr and Lady Black considered, at paragraph 104 of their judgment, that "the rules of natural justice may require a party to be afforded

time to amend his case in a way that cures an otherwise fatal defect of which he had, without fault on his part, previously been unaware". Lord Kerr and Lady Black considered the various ways in which Mr Pathan could have benefitted if he had been notified of the revocation of his sponsor's licence as soon as it had occurred. Lady Arden, who agreed with the majority on this issue, also referred to procedural fairness requiring that an applicant working for his sponsor and who had a valid certificate of sponsorship at the time of application, should have notice of the revocation of the sponsor's licence: see paragraph 56 of her judgment.

[59] The majority of the Supreme Court was not intending, in my judgement, to establish an absolute or universal requirement that the respondent must give the appellant prior notice of something that might affect the consideration of an application with a view to the applicant being able to take steps to address that matter. Rather, as the judgments of the majority of the Supreme Court recognise, the requirements of procedural fairness are flexible and are not set in stone. They are necessarily influenced by the context and the facts. See paragraph 55 of the judgment of Lady Arden and paragraph 104 of the joint judgment of Lord Kerr and Lady Black. Lord Wilson also recognises that the requirements of procedural fairness will vary and the court will imply into a prescribed procedure so much but no more than is required: see paragraph 203 of his judgment. In those circumstances, I do not consider that the majority decision of the Supreme Court requires the imposition of a duty to notify an appellant of a request for additional information and evidence sent to a sponsor of an applicant for leave as a Tier 2 (General) Migrant.

[60] Nor is this a case where the respondent was making adverse findings against an individual and where fairness requires that the individual concerned be told of the possibility of adverse findings and be given the opportunity to respond to the matters giving rise to the adverse findings. This was a case where the Immigration Rules provided that the information could be required to enable the respondent to assess whether a job vacancy was a genuine vacancy. In the absence of that information, she could not make the assessment and could not be satisfied that the vacancy was a genuine one. The case is unlike *In re HK* where the immigration officer considered that an immigrant was over 16 years old and so did not qualify for admission to the United Kingdom as the child under 16 of a person ordinarily resident in the United Kingdom. Procedural fairness required the immigration officer to inform the individual of his suspicions and give him an opportunity to address those matters. Similarly, in Gaima, the respondent considered that a claimant for asylum was not credible because of certain things she was alleged to have done. Those matters were never put to the claimant and the Court of Appeal held that procedural fairness did require that matters relied upon as undermining her credibility should be put to her and she should be given the opportunity to comment. In *Decordova*, a local housing authority was minded to disbelieve a person's account as to why she did not accept an offer of accommodation, namely that she did not want to live in the area as her stepfather who had abused her lived nearby. Procedural fairness required that where a housing authority was minded to disbelieve the account of an individual on a matter that was critical to the issue of whether she should be offered accommodation in a particular area, they were bound to put that matter to the individual and give her the opportunity to comment.

[61] Those situations are very different from the present. Here, there was a decision-making process where, in accordance with the relevant rules, the sponsor

was required to provide evidence of certain matters to enable the respondent to assess whether a job vacancy was a genuine vacancy. The rules provided that, if the information was not provided, the application for leave to remain might be refused. The sponsor was asked to provide the information. It did not do so. The respondent could not therefore be satisfied that the sponsor did require an accounts manager paid £21,000 a year. There was nothing unfair in that process. This was not a case where the respondent was making adverse findings, still less adverse findings on matters within the knowledge of the appellant. It was for the sponsor to provide the information to enable an assessment of whether the vacancy was genuine. It did not provide the information. In those circumstances, there was no allegation or issue that need in fairness to be put to the appellant for comment before the application for leave was refused.

[62] In my judgement, Upper Tribunal Judge Allen was right to hold that the claim of procedural unfairness was not made on the facts of this particular case. Ground 4 of the Grounds of appeal fails.

Conclusion

[63] Applications within section 3C(2)(a) of the 1971 Act may be varied at any time until the application is decided. That occurs when the application is refused and the applicant notified of the refusal. Variations cannot be made after that time. An administrative review is a review of the decision refusing the application not part of the decision-making process. Variations cannot be made after the applicant is notified of the decision and while the process of administrative review is being conducted. There was no procedural unfairness in the way in which the respondent dealt with the application. For those reasons, the appeal should be dismissed.

LORD JUSTICE MALES:
[64] I agree.

LORD JUSTICE FLOYD:
[65] I also agree.

R (ON THE APPLICATION OF ALAM) v SECRETARY OF STATE FOR THE HOME DEPARTMENT; R (ON THE APPLICATION OF RANA) v SECRETARY OF STATE FOR THE HOME DEPARTMENT

COURT OF APPEAL

Floyd, Henderson and Phillips LJJ

[2020] EWCA Civ 1527
16 November 2020

Immigration – leave to remain – curtailment of leave – section 4(1) of the Immigration Act 1971 – notice in writing – service – receipt of notice – procedure and process – judicial review – application for permission

The Claimants, Mr Alam and Mr Rana, were citizens of Bangladesh. They both entered the United Kingdom in 2009 and were granted leave to remain as Tier 4 (General) Students. In December 2014 the University at which Mr Rana was enrolled notified the Home Office that Mr Rana had been withdrawn from the programme due to his failure to progress academically. In September 2015 the sponsor licence of the Academy where Mr Alam was studying was revoked before his extended leave to remain was due to expire. The Secretary of State for the Home Department decided to curtail the Claimants' leave to remain in the United Kingdom.

Section 4(1) of the Immigration Act 1971 ("the 1971 Act") provided that the Secretary of State's power to curtail leave "shall be exercised by notice in writing given to the person affected". Article 8ZA of the Immigration (Leave to Enter and Remain) Order 2000 ("the Order") provided a list of permitted methods by which a section 4(1) notice could be given to the person affected. That list included sending the notice by postal service to a postal address provided by the person. Article 8ZB(1) of the Order created a rebuttable presumption that, if the notice had been sent in accordance with one of the methods listed in Article 8ZA, it would be deemed to be the valid giving of notice to the person affected, unless the contrary was proved.

The Secretary of State sent written notice of the decisions to curtail the Claimants' leave to remain by recorded delivery to each of their last known addresses. The Claimants stated that they did not receive the section 4(1) notices until several years later, when it was drawn to their attention in connection with separate proceedings. The Claimants applied for judicial review of the Secretary of State's curtailment decision. The Upper Tribunal refused permission to apply for judicial review in both cases.

The Claimants' appeals were heard together before the Court of Appeal. The Claimants submitted that, as they had not received notice in writing, the Secretary of State's power to curtail their leave to remain had not been validly exercised in accordance with section 4(1) of the 1971 Act. The Secretary of State argued that, as she had done all that was required of her under the relevant legislation, it was for the Claimants to prove that they were not given notice, and they had no real prospect of doing so.

Held, dismissing the appeals:

(1) The special deeming provision in Article 8ZA(4) of the Order was an attempt to provide for valid service in a case where successive attempts to serve by recorded delivery had failed. In contrast, the methods of service set out in Article 8ZA(1) to (3) did not expressly deem the intended recipient to have received the notice. Rather, they appeared simply to list permitted methods of service. Article 8ZB(1) was plainly a deeming provision which operated when "a notice is *sent*" in accordance with Article 8ZA. That language was apt to cover all the methods of giving notice in writing in 8ZA(2) and (3) except that in 8ZA(2)(a) where the notice was "given by hand" and not "sent", and it did not apply where the deeming provision in Article 8ZA(4) applied. Further, Article 8ZB(1)(a)(i) dealt only with post sent by recorded delivery in the United Kingdom. Article 8ZB(1)(a)(ii) was not confined to recorded delivery but was limited to post sent outside the United Kingdom. There was no provision dealing with time of receipt for post sent by ordinary mail within the United Kingdom. As a result, no presumption applied where the notice in writing was sent by ordinary mail in the United Kingdom. Article 8ZB(1) only created a rebuttable presumption which arose if one of the methods of sending in Article 8ZA was followed. In those circumstances, Article 8ZB(a) deemed the use of the methods of sending in Article 8ZA to be the valid giving of notice and (b) deemed that notice to have been given on the specified day, but left the person affected, or the Secretary of State if the need arose, free to prove that he was not in fact given notice and/or that it was not given on that day (*paras 11 – 19*).

(2) The giving of notice for the purposes of section 4(1) of the 1971 Act and the Order did not require that the intended recipient should have read and absorbed the contents of the notice in writing, merely that it be received. If that were not so, a failure to open an envelope containing the notice, for whatever reason, would mean that notice was not given. Similarly, the recipient did not have to be made aware of the notice. Documents arriving by post would normally be received if they arrived, addressed to the person affected at the dwelling where he or she was living, at least in the absence of positive evidence that mail which so arrived was intercepted. A document received at an address provided to the Secretary of State for correspondence was received by the applicant, even if he did not bother to take steps to collect it. It followed that the burden of proving the negative, non-receipt, in the face of convincing evidence leading to the expectation of receipt, would not be lightly discharged. In particular it would not be discharged by evidence, far less by mere assertion, that the notice did not come to the attention of the person affected. It was not unreasonable to assume that judges in the Administrative Court would often be faced with applications for permission to apply for judicial review based on factual allegations that litigants did not receive notices in writing or other documents curtailing their leave to remain, and that in consequence the exercise by the Secretary of State of her powers in relation to that litigant had not been validly exercised. Some examination of the merits was necessary at the permission stage. The test which should be applied was whether the material before the court raised a factual case

which, taken at its highest, could properly succeed in a contested factual hearing. If so, permission should be granted, subject to discretionary factors such as delay (*paras 29 – 32*).

(3) When considering permission to apply for judicial review in such cases the following points should be considered: (a) where a method of sending within Article 8ZA(2) or (3) of the Order had been followed, the burden fell on the litigant to show that he had a real prospect of establishing that the document was not received in the sense in which the instant Court had interpreted that word; (b) at the permission stage, the litigant would need to do more than show that the notice did not come to his attention, but establish how he proposed to show that it was never actually received; (c) subject to discretionary factors such as delay, the question would be whether the material before the court raised a factual case which, taken at its highest, could properly succeed in a contested factual hearing; and (d) each case would nevertheless depend on its own facts (*para 33*).

(4) Permission to apply for judicial review was correctly refused in Mr Alam's case. The Secretary of State's case that notice of the curtailment decision had not merely been sent to Mr Alam but delivered to him at the place where, as he accepted, he was living was a powerful one which had been fully particularised and supported by contemporaneous documents. In addition, contemporaneous guidance to Home Office officials suggested that a second attempt at service must be undertaken if a curtailment decision was returned undelivered. There was no suggestion that the notice had been returned. That amounted to a strong case that it was received at the address where Mr Alam was living. Against that there was nothing positive to rebut the Secretary of State's case. Taking the evidence before the Judge at its highest, Mr Alam did not have a real prospect of showing that the notice had not been delivered to him, and permission to apply for judicial review was rightly refused. In relation to Mr Rana's case, the Secretary of State's evidence before the Judge that the notice was delivered to Mr Rana's address was compelling. There was no evidence in answer beyond Mr Rana's assertion that he did not receive it. That was plainly not sufficient to show a real prospect of proving that the notice was not delivered (*paras 45 – 49 and 56*).

Cases referred to:

R v Secretary of State for the Home Department and Another ex parte Anufrijeva [2003] UKHL 36; [2004] 1 AC 604; [2003] 3 WLR 252; [2003] 3 All ER 827; [2003] Imm AR 570; [2003] INLR 521
R (FZ) v London Borough of Croydon [2011] EWCA Civ 59; [2011] 1 FLR 2081
R (on the application of Javed) v Secretary of State for the Home Department [2014] EWHC 4426 (Admin)
R (on the application of Mahmood) v Secretary of State for the Home Department (effective service – 2000 Order) IJR [2016] UKUT 57 (IAC); [2016] Imm AR 559
R (on the application of Rahman) v Secretary of State for the Home Department [2019] EWHC 2952 (Admin)
Sun Alliance v London Assurance Co Ltd v Hayman [1975] 1 WLR 177; [1975] 1 All ER 248
Syed (curtailment of leave – notice) [2013] UKUT 144 (IAC)
UKI (Kingsway) Limited v Westminster City Council [2018] UKSC 67

Legislation judicially considered:

Immigration Act 1971, sections 3A, 3B & 4(1)
Immigration (Leave to Enter and Remain) Order 2000, Articles 8, 8ZA & 8ZB
Interpretation Act 1978, section 7
Nationality, Immigration and Asylum Act 2002, section 82(2)

Representation

Mr M Biggs instructed by Hubers Law, for the Claimants;
Mr W Hansen instructed by the Government Legal Department, for the Secretary of State.

Judgment

LORD JUSTICE FLOYD:

[1] These two appeals, which we have heard together, raise the question of what is required "to give notice in writing of" a decision curtailing a person's leave to remain in the United Kingdom. In each appeal the appellant contends that he was not given notice of the curtailment decision, and that in consequence the power of the respondent, the Secretary of State for the Home Department ("the SSHD"), to curtail their leave was not validly exercised. The SSHD contends that, as she has done all that is required of her under the relevant legislation, it is for the appellants to prove that they were not given notice, and they have no real prospect of doing so.

[2] The appellant in the first appeal is Masud Alam. The SSHD wrote to him on 20 October 2015 informing him that his leave had been curtailed so that it now expired on 22 December 2015 ("the October 2015 decision"). Mr Alam says that he did not receive the October 2015 decision until it was brought to his attention in connection with unrelated judicial review proceedings in 2018. On 26 September 2018 he lodged this application for judicial review in the Upper Tribunal ("UT") challenging the October 2015 decision. The proceedings ultimately came before Upper Tribunal Judge ("UTJ") Finch at an oral hearing on 3 June 2019. UTJ Finch refused permission to apply for judicial review in a reserved decision dated 17 June 2019. Permission to appeal to this court was granted by Sir Wyn Williams on 17 February 2020.

[3] The appellant in the second appeal is Masud Rana. The SSHD wrote to him on 24 March 2015 informing him that his leave had been curtailed so that it now expired on 26 May 2015 ("the March 2015 decision"). Mr Rana says that he did not receive the March 2015 decision until it was brought to his attention in connection with other proceedings in 2018. On 4 November 2018 he commenced this application for judicial review in the UT which came before UTJ Freeman on the papers. By a decision dated 7 February 2019 UTJ Freeman refused permission to apply for judicial review and certified the application as totally without merit, thereby precluding an oral hearing. Permission to appeal to this court was given by Newey LJ on 8 November 2019.

Legal framework

[4] The way in which the SSHD may curtail leave to remain is prescribed by section 4(1) of the Immigration Act 1971 ("the 1971 Act"), which provides, so far as material, that this power:

"...shall be exercised by notice in writing given to the person affected".

[5] In *Syed v SSHD* [2013] UKUT 00144 (IAC) UTJ Spencer pointed out that, whilst there were regulations which dealt with the giving of notice in writing of "immigration decisions",[*] there were no corresponding regulations dealing with notice in writing of a decision to *curtail* leave to remain. That was because section 82(2) of the Nationality Immigration and Asylum Act 2002 defined "immigration decision" so as to exclude a decision the effect of which was to leave the applicant with some leave to remain. The notice in writing curtailing Mr Syed's leave had been twice sent by recorded delivery to his last known address and twice returned. In the absence of applicable regulations deeming service by post to be effective, effective notice had not been given to Mr Syed.

[6] Subsequently, in *R (Javed) v SSHD* [2014] EWHC 4426 (Admin), there was evidence that the notice had been sent by recorded delivery to an address which Mr Javed had provided to the SSHD when making a previous application for extension of leave to remain, but had been signed for by someone other than Mr Javed. Neil Garnham QC, sitting as a deputy High Court judge, held that, in the absence of specific regulations, it had not been established that Mr Javed had been given notice of the decision.

[7] Sections 3A and 3B of the 1971 Act, which were inserted by the Immigration and Asylum Act 1999, contain further provisions about leave to remain. Amongst these are section 3B(1) which gives the SSHD power to make further provision by order "with respect to the varying of leave to remain in the United Kingdom"; and section 3B(2)(a) which provides that an order under subsection (1) may provide for "the form or manner in which leave may be ... varied".

[8] The SSHD proceeded to make the Immigration (Leave to Enter and Remain) Order 2000 (SI 2000/1161) ("the 2000 Order"). Article 8 of the 2000 Order as originally made provided that a notice giving or refusing leave to *enter* (as particularly defined) could, instead of being given in writing as required by section 4(1) of the 1971 Act, be given by facsimile or electronic mail; and that in the case of a notice giving or refusing leave to enter the United Kingdom as a visitor, it may be given orally, including by means of a telecommunications system. These provisions did not relate to the curtailment of existing leave to remain.

[9] The 2000 Order was amended with effect from 12 July 2013 to contain further provisions dealing with the giving of notices. It was common ground that these amendments were made with a view to mitigating the effect of the decision in *Syed* and relaxing the requirements for effective service. Article 8ZA as so inserted provides how a section 4(1) notice in writing may be given to the person affected. It is headed "Grant, refusal or variation of leave by notice in writing" and provides so far as material:

---

[*] The Immigration (Notices) Regulations 2003 (SI 2003/658).

"(1)   A notice in writing –

...

(d)   varying a person's leave to enter or remain in the United Kingdom,

may be given to the person affected as required by section 4(1) of the Act as follows.

(2)   The notice may be –

(a)   given by hand;

(b)   sent by fax;

(c)   sent by postal service to a postal address provided for correspondence by the person or the person's representative;

(d)   sent electronically to an e-mail address provided for correspondence by the person or the person's representative;

(e)   sent by document exchange to a document exchange number or address; or

(f)   sent by courier.

(3)   Where no postal or e-mail address for correspondence has been provided, the notice may be sent –

(a)   by postal service to –

(i)   the last-known or usual place of abode, place of study or place of business of the person; or

(ii)   the last-known or usual place of business of the person's representative; or

(b)   electronically to –

(i)   the last-known e-mail address for the person (including at the person's last-known place of study or place of business); or

(ii)   the last-known e-mail address of the person's representative.

(4)   Where attempts to give notice in accordance with paragraphs (2) and (3) are not possible or have failed, when the decision-maker records the reasons for this and places the notice on file the notice shall be deemed to have been given.

(5)   Where a notice is deemed to have been given in accordance with paragraph (4) and then subsequently the person is located, the person shall as soon as is practicable be given a copy of the notice and details of when and how it was given.

(6)   A notice given under this article may, in the case of a person who is under the age of 18 years and does not have a representative, be given to the parent, guardian or another adult who for the time being takes responsibility for the child."

[10] Article 8ZB is headed "Presumptions about receipt of notice." It describes the effect of establishing that one of the methods of sending the notice in writing under Article 8ZA has been utilised:

"(1)   Where a notice is sent in accordance with article 8ZA, it shall be deemed to have been given to the person affected, unless the contrary is proved –

    (a)   where the notice is sent by postal service –

        (i)   on the second day after it was sent by postal service in which delivery or receipt is recorded if sent to a place within the United Kingdom;

        (ii)   on the 28th day after it was posted if sent to a place outside the United Kingdom;

    (b)   where the notice is sent by fax, e-mail, document exchange or courier, on the day it was sent.

(2)   For the purposes of paragraph (1)(a) the period is to be calculated excluding the day on which the notice is posted.

(3)   For the purposes of paragraph (1)(a)(i) the period is to be calculated excluding any day which is not a business day.

(4)   In paragraph (3) 'business day' means any day other than a Saturday, a Sunday, Christmas Day, Good Friday or a day which is a bank holiday under the Banking and Financial Dealings Act 1971 in the part of the United Kingdom to which the notice is sent."

[11] It is worth noting a few points about Articles 8ZA and 8ZB at this stage. First, it is clear that at least the special deeming provision in Article 8ZA(4) was an attempt to provide for valid service in a case like *Syed* where successive attempts to serve by recorded delivery had failed. It allows for what the Home Office sometimes refer to as "service to file", although it is not in any real sense service at all.

[12] Secondly, the deeming provision in respect of failure or impossibility to give notice, paragraph (4) of Article 8ZA, contrasts with the methods of service in paragraphs (1) to (3) of that Article. Paragraphs (1) to (3) do not expressly deem the giving or sending (as the case may be) of the notice in writing to be effective

service. In other words, they do not expressly deem the intended recipient to have received the notice. Rather, they appear simply to list permitted methods of service. In some contexts, provisions which state that service or the giving of notice may be carried out by a particular and specific method are treated as implicitly providing that service or notice by one of those methods amounts to good service or notice in law. In *Sun Alliance v London Assurance Co. Ltd v Hayman* [1975] 1 WLR 177 at 185 Lord Salmon, sitting as a member of the Court of Appeal with Stephenson LJ and McKenna J said:

> "Statutes and contracts often contain a provision that notice may be served on a person by leaving it at his last known place of abode or by sending it to him there through the post. The effect of such a provision is that if notice is served by any of the prescribed methods of service, it is, in law, treated as having been given and received."

[13] It is possible that paragraphs (1) to (3) of Article 8ZA were intended to be treated as operating in the way described by Lord Salmon. So to treat them would be to create a deemed or presumptive giving of notice where the prescribed method is followed. I do not think, however, that this can be correct as a matter of interpretation of Article 8ZA on its own. That is not just because it is difficult to treat paragraphs (1) to (3) as implicitly deeming receipt, when deemed receipt is dealt with explicitly by paragraph (4). Quite apart from that, the methods of service provided for by sub-paragraphs (b), (e) and (f) of Article 8ZA(2) are not specific as to the fax number, document exchange number or couriered address to which the notice in writing must, in each such case, be sent. It would be odd to create a necessary implication of service or notice simply because a document is sent to the person affected at an unspecified fax number. Yet, if this is a deeming provision, the fact that the document had never in fact been delivered would be irrelevant. As UTJ Grubb pointed out in *R (Mahmood) v SSHD (effective service – 2000 Order)* [2016] UKUT 57 (IAC) ("*Mahmood*"), such an interpretation would permit the SSHD to rely on decisions which the intended recipient had never had the opportunity to consider.

[14] Thirdly, and turning to Article 8ZB, Article 8ZB(1) is plainly a deeming provision, although questions arise as to its scope and effect. The deeming provision operates when "a notice is *sent*" in accordance with Article 8ZA. This language is apt to cover all the methods of giving notice in writing in 8ZA(2) and (3) except that in 8ZA(2)(a) where the notice is "given by hand" and not "sent". Further, it does not apply where the deeming provision in Article 8ZA(4) applies. Deemed service will arise under that provision when the decision-maker records the reasons for the impossibility or failure of attempts to give notice on the file. Nothing is sent.

[15] Fourthly, there is a noticeable omission in the deeming provisions associated with postal delivery. Article 8ZB(1)(a)(i) deals only with post sent by recorded delivery *in* the United Kingdom. Article 8ZB(1)(a)(ii) is not confined to recorded delivery, but is limited to post sent *outside* the United Kingdom. There is thus no provision dealing with time of receipt for post sent by ordinary mail within the United Kingdom. The only explanation proffered by counsel in this case was that the omission was deliberate so as to provide an incentive to the Home Office to use recorded delivery. Leaving gaps in legislation seems an odd way of

incentivising good practice by departmental officials. I cannot see any real purpose in the omission.

[16] The reason this omission of UK ordinary post matters is that it would appear that, as a result, no presumption at all applies where the notice in writing is sent by ordinary mail in the United Kingdom. To reach another conclusion one would have to read Article 8ZB(1) as if it contained two parts: the first deeming notice in writing to have been given to the person affected by following any of the specified methods of sending in Article 8ZA (thus including service by ordinary post in the United Kingdom) and the second deeming it to have been given on the specified date in the restricted class of cases expressly mentioned in Article 8ZB. A model for effecting a distinction between service and timing exists in the language of section 7 of the Interpretation Act 1978, but there is no trace of an attempt to effect such a distinction here. Section 7, which it was not suggested could fill this gap, provides:

> "Where an Act authorises or requires any document to be served by post (whether the expression "serve" or the expression 'give' or 'send' or any other expression is used) then, unless the contrary intention appears, the service is deemed to be effected by properly addressing, pre-paying and posting a letter containing the document and, unless the contrary is proved, to have been effected at the time at which the letter would be delivered in the ordinary course of post."

[17] Article 8ZB(1) is, in my view, not open to this disjunctive reading.

[18] A separate but related question is whether the deeming language of Article 8ZB is saying anything about the effectiveness of the giving of notice, or whether it is solely confined to deeming the time of receipt in the class of cases to which it does apply. An argument along these lines was pursued by the SSHD in *Mahmood* as recorded by UTJ Grubb at [51], but appears to have been either abandoned by the SSHD or rejected by the judge. In my judgement, the argument proceeds on a false dichotomy between the giving of notice and receipt of notice, which I will touch on further below.

[19] The appeal was argued on both sides, however, on the basis that the words "unless the contrary is proved" relate to both the giving of the notice in writing and the timing of its receipt. I think that agreement was correct, and its consequence is that Article 8ZB(1) only creates a rebuttable presumption which arises if one of the methods of sending in Article 8ZA is followed. In those circumstances, whilst it is true that the drafting leaves much to be desired, I proceed on the basis that Article 8ZB (a) deems the use of the methods of sending in Article 8ZA to be the valid giving of notice and (b) deems that notice to have given on the specified day, but leaves the person affected (or for that matter the SSHD if the need arises) free to prove (a) that he was not in fact given notice and/or (b) that it was not given on that day.

[20] The issue which really divided the parties on this appeal was what amounts to the giving of notice. On the most generous approach (to the appellants) to this issue, the requirement for the giving of notice could mean that the person affected must become aware of the contents of the decision. On this approach the person affected must not only have the notice in his hands, but must also have opened the envelope or other medium by which it is delivered and read it. The difficulty with this approach is that those who do not trouble to open their mail, or collect

recorded delivery items from the Post Office, or look at their emails, can effectively insulate themselves from being given notice. HHJ Blackett tried to explain how such an approach would work in *R (Rahman) v SSHD* [2019] EWHC 2952 at [20] where he said:

"In ordinary course, the Secretary of State is, therefore, entitled to presume that, provided the notice is given in accordance with article 8ZA, the notice has been given to the person affected and it can be presumed that the recipient thereby becomes aware of the contents. That is the case for good policy reasons. However, the presumption that it was 'given' can be rebutted if the contrary is proved. In my view proving the contrary is not limited to proving that the notice was not sent to the address provided for correspondence. In my view 'proving to the contrary' means that, where the person has not acted in bad faith (that is for example by moving address to avert detection and deliberately not informing the Home Office), demonstrating that he was not given, in the sense of being made aware of the notice, would be sufficient to prove the contrary. As the whole purpose of section 4 of the Immigration Act 1971 is to ensure that a person affected must be told the decision so that he or she may be able to act upon it, such a narrow interpretation would frustrate that purpose."

[21] Mr Biggs, who appeared for the appellants, supported this approach in his skeleton argument. In oral submissions, however, he did not support the good faith/bad faith distinction. In my judgement he was right not to do so, both because there is no basis in the language of the 2000 Order for such a distinction, and because the resultant approach is unworkable. Mr Biggs did recognise, however, that that the court would be unlikely to accept that a person affected had not been given notice when he had had the envelope in his hand but declined to open it.

[22] Mr Biggs also relied on statements in the authorities that in order for notice to be given it had to be "communicated" to the person affected. Thus, in *R (Anufrijeva) v SSHD* [2003] UKHL 36; [2004] 1 AC 604, the appellant asylum seeker had been refused asylum, and consequently lost her entitlement to state benefits, without any communication notifying her of the refusal of her asylum application. The majority of the House of Lords held that the decision to refuse her asylum had not taken effect when it was "recorded" as having been determined, as the SSHD contended. As Lord Steyn explained at paragraphs [26]:

"Notice of a decision is required before it can have the character of a determination with legal effect because the individual concerned must be in a position to challenge the decision in the courts if he or she wishes to do so. This is not a technical rule. It is simply an application of the right of access to justice".

[23] He went on to explain the importance of this principle for the rule of law at [28]:

"This view is reinforced by the constitutional principle requiring the rule of law to be observed. That principle too requires that a constitutional state must accord to individuals the right to know of a decision before their rights can be adversely affected. The antithesis of such a state was described by Kafka: a state where the rights of individuals are overridden by hole in the corner decisions or knocks on doors in the early hours. That is not our system."

[24] *Anufrijeva* was, of course, not concerned with what amounts to the giving of effective notice, because there was no question of any attempt at all having been made to communicate the decision to the appellant. Lord Steyn did, however, at [29], go on to compare the European law approach which requires that the person affected must have the opportunity to make themselves acquainted with the decision:

"In European law the approach is possibly a little more formalistic but the thrust is the same. It has been held to be a 'fundamental principle in the Community legal order ... that a measure adopted by the public authorities shall not be applicable to those concerned before they have the opportunity to make themselves acquainted with it:'"

[25] It was in this context that Lord Steyn explained, at [30], that the underlying principle was one of fairness:

"Until the decision in *Salem* [which was overruled by this decision] it had never been suggested that an uncommunicated administrative decision can bind an individual. It is an astonishingly unjust proposition. In our system of law surprise is regarded as the enemy of justice. Fairness is the guiding principle of our public law. In *R v Commission for Racial Equality, Ex p Hillingdon London Borough Council* [1982] AC 779, 787, Lord Diplock explained the position:

'Where an Act of Parliament confers upon an administrative body functions which involve its making decisions which affect to their detriment the rights of other persons or curtail their liberty to do as they please, there is a presumption that Parliament intended that the administrative body should act fairly towards those persons who will be affected by their decision.'

Where decisions are published or notified to those concerned accountability of public authorities is achieved. Elementary fairness therefore supports a principle that a decision takes effect only upon communication."

[26] These passages do not support the notion that a communication will only be effective if the decision has been read and understood by the person affected. The European law approach described by Lord Steyn speaks in terms of the party affected being given the opportunity to make themselves acquainted with the decision. If Lord Steyn had been contemplating a requirement for the decision to have been read and understood by the person affected before it was communicated to the person affected, he could hardly have considered the broad thrust of the European law as being the same, when that law merely requires that persons affected should "have the opportunity to make themselves acquainted with" the decision.

[27] Lord Millett, at [43], thought that reasonable steps to communicate with the person affected could be enough:

"I do not subscribe to the view that the failure to notify the appellant of the decision invalidated it, but I have come to the conclusion that it could not properly be recorded so as to deprive her of her right to income support until it was communicated to her; *or at least until reasonable steps were taken to do so.*" [emphasis added].

[28] In *UKI (Kingsway) Ltd v Westminster City Council* [2018] UKSC 67; [2019] PTSR 128, Lord Carnwarth cited with approval at [15] the observation of *Lord Salmon in Sun Alliance and London assurance Group v Hayman* (cited above):

"According to the ordinary and natural use of English words, giving a notice means causing a notice to be received. Therefore, any requirement in a statute or a contract for the giving of a notice can be complied with only by causing the notice to be actually received – unless the context or some statutory or contractual provision otherwise provides…".

[29] In my judgement, the giving of notice for the purposes of section 4(1) of the 1971 Act and the 2000 Order does not require that the intended recipient should have read and absorbed the contents of the notice in writing, merely that it be received. If it were not so, a failure to open an envelope containing the notice, for whatever reason, would mean that notice was not given. Similarly, I do not consider that the recipient must be made aware of the notice. Again, a recipient who allows mail to accumulate in a mailbox or on a hall table will not be aware of the notice. Proof of such facts should not enable the person to whom the mail is addressed to establish that the notice was not given, by being received.

[30] Receipt, and thus the giving of notice, can plainly be effected by placing the notice in the hands of the person affected. So much is recognised by Article 8ZA(2)(a). In my judgement, however, receipt in the case of an individual is not so limited. Receipt of an email, for example, will be effected by the arrival of the email in the Inbox of the person affected. Likewise, documents arriving by post will normally be received if they arrive, addressed to the person affected at the dwelling where he or she is living, at least in the absence of positive evidence that mail which so arrives is intercepted. A document received at an address provided to the SSHD for correspondence is received by the applicant, even if he does not bother to take steps to collect it.

[31] It follows that the burden of proving the negative, non-receipt, in the face of convincing evidence leading to the expectation of receipt, will not be lightly discharged. In particular it will not be discharged by evidence, far less by mere assertion, that the notice did not come to the attention of the person affected.

[32] It is not unreasonable to assume that judges in the Administrative Court will often be faced with applications for permission to apply for judicial review based on factual allegations that litigants did not receive notices in writing or other documents curtailing their leave to remain, and that in consequence the exercise by the SSHD of her powers in relation to that litigant have not been validly exercised. Some examination of the merits is necessary at the permission stage. I think that the test which should be applied is whether the material before the court raises a factual case which, taken at its highest, could properly succeed in a contested factual hearing. If so, permission should be granted, subject to

discretionary factors such as delay (compare by way of example *R (FZ) v London Borough of Croydon* [2011] EWCA Civ 59 at [6] to [9]).

[33] Drawing this together, when considering permission to apply for judicial review in such cases the following points should be borne in mind in the light of the above discussion:

(a)   where a method of sending within Article 8ZA (2) or (3) has been followed, the burden falls on the litigant to show he has a real prospect of establishing that the document was not received in the sense in which I have interpreted that word;

(b)   at the permission stage, the litigant will need to do more than show that the notice did not come to his attention, but establish how he proposes to show that it was never actually received in the sense which I have explained;

(c)   subject to discretionary factors such as delay, the question will be whether the material before the court raises a factual case which, taken at its highest, could properly succeed in a contested factual hearing;

(d)   each case will nevertheless depend on its own facts.

The facts of Mr Alam's case

[34] Mr Alam is a national of Bangladesh, born on 1 March 1989. He entered the UK with entry clearance on 1 October 2009 and was then granted leave to remain as a Tier 4 General Student. After successive subsequent applications and grants of leave to remain, his leave was due to expire on 30 July 2016. Before that occurred, on 24 September 2015 the sponsor licence of Bedfordshire Educational Academy where he was studying was revoked.

[35] The October 2015 decision curtailing Mr Alam's leave was addressed to him at 344A Grange Road, London, E13 0HQ ("the Grange Road address") in the sense that this is the address appearing on the letter itself. The letter stated that Mr Alam's leave had been curtailed to 22 December 2015. Under "Reasons for Decision", the decision stated:

"On 24 September 2015 the sponsor licence for Bedfordshire Educational Academy was revoked.

Home Office records have been checked and there is no evidence that you have made a fresh application for entry clearance, leave to enter or remain in the United Kingdom in any capacity.

It is not considered that the circumstances in your case are such that discretion should be exercised in your favour. The Secretary of State has therefore decided to curtail your leave to enter or remain as a Tier 4 Migrant so as to expire on 22 December 2016."

[36] On 30 July 2016, the day his original leave was due to expire, Mr Alam applied for further leave to remain on human rights grounds, but his application

was rejected as invalid by decision of 21 January 2017, which Mr Alam also claimed he never received. He sought to challenge the decision of 21 January 2017 by judicial review. Permission to apply for judicial review was refused, but permission to appeal to this court was granted by Sir Stephen Silber on 5 June 2018. In the course of negotiations to settle that appeal the appellant was provided with a copy of the October 2015 decision curtailing his leave to remain. The appeal was subsequently settled on terms.

Mr Alam contended that he had never received the October 2015 decision and on 11 September his representatives wrote to the SSHD with assertions to that effect. The SSHD replied on 25 September 2018 in a letter which included this:

"(ii) The SSHD submits that the curtailment notice was duly served on your client at his last known address – [the Grange Road address] via recorded delivery (tracking no KX409898502GB) at the time of the notice. The SSHD further submits that the onus was on your client to keep the Home Office updated with any change of addresses.

(iii) The SSHD therefore discharged his duty by serving your client with the curtailment notice at his last known address held by the home office at the time as is required under Sec 3(3)(a) and Sec 4(1) of the Immigration Act 1971."

[37] On 26 September 2018 Mr Alam issued the present judicial review proceedings. At section 7 of his claim form he asserts that he "never received such notice", i.e. the October 2015 notice curtailing his leave. The SSHD filed an acknowledgment of service exhibiting the Home Office General Case Information Database ("GCID") notes. At that time these notes gave an address for Mr Alam as 30 Adelaide Gardens, Romford, RM6 6SS ("the Adelaide Gardens address"). They record that the October 2015 decision was sent to Mr Alam on 19 October 2015 at 15:08 (although the decision is dated 20 October 2015). The decision is recorded as having been despatched by Emma Matthews. The despatch address is "Applicant" and an outgoing recorded delivery number KX409898502GB is quoted. Tracking data for this number is not available, due to the passage of time. The notes record that the decision was sent to Mr Alam "at his last known address".

[38] Mr Alam's amended grounds for permission dated 13 February 2019 sought to challenge the Home Office GCID records relating to sending the October 2015 decision. The grounds also criticised the absence of Royal Mail tracking confirming receipt by Mr Alam and relied on the contention that the presumption created by Article 8ZB of the 2000 Order had been rebutted. On 30 May 2019 Mr Alam applied for permission to rely on a witness statement. Paragraphs 6 and 7 of that witness statement stated:

"6. [The Grange Road address] I resided, it was a shared accommodation. I lived here along with some other flat mates. No one however informed me whether they received [the October 2015 decision] or anyone could have received this notice but did not serve on me.

7. I however believe, as I always maintain very good relations with others, if anyone could have received the said notice, he would have informed me of receiving the said notice. However, no one informed anything in this regard."

The decision of UTJ Finch in Mr Alam's case

[39] UTJ Finch first considered whether the question of whether there had been proper notice of the October 2015 decision was a question of "precedent fact" (as Mr Alam contended) or fell to be assessed by considering whether the SSHD's decision could be challenged on *Wednesbury* principles only. Having referred to a passage in *Mahmood*, she appears to have accepted the SSHD's contention.

[40] At paragraph 18 the judge cited Article 8ZA(2)(c), the provision which records that the notice may be sent by postal service to a postal address provided for correspondence by the person or the person's representative. She then went on to recite that Mr Alam accepted that the Adelaide Road address, which appears in the GCID, "was the one which he provided for service". She also noted the Adelaide Road address was the one which Mr Alam gave as his home address in his recent witness statement dated 29 March 2019. The judge was in error about the facts here, as Mr Hansen, who appeared for the SSHD, accepted. The notice was sent to the Grange Road address, which is where Mr Alam resided at the time.

[41] The judge held that the burden was on Mr Alam to show that the curtailment letter was not delivered ([23]), and that there was no further burden to show that the letter was actually delivered into the hands of the applicant ([24]). She also took judicial notice of the practice of leaving a card giving details of how a recorded delivery item which could not be delivered can be collected ([25]), remarking that there was no record of the letter being returned. She does not, however, go on to explain the relevance of the recorded delivery card to the facts of Mr Alam's case.

[42] At [27] the judge said that she had also considered whether, in the alternative, Mr Alam's witness statement would have rendered the SSHD's decision irrational. She concluded that the witness statement went no further than to make a bare assertion that other people living at "the address" may have signed for the letter and not given it to him or that they would have told him if such a letter had been sent to "the property". Mr Alam had not named any of the individuals concerned or provided any supporting evidence.

[43] She therefore concluded that the decision was not irrational or unlawful. As she had reached this conclusion on "a *Wednesbury* basis" it was not necessary for her to make any further findings as to the applicability of a precedent fact approach. She therefore refused permission to apply for judicial review.

Discussion – Mr Alam

[44] The decision of UTJ Finch is coloured by the dispute as to whether the court is required to look at matters through *Wednesbury* unreasonableness spectacles, or as a matter of "precedent fact". That dispute evaporated in this court when Mr Hansen accepted that the question for us was whether it was arguable that Mr Alam had not been given notice in writing of the October 2015 decision. If that was so, then the SSHD's power to curtail leave had arguably not been validly exercised and it was a proper case for granting permission to apply for judicial review. In my judgement that concession was correct. The court is not, in this

case, concerned with an issue to which the *Wednesbury* test can sensibly be applied. Whether the correct approach is properly labelled "precedent fact" as that term has been used in the authorities is not therefore a matter which needs further exploration.

[45] In my judgement permission to apply for judicial review was nevertheless correctly refused in this case. The SSHD's case that notice of the October 2015 decision had not merely been sent to Mr Alam but delivered to him at the place where, as he accepted, he was living was a powerful one which had been fully particularised and supported by contemporaneous documents, in particular the GCID notes. In addition, Mr Hansen drew our attention to contemporaneous guidance to Home Office officials which suggested that a second attempt at service must be undertaken if a curtailment decision is returned undelivered. There was no suggestion in the GCID notes or elsewhere that the notice had been returned. That all amounts to a strong case that it was received at the address where Mr Alam was living.

[46] Against this there was nothing positive to rebut the SSHD's case. On the view which I have expressed as to the requirement for the giving of notice, it does not avail Mr Alam to say that that the notice did not come to his actual attention. Indeed, to be fair, there is some corroboration for his assertion that he was unaware of the decision in the fact that his application to extend his leave was not made until 30 July 2016, the date when his original leave expired. Had he been aware of the curtailment he would have been likely to apply for further leave within the period of curtailed leave. The focus of the enquiry, however, is on whether the notice had been received. As to that, there is only Mr Alam's assertion that it would have come to his attention had it been delivered. This was based on his belief that, because he always maintained good relations with others, his flatmates would have informed him had they received the notice.

[47] In his skeleton argument Mr Biggs submitted that the effect of this evidence was that Mr Alam had undertaken enquiries as to what might have happened to the notice. In his oral submissions he spontaneously corrected that: but the correction demonstrates the poverty of what is actually said, which amounts to little more than Mr Alam's good relations with his flatmates.

[48] It seems to me that, on the material before the judge, three possibilities needed to be examined. These were (a) that the notice had not in fact been delivered to Mr Alam's address at all; (b) that the notice had been delivered but intercepted by a flatmate and not handed to Mr Alam; (c) that the notice had been delivered but been overlooked or left unopened by Mr Alam himself. There was no evidence of any value to prove non-delivery under (a) and much convincing evidence the other way. Mr Alam had himself discounted the possibility of (b) on the basis of his good relations with his flatmates. That pointed to (c) as a likely explanation. In a flat in multiple occupancy there are ample opportunities for envelopes (even those signed for on receipt) to go unnoticed unless proper care is taken. There is no evidence that Mr Alam conducted any enquiries as to whether any document was delivered at around the relevant time. There is no evidence as to what steps Mr Alam habitually took to ensure he became aware of deliveries. Mr Alam does not even describe his movements at or around the time the delivery would have occurred.

[49] Mr Biggs reminded us that if the judicial review proceeded, Mr Alam would be able to obtain disclosure and apply to cross-examine someone from the Home Office. Given the materials already produced by the SSHD, the prospect

that that course might prove to be fruitful in this case seem to me to be vanishingly small. In my judgement, taking the evidence before the judge at its highest, Mr Alam did not have a real prospect of showing that the notice had not been delivered to him, and permission to apply for judicial review was rightly refused. I would dismiss his appeal.

The facts of Mr Rana's case

[50] Mr Rana is a national of Bangladesh born on 7 September 1989. He entered the United Kingdom on 25 October 2009 with entry clearance as a Tier 4 (General) Student. In January of 2012 he was granted leave to remain as a Tier 4 (General) Student enrolled with BPP University College of Professional Studies ("BPP") until 30 September 2015. On 15 December 2014, BPP contacted the Home Office to notify them that "the applicant has been withdrawn from the programme due to the failure to progress academically". The applicant contacted the SSHD and asked for a "60 day curtailment letter". The SSHD in due course responded by sending a letter to the applicant at Flat 10 Weddell House, Duckett Street, London E1 4LT ("the Weddell House address") dated 24 March 2015 ("the March 2015 decision"). The March 2015 decision curtailed Mr Rana's leave to expire on 26 May 2015.

[51] According to the GCID notes for his case, the March 2015 decision was sent by recorded delivery with a number KR791845689GB. The notes record: "issued ICD 3971 to migrant at: Flat 10 Weddell House" and that "Royal Mail track and trace shows signed for 25 March 2015. Signed name Rana".

[52] On 25 September 2015 Mr Rana applied for an EEA residence card pursuant to the Immigration (EEA) Regulations 2006. His appeal from the refusal of that application was heard on 10 October 2018 and was dismissed, but at the hearing he was provided with a copy of the March 2015 decision and the GCID records.

[53] Mr Rana then issued a letter of claim dated 11 October 2018 in which he challenged the service of the March 2015 decision on the basis that the SSHD bore the burden of proving that Mr Rana had received the decision, and that the SSHD had not discharged this burden. The SSHD responded on 25 October 2018, relying on the GCID records to establish posting of the decision to the Weddell Street address, and its receipt by someone identifying themselves as "Rana". Mr Rana's claim for judicial review and the SSHD's response followed. The SSHD drew attention to the presumptions introduced by the 2000 Order to dispute Mr Rana's contention as to where the burden of proof lay.

[54] In his witness statement Mr Rana said:

"On 25 October 2018, the Respondent responded to the pre-action protocol and states that I signed the 60-day notice post on 25 March 2015. I deny the Respondent's claim and would maintain my position that I never received such letter."

The decision of UTJ Freeman in Mr Rana's case

[55] The decision of UTJ Freeman in Mr Rana's case is short. Having set out the history he said:

"The applicant challenges the 'decision' of 10 October [2018] [that is the date on which he was given the October 2015 decision in the course of his residence card appeal], on the basis that service after the notice has expired was ineffective, which might have been arguable, if that were all; but the original service on 25 March 2015 was unarguably valid, in accordance with article 8ZB of the Immigration (Leave to Enter and Remain) order 2000.

The applicant complains that the Royal Mail tracking reference could not be traced; but the applicant's acknowledgement of service, filed and served on 18 December 2018, points out that the tracking service is only available for 12 to 18 months after delivery. There has been no attempt by the applicant to answer this point, and there is no possible basis on which this claim could succeed."

Discussion – Mr Rana

[56] The SSHD's evidence before UTJ Freeman that the notice was delivered to Mr Rana's address was compelling. There was no evidence in answer beyond Mr Rana's assertion that he did not receive it. That it is plainly not sufficient to show a real prospect of proving that the notice was not delivered. I would dismiss his appeal.

Conclusion

[57] For the reasons I have given, I would dismiss both appeals.

LORD JUSTICE HENDERSON:
[58] I agree.

LORD JUSTICE PHILLIPS:
[59] I also agree.

UNUANE v UNITED KINGDOM

EUROPEAN COURT OF HUMAN RIGHTS (FOURTH SECTION)

Y Grozev (President), I A Motoc, G Kucsko-Stadlmayer, P Pastor Vilanova, T Eicke, J Schukking, A M Guerra Martins (Judges) and I Freiwirth (Deputy Section Registrar)

Application no. 80343/17
24 November 2020

Human rights – Article 8 of the ECHR – private and family life – proportionality – foreign criminals – best interests of the child – serious medical condition – strong ties to partner and children – unduly harsh to separate family

The Applicant was a citizen of Nigeria. He first met his partner, a Nigerian national, in 1992 when they were both living in Nigeria. They married in 1995, but the relationship broke down. In 1998 the Applicant arrived in the United Kingdom as a visitor. He dissolved his marriage and married a Portuguese national in 1999. The Applicant was granted a right of residence in the United Kingdom. His Nigerian partner entered the United Kingdom in December 2000. Shortly thereafter the Applicant re-commenced his relationship with his former partner and they had three children, D, B and C. The couple's eldest child, D, was diagnosed with a rare congenital heart defect as a baby. In November 2009 the Applicant and his partner were convicted of offences relating to the falsification of some 30 applications for leave to remain in the United Kingdom. The Applicant was sentenced to five and a half years of imprisonment, while his partner was sentenced to 18 months imprisonment.

In June 2014 the Secretary of State for the Home Department made a deportation order against the Applicant and his partner pursuant to section 32(5) of the UK Borders Act 2007. A deportation order was also made against B and C as dependent family members of the Applicant's partner. At that time D was a British citizen, but B and C were not. The Secretary of State considered that D could voluntarily depart the United Kingdom to continue his family life with his parents and siblings in Nigeria, where he could avail himself of treatment for his heart condition. The Applicant appealed on the ground that his deportation to Nigeria would be in breach of Article 8 of the ECHR. He argued that the Secretary of State had given insufficient weight to his children's best interests. The Applicant's partner, together with B and C, appealed on similar grounds.

In dismissing the Applicant's appeal, the First-tier Tribunal ("FtT") treated his family as his dependants, whose appeals fell to be determined in line with his. The Upper Tribunal ("UT") found that the FtT had made a material error of law by treating the appeals as indivisible. The UT set aside the decision of the FtT and reheard the appeals. The UT found that it was in the best interests of B and C to remain in the United Kingdom with both parents. The UT acknowledged that there was clear evidence that the surgery D required in the future was not available in Nigeria and that it would not be possible for him to return to the United Kingdom from Nigeria for the surgery as medical treatment under the NHS was residence based. Having accepted that D could not leave the United Kingdom, the UT considered that it would be undesirable to split the siblings. The UT allowed the appeals of the Applicant's partner and children on the ground that separating them would be "unduly harsh" on the children. The UT did not find very compelling circumstances outweighing the Applicant's deportation and dismissed his appeal. The Court of Appeal refused permission to appeal. The Applicant was deported in February 2018.

Held, finding a violation of Article 8 of the ECHR;

(1) The Government had accepted before the UT as well as before the Court that the Applicant's deportation would constitute an interference with his rights under Article 8(1) of the ECHR. Moreover, it was not in doubt that the deportation order was "in accordance with the law" and "in pursuit of a legitimate aim" for the purposes of Article 8(2) of the ECHR. Consequently, the principal issue to be determined was whether the Applicant's deportation was "necessary in a democratic society", or, in other words, whether the deportation order struck a fair balance between the Applicant's Convention rights and the community's interests (*para 77*).

(2) The criteria which emerged from the case law in *Boultif v Switzerland* 2001 ECHR 54273/00 and *Üner v Netherlands* 2006 ECHR 46410/99 was primarily meant to facilitate the application of Article 8 in expulsion cases by domestic courts. Nevertheless, in applying those criteria, the respective weight to be attached to them would inevitably vary according to the specific circumstances of each case: *Maslov v Austria* 2008 ECHR 1638/03 and *AA v United Kingdom* 2011 ECHR 8000/08 considered. In the light of the relevant domestic case law, the Immigration Rules HC 395 (as amended) did not necessarily preclude the domestic courts and tribunals from employing the *Boultif* criteria for the purpose of assessing whether an expulsion measure was necessary and proportionate. In the instant case, the UT had neither made any substantial further findings adverse to the Applicant nor conducted a separate balancing exercise as required by the Court's case law under Article 8 of the ECHR. In fact, the UT had merely noted that it could not allow his appeal on the basis that paragraph 398 of the Immigration Rules "imposed requirements" to identify "very compelling circumstances" over and above the accepted genuine and subsisting parental relationship with the children, something which the Applicant could not establish. It therefore fell to the Court, in exercise of its supervisory jurisdiction, to give the final ruling on whether an expulsion measure was reconcilable with Article 8 of the ECHR (*paras 78 – 85*).

(3) The Applicant had been convicted of offences that were undoubtedly serious, as evidenced by the length of the prison sentence. Furthermore, it was not his first criminal conviction in the United Kingdom. In February 2005 he had been convicted of obtaining a money transfer by deception, for which he was sentenced to a period of unpaid work and ordered to pay a fine. That being said, the Court had tended to consider the seriousness of a crime not merely by reference to the length of the sentence imposed, but rather by reference to the nature and circumstances of the particular criminal offence or offences committed by the applicant in question and their impact on society as a whole. In that context, the Court had consistently treated crimes of violence and drug-related offences as being at the most serious end of the criminal spectrum. In any event, the fact that

the offence committed by an applicant was at the more serious end of the criminal spectrum was not in and of itself determinative of the case. Rather, it was just one factor which had to be weighed in the balance, together with the other criteria which emerged from the judgments in *Boultif* and *Üner* (*paras 86 and 87*).

(4) The UT had weighed those other criteria in the balance, albeit exclusively with reference to the Applicant's partner. Having concluded that it would be in the best interests of the children to remain in the United Kingdom with both of their parents and that it would be "unduly harsh" to separate them, the UT had allowed the Applicant's partner's appeal and those of the children under Article 8 of the ECHR. Although many of the factors relevant to the Applicant's partner's appeal had been essentially the same as those relevant to his own, his appeal had been dismissed on the sole basis that there had been no "very compelling circumstances" over and above those which had applied in respect of his partner. That conclusion was not reconcilable with Article 8 of the ECHR. The UT had acknowledged the strength of the Applicant's ties to his partner and children, all of whom would stay in the United Kingdom. It had also acknowledged that his partner and children needed him, and that need for parental support had been particularly acute in the case of D on account of his medical condition and forthcoming surgery. Finally, it had accepted that it was in the best interests of the children for him to remain in the United Kingdom, a factor which had to be accorded significant weight. Having regard to those careful and detailed findings by the UT which had to carry significant weight in the overall assessment of proportionality, in the circumstances, the seriousness of the particular offences committed by the Applicant were not of a nature or degree capable of outweighing the best interests of the children so as to justify his expulsion. The Applicant's deportation had therefore been disproportionate to the legitimate aim pursued and as such had not been "necessary in a democratic society" (*paras 88 and 89*).

Cases referred to:

AA v United Kingdom 2011 ECHR 8000/08; [2012] Imm AR 107; [2012] INLR 1
AW Khan v United Kingdom 2010 ECHR 47486/06; (2010) 50 EHRR 47; [2010] Imm AR 40; [2010] INLR 567
Abdulaziz, Cabales and Balkandali v United Kingdom 1985 ECHR 9214/80, ECtHR; (1985) 7 EHRR 471
Alam v Denmark 2017 ECHR 33809/15; (2017) 65 EHRR SE10
Baghli v France 1999 ECHR 34374/97; (2001) 33 EHRR 32
Boujlifa v France 1997 ECHR 25404/94, ECtHR; (2000) 30 EHRR 419
Boultif v Switzerland 2001 ECHR 54273/00; (2001) 33 EHRR 50
Dalia v France 1998 ECHR 26102/95, ECtHR; (2001) 33 EHRR 26
Hamesevic v Denmark 2017 ECHR 25748/15
Hesham Ali (Iraq) v Secretary of State for the Home Department [2016] UKSC 60; [2016] 1 WLR 4799; [2017] 3 All ER 20; [2017] Imm AR 484; [2017] INLR 109
Izuazu (Article 8 – new rules) [2013] UKUT 45 (IAC); [2013] Imm AR 453; [2013] INLR 733
Jeunesse v Netherlands 2014 ECHR 12738/10; (2015) 60 EHRR 17
Krasniqi v Austria 2017 ECHR 41697/12
Lukic v Germany 2011 ECHR 25021/08
MF (Article 8 – new rules) Nigeria [2012] UKUT 393 (IAC); [2013] Imm AR 256

MF (Nigeria) v Secretary of State for the Home Department [2013] EWCA Civ 1192; [2014] 1 WLR 544; [2014] 2 All ER 543; [2014] Imm AR 211; [2014] INLR 18

Maslov v Austria 2008 ECHR 1638/03; (2008) 47 EHRR 20; [2009] INLR 47

NA (Pakistan) v Secretary of State for the Home Department; Secretary of State for the Home Department v KJ (Angola), WM (Afghanistan) and MY (Kenya) [2016] EWCA Civ 662; [2017] 1 WLR 207; [2017] Imm AR 1; [2016] INLR 587

Ndidi v United Kingdom 2017 ECHR 41215/14

Odelola v Secretary of State for the Home Department [2009] UKHL 25; [2009] 1 WLR 1230; [2009] 3 All ER 1061; [2010] Imm AR 59; [2009] INLR 401

R (on the application of Agyarko) v Secretary of State for the Home Department; R (on the application of Ikuga) v Secretary of State for the Home Department [2017] UKSC 11; [2017] 1 WLR 823; [2017] 4 All ER 575; [2017] 3 CMLR 3; [2017] Imm AR 764; [2017] INLR 548

Slivenko v Latvia 2003 ECHR 48321/99; (2004) 39 EHRR 24

Üner v Netherlands 2006 ECHR 46410/99; (2007) 45 EHRR 14; [2007] Imm AR 303; [2007] INLR 273

Legislation and international instruments judicially considered:

Borders, Citizenship and Immigration Act 2009, section 55
European Convention on Human Rights, Articles 8, 13 & 41
Human Rights Act 1998, sections 2, 3 & 6
Immigration Act 1971, section 3(5)
Immigration Rules HC 395 (as amended), paragraphs A362 & A398 – 399A
Nationality, Immigration and Asylum Act 2002, section 117C
UK Borders Act 2007, sections 32 & 33

Representation

Ms N Burgess, lawyer for the Joint Council for the Welfare of Immigrants, for the Applicant;
Ms P Fudakowska, Agent of the Foreign and Commonwealth Office, for the United Kingdom Government.

JUDGMENT

INTRODUCTION

[1] The applicant complained under Article 8 of the Convention that his deportation to Nigeria disproportionately interfered with his family and private life. He further complained, under Article 8 of the Convention taken alone and/or read together with Article 13 of the Convention, that domestic law had prevented the relevant decision-makers from conducting a detailed proportionality assessment.

THE FACTS

[2] The applicant, Mr Charles Unuane, is a Nigerian national who was born in 1963. He is represented before the Court by Ms N. Burgess of the Joint Council for the Welfare of Immigrants, a lawyer practising in London.

[3] The Government were represented by their Agent, Ms P. Fudakowska of the Foreign and Commonwealth Office.

[4] The facts of the case, as submitted by the parties, may be summarised as follows.

A. Background

[5] The applicant is a Nigerian national born in 1963. He has three children with his Nigerian partner: D (born 2002); B (born 2004); and C (born 2006). While D has been a British citizen throughout, B and C have since also been registered as British citizens. Shortly after birth D was diagnosed with pulmonary atresia with intact ventricular septum, a rare congenital heart defect.

[6] The applicant first met his current partner in 1992 when both were living in Nigeria. They married in 1995, but the relationship broke down in 1998. In 1998, the applicant came to the United Kingdom as a visitor, whereupon he commenced a relationship with a Portuguese national. In 1999, the applicant dissolved his marriage with his partner and married the Portuguese national. The applicant was granted a right of residence in August 1999. In December 2000, the applicant's Nigerian partner entered the United Kingdom and shortly thereafter he recommenced his relationship with her. Their three children were born thereafter.

[7] In February 2005 the applicant was convicted of obtaining a money transfer by deception. He was sentenced to a period of unpaid work and ordered to pay a fine. In November 2009 the applicant and his partner were both convicted of offences relating to the falsification of some thirty applications for leave to remain in the United Kingdom. The applicant was ultimately sentenced to a period of five years and six months imprisonment, while his partner was sentenced to eighteen months imprisonment.

[8] The applicant's custodial sentence ended on 26 October 2012. Thereafter he remained in immigration detention until 6 November 2012.

B. Deportation proceedings

[9] On 2 June 2014, the Secretary of State for the Home Department made a deportation order against the applicant. Pursuant to section 32(5) of the United Kingdom Borders Act 2007 ("the 2007 Act") the Secretary of State was required to make a deportation order in respect of foreign criminals sentenced, *inter alia*, to a period of imprisonment of at least twelve months. The Secretary of State considered that the applicant was a foreign criminal as defined by section 32(1) of the 2007 Act and accordingly his deportation, by virtue of section 32(4) of the 2007 Act, was deemed to be conducive to the public good. A further deportation order was made against the applicant's partner for the same reasons. In addition, a deportation order was made against B and C as dependent family members of the applicant's partner. At the time, unlike D, B and C were not yet British citizens.

[10] On 16 June 2014 the Secretary of State provided reasons for her decision. The Secretary of State considered the applicant's family and private life rights

under Article 8 of the Convention in line with the Immigration Rules. By virtue of paragraph 398 of the Immigration Rules (see paragraphs 29–34 below), where a person had been sentenced to a period of imprisonment of at least four years, the person would be required to show "exceptional circumstances" outweighing the public interest before his or her Article 8 claim could succeed. The applicant had been sentenced to a period of imprisonment of at least four years. In relation to the impact on D, the Secretary of State considered that he could voluntarily depart the United Kingdom to continue his family life with his parents and siblings in Nigeria, where he could avail himself of treatment for his heart condition. Accordingly, the Secretary of State concluded that the applicant had failed to demonstrate any exceptional circumstances to outweigh the public interest in favour of deportation.

C. The appeal proceedings

[11] The applicant appealed the Secretary of State's decision on the grounds that he had an established family life and private life in the United Kingdom and his deportation to Nigeria would be in breach of Article 8 of the Convention. In particular, the applicant argued that the Secretary of State had given insufficient weight to the applicant's children, particularly D, who was a British citizen. The applicant's partner, together with B and C, also appealed on similar grounds.

[12] On 9 February 2015 the First-tier Tribunal dismissed the applicant's appeal. The First-tier Tribunal treated the applicant's family as his dependents, whose appeal fell to be determined in line with his. This meant that the applicant's partner could not succeed if the applicant himself did not succeed. In March 2015 the First-tier Tribunal granted the applicant permission to appeal the decision.

[13] On 28 January 2016 the Upper Tribunal allowed the applicant's appeal. The Upper Tribunal found that the First-tier Tribunal had made a material error of law by treating the appeals as indivisible. The Upper Tribunal set aside the decision of the First-tier Tribunal and listed the appeals to be heard again by the Upper Tribunal.

D. Decision of the Upper Tribunal of 5 October 2016

[14] On 4 June 2016 the Upper Tribunal heard the appeals of the applicant, his partner and B and C. It gave judgment on 5 October 2016.

[15] The medical evidence presented to the Upper Tribunal consisted of a report prepared by a consultant paediatric cardiologist at a leading children's hospital, who had been responsible for D's treatment throughout, dated February 2016. This report explained that D had already undergone three open heart operations and that he would require further open heart surgery in order to replace a tube between the right ventricle and the lung arteries in the "reasonably near future". The report suggested that this could be required at some point in the next three to four years. The report further stated that the necessary surgery would not be available in Nigeria and accordingly sending D to Nigeria would have a "significant impact on his long-term future". The report's conclusion that the necessary surgery would not be available in Nigeria was not challenged by the Secretary of State.

[16] The applicant further relied on the content of a report by the Offender Assessment System, in which the Probation Service apparently indicated that he

was at "no risk of reoffending". However, his representatives were unable to produce a copy of the report.

[17] In addition, there was evidence before the Tribunal that the applicant's parents and five of his siblings still lived in Nigeria, as did his partner's mother and five of her siblings.

[18] The Upper Tribunal's determination began by considering the appeals on behalf of the children B and C, who had lived all their lives in the United Kingdom. They had no experience of life in Nigeria and, as their parents were not "well-connected" there, they would be unlikely to go back to "good circumstances". It therefore had "no hesitation" in saying that it was in the best interest of the children for them to remain in the United Kingdom with both their parents, who, notwithstanding their criminal activities, had managed to produce well-adjusted children. According to the Tribunal, it would be facile to pretend that the applicant had not contributed to this success. Nevertheless, it did not follow that any of the parties should be allowed to remain. The Tribunal then considered the position of D. It acknowledged that there was clear evidence that the necessary surgery which he would require in the future was not available in Nigeria. Furthermore, given that medical treatment under the National Health Service was residence-based, it would not be possible for D to go to Nigeria and return to the United Kingdom at some point in the future for the surgery. In any event, as D was a British citizen and a minor, he could not be expected to leave the United Kingdom. The Tribunal further accepted that on account of his medical condition and forthcoming surgery his need for parental support was enhanced and "as a matter of informed common sense, it would be good for him to have the support of his mother at that time just as it would be good for the mother to be able to be near him". Having accepted that D could not leave the United Kingdom, the Tribunal considered that it would be undesirable to split the siblings. It therefore concluded, having regard to the Immigration Rules with reference to Article 8 of the Convention, that the appeals of the applicant's partner and minor children were allowable because the effect of separating them would be "unduly harsh" on the children.

[19] In relation to the applicant, the Tribunal concluded that they could not allow his appeal despite the fact that the "arguments in favour of his remaining for the sake of the children are in some cases the same as the case of the [wife]. The wife needs him and she is staying. The boys need him". Nevertheless, the Tribunal concluded that:

"... Parliament has imposed requirements on the Article 8 balancing exercise which we have to follow. Paragraph 398 of HC395 requires that in a case where a person has been sentenced to at least four years' imprisonment (as has the first Appellant) then the public interest in deportation will outweigh other factors unless there are 'very compelling circumstances over and above those described in paragraphs 399 and 399A'.

These are Rules that deal with people in genuine and subsisting parental relationships with the children and who have been in the United Kingdom for a long time themselves. We are quite satisfied that there is a genuine and subsisting parental relationship with the children but there are no 'very compelling circumstances over and above those described at paragraphs 399 and 399A'.

We raised the point with Counsel at the beginning of the hearing. It is no discredit to him that he was not really able to point to anything that would satisfy the requirements of this Rule. The point is echoed in Section 117C of the Nationality, Immigration and Asylum Act 2002 which requires that in the case of a person sentenced to at least four years' imprisonment 'the public interest requires deportation unless there are very compelling circumstances, over and above those described in Sections 1 and 2'.

For similar reasons, there are no such very compelling circumstances here."

[20] The applicant's appeal was therefore dismissed.

E. Subsequent proceedings

[21] The applicant sought permission to appeal the Upper Tribunal's decision on the ground, *inter alia*, that it did not consider the relevant "Strasbourg factors" which, following the judgment of the Supreme Court in *Hesham Ali v Secretary of State for the Home Department* (see paragraphs 46–49 below), ought to have fed into its analysis. By a decision dated 2 October 2017, the Court of Appeal refused permission to appeal as it considered that the decision under challenge contained "no arguable errors of law".

[22] The applicant was deported on 27 February 2018.

RELEVANT LEGAL FRAMEWORK AND PRACTICE

A. Domestic law and practice

1. The Human Rights Act 1998

[23] Section 2 of the Human Rights Act 1998 provides that, in determining any question that arises in connection with a Convention right, courts and tribunals must take into account any case-law from this Court so far as it is relevant to the proceedings in which that question has arisen.

[24] Section 3(1) provides that primary and subordinate legislation must be read and given effect in a way which is compatible with Convention rights so far as it is possible to do so and section 6(1) makes it unlawful for a public authority to act in a way which is incompatible with a Convention right.

2. Deportation of a foreign criminal

(a) The Immigration Act 1971

[25] Section 3(5) of the Immigration Act 1971 provides that a person who is not a British citizen is liable to deportation from the United Kingdom if (a) the Secretary of State deems his deportation to be conducive to the public good, or (b) another person to whose family he belongs is or has been ordered to be deported.

(b) The United Kingdom Borders Act 2007

[26] Section 32(4) and (5) of the United Kingdom Borders Act 2007 provides that, subject to section 33, the Secretary of State "must" make a deportation order in respect of a "foreign criminal", and, for the purposes of section 3(5)(a) of the

Immigration Act 1971, the deportation of a foreign criminal is conducive to the public good. A foreign criminal is defined as a person who is not a British citizen, who has been convicted in the United Kingdom of an offence and sentenced to a period of imprisonment of at least twelve months.

[27] According to section 33, section 32(4) and (5) does not apply where the removal of the foreign criminal in pursuance of the deportation order would breach his rights under either the Refugee Convention or the European Convention on Human Rights.

(c) Borders, Citizenship and Immigration Act 2009

[28] Section 55 of the Borders, Citizenship and Immigration Act 2009 places the Secretary of State for the Home Department under a duty to make arrangements for ensuring that any functions in relation to immigration, asylum or nationality are discharged having regard to the need to safeguard and promote the welfare of children who are in the United Kingdom.

(d) The Immigration Rules

[29] As the House of Lords confirmed in its judgment in *Odelola v Secretary of State for the Home Department* [2009] UKHL 25 (*per* Lord Hoffmann at paragraph 6), the Immigration Rules are detailed statements by the Secretary of State for the Home Department which set out how she proposes to exercise the power of the executive to control immigration. They are not subordinate legislation but they do create legal rights: for example, under section 84(1) of the Nationality, Immigration and Asylum Act 2002, one may appeal against an immigration decision on the ground that it is not in accordance with the Immigration Rules.

[30] On 9 July 2012 the Secretary of State amended the Immigration Rules to include new rules on deportation. The new rules provided as follows:

"Where Article 8 is raised in the context of deportation under Part 13 of these Rules, the claim under Article 8 will only succeed where the requirements of these Rules as at 9 July 2012 are met, regardless of when the notice of intention to deport or the deportation order, as appropriate, was served."

[31] Paragraphs 398 to 399A set out the situations in which a foreign criminal's private and/or family life would be deemed to outweigh the public interest in effecting his or her deportation. In the case of offenders sentenced to between twelve months and four years' imprisonment, the new rules identified a number of situations in which the public interest in deportation would be outweighed. However, for more serious offenders sentenced to four or more years' imprisonment, the public interest in deportation would only be outweighed in "exceptional circumstances".

[32] The Explanatory Memorandum stated that:

"The new Immigration Rules will reform the approach taken as a matter of public policy towards ECHR Article 8 – the right to respect for family and private life – in immigration cases. The Immigration Rules will fully reflect the factors which can weigh for or against an Article 8 claim. The rules will set proportionate requirements that reflect the Government's and Parliament's view of how individuals' Article 8 rights should be qualified in the public interest to safeguard the economic well-being of the UK by controlling immigration and to protect the public against foreign criminals. This will mean that failure to meet the requirements of the rules will normally mean failure to establish an Article 8 claim to enter or remain in the UK, and no grant of leave on that basis. Outside exceptional cases, it will be proportionate under Article 8 for an applicant who fails to meet the requirement of the rules to be removed from the UK."

[33] On 13 June 2012, the Home Office issued a statement entitled "Immigration Rules on Family and Private Life: Grounds of Compatibility with Article 8 of the European Convention on Human Rights". According to the statement:

"The intention is that the Rules will state how the balance should be struck between the public interest and individual right, taking into account relevant case law, and thereby provide for a consistent and fair decision-making process. Therefore, if the Rules are proportionate, a decision taken in accordance with the Rules will, other than in exceptional cases, be compatible with A8."

[34] The statement concluded that "[i]t is the Department's view that the new Rules on family and private life are compatible with ECHR Article 8".

(e) Nationality, Immigration and Asylum Act 2002

[35] Section 19 of the Immigration Act 2014 inserted Part 5A (Sections 117A to 117D) into the Nationality, Immigration and Asylum Act 2002, which came into force on 28 July 2014. Part 5A applies where a court or tribunal is required to determine whether a decision made under the Immigration Acts breaches a person's right to respect for private and family life under Article 8 of the Convention. In cases concerning the deportation of foreign criminals a court or tribunal must have regard to the considerations listed in section 117C, which provides as relevant:

"117C Article 8: additional considerations in cases involving foreign criminals

(1)   The deportation of foreign criminals is in the public interest.

(2)   The more serious the offence committed by a foreign criminal, the greater is the public interest in deportation of the criminal.

(3)   In the case of a foreign criminal ("C") who has not been sentenced to a period of imprisonment of four years or more, the public interest requires C's deportation unless Exception 1 or Exception 2 applies.

(4)   Exception 1 applies where –

(a)   C has been lawfully resident in the United Kingdom for most of C's life,

(b)   C is socially and culturally integrated in the United Kingdom, and

(c)   there would be very significant obstacles to C's integration into the country to which C is proposed to be deported.

(5)   Exception 2 applies where C has a genuine and subsisting relationship with a qualifying partner, or a genuine and subsisting parental relationship with a qualifying child, and the effect of C's deportation on the partner or child would be unduly harsh.

(6)   In the case of a foreign criminal who has been sentenced to a period of imprisonment of at least four years, the public interest requires deportation unless there are very compelling circumstances, over and above those described in Exceptions 1 and 2."

(f) The Immigration Rules as further amended in July 2014

[36] On 10 July 2014, the Secretary of State laid before Parliament a Statement of Changes in Immigration Rules (HC 532), which made further amendments to the rules on deportation. Paragraph A362 of the Immigration Rules states:

"Where Article 8 is raised in the context of deportation under Part 13 of these Rules [paragraphs A362 to 400], the claim under Article 8 will only succeed where the requirements of these rules as at 28 July 2014 are met, regardless of when the notice of intention to deport or the deportation order, as appropriate, was served."

[37] The test in the amended rules echoes the test contained in section 117C of the Nationality, Immigration and Asylum Act 2002. In particular, paragraphs A398 to 399A state:

"Deportation and Article 8

A398. These rules apply where:

(a)   a foreign criminal liable to deportation claims that his deportation would be contrary to the United Kingdom's obligations under Article 8 of the Human Rights Convention;

(b)   a foreign criminal applies for a deportation order made against him to be revoked.

398. Where a person claims that their deportation would be contrary to the UK's obligations under Article 8 of the Human Rights Convention, and

(a)   the deportation of the person from the UK is conducive to the public good and in the public interest because they have been convicted of an offence for which they have been sentenced to a period of imprisonment of at least 4 years;

(b)   the deportation of the person from the UK is conducive to the public good and in the public interest because they have been convicted of an offence for which they have been sentenced to a period of imprisonment of less than 4 years but at least 12 months; or

(c)   the deportation of the person from the UK is conducive to the public good and in the public interest because, in the view of the Secretary of State, their offending has caused serious harm or they are a persistent offender who shows a particular disregard for the law, the Secretary of State in assessing that claim will consider whether paragraph 399 or 399A applies and, if it does not, the public interest in deportation will only be outweighed by other factors where there are very compelling circumstances over and above those described in paragraphs 399 and 399A.

399. This paragraph applies where paragraph 398 (b) or (c) applies if –

(a)   the person has a genuine and subsisting parental relationship with a child under the age of 18 years who is in the UK, and

    (i)   the child is a British Citizen; or

    (ii)   the child has lived in the UK continuously for at least the 7 years immediately preceding the date of the immigration decision; and in either case

        (a)   it would be unduly harsh for the child to live in the country to which the person is to be deported; and

        (b)   it would be unduly harsh for the child to remain in the UK without the person who is to be deported; or

(b)   the person has a genuine and subsisting relationship with a partner who is in the UK and is a British Citizen or settled in the UK, and

    (i)   the relationship was formed at a time when the person (deportee) was in the UK lawfully and their immigration status was not precarious; and

    (ii)   it would be unduly harsh for that partner to live in the country to which the person is to be deported, because of compelling circumstances over and above those described in paragraph EX.2. of Appendix FM; and

    (iii)   it would be unduly harsh for that partner to remain in the UK without the person who is to be deported.

399A. This paragraph applies where paragraph 398(b) or (c) applies if –

(a)   the person has been lawfully resident in the UK for most of his life; and

(b)   he is socially and culturally integrated in the UK; and

(c)   there would be very significant obstacles to his integration into the country to which it is proposed he is deported."

[38] Following the 2014 amendment, the "exceptional circumstances" test in Paragraph 398 (see paragraph 31 above) became the "very compelling circumstances" test.

3. Judicial interpretation of paragraphs 398 to 399A of the Immigration Rules

(a) MF (Nigeria)

[39] In both *MF (Article 8 – new rules) Nigeria* [2012] UKUT 393 (IAC) (31 October 2012) and *Izuazu (Article 8 – new rules) Nigeria* [2013] UKUT 45 (IAC) (30 January 2013) the Upper Tribunal indicated that in cases to which the Immigration Rules applied, judges should adopt a two stage approach. First, they should consider whether a claimant was able to benefit under the applicable provisions of the Immigration Rules designed to address Article 8 claims. Where the claimant did not meet the requirements of the Rules it would then be necessary to make an assessment of Article 8 applying the criteria established by law.

[40] In *MF (Nigeria)* the Tribunal held as follows:

"38. Whilst for the above reasons we consider that we are obliged by primary legislation to continue (ordinarily) to adopt a two-stage approach, we acknowledge that in practice where Article 8-specific provisions of the rules have application, the second stage assessment will take a different hue. It will now resemble that conducted under the rules to a greater or lesser extent. Clearly, if the new rules perfectly mirrored Strasbourg jurisprudence as interpreted by our higher courts, the second stage judicial exercise would largely cover the same canvas. The difficulty is that the new rules do not obviously constitute a perfect mirror. We do not seek in this decision to gauge the extent of the difference, but one particular difference is of great importance in the present case. This relates to their methodology. They do not set out in full the *Boultif* criteria (*Boultif v Switzerland*, 54273/00; [2001] ECHR 497) as restated by the Grand Chamber in *Maslov v Austria* 1683/03; [2008] ECHR 546 (see Appendix A). It is possible to read the new rules as encompassing some of these criteria, but the decision-maker is not mandated or directed to take all of them into account."

[41] The Upper Tribunal's decision in *MF (Nigeria)* was the subject of an appeal to the Court of Appeal (*MF (Nigeria) v Secretary of State for the Home Department* [2013] EWCA Civ 1192 (8 October 2013)). The court disagreed with the Upper Tribunal's approach to and interpretation of the Immigration Rules. Rather than adopt a two-stage approach, it held that the new Rules were a "complete code" and the exceptional circumstances to be considered in the balancing exercise involved the application of a proportionality test as required by the Strasbourg jurisprudence. Therefore, in the case of a foreign prisoner to whom paragraphs 399 and 399A did not apply, very compelling reasons would be required to outweigh the public interest in deportation. These compelling reasons were the "exceptional circumstances".

[42] With regard to the meaning of "exceptional circumstances", Lord Dyson, delivering the judgment of the Court, stated that:

"43. The word 'exceptional' is often used to denote a departure from a general rule. The general rule in the present context is that, in the case of a foreign prisoner to whom paras 399 and 399A do not apply, very compelling reasons will be required to outweigh the public interest in deportation. These compelling reasons are the 'exceptional circumstances'.

44. We would, therefore, hold that the new rules are a complete code and that the exceptional circumstances to be considered in the balancing exercise involve the application of a proportionality test as required by the Strasbourg jurisprudence. We accordingly respectfully do not agree with the UT that the decision-maker is not 'mandated or directed' to take all the relevant Article 8 criteria into account (para 38).

45. Even if we were wrong about that, it would be necessary to apply a proportionality test outside the new rules as was done by the UT. Either way, the result should be the same. In these circumstances, it is a sterile question whether this is required by the new rules or it is a requirement of the general law. What matters is that it is required to be carried out if paras 399 or 399A do not apply.

46. There has been debate as to whether there is a one stage or two stage test. If the claimant succeeds on an application of the new rules at the first hurdle, i.e. he shows that para 399 or 399A applies, then it can be said that he has succeeded on a one stage test. But if he does not, it is necessary to consider whether there are circumstances which are sufficiently compelling (and therefore exceptional) to outweigh the public interest in deportation. That is an exercise which is separate from a consideration of whether para 399 or 399A applies. It is the second part of a two stage approach which, for the reasons we have given, is required by the new rules. The UT concluded (para 41) that it is required because the new rules do not fully reflect Strasbourg jurisprudence. But either way, it is necessary to carry out a two stage process."

(b) *NA (Pakistan)*

[43] In June 2016 the Court of Appeal gave judgment in the case of *NA (Pakistan) v Secretary of State for the Home Department* [2016] EWCA Civ 662. It considered whether the "very compelling" circumstances could be of a kind mentioned in the Exceptions:

"The phrase used in section 117C(6), in para. 398 of the 2014 rules and which we have held is to be read into section 117C(3) does not mean that a foreign criminal facing deportation is altogether disentitled from seeking to rely on matters falling within the scope of the circumstances described in Exceptions 1 and 2 when seeking to contend that 'there are very compelling circumstances, over and above those described in Exceptions 1 and 2'. As we have indicated above, a foreign criminal is entitled to rely upon such matters, but he would need to be able to point to features of his case of a kind mentioned in Exceptions 1 and 2 (and in paras. 399 or 399A of the 2014 rules), or features falling outside the circumstances described in those Exceptions and those paragraphs, which made his claim based on Article 8 especially strong.

In the case of a serious offender who could point to circumstances in his own case which could be said to correspond to the circumstances described in Exceptions 1 and 2, but where he could only just succeed in such an argument, it would not be possible to describe his situation as involving very compelling circumstances, over and above those described in Exceptions 1 and 2. One might describe that as a bare case of the kind described in Exceptions 1 or 2. On the other hand, if he could point to factors identified in the descriptions of Exceptions 1 and 2 of an especially compelling kind in support of an Article 8 claim, going well beyond what would be necessary to make out a bare case of the kind described in Exceptions 1 and 2, they could in principle constitute 'very compelling circumstances, over and above those described in Exceptions 1 and 2', whether taken by themselves or in conjunction with other factors relevant to application of Article 8.

An interpretation of the relevant phrase to exclude this possibility would lead to violation of Article 8 in some cases, which plainly was not Parliament's intention."

[44] The court further observed that:

"Although there is no 'exceptionality' requirement, it inexorably follows from the statutory scheme that the cases in which circumstances are sufficiently compelling to outweigh the high public interest in deportation will be rare. The commonplace incidents of family life, such as ageing parents in poor health or the natural love between parents and children, will not be sufficient."

[45] The court also considered the role to be played by the Strasbourg jurisprudence:

"Against that background, one may ask what is the role of the Strasbourg jurisprudence? In particular, how does one take into account important decisions such as *Üner v Netherlands* (2007) 45 EHRR 14 and *Maslov v Austria*? Mr Southey QC, who represents KJ and WM, rightly submits that the Strasbourg authorities have an important role to play. Mr Tam rightly accepted that this is correct. The answer is that the Secretary of State and the tribunals and courts will have regard to the Strasbourg jurisprudence when applying the tests set out in our domestic legislation. For example, a tribunal may be considering whether it would be 'unduly harsh' for a child to remain in England without the deportee; or it may be considering whether certain circumstances are sufficiently 'compelling' to outweigh the high public interest in deportation of foreign criminals. Anyone applying these tests (as required by our own rules and legislation) should heed the guidance contained in the Strasbourg authorities. As we have stated above, the scheme of Part 5A of the 2002 Act and paras. 398–399A of the 2014 rules is to ensure compliance with the requirements of Article 8 through a structured approach, which is intended to ensure that proper weight is given to the public interest in deportation whilst also having regard to other relevant factors as identified in the Strasbourg and domestic case-law. The new regime is not intended to produce violations of Article 8."

(c) *Hesham Ali v Secretary of State for the Home Department*

[46] In *Hesham Ali v Secretary of State for the Home Department* [2016] UKSC 60 (16 November 2016), the Supreme Court provided guidance on how tribunals and courts should approach decision-making in the context of immigration cases involving Article 8 of the Convention. The leading judgment was given by Lord Reed, with whom Lord Neuberger of Abbotsbury, Lord Thomas of Cwmgiedd, Baroness Hale of Richmond, Lord Kerr of Tonaghmore, Lord Wilson and Lord Hughes agreed. He stated, insofar as is relevant:

"*Administrative decision-making*

36. Considering the new rules in the light of the guidance given by the European court, rule 397 makes it clear that a deportation order is not to be made if the person's removal would be incompatible with the ECHR. Where Article 8 claims are made by foreign offenders facing deportation, rule 398 explains that the Secretary of State will first consider whether rule 399 or 399A applies. Those rules, applicable where offenders have received sentences of between 12 months and four years, provide guidance to officials as to categories of case where it is accepted by the Secretary of State that deportation would be disproportionate. The fact that a claim under Article 8 falls outside rules 399 and 399A does not, however, mean that it is necessarily to be rejected. That is recognised by the concluding words of rule 398, which make it clear that a claim that deportation would be contrary to Article 8 will not be rejected merely because rules 399 and 399A do not apply, but that 'it will only be in exceptional circumstances that the public interest in deportation will be outweighed by other factors.

…

38. The implication of the new rules is that rules 399 and 399A identify particular categories of case in which the Secretary of State accepts that the public interest in the deportation of the offender is outweighed under Article 8 by countervailing factors. Cases not covered by those rules (that is to say, foreign offenders who have received sentences of at least four years, or who have received sentences of between 12 months and four years but whose private or family life does not meet the requirements of rules 399 and 399A) will be dealt with on the basis that great weight should generally be given to the public interest in the deportation of such offenders, but that it can be outweighed, applying a proportionality test, by very compelling circumstances: in other words, by a very strong claim indeed, as Laws LJ put it in *SS (Nigeria)*. The countervailing considerations must be very compelling in order to outweigh the general public interest in the deportation of such offenders, as assessed by Parliament and the Secretary of State. The Strasbourg jurisprudence indicates relevant factors to consider, and rules 399 and 399A provide an indication of the sorts of matters which the Secretary of State regards as very compelling. As explained at para 26 above, they can include factors bearing on the weight of the public interest in the deportation of the particular offender, such as his conduct since the offence was committed, as well as factors relating to his private or family life. Cases falling within the scope of section 32 of the 2007 Act in which the public interest in deportation is outweighed, other than those

specified in the new rules themselves, are likely to be a very small minority (particularly in non-settled cases). They need not necessarily involve any circumstance which is exceptional in the sense of being extraordinary (as counsel for the Secretary of State accepted, consistently with *Huang* [2007] 2 AC 167, para 20), but they can be said to involve 'exceptional circumstances' in the sense that they involve a departure from the general rule.

...

Appellate decision-making

...

46. ... It is the duty of appellate tribunals, as independent judicial bodies, to make their own assessment of the proportionality of deportation in any particular case on the basis of their own findings as to the facts and their understanding of the relevant law. But, where the Secretary of State has adopted a policy based on a general assessment of proportionality, as in the present case, they should attach considerable weight to that assessment: in particular, that a custodial sentence of four years or more represents such a serious level of offending that the public interest in the offender's deportation almost always outweighs countervailing considerations of private or family life; that great weight should generally be given to the public interest in the deportation of a foreign offender who has received a custodial sentence of more than 12 months; and that, where the circumstances do not fall within rules 399 or 399A, the public interest in the deportation of such offenders can generally be outweighed only by countervailing factors which are very compelling, as explained in paras 37–38 above.

...

50. In summary, therefore, the tribunal carries out its task on the basis of the facts as it finds them to be on the evidence before it, and the law as established by statute and case law. Ultimately, it has to decide whether deportation is proportionate in the particular case before it, balancing the strength of the public interest in the deportation of the offender against the impact on private and family life. In doing so, it should give appropriate weight to Parliament's and the Secretary of State's assessments of the strength of the general public interest in the deportation of foreign offenders, as explained in paras 14, 37–38 and 46 above, and also consider all factors relevant to the specific case in question. The critical issue for the tribunal will generally be whether, giving due weight to the strength of the public interest in the deportation of the offender in the case before it, the Article 8 claim is sufficiently strong to outweigh it. In general, only a claim which is very strong indeed – very compelling, as it was put in *MF (Nigeria)* – will succeed.

A complete code?

51. In *MF (Nigeria)* [2014] 1 WLR 544 the Court of Appeal described the new rules set out in para 23 above as 'a complete code' for Article 8 claims (para 44). That expression reflected the view that the concluding words of rule 398

required the application of a proportionality test in accordance with the Strasbourg jurisprudence, taking into account all the Article 8 criteria and all other factors which were relevant to proportionality (para 39). On that basis, the court commented that the result should be the same whether the proportionality assessment was carried out within or outside the new rules: it was a sterile question whether it was required by the rules or by the general law (para 45).

52. The idea that the new rules comprise a complete code appears to have been mistakenly interpreted in some later cases as meaning that the Rules, and the Rules alone, govern appellate decision-making. Dicta seemingly to that effect can be found, for example, in *LC (China) v Secretary of State for the Home Department* [2014] EWCA Civ 1310; [2015] Imm AR 227, para 17, and *AJ (Angola) v Secretary of State for the Home Department* [2014] EWCA Civ 1636, para 39.

53. As explained at para 17 above, the Rules are not law (although they are treated as law for the purposes of section 86(3)(a) of the 2002 Act), and therefore do not govern the determination of appeals, other than appeals brought on the ground that the decision is not in accordance with the Rules: see para 7 above. The policies adopted by the Secretary of State, and given effect by the Rules, are nevertheless a relevant and important consideration for tribunals determining appeals brought on Convention grounds, because they reflect the assessment of the general public interest made by the responsible minister and endorsed by Parliament. In particular, tribunals should accord respect to the Secretary of State's assessment of the strength of the general public interest in the deportation of foreign offenders, and also consider all factors relevant to the specific case before them, as explained at paras 37–38, 46 and 50 above. It remains for them to judge whether, on the facts as they have found them, and giving due weight to the strength of the public interest in deportation in the case before them, the factors brought into account on the other side lead to the conclusion that deportation would be disproportionate."

[47] Lord Thomas, in a separate opinion, stated:

"83. One way of structuring such a judgment would be to follow what has become known as the 'balance sheet' approach. After the judge has found the facts, the judge would set out each of the 'pros' and 'cons' in what has been described as a 'balance sheet' and then set out reasoned conclusions as to whether the countervailing factors outweigh the importance attached to the public interest in the deportation of foreign offenders.

84. The use of a 'balance sheet' approach has its origins in Family Division cases (see paras 36 and 74 of the decision of the Court of Appeal *In re B-S (Children) (Adoption Order: Leave to Oppose)* [2014] 1 WLR 563). It was applied by the Divisional Court in *Polish Judicial Authority v Celinski* [2016] 1 WLR 551 to extradition cases where a similar balancing exercise has to be undertaken when Article 8 is engaged – see paras 15–17. Experience in extradition cases has since shown that the use of the balance sheet approach has greatly assisted in the clarity of the decisions at first instance and the work of appellate courts."

[48] In a separate opinion, Lord Kerr said the following:

"A consistent thread running through the cases which I have discussed (and others which preceded them such as *Benhebba v France* (Application No 53441/99) (unreported) 10 July, 2003 and *Mehemi v France* (1997) 30 EHRR 739) is the need to review and assess a number of specifically identified factors in order to conduct a proper Article 8 inquiry. Another theme is that this examination must be open textured so that sufficient emphasis is given to each of the factors as they arise in particular cases. Of their nature factors or criteria such as these cannot be given a pre-ordained weight. Any attempt to do that would run counter to the essential purpose of the exercise. ...

116. ECtHR jurisprudence does not expressly forbid the making of policies in relation to the normal circumstances in which expulsion of foreign criminals should take place but it has not sanctioned the setting of policy standards as to how Article 8 might be applied.

...

120. The ECtHR cases do not permit a national policy which limits or dictates the weight to be given to the *Boultif* factors in the Article 8 balancing exercise. This is clear from, for example, the court's judgment in *Üner* where in para 60 it said '... that all the [*Boultif*] factors ... should be taken into account in all cases concerning settled migrants who are... be expelled and/or excluded following a criminal conviction'. When it comes to applying Article 8, therefore, as opposed to following a purely domestic policy, it is not open to the state to say that some of the *Boultif* factors should not be taken into account or should be subservient to others. If those factors are relevant to a potential deportee's situation, they must be taken into account and they must be given the weight that they deserve, following an open-ended and rounded evaluation of the case."

[49] He continued:

"Many who fall outside the categories set out in the rules enjoy a full family or private life in every sense. The significance of that inescapable truth is that, under the 2012 Immigration Rules, anyone who does not come within any of the specified categories and who is liable to deportation as a result of their status as a foreign criminal must demonstrate 'exceptional circumstances' in order to outweigh the statutorily imposed public interest in their deportation. That requirement runs directly counter to a proper assessment of whether an interference with the right to respect for family or private life on the part of those who do not come within one of the exemptions is justified."

(d) *R (on the application of Agyarko) v Secretary of State for the Home Department* [2017] UKSC 11

[50] In *R (on the application of Agyarko)* Lord Reed summarised the position thus:

"Cases are not, therefore, to be approached by searching for a unique or unusual feature, and in its absence rejecting the application without further examination.

Rather, as the Master of the Rolls made clear, the test is one of proportionality. The reference to exceptional circumstances in the European case law means that, in cases involving precarious family life, 'something very compelling ... is required to outweigh the public interest', applying a proportionality test. The Court of Appeal went on to apply that approach to the interpretation of the Rules concerning the deportation of foreign criminals, where the same phrase appears; and their approach was approved by this court, in that context, in *Hesham Ali*."

B. International law and practice

[51] The relevant texts adopted by the Council of Europe in the field of immigration are set out in *Üner v the Netherlands* [GC], no. 46410/99, §§ 35–38, ECHR 2006 XII.

THE LAW

I. ALLEGED VIOLATION OF ARTICLE 8 OF THE CONVENTION

[52] The applicant complained that his deportation constituted a disproportionate interference with his right to respect for his family and private life and that the Upper Tribunal, in searching for "very compelling circumstances", did not conduct a proper assessment of his rights under Article 8 of the Convention.

[53] Article 8 reads as follows:

"1. Everyone has the right to respect for his private and family life, his home and his correspondence.

2. There shall be no interference by a public authority with the exercise of this right except such as is in accordance with the law and is necessary in a democratic society in the interests of national security, public safety or the economic well-being of the country, for the prevention of disorder or crime, for the protection of health or morals, or for the protection of the rights and freedoms of others."

A. Admissibility

[54] The Government submitted that the applicant's complaint under Article 8 of the Convention should be declared inadmissible as it was manifestly ill-founded.

[55] In the Court's view, however, this complaint is neither manifestly ill founded nor inadmissible on any other grounds listed in Article 35 of the Convention. It must therefore be declared admissible.

B. Merits

1. The parties' submissions

(a) The applicant

[56] The applicant contended that the domestic authorities did not carry out an adequate assessment of the proportionality of his removal, since they did not properly balance his right to respect for his private and family life with the public interest in deportation. In his view, Article 8 required an assessment of whether an interference was in accordance with the law and was necessary in a democratic society for one of the proscribed aims in Article 8 § 2. Whether an interference was "necessary" in turn required a consideration of whether an interference was "proportionate". In other words, a balancing exercise was required when applying Article 8 § 2 of the Convention, and section 117C and paragraph 398 were inimical to such an approach.

[57] Although the applicant acknowledged that the Supreme Court had now endorsed the "balance-sheet approach" (see paragraph 47 above), he nevertheless submitted that in his case the Tribunal had not carried out such a "free-wheeling" balancing exercise. On the contrary, the exercise carried out by the authorities was quite different. Rather than give thorough and careful consideration of the proportionality test required by the Convention, they inquired whether there were very compelling circumstances over and above those identified in Exceptions 1 and 2. The applicant could only rely on Exception 2, which required deportation to be "unduly harsh" on a British child with whom he had a genuine and subsisting relationship. However, as he had to show very compelling circumstances over and above that exception, he could only succeed if the impact of his deportation on his son was "extra unduly harsh". Such a concept lacked the clarity necessary to protect the individual against arbitrary interference. Furthermore, for persons sentenced to more than four years the risk of re-offending could only be taken into account if it amounted to a "very compelling circumstance". This was not consistent with Article 8 § 2.

[58] The applicant further argued that pursuant to section 117C and paragraph 398, the domestic decision-maker was unable to adjust the weight of the public interest according to the nature and seriousness of the crimes involved. All foreign criminals with sentences of up to four years were lumped together in one group, and those with sentences of over four years were lumped together in another group, and there was no scope for the public interest to vary within either group, no matter the length of the sentence, the seriousness of the crime, or the risk of reconviction. Such an approach was incompatible with the difficult evaluative exercise required by Article 8 of the Convention.

[59] The applicant relied on the dissenting opinion of Lord Kerr in *Hesham Ali*, in which he made it clear that the Convention did not permit a national policy which limited or dictated the weight to be given to the *Boultif* factors in the Article 8 balancing exercise. In Lord Kerr's view, the quest to strike the appropriate balance should not be encumbered by pre emptive considerations of exceptionality (see paragraphs 48–49 above).

[60] Finally, the applicant argued that in any event his deportation had disproportionately interfered with his right to respect for his family life. Carrying out the proper balancing exercise, he had enjoyed a genuine and subsisting relationship with his children established at a time when he had leave to remain;

the children were going to suffer financial hardship on account of his deportation; they would also suffer emotionally on account of his absence, especially his eldest son, who would need further heart surgery in the foreseeable future; the children's mother would also suffer emotionally; and the applicant had been at low risk of re-offending.

(b) The Government

[61] The Government argued that where there was serious criminality, attracting substantial terms of imprisonment, the public interest in favour of expulsion carried great weight (*Boultif v Switzerland*, no. 54273/00, ECHR 2001 IX, *Üner v the Netherlands* [GC], no. 46410/99, § 54, ECHR 2006 XII and *Maslov v Austria* [GC], no. 1638/03, ECHR 2008). Therefore, in cases of serious criminality, expulsion would be compatible with Article 8 in the absence of private and family life factors of commensurately compelling weight. Furthermore, while the Court had repeatedly emphasised that the best interests of the child are paramount, in the context of the removal of a non-national parent as a consequence of a criminal conviction it had indicated that the decision first and foremost concerns the offender and, as a consequence, the nature and seriousness of the offence committed or the offending history might outweigh the other criteria (*Jeunesse v the Netherlands* [GC], no. 12738/10, 3 October 2014 para 109).

[62] Paragraph 398 of the Immigration Rules and section 117C of the Nationality, Immigration and Asylum Act 2002 ("the 2002 Act") were designed to reflect the public interest in the deportation of serious and/or persistent offenders, while recognising that there would be cases where the making of a deportation order would be incompatible with Article 8 of the Convention. In the Government's view, their proper application was consistent with the principles laid down by the Court and facilitated the striking of a fair balance in individual cases. Moreover, by providing a framework for the domestic decision-maker, those provisions also proved a safeguard against arbitrariness and inconsistent decision-making.

[63] The Government further argued that the framework provided by the Immigration Rules and the 2002 Act did not in any way prevent the domestic authorities from considering the criteria in *Boultif*, *Üner* and *Maslov*, or any other factors upon which an individual wished to rely. Rather, it ensured that the domestic decision-maker appreciated that in a case of serious offending, the family and/or private life factors relied upon by the applicant would need to be commensurately weighty before the striking of a fair balance under Article 8 precluded expulsion. In this regard, the domestic courts had repeatedly made clear that paragraph 398 of the Immigration Rules and section 117C of the 2002 Act provided scope for all relevant factors to be taken into account in the proportionality assessment whilst at the same time ensuring that when the balance came finally to be struck, the public interest was accorded its proper weight. Critically, the domestic courts had repeatedly held that the legislative provisions had to be interpreted and applied so as to produce a result that was, in the individual case, compatible with Article 8 of the Convention (see, for example, *NA (Pakistan) & Ors v Secretary of State for the Home Department* [2016] EWCA Civ 662 at paragraph 45 above).

[64] In addition, the domestic courts had clarified that the "very compelling circumstances" test did not provide a comprehensive list of the factors to be taken

into account. On the contrary, all relevant factors, including, for example, evidence of reform and rehabilitation, were to be looked at cumulatively and placed in the balance – and could, therefore, outweigh the public interest in deporting a foreign national who had been involved in criminal offending. Indeed, the domestic courts had made it clear that in giving effect to the domestic legislative scheme, the Tribunal had to continue to strike the proportionality balance by applying the principles laid down in *Boultif, Üner* and *Maslov*; and in *Hesham Ali v Secretary of State for the Home Department* the Supreme Court held that the domestic legislative scheme governing deportation "can and should" accommodate a "balance sheet approach" (see paragraph 47 above).

[65] Moreover, the "unduly harsh" test focused simply on the impact on the child, and provided a domestic exception to deportation, in cases where the parent's offending attracted a sentence of less than four years, even if deportation would not be disproportionate once the nature and severity of the offending was weighed in the balance. Even where an individual did not succeed on any of the specific statutory domestic exceptions to deportation (including the "unduly harsh" exception), the Tribunal nevertheless had to ultimately consider whether deportation would be disproportionate.

[66] It therefore followed that a full proportionality balancing exercise always had to be conducted, preferably by way of a "balance sheet exercise", and that even where the "unduly harsh" test was not satisfied, an individual could still succeed on Article 8 grounds once all the factors in his or her favour were weighed against the public interest in deportation, having regard to the nature and severity of the offending, on the basis of the guiding principles laid down by the Court.

[67] In the case at hand, the Government submitted that the Upper Tribunal, in a careful and detailed decision extending to 118 paragraphs, had considered the relevant facts. It did not, however, allow the applicant's appeal. Having assessed all the circumstances, the Upper Tribunal did not consider that they were sufficiently compelling to outweigh the public interest in the applicant's deportation, given the seriousness of his offending.

[68] In the Government's view, the Upper Tribunal was entitled to reach that conclusion. The applicant had been given community punishment for his first offence of deception in 2005, but nevertheless went on to commit far more serious offences of dishonesty, which involved undermining immigration control on a substantial scale. Thus, there was a weighty public interest in the applicant's deportation, and the Upper Tribunal was correct in so concluding.

[69] Should the Court disagree, and conclude that the Upper Tribunal's conclusion fell outside the ambit of the margin of appreciation on the facts of the case, the Government submitted that that could not be attributed to the domestic legislative scheme, since neither Rule 398 nor section 117C compelled the domestic decision-makers, courts or tribunals to reach conclusions that were not in conformity with Article 8. In this regard, the Government reiterated that both the Court of Appeal and Upper Tribunal had made clear that the relevant provisions of domestic law called for a "wide-ranging evaluative exercise … in the case of all foreign criminals, in order to ensure that Part 5A of the 2002 Act produces, in each case, a result that is compatible with the United Kingdom's obligations under Article 8 of the ECHR".

2. The Court's assessment

(a) General principles

[70] The State is entitled, as a matter of international law and subject to its treaty obligations, to control the entry of aliens into its territory and their residence there (see, among many other authorities, *Üner*, cited above, § 54; *Abdulaziz, Cabales and Balkandali v the United Kingdom*, 28 May 1985, § 67, Series A no. 94, and *Boujlifa v France*, 21 October 1997, § 42, Reports of Judgments and Decisions 1997‑VI). The Convention does not guarantee the right of an alien to enter or to reside in a particular country and, in pursuance of their task of maintaining public order, Contracting States have the power to expel an alien convicted of criminal offences. However, their decisions in this field must, in so far as they may interfere with a right protected under paragraph 1 of Article 8, be in accordance with the law and necessary in a democratic society, that is to say, justified by a pressing social need and, in particular, proportionate to the legitimate aim pursued (see *Üner*, cited above, § 54; see also *Boultif*, cited above, § 46, and *Slivenko v Latvia* [GC], no. 48321/99, § 113, ECHR 2003-X).

[71] These principles apply regardless of whether an alien entered the host country as an adult or at a very young age, or was perhaps even born there (see *Üner*, cited above, § 55).

[72] Nonetheless, even though Article 8 of the Convention does not contain an absolute right for any category of alien not to be expelled, the Court's case‑law amply demonstrates that there are circumstances where the expulsion of an alien will give rise to a violation of Article 8 of the Convention (see *Üner*, cited above, § 57, and the references therein). In *Boultif* the Court elaborated the relevant criteria which it would use in order to assess whether an expulsion measure was necessary in a democratic society and proportionate to the legitimate aim pursued. These criteria are the following:

- the nature and seriousness of the offence committed by the applicant;

- the length of the applicant's stay in the country from which he or she is to be expelled;

- the time elapsed since the offence was committed and the applicant's conduct during that period;

- the nationalities of the various persons concerned;

- the applicant's family situation, such as the length of the marriage, and other factors expressing the effectiveness of a couple's family life;

- whether the spouse knew about the offence at the time when he or she entered into a family relationship;

- whether there are children of the marriage, and if so, their age; and

- the seriousness of the difficulties which the spouse is likely to encounter in the country to which the applicant is to be expelled.

[73] In *Üner*, the Court made explicit two further criteria implicit in those identified in *Boultif*:

• the best interests and well-being of the children, in particular the seriousness of the difficulties which any children of the applicant are likely to encounter in the country to which the applicant is to be expelled; and

• the solidity of social, cultural and family ties with the host country and with the country of destination.

[74] All the above factors should be taken into account in all cases concerning settled migrants who are to be expelled and/or excluded following a criminal conviction (see *Üner*, cited above, § 60).

[75] In assessing whether an interference with a right protected by Article 8 was necessary in a democratic society and proportionate to the legitimate aim pursued, the Contracting States enjoy a certain margin of appreciation (see *Slivenko*, cited above, § 113, and *Boultif*, cited above, § 47). However, as the State's margin of appreciation goes hand in hand with European supervision, the Court is empowered to give the final ruling on whether an expulsion measure is reconcilable with Article 8 (see *Maslov v Austria* [GC], no. 1638/03, § 76, ECHR 2008).

[76] The requirement for "European supervision" does not mean that in determining whether an impugned measure struck a fair balance between the relevant interests, it is necessarily the Court's task to conduct the Article 8 proportionality assessment afresh. On the contrary, in Article 8 cases the Court has generally understood the margin of appreciation to mean that, where the independent and impartial domestic courts have carefully examined the facts, applying the relevant human rights standards consistently with the Convention and its case-law, and adequately balanced the applicant's personal interests against the more general public interest in the case, it is not for it to substitute its own assessment of the merits (including, in particular, its own assessment of the factual details of proportionality) for that of the competent national authorities. The only exception to this is where there are shown to be strong reasons for doing so (see *Ndidi v the United Kingdom*, no. 41215/14, § 76, 14 September 2017; *Hamesevic v Denmark* (dec.), no. 25748/15, § 43, 16 May 2017; and *Alam v Denmark* (dec.), no. 33809/15, § 35, 6 June 2017).

(b) Application of the general principles to the case at hand

[77] In the present case the Government accepted before the Upper Tribunal as well as before this Court that the applicant's deportation would constitute an interference with his rights under Article 8 § 1 of the Convention. Moreover, it does not appear to be in doubt that the deportation order was "in accordance with the law" and "in pursuit of a legitimate aim" (the prevention of disorder and crime) for the purposes of Article 8 § 2 of the Convention. Consequently, the principal issue to be determined is whether the applicant's deportation would be "necessary in a democratic society", or, in other words, whether the deportation order struck a fair balance between the applicant's Convention rights on the one hand and the community's interests on the other (see *Ndidi*, § 74, *Slivenko*, § 113, and *Boultif*, § 47, judgments cited above). In that respect the applicant has made two distinct complaints: that due to the requirements of paragraphs 398 and 399 of the Immigration Rules, the Upper Tribunal was not able to conduct a thorough assessment of the proportionality of his deportation; and that his deportation from the United Kingdom disproportionately interfered with his right to respect for his family and private life.

(i) The Immigration Rules

[78] The Court would stress that the criteria which emerge from the Court's case-law and which are spelled out in the *Boultif* and *Üner* judgments are primarily meant to facilitate the application of Article 8 in expulsion cases by domestic courts. Furthermore, the Court reiterates that nevertheless, in applying these criteria, the respective weight to be attached to them will inevitably vary according to the specific circumstances of each case (see *Maslov*, cited above, § 70 and *AA v the United Kingdom*, no. 8000/08, § 57, 20 September 2011).

[79] As a consequence, where the domestic courts properly apply Article 8 of the Convention with reference to the criteria which emerge from the aforementioned judgments, the Court will only substitute its own assessment of the merits where there are shown to be strong reasons for doing so (see *Ndidi*, cited above, § 76). On the other hand, where such "strong reasons exist", or where the domestic courts do not carefully examine the facts, apply the relevant human rights standards consistently with the Convention and the Court's case-law, and adequately balance the interests of the applicant against those of the general public, the Court remains empowered to give the final ruling on whether an expulsion measure is reconcilable with Article 8 (see *Maslov*, cited above, § 76).

[80] In the present case the applicant argues that the Tribunal was precluded by the Immigration Rules from conducting such an assessment and that the Tribunal's only discretion outside the Rules would be to consider whether there existed "exceptional circumstances" or, following the 2014 amendment, "very compelling circumstances". As Lord Kerr observed, such a requirement would appear to run directly counter to a proper assessment of whether an interference with the right to respect for family or private life on the part of those who do not come within one of the exemptions is justified (see paragraphs 48–49 above).

[81] That being said, the domestic courts have confirmed, and the Government has reiterated before this Court, that the Immigration Rules and section 117C of the Nationality, Immigration and Asylum Act 2002 provide scope for all relevant factors to be taken into account in the proportionality assessment and that, in considering whether "exceptional" or "very compelling circumstances" exist, the authorities should consider the proportionality test required by this Court. In *MF (Nigeria)*, the Court of Appeal found that "the exceptional circumstances to be considered in the balancing exercise involve the application of a proportionality test as required by the Strasbourg jurisprudence (see paragraph 42 above). In *NA (Pakistan)*, the Court of Appeal held that any court or tribunal applying the tests required by the Immigration Rules and the 2002 Act "should heed the guidance contained in the Strasbourg authorities" since the scheme of Part 5A of the 2002 Act and paragraphs 398–399A of the Immigration Rules was "to ensure compliance with the requirements of Article 8 through a structured approach, which is intended to ensure that proper weight is given to the public interest in deportation whilst also having regard to other relevant factors as identified in the Strasbourg and domestic case-law" (see paragraph 45 above).

[82] Furthermore, in *Hesham Ali* (see paragraphs 46–49 above) the Supreme Court made it clear that it was "the duty of appellate tribunals, as independent judicial bodies, to make their own assessment of the proportionality of deportation in any particular case on the basis of their own findings as to the facts and their understanding of the relevant law", although it acknowledged that in doing so "they should attach considerable weight to [the policy adopted by the Secretary of State]." Lord Thomas, in a separate opinion, recommended that tribunals conducting the proportionality assessment "follow what has become known as the 'balance sheet' approach". The "balance-sheet" approach requires a judge, having found the facts, to set out each of the "pros" and "cons" and then set out reasoned conclusions as to whether the countervailing factors outweigh the importance attached to the public interest in the deportation of foreign offenders. This has since been affirmed in *R (on the application of Agyarko)* (see paragraph 50 above).

[83] In light of the foregoing, the Court does not consider that the Immigration Rules necessarily preclude the domestic courts and tribunals from employing the *Boultif* criteria for the purpose of assessing whether an expulsion measure was necessary and proportionate.

(ii) The applicant's deportation

[84] In the context of the present case the Upper Tribunal neither made any substantial further findings adverse to the applicant nor conducted a separate balancing exercise as required by the Court's case law under Article 8. In fact, the Upper Tribunal merely noted that it "cannot allow his appeal" on the basis that paragraph 398 of the Immigration Rules "imposed requirements" to identify "very compelling circumstances" over and above the accepted genuine and subsisting parental relationship with the children, something which the applicant could not establish.

[85] In light of the above, it therefore falls to the Court, in exercise of its supervisory jurisdiction, to give the final ruling on whether an expulsion measure is reconcilable with Article 8.

[86] In this context, the Court notes that in November 2009 the applicant was convicted of offences relating to the falsification of some thirty applications for leave to remain in the United Kingdom for which he was sentenced to a period of five years and six months imprisonment (see paragraph 7 above). The offence was undoubtedly serious, as evidenced by the length of the prison sentence. Furthermore, it was not his first criminal conviction in the United Kingdom. In February 2005 he had been convicted of obtaining a money transfer by deception, for which he was sentenced to a period of unpaid work and ordered to pay a fine (see paragraph 7 above).

[87] That being said, the Court has tended to consider the seriousness of a crime in the context of the balancing exercise under Article 8 of the Convention not merely by reference to the length of the sentence imposed but rather by reference to the nature and circumstances of the particular criminal offence or offences committed by the applicant in question and their impact on society as a whole. In that context, the Court has consistently treated crimes of violence and drug-related offences as being at the most serious end of the criminal spectrum (see, for example, *Maslov*, cited above, § 85; *AW Khan v the United Kingdom*, no. 47486/06, § 40, 12 January 2010; *Dalia v France*, 19 February 1998, § 54, Reports of Judgments and Decisions 1998 I; and *Baghli v France*, no. 34374/97,

§ 48, ECHR 1999 VIII but see also *Lukic v Germany*, no, 25021/08, 20 September 2011 involving multiple convictions for fraud). In any event, the fact that the offence committed by an applicant was at the more serious end of the criminal spectrum is not in and of itself determinative of the case. Rather, it is just one factor which has to be weighed in the balance, together with the other criteria which emerge from the judgments in *Boultif* and *Üner*.

[88] In the present case the Upper Tribunal did weigh those other criteria in the balance, albeit exclusively with reference to the applicant's partner. After all, having concluded that they had no hesitation in saying that it would be in the best interests of the children to remain in the United Kingdom with both of their parents and that it would be "unduly harsh" to separate them, they allowed his partner's appeal and those of the minor children including under Article 8 of the Convention. Although many of the factors relevant to applicant's partner's appeal were essentially the same as those relevant to his own, his appeal was dismissed on the sole basis there were no "very compelling circumstances" over and above those which had applied in respect of his partner.

[89] In the Court's view, this conclusion is not reconcilable with Article 8 of the Convention. The Upper Tribunal itself acknowledged the strength of the applicant's ties to his partner and children, all of whom would stay in the United Kingdom. It also acknowledged that his partner and children needed him, and this need for parental support was particularly acute in the case of D on account of his medical condition and forthcoming surgery. Finally, it accepted that it was in the best interests of the children for him to remain in the United Kingdom, a factor which, according to the Court's case-law, must be accorded significant weight (see *Krasniqi v Austria*, no. 41697/12, § 47 25 April 2017). Having regard to these careful and detailed findings by the Upper Tribunal, which must carry significant weight in the overall assessment of proportionality, the Court considers that in the circumstances of the present case the seriousness of the particular offence(s) committed by the applicant was not of a nature or degree capable of outweighing the best interests of the children so as to justify his expulsion. It therefore considers that the applicant's deportation was disproportionate to the legitimate aim pursued and as such was not "necessary in a democratic society".

[90] There has accordingly been a violation of Article 8 of the Convention.

II. ALLEGED VIOLATION OF ARTICLE 13 OF THE CONVENTION READ TOGETHER WITH ARTICLE 8

[91] The applicant further complained that he did not have an effective remedy before a national authority for the breach of his rights under Article 8 of the Convention.

[92] Article 13 of the Convention provides as follows:

"Everyone whose rights and freedoms as set forth in [the] Convention are violated shall have an effective remedy before a national authority notwithstanding that the violation has been committed by persons acting in an official capacity."

[93] However, the applicant was able to appeal against the deportation order, first to the First-tier Tribunal and then to the Upper Tribunal. From the Upper Tribunal, he was able to seek permission to appeal to the Court of Appeal, and in

doing so he was able to argue that the Tribunal had not considered all the factors relevant to the Article 8 proportionality assessment. He was not, therefore, denied an effective remedy within the meaning of Article 13 of the Convention and this complaint must be declared inadmissible as manifestly ill-founded pursuant to Article 35 § 3(a) of the Convention.

III. APPLICATION OF ARTICLE 41 OF THE CONVENTION

[94] Article 41 of the Convention provides:

"If the Court finds that there has been a violation of the Convention or the Protocols thereto, and if the internal law of the High Contracting Party concerned allows only partial reparation to be made, the Court shall, if necessary, afford just satisfaction to the injured party."

A. Damage

[95] The applicant claimed twenty-five thousand euros (EUR) in respect of non-pecuniary damage.

[96] The Court considers that the applicant must have suffered distress and anxiety as a result of his deportation and separation from his family. Making an assessment on an equitable basis it awards the applicant EUR 5,000 under the head of non-pecuniary damage, plus any tax that may be chargeable.

B. Costs and expenses

[97] The applicant also claimed "costs and expenses, to be particularised on an up-to-date basis in line with section 4 of the Practice Direction on just satisfaction claims in the event of this application being declared admissible". No further particulars of his claim have been submitted to the Court.

[98] Both the Practice Direction to which the applicant refers and Rule 60 of the Rules of Court provide that an applicant who wishes to obtain an award of just satisfaction under Article 41 of the Convention must submit itemised particulars of all claims, together with any relevant supporting documents, within the time-limit fixed for the submission of his or her observations on the merits unless the President of the Chamber directs otherwise. If the applicant fails to comply with this requirement the Chamber may reject the claims in whole or in part.

[99] The applicant was therefore required to submit itemised particulars of his claim for costs and expenses within the time-limit fixed for the submission of his observations on the merits. As he did not do so, the Court rejects any claim for costs and expenses.

C. Default interest

[100] The Court considers it appropriate that the default interest rate should be based on the marginal lending rate of the European Central Bank, to which should be added three percentage points.

FOR THESE REASONS, THE COURT, UNANIMOUSLY,

1. *Declares* the complaint concerning Article 8 of the Convention admissible and the remainder of the application inadmissible;

2. *Holds* that there has been a violation of Article 8 of the Convention;

3. *Holds*

    (a) that the respondent State is to pay the applicant, within three months from the date on which the judgment becomes final in accordance with Article 44 § 2 of the Convention, the following amount, to be converted into the currency of the respondent State at the rate applicable at the date of settlement:

    > EUR 5,000 (five thousand euros), plus any tax that may be chargeable, in respect of non-pecuniary damage;

    (b) that from the expiry of the above-mentioned three months until settlement simple interest shall be payable on the above amount at a rate equal to the marginal lending rate of the European Central Bank during the default period plus three percentage points;

4. *Dismisses* the remainder of the applicant's claim for just satisfaction.

Done in English, and notified in writing on 24 November 2020, pursuant to Rule 77 §§ 2 and 3 of the Rules of Court.

Ilse Freiwirth	Yonko Grozev
Deputy Registrar	President

EOG v SECRETARY OF STATE FOR THE HOME DEPARTMENT

ADMINISTRATIVE COURT

Mostyn J

[2020] EWHC 3310 (Admin)
3 December 2020

Human rights – Article 14 of the ECHR – prohibition of discrimination – Home Office policies and concessions – NRM referrals – potential victims of trafficking – recipient of positive reasonable grounds decision – delays in conclusive grounds decisions – protection from removal – Article 10.2 of the Trafficking Convention – unlawful lacuna in Home Office policy – interim discretionary leave policy required

The Claimant entered the United Kingdom in September 2017 having been granted a Tier 5 Youth Mobility Scheme Visa valid until 20 September 2019. In April 2018 she fell under the control of a man who abused her and forced her into prostitution until she managed to escape. On 11 September 2018 she was referred into the National Referral Mechanism ("NRM") as a potential victim of trafficking. She received a negative reasonable grounds decision within six days. The NRM agreed to reconsider that decision. On 11 June 2019 the Claimant received a positive reasonable grounds decision. She started working with a trafficking support organisation on 25 June 2019. She was forced to give up her employment on 14 September 2019 as her leave to remain lapsed before she had been recognised as a victim of trafficking or could be considered for discretionary leave to remain. She had not worked since and was dependent on payments from the state.

In December 2019 the Claimant applied for judicial review of the Secretary of State for the Home Department's policy concerning leave to remain for suspected victims of trafficking who had been referred to the NRM. By the time of that application the Claimant had still not received a conclusive grounds decision. Relying on Article 10.2 of the European Convention on Action against Trafficking in Human Beings 2005 ("the Trafficking Convention"), the Claimant argued that, in circumstances where such delays arose, it was incumbent on the Secretary of State to include terms within the existing policy which regulated the leave position of a person who had received a positive reasonable grounds decision. Specifically, she claimed that discretionary leave, in some form, should be granted. The Claimant argued that Article 10.2 made abundantly clear that following a reasonable grounds decision discretionary leave to remain, in some form, must be granted to that person. She claimed that an obligation not to remove must mean the same as an authorisation to stay and an authorisation to stay could only be expressed by a grant of discretionary leave.

The Court considered whether the policy of excluding a recipient of a reasonable grounds decision from a grant of discretionary leave was unlawful and whether the Secretary of State's refusal to treat the Claimant's referral into the NRM as an application to vary her existing visa leave, thereby extending that leave under section 3C of the Immigration Act 1971, was unlawful. The Court also considered whether as a non-British, non-EEA national the Claimant was treated less favourably than a British or EEA national for the purposes of Article 14 of the ECHR and whether that discrimination also rendered the policy unlawful.

Held, granting the application:

(1) The Claimant did not receive a conclusive grounds decision until 28 April 2020, 595 days after her initial referral to the NRM. That conclusive grounds decision should have led to an automatic consideration of discretionary leave, yet the Claimant had not been granted or refused such leave. Two hundred and eleven days had elapsed since the conclusive grounds decision without a decision having been made about discretionary leave. The Claimant had been forced to give up her employment more than a year after her referral into the NRM. Even allowing for management and resource difficulties, any reasonable estimation of the likely timescales for decisions on reasonable grounds, conclusive grounds and discretionary leave would have led to the conclusion that they would have been completed with plenty of time to spare within a year. The Claimant must have had a reasonable expectation that she would have been able to continue with her work once her visa had expired. Instead she was forced to give up her employment and was cast into the "hostile environment" mandated by the Immigration Act 2014 for overstayers and other illegal migrants. As a result of the Secretary of State's delay the Claimant found herself in a most unhappy situation where she, as an overstayer, was branded a criminal, deprived of access to basic services, unemployed, dehumanised and penalised. The treatment meted out to her was far removed from the idea of social and psychological recovery (*paras 29 – 33*).

(2) The merit or otherwise of the claim had to be judged in the specific factual context where all referrals to the NRM appeared to be beset by extreme delay and where those delays arguably had resulted in unacceptable treatment of the Claimant. If there had been no delays, and if the Claimant's referral to the NRM had been processed within the timescales advertised in the two policy documents, then she would have had no case to bring before the Court. Well before her visa ran out, she would have received her conclusive grounds decision together with a decision on discretionary leave. One way or another her position would have been certain. She would either have been lawfully continuing to work; or she would have been preparing to return to her homeland if she had not already done so (*paras 36 and 37*).

(3) There was an unlawful lacuna in the existing policy inasmuch as it failed to implement the obligation in Article 10.2 of the Trafficking Convention formally to protect persons in receipt of a positive reasonable grounds decision from removal from the United Kingdom's national territory pending the conclusion of the process. Suffering such persons to remain as overstayers, or as illegal immigrants, did not fulfil the obligation. The Secretary of State had to formulate a policy that granted such persons interim discretionary leave on such terms and conditions as were appropriate both to their existing leave positions and to the likely delay that they would face. It was not for the Court to prescribe what the terms and conditions should be. Constitutionally that was a matter reserved to the Secretary of State. The terms and conditions did, however, have to be lawful and that meant

that someone in the position of the Claimant, who had a time-limited right to work, should not have the arbitrary adverse consequence of a removal of that right meted out to her simply by virtue of the delays that she was likely to face. What interim discretionary leave policy the Secretary of State should formulate in relation to those potential victims who had no leave of any type to be in the United Kingdom would be a matter for her to decide (*paras 48 and 49*).

(4) The discrimination claim had no substance whatsoever. A non-British, non-EEA potential victim of trafficking was not a qualifying status for the purposes of Article 14 of the ECHR. If that was wrong and if there was differential treatment, then it was abundantly objectively justified as it related to the immigration conditions of the Claimant and her comparator. It was indisputable that it was objectively justified to dispense different treatment to two people in otherwise identical positions by reference to their immigration statuses. That was the very essence of immigration control (*para 51*).

Cases referred to:

Balajigari and Others v Secretary of State for the Home Department [2019] EWCA Civ 673; [2019] 1 WLR 4647; [2019] 4 All ER 998; [2019] Imm AR 1152; [2019] INLR 619
MS (Pakistan) v Secretary of State for the Home Department [2020] UKSC 9; [2020] 1 WLR 1373; [2020] 3 All ER 733; [2020] Imm AR 967; [2020] INLR 460
R (on the application of O) v Secretary of State for the Home Department [2019] EWHC 148 (Admin)
R (on the application of PK (Ghana)) v Secretary of State for the Home Department [2018] EWCA Civ 98; [2018] 1 WLR 3955; [2018] Imm AR 961

Legislation and international instruments judicially considered:

European Convention on Action against Trafficking in Human Beings 2005, Articles 1, 10 & 14
European Convention on Human Rights, Articles 4 &14
Immigration Act 1971, sections 3C, 24 & 24B
Immigration Act 2014, sections 22 & 40
Modern Slavery Act 2015, section 49
National Health Service Act 2006, section 175
Road Traffic Act 1988, sections 97 & 99

Representation

Ms A Weston QC and *Ms M Butler* instructed by Duncan Lewis Solicitors, for the Claimant;
Mr R Tam QC and *Mr W Irwin* instructed by the Government Legal Department, for the Secretary of State.

Judgment

MR JUSTICE MOSTYN:

[1] The Council of Europe Convention on Action against Trafficking in Human Beings ("ECAT") was signed in Warsaw on 16 May 2005. Its paramount objectives, as stated in its recitals, are respect for victims' rights; protection of victims; and action to combat trafficking. In a similar vein, Article 1 provides that the purposes of ECAT are (a) to prevent and combat trafficking in human beings and (b) to protect the human rights of the victims of trafficking and to design a comprehensive framework for the protection and assistance of victims and witnesses.

[2] Although ECAT has not been formally incorporated into our domestic law it has been held that a failure by the government to apply its principles will be justiciable (see, for example, *R (PK (Ghana)) v Home Secretary* [2018] 1 WLR 3955 and *MS (Pakistan) v Secretary of State for the Home Department* [2020] UKSC 9 at [20]). Further, the Modern Slavery Act 2015 states in its explanatory notes that the Act was passed against the backdrop of ECAT and other international instruments and that the guidance that the Secretary of State is obliged to issue under section 49 must take into account the international requirements set out in the Convention. The latest version of that guidance (version 1.02) was re-issued in August 2020 ("the Main Guidance").

[3] Therefore, ECAT is as close to being incorporated in our domestic law, without actually being so, as it is possible to be.

[4] The obligations imposed by ECAT are discussed and explained in its Explanatory Report also dated 16 May 2005 ("the Explanatory Report") and have been further considered in authorities stretching to the Supreme Court.

[5] I will also be referring to a further piece of guidance: *Discretionary Leave Considerations for Victims of Modern Slavery* the latest version of which (3.0) was issued on 9 October 2020 ("the DL Guidance").

[6] Those documents and authorities set out how this country has sought to comply with its international obligations. The arrangements that have been made are well-known. They are pithily summarised by Baroness Hale of Richmond in *MS (Pakistan) v Home Secretary* at [2].

[7] In this country a person who is a suspected victim of trafficking is referred to the National Referral Mechanism ("NRM"). This is a body within the Home Office which acts as the competent authority for the purposes of ECAT. Its creation was by executive action alone; it has no statutory origin. Its staff must be trained and qualified in preventing and combatting trafficking. Using legislative and other measures it must seek to "identify" the referred person as a victim. Article 10 provides that the process of identification has two stages. First, there is a preliminary sift to determine if there are "reasonable grounds" to believe that a person has been a victim of trafficking (see the Explanatory Report at paras 131 and 132). If that decision is positive then the potential victim:

i)   cannot be removed from this country (see Article 10.2 and the Explanatory Report at para 132);

ii)   gains the benefit of the "recovery and reflection period" referred to in Article 13 which must last at least 30 days (but which probably should be longer (see the Explanatory Report at para 177)) and which is set at 45 days in this country (see the Main Guidance at paras 7.1 and 7.2); and

iii)   gains entitlement to the assistance specified in Article 12(1) and (2) (see the Explanatory Report at paras 135 and 147).

[8] The assistance to be afforded to potential victims under Articles 12.1 and 12.2 is that which is necessary for them in their physical, psychological and social recovery. At a minimum it includes (i) money for accommodation and psychological and material assistance; (ii) access to emergency medical treatment; (iii) access to education for children; and (iv) a general obligation to take account of the victim's safety and protection needs. The Explanatory Report states at para 150:

"The aim of the assistance provided for in sub-paragraphs (a) to (f) [of Article 12.1] is to "assist victims in their physical, psychological and social recovery". The authorities must therefore make arrangements for those assistance measures while bearing in mind the specific nature of that aim."

The obligation on the state to assist potential victims awaiting a conclusive grounds decision in their physical, psychological and social recovery is at the heart of the dispute in this case.

[9] For most potential victims these obligations are largely met by the government paying for accommodation; providing a weekly subsistence allowance of £65; and affording access to the NHS and education for children.

[10] Although it is not stated explicitly, it is obvious that an underlying principle of ECAT and its Explanatory Report is that the preliminary reasonable grounds decision should be taken very quickly. This imperative of expedition is reflected in the Main Guidance paras 7.2, 14.48 and 14.57 where it is stated that a reasonable grounds decision should be made within five working days "wherever possible".

[11] The second stage of the process of identification is for the Single Competent Authority ("SCA"), the decision-making arm of the NRM, to decide on the balance of probability if the referred person is indeed a victim of trafficking. This is known as the "conclusive grounds" decision.

[12] A positive conclusive grounds decision gives rise to an entitlement to a 45-day run-off of the interim support referred to above (see the Main Guidance at paras 7.1 and 7.2). More significantly, it opens the door under Article 14 to the possibility of the issue of a renewable residence permit. I shall deal with this in detail below. A conclusive grounds decision also allows for the meeting of long-term recovery needs for those with such needs.

[13] It is implicit in the terms of ECAT that the conclusive grounds decision should be taken in a reasonable time. In *R (O) v SSHD* [2019] EWHC 148 (Admin) Garnham J at [67] stated:

"... decisions must be taken in a reasonable time. What is reasonable, however, will turn on the nature of the power being exercised, the effect of exercising, and failing to exercise, the power, and all the circumstances of the case."

[14] The need to make a conclusive grounds decision in a reasonable time is reflected in the Main Guidance. At para 7.1 it states:

"The SCA will make a Conclusive Grounds decision no sooner than 45 calendar days after the reasonable grounds decision, to determine whether 'on the balance of probabilities' there are sufficient grounds to decide that the individual is a victim of modern slavery. This decision is based on evidence made available to the SCA. Following a positive Conclusive Grounds decision, victims will be exited from support only when appropriate to do so. Victims with a positive Conclusive Grounds decision will receive at least 45 calendar days of support during the move-on support period."

Para 7.2 states:

"Conclusive Grounds decision is made by the SCA. The Conclusive Grounds decision should generally be made *as soon as possible* after 45 calendar days."

At para 14.77 it states:

"There is no target to make a Conclusive Grounds decision within a specific timeframe. A Conclusive Grounds decision should be made *as soon as possible* after the 45-calendar day Recovery Period has ended, unless the SCA has received a request to delay the decision. The 45-day period begins when the SCA makes a positive Reasonable Grounds decision. The SCA is responsible for making a Conclusive Grounds decision."

And at para 14.243:

"To make sure that a Conclusive Grounds decision can be made *as near as possible* to day 45 (although that may not be possible in every case), a review date for day 30 should be set to:

• monitor progress on the case

• check it is on target for a conclusive decision."

[Emphasis added]

[15] I turn to residence permits. Under Article 14 of ECAT a residence permit "shall be issued to a victim" where the competent authority considers that their stay in the national territory is "necessary owing to their personal situation" or where it is considered that their stay is "necessary for the purposes of cooperation with the authorities in investigation or criminal proceeding." For the purposes of Article 14 a "victim" is someone who has had the benefit of a conclusive grounds decision, not merely a reasonable grounds decision.

[16] In this country the victims who will be seeking a residence permit under Article 14 will be those who are not British or EEA citizens.

[17] The Explanatory Report para 181 explains how the immediate return of a victim to his or her country of origin is unsatisfactory both for the victim and the law enforcement authorities combating the trafficking. It explains how a return may lead the victim back into the hands of traffickers; how it is unlikely to deter other victims from falling into the same trap; and how it may expose victims to a risk of reprisal. From the law-enforcement perspective the availability of residence permits is a measure calculated to encourage victims to cooperate. Para 183

expresses the first ground where it would be reasonable to grant a residence permit as: "the victim's personal circumstances must be such that it would be unreasonable to compel them to leave the national territory". Para 184 explains that the personal situation requirement will take in a range of situations, such as the victim's safety, state of health, family situation or some other factor which should be considered.

[18] The issue of a residence permit pursuant to Article 14 triggers the further entitlements referred to in Articles 12.3 and 12.4. Those entitlements are: (a) access to necessary medical or other assistance to which the victim does not have adequate resources and access; and (b) in accordance with nationally devised rules, access to the labour market and to vocational training and education. The entitlements are only available to victims who are "lawfully resident" in the state in question. The Explanatory Report at para 165 explains that lawful residence covers those victims issued with residence permits under Article 14. Para 166 goes on to say:

> "[Article 12.4] provides that each Party is to adopt the rules under which victims lawfully resident in the Party's territory are allowed access to the labour market, to vocational training and to education. In the drafters' view these measures are desirable for helping victims reintegrate socially and more particularly take greater charge of their lives. However, ECAT does not establish an actual right of access to the labour market, vocational training and education. It is for the Parties to decide the conditions governing access. As in paragraph 3, the words 'lawfully resident' refer, for instance, to victims who have a residence permit referred to in Article 14 or who have the Party's nationality. The authorisation referred to need not involve issuing an administrative document to the person concerned that allows them to work."

[19] ECAT does not establish an absolute right of the beneficiary of a residence permit under Article 14 to work but, rather, mandates that the contracting states should devise rules whereby such persons can access the labour market. However, that distinction is of no relevance in this country as the relevant policy here permits a victim who has received our version of an Article 14 residence permit to work in any field and to access public funds.

[20] The policy in this country is set out in the DL Guidance. The Article 14 residence permit will be a grant of discretionary leave. The standard grant is for 30 months. The decision whether to grant discretionary leave is made by the SCA. Consistently with the terms of Article 14, consideration of whether there should be a grant of discretionary leave will only arise once there has been a positive conclusive grounds decision.

[21] Page 6 of the DL Guidance states that a victim will not qualify for discretionary leave solely because the SCA has confirmed that he or she is a victim of modern slavery. It says: "there must be reasons based on their individual circumstances to justify a grant of discretionary leave". It states at page 7:

> "Discretionary leave may be considered under this specific policy where the SCA has made a positive conclusive grounds decision that an individual is a victim of modern slavery and they satisfy one of the following criteria:
>
> • leave is necessary owing to personal circumstances

- leave is necessary to pursue compensation

- victims who are helping police with their enquiries."

And at page 11:

"A positive conclusive grounds decision does not result in an automatic grant of immigration leave. However, unless the confirmed victim has an outstanding asylum claim at the time the positive conclusive grounds decision is made, *automatic consideration should normally be given at the same time, or as soon as possible afterwards,* to whether a grant of discretionary leave is appropriate under this policy." [Emphasis added]

[22] Therefore, it can be seen that the policy which has been adopted, reflecting the tacit imperative of expedition inherent in ECAT, is that a conclusive grounds decision should be made "as soon as possible" after the 45-day recovery period has finished. And that a decision about discretionary leave, where that is relevant, should be made at the same time as the conclusive grounds decision or "as soon as possible" thereafter.

[23] In *R (O) v SSHD* a wholesale attack was mounted against the NRM on the grounds that it was beset by systemic, chronic delay and as such its functioning was irrational in public law terms and therefore unlawful. Between [41] and [45] Garnham J analysed the statistics as they stood in the final quarter of 2018. The statistics revealed great delays. However, at [99] Garnham J held on the evidence before him:

"Furthermore, it appears from the evidence and the agreed statistics that the position is now improving. The problems appear to have been identified and resources are being devoted to improving the speed at which cases are determined."

[24] In the case before me I have been directed by a witness statement made by Nicola Simpson, the head of the NRM Sustainability and Policy Team, to a URL* which allowed the download of an Excel spreadsheet prepared by government statisticians containing a wealth of information about the functioning of the NRM. From that it has been possible to extract data which undermines the belief of Garnham J that things were improving. On any view things have gone from bad to worse.

[25] I have also seen a letter from the Independent Anti-slavery Commissioner, Dame Sara Thornton, to Victoria Atkins MP, the Parliamentary Undersecretary for Safeguarding and Vulnerability, dated 18 October 2019. This letter reveals the scale, past and present, of the backlog of unresolved cases at the NRM.

---

* https://www.gov.uk/government/statistics/modern-slavery-national-referral-mechanism-and-duty-to-notify-statistics-uk-quarter-2-2020-april-to-june

[26] I set out in the following table the pertinent data extracted from the above-mentioned sources:

	2017	2018	2019
No. of cases referred to NRM	5,141	6,986	10,620
No. of reasonable grounds decisions	4,830	6,826	10,423
No. of conclusive grounds decisions	1,873	3,254	3,608
Average (mean) no. of days to reach CG decision	356	462	462
Backlog	N/A	7,000	9,000

[27] This table, and the underlying data, make for very dispiriting reading. The table shows a remorseless increase in cases referred to the NRM. While it is true that the number of reasonable grounds decisions has matched the incoming caseload, the same cannot be said of conclusive grounds decisions. There was an increase in such decisions between 2017 and 2018 but the number in 2018 was only about half of what was needed to deal with the volume of incoming cases; and in 2019 it was only just over a third. Hence the increase in the backlog from 7,000 to 9,000 cases which at the current disposal rate will take between two and three years to conclude. The present average (mean) number of 462 days (i.e.15 months) to dispose conclusively of cases will inevitably worsen given the scale of the backlog.

[28] The data also belies Garnham J's projection in [41], based on the statistical evidence before him, that in 2018 the number of referrals would fall to 4,245 as well as his projection in [43] that the average length of time for making a conclusive grounds decision was falling. He estimated that for 2017 the average length of time for making such a decision had fallen to 327 days. In fact, it was 356 days, and rose sharply in 2018 to 462 days where it stayed for 2019.

[29] These delays are mirrored by the personal experience of the claimant in this case. She was referred to the NRM on 11 September 2018. She did receive a reasonable grounds decision, albeit negative, within six days. The NRM agreed to reconsider that decision. It took, remarkably, until 11 June 2019 for the claimant to receive a positive reasonable grounds decision. That was 273 days after her initial referral to the NRM. By the time that she made her judicial review application on 11 December 2019, 456 days after her initial referral, she had not received a conclusive grounds decision. She did not receive a conclusive grounds decision until 28 April 2020, an astonishing 595 days after her initial referral to the NRM. That conclusive grounds decision should have led to an automatic consideration of discretionary leave yet at the date I write this judgment, 26 November 2020, she has not yet been granted or refused such leave. 211 days have elapsed since the conclusive grounds decision without a decision having been made about discretionary leave. An astonishing 806 days have elapsed between her initial referral to the NRM and today.

[30] The effect of these delays has been to hit the claimant very hard. She entered this country on 20 September 2017 having been granted a Tier 5 Youth Mobility Scheme Visa, which entitled her to work and which was valid until 20 September 2019. Unfortunately, in April 2018 she fell under the domination of a man who abused her sexually and forced her into prostitution. Eventually she managed to escape, and as stated above, on 11 September 2018 she was referred into the NRM. On 25 June 2019 the claimant started work with a trafficking

support organisation. She was able to do so because her visa remained unexpired. She very much enjoyed this work and on any view her ability to do it was an important component in her psychological and social recovery with which the state was obligated to assist her under the terms of the Convention. However, as stated above, her visa was due to expire on 20 September 2019. Therefore, a few days before that, on 14 September 2019, she ceased work, and has not worked since. Since then she has been dependant on payments from the state.

[31] 14 September 2019 was more than a year after her referral into the NRM. Even allowing for management and resource difficulties any reasonable estimation of the likely timescales for decisions on reasonable grounds, conclusive grounds and discretionary leave would have led to the conclusion that they would have been completed with plenty of time to spare within a year. The claimant therefore must have had a not unreasonable expectation that she would have been able to have continued with her work once her visa had expired because by then, surely, she would have reasoned, she would have gained discretionary leave.

[32] But no. Instead the claimant was forced to give up her employment and was cast into the "hostile environment" mandated by the Immigration Act 2014 for overstayers and other illegal migrants. The features of this environment were well described in *R (Balajigari) v SSHD* [2019] 1 WLR 4647 by Underhill LJ at [81]:

> "Secondly, Mr Biggs relied on the legal consequences for an applicant who remained in the UK without leave, which have been rendered more severe by the so-called "hostile environment" provisions introduced by the Immigration Act 2014. It is, in the first place, a criminal offence to be in the UK without leave to remain: see section 24 of the Immigration Act 1971. As regards practical consequences, a person without leave faces severe restrictions on their right to work (see section 24B of the 1971 Act), to rent accommodation (section 22 of the 2014 Act), to have a bank account (section 40 of the 2014 Act) and to hold a driving licence (sections 97, 97A and 99 of the Road Traffic Act 1988); nor will they be entitled to free treatment from the NHS: section 175 of the National Health Service Act 2006. He submitted that those consequences are bound to have a serious impact on a migrant's private life irrespective of any removal action."

[33] So it can be seen as a result of the defendant's delay the claimant finds herself in a most unhappy situation where she, as an overstayer, is branded a criminal (although no one has seriously suggested she would actually be prosecuted), deprived of access to basic services, unemployed, dehumanised and penalised. She has filed some moving evidence describing her sense of failure and emotional isolation since she has been deprived of the opportunity to work. The treatment meted out to her is far removed from the idea of social and psychological recovery.

[34] The claimant's claim for judicial review argues that her predicament on 11 December 2019 was the consequence of the application to her of an unlawful policy by the defendant. Specifically, she argues that (1) the defendant's policy of excluding a recipient of a reasonable grounds decision from a grant of discretionary leave is unlawful and (2) the defendant's refusal to treat a referral into the NRM as an application to vary her existing visa leave, thereby extending that leave under section 3C Immigration Act 1971, is likewise unlawful. Further,

she argues that as a non-British, non-EEA national she is treated less favourably than a British or EEA national for the purposes of Article 14 of the European Convention on Human Rights and this discrimination also renders the policy unlawful.

[35] The claimant has been careful not to rerun the arguments based on chronic systemic delays unsuccessfully mounted by Ms Lieven QC in *R(O) v SSHD*. Ms Weston QC recognises that a judicial review based on delay is always a very steep climb requiring clear proof of irrationality. Rather, Ms Weston QC has been careful to confine the claim in the way I have set out above.

[36] However, the merit or otherwise of the claim has to be judged in the specific factual context where all referrals to the NRM appear to be beset by extreme delay and where those delays arguably have resulted in unacceptable treatment being meted out to this claimant.

[37] If there had been no delays, and if the claimant's referral to the NRM had been processed within the timescales advertised in the two policy documents, then she would have had no case to bring before this court. Well before her visa ran out she would have received her conclusive grounds decision together with a decision on discretionary leave. One way or another her position would have been certain. She would either have been lawfully continuing to work; or she would have been preparing to return to her homeland if she had not already done so.

[38] Therefore, the argument of Ms Weston QC was refined during her oral submissions. She argued that in circumstances where such gross delays arose it was incumbent on the defendant to include within the existing policy terms which regulated the leave position of a person who had received a positive reasonable grounds decision. Ms Weston QC placed strong reliance on Article 10.2. This provides:

"Article 10 – Identification of the victims

2. Each Party shall adopt such legislative or other measures as may be necessary to identify victims as appropriate in collaboration with other Parties and relevant support organisations. Each Party shall ensure that, if the competent authorities have reasonable grounds to believe that a person has been victim of trafficking in human beings, that person shall not be removed from its territory until the identification process as victim of an offence provided for in Article 18 of this Convention has been completed by the competent authorities and shall likewise ensure that that person receives the assistance provided for in Article 12, paragraphs 1 and 2."

[39] This makes abundantly clear, she argues, that following a reasonable grounds decision discretionary leave to remain, in some form, must be granted to that person. An obligation not to remove must mean the same as an authorisation to stay. And an authorisation to stay can only be expressed by a grant of discretionary leave. Yet, a decision on reasonable grounds says nothing about being allowed to stay at that point in time. The decision dated 11 June 2019 sent to the claimant only addressed the future. It said: "if you are not a UK or EU/EEA national, and you receive a positive decision at Conclusive Grounds stage, then we will consider whether you will qualify for Discretionary Leave under the Modern Slavery policy."

[40] Ms Weston QC bolsters her argument about the meaning of Article 10.2 by reliance on some rather ambiguous drafting in Article 13.1. As explained above, this provides for a recovery and reflection period, set at 45 days in this country, to start immediately following a positive reasonable grounds decision. Article 13.1 provides:

> **"Article 13 – Recovery and reflection period**
>
> 1. Each Party shall provide in its internal law a recovery and reflection period of at least 30 days, when there are reasonable grounds to believe that the person concerned is a victim. Such a period shall be sufficient for the person concerned to recover and escape the influence of traffickers and/or to take an informed decision on cooperating with the competent authorities. During this period it shall not be possible to enforce any expulsion order against him or her. This provision is without prejudice to the activities carried out by the competent authorities in all phases of the relevant national proceedings, and in particular when investigating and prosecuting the offences concerned. *During this period,* the Parties shall authorise the persons concerned to stay in their territory."

Ms Weston QC argues that the mention of "this period" in the final sentence (which I have underlined) refers to, and is governed by, the scenario in the immediately preceding sentence namely the time taken to undertake the activities carried out by the competent authorities in all phases of the relevant national proceedings. Ms Weston QC says that "these activities" plainly extend to reaching a conclusive grounds decision. Therefore, in that period the state must authorise the person to stay here. That can only be done by a grant of discretionary leave.

[41] Although this is a respectable argument I do not agree with it. Nor do I think it is necessary to enable the primary argument about the meaning of Article 10.2 to succeed. Although the drafting is ambiguous it seems to me that the reference to "this period" in the final sentence is indeed to the recovery and reflection period. Article 13 is about the recovery and reflection period and nothing else. Had the final sentence been referring to a different period it would have said "that period" to distinguish it from the period referred to in the heading of the Article and in its first three sentences.

[42] Reverting to her primary argument, Ms Weston QC submits that the absence of the grant of any kind of leave, however limited, to the beneficiary of a reasonable grounds decision is a fatal failure to implement the clear requirement not to remove such a person from the national territory as provided for in Article 10.2. As pointed out by Underhill LJ in *Balajigari* it is a criminal offence for anyone who is not a British or EEA citizen to be in this country without leave. It is unthinkable, it is argued, that a government agency whose obligation is to promote the psychological and social recovery of potential victims of trafficking should withhold interim leave from such people and force them into the status of criminality and exposure to the chill winds reserved for overstayers and other illegal immigrants.

[43] Ms Weston QC argues that any new policy would necessarily have to deal with those potential victims who had no leave as well as those potential victims who, like the claimant, had extant leave entitling them to work. As regards the latter class Ms Weston QC argues that the new policy should apply the principle embodied in section 3C of the Immigration Act 1971 and treat the reasonable grounds decision as having the effect of extending the existing leave until the process was concluded.

[44] Mr Tam QC argues that the true complaint of the claimant is about the delay that she has suffered at each stage of her journey through the system. He does not dispute that the data appears to show a further deterioration since Garnham J considered the statistics in late 2018. He accepts that the delay in dealing with all three stages of the claimant's progress has been most regrettable. However, he argues that this attack on the policy is completely misplaced when there were remedies available to the claimant in respect of the delay that she was suffering. First, she could have sought discretionary leave outside the Immigration Rules on the ground that she was a potential victim of trafficking and had been waiting an unconscionably long time for a conclusive grounds decision. Had she made that application before her visa expired then section 3C would have operated to have extended that leave until her application was determined.

[45] Second, she could make a claim for humanitarian protection or asylum if she feared harm were she to be made to return to her homeland. Third, and similarly, she could make a human rights claim relying on Article 4 of the European Convention on Human Rights were she to be returned to her homeland. If she had made either of the latter two applications then an adverse decision would have attracted a right of appeal to the First-Tier Tribunal. Therefore, as she had these alternative routes of challenge it would be inappropriate for the court to allow a more wide-ranging attack on the policy itself.

[46] As for the attacks on the policy Mr Tam QC argues that it has been formulated precisely in accordance with the state's international obligations under ECAT. By its terms ECAT contemplates that a potential victim of trafficking might simultaneously be present illegally in the national territory and still require protection and recovery. See, for example, Article 13.1, which contemplates the temporary suspension of an expulsion order.

[47] In her reply Ms Weston QC characterised the three potential applications that Mr Tam QC suggests her client might make as being straw men which required dismantling. Under the existing published policy for the grant of discretionary leave outside the Immigration Rules the criterion is very stringent. Compelling compassionate grounds must be demonstrated and even then the grant of leave will be very sparingly exercised. She maintains that her client would have no chance whatsoever of being granted leave on that ground. Similarly, the two latter claims that Mr Tam QC trailed would be essentially impossible having regard to the fact that her homeland is New Zealand. Any decision-maker would safely assume she would receive full protection in New Zealand if she faced any harm.

[48] My conclusion is as follows. I agree with Ms Weston QC that there is an unlawful lacuna in the existing policy inasmuch as it fails to implement the obligation in Article 10.2 formally to protect persons in receipt of a positive reasonable grounds decision from removal from this country's national territory pending the conclusion of the process. Suffering such persons to remain as overstayers, or as illegal immigrants, does not fulfil the obligation. The defendant must formulate a policy that grants such persons interim discretionary leave on such terms and conditions as are appropriate both to their existing leave positions and to the likely delay that they will face. It is not for me to prescribe what such terms and conditions should be. I agree with Mr Tam QC that constitutionally that is a matter reserved to the defendant. However, the terms and conditions must

obviously be lawful and this would mean that someone in the position of the claimant, who has a time-limited right to work, should not have the arbitrary adverse consequence of a removal of that right meted out to her simply by virtue of the delays that she is likely to face.

[49] What interim discretionary leave policy the defendant should formulate in relation to those potential victims who have no leave of any type to be here will be a matter for her to decide.

[50] I therefore will grant a declaration which incorporates my decision set out in para 48 above. I ask counsel to seek to agree the terms of the declaration. If they cannot do so then I will rule on any disputed wording.

[51] Having made my primary decision, I can deal with the discrimination claim extremely shortly. For the reasons given by Mr Tam QC I am completely satisfied that this claim has no substance whatsoever. I do not accept that a non-British, non-EEA potential victim of trafficking is a qualifying status for the purposes of Article 14 of the European Convention on Human Rights. If I am wrong about that and if there is differential treatment then in my judgement it is abundantly objectively justified as it relates to the immigration conditions of the claimant and her comparator. It is indisputable that it is objectively justified to dispense different treatment to two people in otherwise identical positions by reference to their immigration statuses. That is the very essence of immigration control. I agree that this ground is devoid of merit.

[52] That is my judgment.

YD (ALGERIA) v SECRETARY OF STATE FOR THE HOME DEPARTMENT

COURT OF APPEAL

Peter Jackson, Asplin and Lewis LJJ

[2020] EWCA Civ 1683
14 December 2020

Asylum – internal relocation – persecution – would not live as an openly gay man – social, cultural and religious reasons – not sufficient to amount to persecution – human rights – Article 8 of the ECHR – no significant obstacles to reintegration – risk on return – homosexuals – Algeria – family members – OO (Gay men) Algeria *CG [2016] UKUT 65 (IAC) approved*

The Claimant, a citizen of Algeria, entered the United Kingdom in 2012 when he was 15 years old. He claimed asylum on the ground that he had a well-founded fear of persecution in Algeria because he was homosexual. He recounted that his parents had died when he was six years old and, thereafter, he had lived with his uncle, with whom he had a troubled relationship. When the Claimant was aged 13, he had formed a sexual relationship with A, a 14-year-old boy. A's mother had discovered the relationship and said that she would tell the Claimant's uncle. The Claimant lived on the streets for a while before meeting someone who helped him travel to the United Kingdom. The Claimant asserted that, if returned to Algeria, he feared that his uncle would kill him and that he would be generally treated badly and be in danger because of his homosexuality. The Secretary of State for the Home Department refused the claim but granted the Claimant discretionary leave to remain ("LTR") for one year. The Claimant's further application for LTR was refused in October 2015.

On appeal, the First-tier Tribunal ("FtT") accepted the Claimant's account and found that he was gay. It summarised the country guidance in *OO (Gay men) Algeria* CG [2016] UKUT 65 (IAC) and noted that the Algerian state did not actively seek out gay men to take any form of action against them, either by prosecution or subjecting them to other forms of persecutory ill-treatment. The FtT held that the Claimant did have a well-founded fear of persecution in his home area in Algeria because of the risk posed by his uncle, and the state would be unwilling to protect him from that risk. It found however that the Claimant would not be at risk if he were to relocate within Algeria and there were no features in the case that would make relocation unreasonable or unduly harsh. The FtT found that in Algeria the Claimant would not choose to express himself as a gay person because of a respect for the social norms, traditions and religion. In relation to Article 8 of the ECHR, the FtT accepted that the Claimant had established a private life in the United Kingdom but held that he did not meet the requirements of paragraph 276ADE of the Immigration Rules HC 395 (as amended) because there were no significant obstacles to him re-integrating in Algeria. The Upper Tribunal ("UT") dismissed the Claimant's appeal against the FtT's decision.

On appeal, the Claimant submitted first, that the UT erred in its application of the principles established in *HJ (Iran) v Secretary of State for the Home*

Department [2010] UKSC 31, in that it failed adequately to consider the cumulative impact of the consequences that a gay man living openly in Algeria would or might face. He argued that it was necessary to consider whether the effects of the long-term concealment or suppression of a gay man's sexual orientation, for fear of the consequences of living openly, irrespective of whether those amounted to persecution, could themselves be sufficiently serious to amount to persecution. He submitted that *OO (Algeria)*, upon which the UT had relied, was itself flawed because, *inter alia*, the UT in that case had focussed on the risk of physical violence and failed to consider other types of treatment which, cumulatively, might constitute persecution. Secondly, the Claimant submitted that the UT erred in concluding that internal relocation within Algeria would not be unduly harsh. Thirdly, he submitted that the UT had erred in its approach to Article 8 of the ECHR, particularly when considering that there were no significant obstacles to him re-integrating in Algeria.

Held, dismissing the appeal:

(1) On any fair reading of the decision in *OO (Algeria)*, it was clear that the UT did not limit its consideration to the risk of physical violence. The review of the evidence covered criminalisation of homosexual acts, the risk of prosecution, the risk of physical attacks from the authorities, discrimination in the provision of services and employment and attitudes to homosexuality. Given the structure of the decision, the evidence it considered, and its conclusions, it was clear that the UT considered whether there was reliable evidence of physical violence and other forms of conduct in order to determine whether gay men in Algeria had a well-founded fear of persecution. It was also clear that the UT considered the cumulative effect of the treatment that occurred. It did not use the word "cumulatively", and it could have expressed its conclusions more fully in that respect, but the issue was one of substance rather than form. In substance, the UT in *OO (Algeria)* considered matters cumulatively as well as individually (*paras 43 – 45*).

(2) There was no substance to the criticism that the UT in the instant case erred by failing to consider how a gay man living openly as such in Algeria would be treated. The UT expressly said that any assessment had to be informed by the decision in *HJ (Iran)* and stated it must ask itself whether it was 'satisfied on the available evidence that gay people who lived openly would be liable to persecution'. It identified the relevant principle and applied that to the evidence before it. There were difficulties in doing that, as the evidence was that most gay men in Algeria did not live openly and many would not identify themselves as gay for societal, cultural and religious reasons. There was no doubt however that the UT sought to determine how gay men who lived openly would be treated. Different societies at different times had taken different views as to homosexuality. The Refugee Convention was intended to provide protection only in the circumstances agreed by the contracting parties. The fact that homosexual acts were criminalised in a particular country was not, of itself, recognised as giving rise to a well-founded fear of persecution. The UT here, and in *OO (Algeria)*, correctly understood the question it had to consider and reached findings of fact which the instant Court must respect. The UT was entitled to conclude that, outside the family home, a gay man in Algeria would not have a

well-founded fear of persecution by reason of his sexual orientation (*paras 46 – 50*).

(3) The Claimant's submission that the very fact of being forced to conceal or suppress one's sexual orientation might give rise to harm which reached the threshold of persecution needed to be set in context. The country guidance was that gay men did not live openly in Algeria because of social, cultural and religious norms in a conservative society, subject to strict Islamic values. The fact that a gay man would not live openly in Algeria for those reasons was not enough to amount to persecution. That conclusion was consistent with the decision in *HJ (Iran)*. If the fact that a gay man concealed his sexual orientation was enough to establish persecution, that would have been the basis of the Supreme Court's decision. Instead, Lord Roger recognised that there were three questions: was the applicant gay, would a gay man who lived openly be liable to persecution in the country of nationality, and what would the person do on return? If he would not live openly, a tribunal would have to ask why, and if that were the result of social pressures, then his application for refugee status would fail. In the instant case, the fact of concealment resulted from societal pressures, not from the actions of the state. The state was not under a duty to protect a gay man from societal, cultural or religious values which were hostile to homosexuality but did not manifest themselves in ill-treatment of the kind to amount to persecution. Finally, on the facts of the case, there was no evidence that concealment by the Claimant of his sexual orientation would result in psychological harm (*paras 51 – 55*).

(4) In relation to the second ground of appeal, the sole question was whether it was unduly harsh to require the Claimant to relocate within Algeria, where he would choose not to live openly as a gay man. Life would clearly be different, and probably immeasurably better, for the Claimant if he were to live in a country where the society and social, cultural and religious pressures, did not compel him to decide to conceal his sexual orientation. The Refugee Convention was not, however, intended to guard or protect an individual from such pressures. The UT and FtT were entitled to conclude that it would not be unduly harsh for the Claimant to relocate within Algeria. Furthermore, the UT's observations in *OO (Algeria)* on that question were not flawed. The UT was dealing with a situation where it found that gay men would not live openly, not because of a fear of persecution, but due to other reasons. In those circumstances, there would need to be something arising from an individual's personal circumstances which would make it unreasonable and unduly harsh to expect him to relocate to avoid the risk of persecution from his family. There was nothing inconsistent in that summary with the test on relocation expressed in *Januzi and Others v Secretary of State for the Home Department* [2006] UKHL 5 and *Secretary of State for the Home Department v AH (Sudan) and Others* [2007] UKHL 49, provided that the tribunal kept in mind the need to consider all the relevant circumstances of the claimant and his country of origin (*paras 62 and 65 – 66*).

(5) The Claimant was born in Algeria and lived there until he was 15. He had acquired skills and experience in the United Kingdom and demonstrated self-reliance and initiative: *Kamara v Secretary of State for the Home Department* [2016] EWCA Civ 813 distinguished. In those circumstances, the UT was entitled to conclude that the Claimant would be capable of adapting to life in Algeria. The fact that he would not live an openly gay life would be a severely limiting feature on aspects of his life in Algeria, but it did not provide a very significant obstacle to his re-integration (*paras 69 – 71*).

Cases referred to:

HJ (Iran) v Secretary of State for the Home Department; HT (Cameroon) v Secretary of State for the Home Department [2010] UKSC 31; [2011] 1 AC 596; [2010] 3 WLR 386; [2011] 2 All ER 591; [2010] Imm AR 729; [2010] INLR 425

Horvath v Secretary of State for the Home Department [2000] UKHL 37; [2001] 1 AC 489; [2000] 3 WLR 379; [2000] 3 All ER 577; [2000] Imm AR 552; [2000] INLR 239

Hysi v Secretary of State for the Home Department [2005] EWCA Civ 711; [2005] INLR 602

J v Secretary of State for the Home Department [2006] EWCA Civ 1238; [2007] Imm AR 73

Januzi v Secretary of State for the Home Department; Hamid v Secretary of State for the Home Department; Gaafar v Secretary of State for the Home Department; Mohammed v Secretary of State for the Home Department [2006] UKHL 5; [2006] 2 AC 426; [2006] 3 All ER 305; [2006] Imm AR 252; [2006] INLR 118

Johar and Others v Union of India and Others (2018) SCC 781 (Supreme Court of India)

Minister voor Immigratie en Asiel v X and Y; Z v Minister voor Immigratie en Asiel (Cases C-199/12 to C-201/12)

OO (Gay men) Algeria CG [2016] UKUT 65 (IAC)

R (on the application of SG (Iraq)) v Secretary of State for the Home Department [2012] EWCA Civ 940; [2013] 1 WLR 41; [2012] Imm AR 953; [2013] INLR 214

Secretary of State for the Home Department v AH (Sudan) and Others [2007] UKHL 49; [2008] 1 AC 678; [2007] 3 WLR 832; [2008] 4 All ER 190; [2008] Imm AR 289; [2008] INLR 100

Secretary of State for the Home Department v Kamara [2016] EWCA Civ 813; [2016] 4 WLR 152

TK (gay man) St Lucia [2019] UKUT 92 (IAC)

Legislation and international instruments judicially considered:

Convention relating to the Status of Refugees, Article 1A(2)
Directive 2004/83/EC ("the Qualification Directive"), Article 9
European Convention on Human Rights, Article 8
Immigration Rules HC 395 (as amended), paragraph 276ADE

Representation

Mr R Husain QC, *Ms R Chapman, Ms L Hooper* and *Ms E Mitchell* instructed by Bindmans LLP, for the Claimant;
Mr S Singh QC instructed by the Government Legal Department, for the Secretary of State;
Ms M Demetriou QC and *Mr T Pascoe* instructed by Baker & McKenzie LLP, for the UNHCR as Intervener.

JUDGMENT

LORD JUSTICE LEWIS (with whom Lord Justice Peter Jackson and Lady Justice Asplin agree):

INTRODUCTION

[1] This is an appeal against a decision of the Upper Tribunal (Immigration and Asylum Chamber) dated 21 November 2017 dismissing an appeal against a decision of the First-tier Tribunal. That tribunal had dismissed the appellant's appeal against a decision of the respondent of 13 October 2015 refusing him leave to remain in the United Kingdom. In essence, the respondent rejected the appellant's claim that, as a gay man, he would be subjected to persecution were he to be returned to Algeria and his claim that return would be incompatible with his right to respect for his private and family life guaranteed by Article 8 of the Convention for the Protection of Human Rights and Fundamental Freedoms ("the Convention").

[2] In summary, the Upper Tribunal followed an earlier decision of the Upper Tribunal, *OO (Gay men) (Algeria)* CG [2016] UKUT 00065, giving country guidance on the conditions in Algeria for gay men. That earlier decision concluded that, outside the family, gay men would not face treatment amounting to persecution in Algeria. Further, it concluded that very few gay men lived openly as such in Algeria as a consequence of cultural, religious and social pressures.

[3] The issues that arise on this appeal are whether the Upper Tribunal in *OO (Algeria)* wrongly equated persecution with a risk of being subjected to physical violence and also failed to consider, cumulatively, the impact of the treatment that gay men would face in Algeria. Further, the appeal raises the issues of whether it would be unduly harsh to require the appellant to relocate within Algeria or whether returning him to Algeria would amount to a disproportionate interference with his rights under Article 8 of the Convention given that he would conceal his sexual orientation if he returned to live in Algeria.

THE FACTS

The background

[4] The appellant, YD, is an Algerian citizen born on 3 January 1997. He entered the United Kingdom illegally in July 2012 when he was 15 years of age. He claimed asylum on the basis that as a homosexual male he had a well-founded fear of persecution if he were to be returned to Algeria.

[5] The background to the claim was as follows. The appellant's parents died in a car crash when he was six and he went to live with his uncle. That relationship became troubled and the appellant was told to leave the home when he was about 12 years old. He became homeless for some months. He met another boy, Anis, and went to stay with him. They formed a sexual relationship. The appellant was 13 and the boy was 14. The boy's mother discovered them having sex. She told the appellant to leave the house and said that she would tell his uncle about the relationship. The appellant returned to living on the streets and subsequently met a person who helped him travel to the United Kingdom.

The asylum claim

[6] The basis of the claim for asylum was that the appellant feared that his uncle would kill him because of his homosexuality and that he would be judged and treated badly, and would be in danger, in Algeria. That claim was refused on 8 July 2013 but the appellant was granted discretionary leave to remain for one year. He applied for further leave to remain. That was refused on 13 October 2015. The appellant appealed to the First-tier Tribunal.

The appeal to the First-tier Tribunal

[7] The appellant provided a written statement for the First-tier Tribunal together with two other witness statements made earlier. In the witness statement prepared for the tribunal hearing, he said that he believed that his uncle would find him and kill him if he were returned to Algeria. He said that he would not be accepted in Algeria. He had lived for four years in the United Kingdom and he felt good about himself and did not feel ashamed about his sexuality. He said people in the United Kingdom were very open minded and he did not have to worry about his behaviour or how people viewed him. The situation would be very different in Algeria and he did not think he would be able to cope with that. He would be rejected by society, mistreated and abused, and did not believe the police would protect him. He had had one relationship with one male in the United Kingdom. That man made a witness statement and gave evidence before the tribunal confirming that he and the appellant were in a relationship although they did not live together. The appellant gave oral evidence and the decision of the First-tier Tribunal records a summary of his oral evidence.

[8] The tribunal first found as a fact that the appellant was gay and was in a relationship with a man. The tribunal was also satisfied that the appellant had had a relationship in Algeria with Anis as he had described and that that relationship had been discovered. Secondly, the First-tier Tribunal summarised the earlier country guidance about the conditions facing gay men in Algeria given in *OO (Algeria)*. It noted that the authorities do not seek to prosecute gay men and there was no real risk of prosecution even when authorities became aware of homosexual behaviour. The state did not actively seek out gay men to take any form of action against them either by prosecution or subjecting them to other forms of persecutory ill-treatment. Sharia law was not applied to gay men. It noted that the earlier decision said that:

"the only risk of ill-treatment at a level to become persecutory likely to be encountered by a gay man in Algeria, is at the hands of his own family after they discovered that he is gay. There is no reliable evidence such as to establish that a gay man identified as such faces a real risk of persecutory treatment from persons outside his own family."

[9] It noted the earlier decision stated that where a gay man had to flee his family home to avoid persecution from family members, he would attract no real risk of persecution in his place of relocation because, generally, he would not live as a gay man. It would be a question of whether the individual could show that, due to his individual circumstances, it would be unreasonable and unduly harsh to expect him to relocate within Algeria.

[10] Against that background, the First-tier Tribunal held so far as material to the present appeal that:

"23. Firstly, I find in view of the problems that the Appellant had with his uncle and with Anis's mother, that there is a real risk of violent and persecutory ill-treatment of the Appellant from his uncle and from Anis's parents. It therefore follows that the Appellant will not be able to live in the local area, bearing in mind the problems that he had had and the feedback that his uncle has had from his sexual encounters with Anis. However, the Tribunal [in *OO*] went on to state at paragraph 177, that once the gay son has left the family home and re-established himself elsewhere, there is no real risk that family members would pursue him to that place of relocation and so generally that risk of persecution can be avoided by the availability of a safe and reasonable internal relocation alternative. I find bearing in mind that there is no indication that the Appellant's uncle or Anis's parents have influence all over the whole of Algeria would be able to reach the Appellant if he is to relocate. It cannot be said that the Appellant's uncle or Anis's parents would pursue the Appellant to a place of relocation.

24. The question I have to consider is whether it is reasonable for the Appellant to relocate taking away the issue of his uncle and Anis's parents. Considering that question I have taken into account the submissions made by [counsel for the appellant] with reference to *HJ (Iran)*. At paragraph 82, the Supreme Court outlines the approach to be followed by Tribunals. The court stated that the Tribunal must first ask whether it is satisfied on the evidence that the Appellant is gay. I find that in this particular case I have found that the Appellant is gay. The Tribunal must then ask itself whether it is satisfied on the available evidence that gay people who live openly would be liable to persecution in the applicant's country of nationality. In this case the country guidance case is the point of reference and in that case the Tribunal found that although the Algerian Criminal Code makes homosexual behaviour unlawful, the authorities do not seek to prosecute gay men and there is no real risk of persecution, even the authorities become aware of such behaviour.

25. The Tribunal also found that Sharia law is not applied against gay men in Algeria and that the criminal law is entirely secular and discloses no manifestation at all of Sharia law in its application. I therefore find that other than outside the Appellant's family members, the country guidance case decides that there is no reliable evidence to establish that a gay man identified as such faces a real risk of persecutory ill-treatment from person's outside his own family.

26. The question I have to consider is that if the Appellant was to return to Algeria how would he live. The question for consideration is whether he would live discreetly in order to avoid persecution. The Appellant stated in evidence that he feels free to live openly as a gay person in the UK and that he would not be able to do this in Algeria. He said that he would be in danger. However, this is contrary to the evidence which has been considered in the country guidance case and for which the conclusion has been reached that if the Appellant chooses to live discreetly in Algeria he would be driven by respect for social

laws and a desirirable (*sic*) to avoid attracting disapproval of a type that falls well below the threshold of persecution.

...

29. Having considered all the evidence before me, I find that if the Appellant was to return to Algeria today he would obviously not live openly as a gay person. I find that the Appellant would not want to express himself as a gay person in Algeria not necessarily because of persecution, but also because of the fact that respect for the social norms and traditions and religion as he himself expressed in evidence. The Appellant stated that his sexual orientation would put him in danger however, the country guidance case states that this is not the case and therefore his subjective evidence does not stand up with the background evidence as analysed in the country guidance case. And that there is no particular characteristics in the Appellant's case that would make relocation for him unreasonable or unduly harsh.

30. The Appellant has been in the UK now for about four years and has a way of life which would enable him to adapt to any place he decides to relocate to. For the reasons I have stated the Appellant does not succeed on his asylum claim, his case would also fail under Article 2 and Article 3 of the Human Rights Convention. With regard to Article 8, I find that the Appellant does not have any family life in the United Kingdom. He also does not have any children in the United Kingdom and his case cannot succeed under the family life aspect of Appendix FM of the Immigration Rules. With regards to paragraph 276ADE, I accept that the Appellant has a private life however with regard to the findings that I have made applying the country guidance case, I find that there would be no significant obstacles with the Appellant reintegrating back into Algeria."

[11] The First-tier Tribunal therefore dismissed the appellant's asylum claim and his human rights claim.

The appeal to the Upper Tribunal

[12] The appellant appealed to the Upper Tribunal on five grounds of which only three are material for present purposes. The first was that the First-tier Tribunal misapplied the judgment of the Supreme Court in *HJ (Iran)*. As the Upper Tribunal noted, this was in effect a challenge to the country guidance decision in *OO (Algeria)* contending that the Upper Tribunal there had applied too narrow a definition of persecution. The Upper Tribunal held:

"9. At the heart of the criticism of the Tribunal's decision in *OO (Algeria)* is the contention that the Tribunal applied to narrow a definition of persecution. It is said that self- repression of sexual orientation as a reaction to social stigma, ostracism and discrimination can amount to persecution or a violation of human rights. So, if applicants for asylum require, for their own protection against such reactions, to exercise self-restraint by avoiding behaviour which would identify sexual orientations, that is capable of constituting persecution. Reference is made to what Lord Rodger said at paragraph 78 of *HJ (Iran)* that what is protected is the right of gay people to be as free as their straight equivalents to live their lives in the ways that is natural to them, without fear of persecution.

10. We do not consider these criticisms to be well-founded. The Tribunal had full regard to the Supreme Court's decision in *HJ (Iran)*. The Supreme Court highlighted a distinction to be made when considering the question whether someone living discreetly as a gay person amounts to persecution. Social pressures do not amount to persecution and the convention does not offer protection against them. However, as stated at paragraph 82, if a material reason for the applicant living discreetly on his return would be a fear of persecution which would follow if he were to live openly as a gay man then the application should be accepted. There is nothing in *OO (Algeria)* that runs contrary to that approach. The Tribunal carefully assessed the evidence and found that it was not established that gay people in Algeria would be subjected to any harm of sufficient intensity and duration capable of amounting to persecution...."

[13] Ground 4 was a challenge to the finding that it would not be unduly harsh for the appellant to relocate internally within Algeria. In the appellant's skeleton argument for the tribunal this was put on the basis that it was unduly harsh to expect a gay man who wished to live openly free from persecution to relocate to a place where he would continue to experience serious harm and be required to conceal and self-suppress. Further, it was said that the First-tier Tribunal failed to consider whether the appellant could live a relatively normal life without discrimination in the context of the country concerned. The Upper Tribunal dealt with this in the following way:

"20. Ground 4 contends that the judge erred in finding that it would not be unduly harsh for the appellant to relocate internally within Algeria. The first reason given is that, since the appellant would have to supress or conceal his sexual orientation wherever he lived in Algeria that would necessarily make relocation unreasonable or unduly harsh. However, that is contrary to what the Tribunal found in *OO (Algeria)*. Secondly, it is said that there was no evidential basis for the finding at paragraph 30 that the appellant could adapt to any place he decided to relocate to. The judge states at paragraph 30 that the appellant had now been in the UK for 4 years and had a way of life which would enable him to ... adapt. This is against the background that the appellant had been born and brought up in Algeria and had not left that country until he was 15. Since arriving in Britain 4 years ago, he has completed a hairdressing course and gained experience in hairdressing salons. He has thus not only lived independently in a foreign country for a significant period of time during his formative years but had demonstrated self-reliance and initiative. Upon the evidence before him the judge was entitled to come to the view that there was nothing in the appellant's circumstances which would make relocation in Algeria unduly harsh."

[14] Ground 3 concerned a complaint about the way in which the First-tier Tribunal dealt with the evidence relating to the relationship in the United Kingdom. That ground was rejected and there is no appeal against that decision. Ground 5, which the Upper Tribunal dealt with together with ground 3, challenged the finding, amongst other things, that there were no significant obstacles to the appellant's re-integration within Algeria. The Upper Tribunal set out at paragraph 19 of its judgment the findings of the First-tier Tribunal on that matter and said:

"….Those include the finding that the appellant would not live openly as a gay person for reasons other than a fear of persecution. He had also found that the appellant was capable of adapting to Algeria (See our discussion … on ground of appeal 4)…."

[15] In the light of those, and other matters, the Upper Tribunal held that the First-tier Tribunal had not erred in concluding that there were no significant obstacles to the Appellant's re-integration in Algeria. The Upper Tribunal therefore dismissed the appeal.

The present proceedings

[16] The appellant appeals against the decision of the Upper Tribunal with permission from Irwin LJ. He was granted permission to amend his grounds of appeal at the hearing. The United Nations High Commissioner for Refugees was given permission to intervene by making written and oral submissions at the hearing. We are grateful to the Commissioner for the assistance provided and to all counsel for their written and oral submissions.

THE GROUNDS OF APPEAL

[17] There are three grounds of appeal. Ground 1 alleges that the Upper Tribunal erred in its application of the principles established by the Supreme Court in *HJ (Iran) v Secretary of State* [2011] 2 AC 596 and that it reached its conclusion in light of the country guidance given in *OO (Algeria)* which was itself flawed. In particular, it is said that:

"[A] The Upper Tribunal (in both *OO (Algeria)* and the present case) failed to consider, adequately or at all, the cumulative impact of the consequences a gay man living openly in Algeria would or may face. Had the Tribunal done so, then, on the basis of the findings of fact made in *OO (Algeria)*, it may well have concluded that a gay man living openly would face a real risk of consequences which, taken together, would be sufficiently serious to amount to persecution. Indeed, in the Appellant's submission, this was the only conclusion reasonably available.

[B] The Upper Tribunal (in both *OO (Algeria)* and the present case) failed to consider, adequately or at all, whether the effects of the long term concealment or suppression of a gay man's sexual orientation, for fear of the consequences of living openly (irrespective of whether these amounted to persecution) and in the context of pervasive societal stigma and shame, could themselves be sufficiently serious to amount to persecution. Had the Tribunal done so, it may well have concluded that the overall impact was capable of reaching this threshold, and that it was reached in the Appellant's case. Indeed, in the Appellant's submission, this was the only conclusion reasonably available."

[18] Ground 2 contends that the Upper Tribunal erred in concluding that internal relocation within Algeria would not be unduly harsh and reached the conclusion in the light of the country guidance in *OO (Algeria)* which was itself flawed and:

"In particular the Appellant contends that the Upper Tribunal (in both *OO (Algeria)* and the present case) failed to consider, adequately or at all, whether the effects of the long term concealment or suppression of a gay man's sexual orientation, for fear of the consequences of living openly (irrespective of whether these amounted to persecution) and in the context of pervasive societal stigma and shame, could either render, or contribute to rendering, internal relocation unduly harsh."

[19] Ground 3 contended that the Upper Tribunal erred in its approach to Article 8 of the Convention and paragraph 276ADE of the Immigration Rules and:

"In particular, the Appellant submits that the Tribunal failed to consider, adequately or at all, the full range of circumstances relevant to the extent of the interference with his Article 8 rights and the significance of the obstacles to integration on return. These circumstances necessarily included the fact that the Appellant would be constrained by fear (irrespective of whether this amounted to a fear of persecution) to engage in long-term, active, and comprehensive concealment of a fundamental aspect of his identity. Had the Tribunal given these circumstances proper consideration, it may well have concluded that the appeal on one or both of these grounds was made out. Indeed, in the Appellant's submission, this was the only conclusion reasonably available."

THE FIRST ISSUE – THE PROPER APPROACH TO THE MEANING OF PERSECUTION

[20] Mr Husain QC on behalf of the Appellant submitted that the Upper Tribunal erred in *OO (Algeria)* in its approach to the interpretation of persecution within the meaning of the Refugee Convention. In particular, he submitted that the Upper Tribunal in that case failed to consider the cumulative effect of the consequences of the treatment faced by gay men in Algeria. Further, he submitted that the Upper Tribunal in *OO (Algeria)* focussed on the risk of physical violence and failed to consider other types of treatment which, cumulatively, might constitute persecution. It had failed to consider matters such as social stigma, discrimination, and harassment or threats of violence. In addition, the fact that homosexual activity was criminalised was itself a significant violation of a person's dignity. He relied on a series of judgments from this jurisdiction, and other jurisdictions around the world, to demonstrate that such matters were properly to be taken into account when considering what conduct amounted to persecution and the gravity with which the courts considered the violation of a person's dignity and right to live as he or she chooses. He further submitted that the Upper Tribunal also failed to address the question of how men who lived an openly gay life in Algeria would be treated. As the decision in *OO (Algeria)* was flawed, the decision of the Upper Tribunal in the present case, which relied on that decision was equally flawed.

[21] In relation to ground 1B, Mr Husain submitted that the fact of having to conceal or supress one's sexual orientation gave rise to harm which amounted to persecution. He submitted that the reason why the state was responsible for the fact of concealment where that arose from cultural, social or religious norms was that in part the state had contributed to that by criminalising homosexual activities.

It was wrong to sever one aspect of the state's activities from other factors giving rise to the need for concealment.

[22] Ms Demetriou QC for the Commissioner submitted that the Upper Tribunal in *OO (Algeria)* had erred by concluding that, since the evidence fell short of establishing a real risk of physical attacks on gay men, they faced no real risk of persecution. The Upper Tribunal should have considered cumulatively whether all the consequences of living openly as a gay man in Algeria met the threshold of persecution. She relied upon the *UNHCR Handbook*, and the *UNHCR Guidelines on Claims on Sexual Orientation and/or Gender Identity* (issued on 23 October 2012 and annexed to the Handbook) as an aid for interpreting the Refugee Convention. Paragraph 53 of the Handbook stated that various measures not in themselves amounting to persecution could, in combination with other measures or adverse factors, amount to persecution. The Guidelines refer to situations where the cumulative effect of restrictions on the exercise of human rights in a range of fields and of discrimination in matters such as employment could, in certain circumstances, amount to persecution. It was wrong, therefore, to focus solely on the risk of physical violence and wrong not to make a cumulative assessment of the measures affecting those who lived openly gay lives in Algeria. She submitted that the Upper Tribunal had effectively done that and relegated matters relating to stigma, ostracism, discrimination and other matters to questions of merely social mores rather than considering whether they were aspects of treatment capable of constituting persecution.

[23] Mr Singh QC for the respondent submitted that the Upper Tribunal in *OO (Algeria)* had not made the errors alleged. It had considered all the evidence and found that, although homosexual activity was criminalised, prosecutions were rare. There was no evidence of abuse or arrest or blackmail or other ill-treatment on the part of the police. There would be a hostile reaction from family members to a gay male member of the family and that may lead to violence from which, it was accepted, the state would not protect the victim. There was however no reliable evidence before the Upper Tribunal of violence or other treatment crossing the threshold of persecutory treatment. The adverse reaction to homosexual behaviour would not be at anything other than a low level and well below the level that constituted persecution. The Upper Tribunal had considered all the evidence. While it had not used the word "cumulative", that was a criticism of form not substance as that was, in essence, what the Upper Tribunal had done. It had not excluded acts falling short of violence. It had considered a wide range of matters albeit that evidence of violence might more easily establish a risk of persecution. Further, given that very few gay men lived openly gay lives in Algeria, it had sought to consider such evidence as was available to the response to demonstrations of public homosexual behaviour and reactions to persons believed to be gay and had considered why gay men did not live openly gay lives and concluded that was not because of a fear of persecution but societal, cultural and religious norms. The fact that a person concealed his sexual orientation in these circumstances did not amount to persecution. That was, in effect, to seek to use a person's sexual orientation as justifying a finding of persecution when the person would not in fact have been a victim of persecution and would not otherwise qualify as a refugee under the Refugee Convention.

Discussion

The legal framework

[24] In broad terms, the Convention relating to the Status of Refugees ("the Refugee Convention") is intended to provide protection to persons with a well-founded fear of persecution on defined grounds either from the state, or through those acting on its behalf, or from the acts of other non-state actors where the state is unwilling or unable to provide protection against such treatment (see, generally, *Horvath v Secretary of State for the Home Department* [2001] AC 489).

[25] Article 1A(2) of the Refugee Convention as amended defines, so far as material to this appeal, a refugee as any person who:

"… owing to well-founded fear of being persecuted for reasons of race, religion, nationality, membership of a particular social group or political opinion, is outside the country of his nationality and is unable, or owing to such fear, is unwilling to avail himself of the protection of that country…"

[26] There is ultimately a single question to be asked: does the individual have a well-founded fear of being persecuted if returned to his own country for a reason specified in Article 1A(2) of the Refugee Convention?

[27] In answering that single question, one of the matters to be considered is whether the treatment which the individual fears amounts to persecution. There is no definition in the Refugee Convention of what constitutes persecution. Certain actions may be readily identified as amounting to persecution such as killing, serious acts of physical or sexual violence against the individual, or torture on the part of state agents (or a failure to protect against such acts). Other acts can amount to persecution where their nature, intensity and duration give rise to sufficiently serious harm bearing in mind the circumstances and characteristics of the person concerned. Further, even if actions considered individually would not amount to persecution, such actions may in certain cases, when considered cumulatively with other actions, amount to persecution.

[28] For present purposes, the parties accept that an appropriate approach to the meaning of persecution is set out in Article 9 of Council Directive 2004/83/EC of 29 April 2004 on minimum standards for the qualification and status of third country nationals or stateless persons as refugees or as persons who otherwise need international protection and the content of the protection granted ("the Directive"). It is in the following terms:

"Article 9 Acts of persecution

1.   Acts of persecution within the meaning of article 1 A of the Geneva Convention must:

(a)   be sufficiently serious by their nature or repetition as to constitute a severe violation of basic human rights, in particular the rights from which derogation cannot be made under Article 15(2) of the European Convention for the Protection of Human Rights and Fundamental Freedoms; or

(b) be an accumulation of various measures, including violations of human rights which is sufficiently severe as to affect an individual in a similar manner as mentioned in (a).

2. Acts of persecution as qualified in paragraph 1, can, *inter alia*, take the form of:

(a) acts of physical or mental violence, including acts of sexual violence;

(b) legal, administrative, police, and/or judicial measures which are in themselves discriminatory or which are implemented in a discriminatory manner;

(c) prosecution or punishment, which is disproportionate or discriminatory;

(d) denial of judicial redress resulting in a disproportionate or discriminatory punishment;

(e) prosecution or punishment for refusal to perform military service in a conflict, where performing military service would include crimes or acts falling under the exclusion clauses as set out in Article 12(2);

(f) acts of a gender-specific or child-specific nature.

3. In accordance with Article 2(c), there must be a connection between the reasons mentioned in Article 10 and the acts of persecution as qualified in paragraph 1."

[29] A number of features emerge from Article 9 of the Directive. First the acts must be sufficiently serious in order to amount to acts of persecution. That appears from the reference in Article 9(1)(a) to the acts amounting to "sufficiently serious" breaches constituting a severe violation of basic human rights or in Article 9(1)(b) to an accumulation of measures which is "sufficiently severe" as to affect the individual in the same manner as the acts referred in Article 9(1)(a). Secondly, acts of persecution can take a wide range of forms and are not limited to (but will include) the infliction of death or serious physical or mental violence. A non-exhaustive list of actions capable in appropriate circumstances of constituting persecution is given in Article 9(2) of the Directive. Further, whilst some actions are necessarily ones carried out by, or on behalf of, the state (e.g. legal, administrative, police or judicial measures or prosecution or punishment), others may be carried out by state agents or by other individuals, such as acts of physical or mental violence, including sexual violence, or acts of a gender-specific or child-specific nature. Where the acts are done by non-state agents, the question of whether the state is able and willing to provide sufficient protection against such acts would arise. Thirdly, persecution may arise from individual acts or from an accumulation of different acts.

[30] The well-founded fear must be of persecution for a reason specified in Article 1A(2) of the Refugee Convention. That includes persecution for reasons of membership of a particular social group. It is accepted that homosexuals form a particular social group and if a person had a well-founded fear of persecution by

reason of the fact that he or she was homosexual that would fall within the scope of Article 1A(2).

[31] The courts have had to consider the question of whether a person could claim to be a refugee if he or she could take action to avoid becoming the victim of persecution if returned. That question was considered in the context of gay men in *HJ (Iran) v Secretary of State for the Home Department* [2011] 1 A.C. 596, which concerned a gay man from Iran and a gay man from Cameroon. If they lived as openly gay men in their respective countries, they would face treatment which amounted to persecution. In the case of Iran, a gay man faced the risk of prosecution and hanging. In the case of Cameroon, the appellant, HT, was a gay man who was seen kissing his partner. He had been the subject of a violent attack by persons armed with sticks and a knife who had pulled off his clothes and tried to cut off his penis. Police officers arrived but did not protect him against attack. Instead, they joined in the attack and punched and kicked him.

[32] The issue for the Supreme Court in HJ was whether the Court of Appeal was correct in *J v Secretary of State of State for the Home Department* [2007] Imm AR 73 in holding that a gay man would not have a well-founded fear of persecution if he could reasonably be expected to tolerate living discreetly in his country of origin, that is, if he could reasonably be expected to conceal the fact that he was gay and thereby avoid the risk of persecution. The Supreme Court held that that approach was not correct: see *per* Lord Hope at paragraphs 23 to 29 and *per* Lord Rodger, with whom Lord Walker, Lord Collins and Dyson JSC agreed, at paragraphs 73 to 81. As Lord Rodger expressed it at paragraph 69:

"... if a person has a well-founded fear that he would suffer persecution on being returned to his country of nationality if he were to live openly as a gay man, then he is to be regarded as a refugee for purposes of the Convention, even though, because of the fear of persecution, he would in fact live discreetly and so avoid suffering any actual harm".

[33] The Supreme Court recognised, however, a distinction between a situation where a gay man conceals his sexual orientation because, in part at least, he fears that he will be persecuted if he lives openly as a gay man and a situation where a gay man chooses to live in a way that does not disclose his sexual orientation. That requires the court or tribunal to ask why a gay man would conceal his sexual orientation on his return to his country of origin. If he were to do that in reaction to "family or social pressures" (*per* Lord Hope at paragraph 22) or "social pressures" (*per* Lord Rodger at paragraph 82) that would not amount to persecution and the Refugee Convention would not offer protection against return to the country of nationality. In the light of that, Lord Rodger gave the following guidance to tribunals on the approach to be adopted at paragraph 82 of his judgment in *HJ (Iran)*:

"The approach to be followed by tribunals

82. When an applicant applies for asylum on the ground of a well-founded fear of persecution because he is gay, the tribunal must first ask itself whether it is satisfied on the evidence that he is gay, or that he would be treated as gay by potential persecutors in his country of nationality. If so, the tribunal must then ask itself whether it is satisfied on the available evidence that gay people who

lived openly would be liable to persecution in the applicant's country of nationality. If so, the tribunal must go on to consider what the individual applicant would do if he were returned to that country. If the applicant would in fact live openly and thereby be exposed to a real risk of persecution, then he has a well-founded fear of persecution – even if he could avoid the risk by living "discreetly". If, on the other hand, the tribunal concludes that the applicant would in fact live discreetly and so avoid persecution, it must go on to ask itself why he would do so. If the tribunal concludes that the applicant would choose to live discreetly simply because that was how he himself would wish to live, or because of social pressures, e g, not wanting to distress his parents or embarrass his friends, then his application should be rejected. Social pressures of that kind do not amount to persecution and the Convention does not offer protection against them. Such a person has no well-founded fear of persecution because, for reasons that have nothing to do with any fear of persecution, he himself chooses to adopt a way of life which means that he is not in fact liable to be persecuted because he is gay. If, on the other hand, the tribunal concludes that a material reason for the applicant living discreetly on his return would be a fear of the persecution which would follow if he were to live openly as a gay man, then, other things being equal, his application should be accepted. Such a person has a well-founded fear of persecution. To reject his application on the ground that he could avoid the persecution by living discreetly would be to defeat the very right which the Convention exists to protect – his right to live freely and openly as a gay man without fear of persecution. By admitting him to asylum and allowing him to live freely and openly as a gay man without fear of persecution, the receiving state gives effect to that right by affording the applicant a surrogate for the protection from persecution which his country of nationality should have afforded him."

[34] Lord Walker (at paragraph 98), Lord Collins (at paragraph 100) and Dyson JSC (at paragraph 132) expressly agreed that the approach to be followed by tribunals should be as set out by Lord Rodger in paragraph 82 of his judgment. Lord Hope set out the test to be adopted by tribunals in materially similar terms in paragraph 35 of his judgment.

The judgment of the Upper Tribunal in OO (Algeria)
[35] In *OO (Algeria)* the Upper Tribunal considered the current situation in Algeria in order, amongst other things, to give country guidance on the risks faced in that country by gay men. The system of country guidance cases is described by Stanley Burnton LJ at paragraphs 45 to 46 of his judgment *R (SG (Iraq)) v Secretary of State for the Home Department* [2013] 1 W.L.R. 41. In essence, a determination intended to be guidance on the situation in a particular country will be reached after consideration of the representations of the parties, and expert and factual evidence, and is aimed at arriving at reliable, accurate descriptions of the conditions in a country and the risk on return. Decision-makers and tribunals are required to take country guidance determinations into account and to follow them unless there are very strong grounds supported by cogent evidence for not doing so. In view of the criticisms made of the decision in *OO (Algeria)*, it is necessary to consider that decision in detail.
[36] The appellant in *OO (Algeria)* claimed to be a bisexual man who had a well-founded fear of persecution by reason of his sexual orientation if he were

returned to Algeria. The Upper Tribunal heard oral evidence from the appellant, and from one expert witness, and had written evidence from a second expert witness. They also heard evidence from a person who was a gay man from Algeria who lived in France and was well placed to express informed views on the issues in the case.

[37] The Upper Tribunal set out the legal framework and the terms of Article 9 of the Directive at paragraph 10 of its judgment. It then set out paragraph 82 of the judgment of Lord Rodger in *HJ (Iran)*. It then proceeded to consider the evidence of Dr Seddon, one of the experts, the written evidence of another expert, Ms Pargeter, and other evidence including that of the person who was a gay Algerian and now lived in France. It considered their evidence under a series of headings, including the risks of prosecutions of gay men, the applicability of Sharia law, the risk of targeted or arbitrary attacks or abusive treatment by the police, the range of adverse responses to homosexual behaviour, attitudes to gay men and discrimination (including in respect of medical treatment and discrimination in the work place), and it considered evidence on living as a gay man in Algeria and the reasons for discretion or concealment of sexual identity. Finally, it dealt with the documentary evidence including reports from the United States State Department, country information from the UK Border Agency, and other reports.

[38] The Upper Tribunal then set out its conclusions on the evidence under a series of headings. First, in relation to the prosecution of gay men, it had already noted that the Algerian criminal code criminalised all homosexual acts, although more severe penalties were imposed where the acts were done in public or where one participant was under 18 years of age (see paragraph 19 of its judgment). The Upper Tribunal was satisfied on the evidence that the Algerian authorities did not generally prosecute a person for homosexual behaviour even when that came to the attention of the public or the authorities. The evidence in fact pointed the other way (see paragraphs 141–143 of its judgment). It concluded that the evidence did not establish that Sharia law providing for severe punishment was applied to gay men in Algeria. The Upper Tribunal concluded that there was no reliable evidence to establish a risk of targeted or arbitrary attacks on gay men or abusive treatment by police. Some gay men did experience violence at the hands of family members when they disclosed to them that they were gay or that was discovered. But outside the family, the evidence did not establish that gay men faced a real risk of being subjected to violent attack by the authorities or by members of the public who came to know that a man was gay (see paragraph 153 of its judgment). The Upper Tribunal concluded that there was a range of responses experienced by gay men who were recognised as such although in most, possibly nearly all, cases this would involve expressions of disapproval and fell a long way short of establishing that responses would involve physical ill-treatment (outside of the family). It referred to the evidence that social responses ranged from mockery and stigmatisation to outright hostility. At paragraph 162, the Upper Tribunal said this:

"162. Drawing all of this together we are satisfied that the evidence clearly demonstrates that there will be a range of responses to displays of homosexual behaviour outside the family context, but while the risk of a physical attack cannot be excluded, generally the response will be at the lower end of that range. Where the response is at the upper end of the possible range of responses, that is likely to be because open displays of affection in public are simply not tolerated, whether that be by heterosexual couples or homosexual couples."

[39] The Upper Tribunal considered whether gay men in Algeria were able to live openly as gay. It noted that few gay men chose to live openly there and that that was the result of a number of considerations including cultural, religious and societal views, the intense and deep rooted and near universal disapproval of homosexuality that prevails in Algeria, and near universal adherence to and respect for social and religious mores. It concluded on the evidence that the choice to live discreetly as a gay man was not generally driven by a need to avoid persecution but by social pressures of the type contemplated in *HJ (Iran)* (see paragraph 168).

[40] The Upper Tribunal set out its country guidance at paragraphs at 172 to 190, the material parts of which are in the following terms.

"172. Although the Algerian Criminal Code makes homosexual behaviour unlawful, the authorities do not seek to prosecute gay men and there is no real risk of prosecution, even when the authorities become aware of such behaviour. In the very few cases where there has been a prosecution for homosexual behaviour, there has been some other feature that has given rise to the prosecution. The state does not actively seek out gay men in order to take any form of action against them, either by means of prosecution or by subjecting gay men to other forms of persecutory ill-treatment.

173.   Sharia law is not applied against gay men in Algeria. The criminal law is entirely secular and discloses no manifestation, at all, of Sharia law in its application.

174.   Algeria is an extremely conservative society where behaviour is regulated by reference to the strict Islamic values endorsed by the state. It is not just open displays of affection by gay men that are not tolerated but such behaviour by heterosexual couples also, particularly between unmarried heterosexual couples. Because there is general adherence to strict Islamic doctrine, which includes a similar intolerance to extra-marital sexual relations, young unmarried men do not have access to women and so may have resort to same-sex liaisons. This is not seen as homosexual conduct but pragmatism in achieving sexual gratification. Indeed, there is some evidence that where one of the same sex partners is perceived to be 'dominant' he will be admired as virile and masculine.

175.   There are, undoubtedly, gay men in Algeria and there is no reason to suppose that they do not represent a similar proportion of the population as in other countries. Therefore, it is remarkable that there is little evidence of gay men living openly as such anywhere in Algeria. That much is accepted by the respondent.

176.   It is conceded by the respondent that where a gay man does face a real risk of persecution, which, when such occurs, is likely to be from his own family members, there is no sufficiency of protection available from the police or other state authorities.

177.   There is a real risk of violent and persecutory ill-treatment of gay men from family members, motivated by the deep sense of shame and dishonour

perceived to be brought upon the family as a consequence of it becoming known in the neighbourhood that there is within the household a gay son. There is a risk of that being the case throughout Algerian society, but it is clear from the evidence that that is especially the case in the less affluent and densely populate neighbourhoods where, typically, values will be conservative and non-secular and households are under close scrutiny from neighbours. But once the gay son has left the family home and re-established himself elsewhere there is no real risk that family members will pursue him to that place of relocation, and so generally that risk of persecution can be avoided by the availability of a safe and reasonable internal relocation alternative.

178.   Typically, a gay man in Algeria will first encounter problems when his family becomes aware that he is gay, either because he 'comes out' to his family, perhaps when resisting pressure to marry, which is something expected of all Algerian men when they reach marriageable age, or because his sexual orientation has come to the attention of family members for other reasons. In such a situation, some, but certainly not all, gay men may face a real risk of persecution. There is some evidence that 'caring and concerned' fathers will beat and otherwise 'discipline' gay sons in an attempt to 'straighten them out' for their own good. Very few families will be prepared to accept and tolerate the fact of a son's homosexuality. Those that do are likely to be educated, secular, middles class families, living in more prosperous lower density area.

179.   Where, exceptionally, a family is prepared to accept the homosexuality of their son that does not enable the son to manifest his sexual orientation outside the family home. He will choose to conceal it, not to avoid persecution, (there being no adequate or sufficient evidence of such taking place) but to protect the reputation of his family within the local neighbourhood and because he is likely to feel ashamed of having the sexual preferences that he does and will wish to avoid damaging relationships with friends, work colleagues and others.

180.   As there is no sufficiency of protection available, the next question is whether the gay son whose family is not prepared to tolerate him living as a gay man, can relocate elsewhere in Algeria to avoid ill-treatment from family members and if so whether it will be reasonable to expect him to do so. If it is not reasonable then having travelled to the UK, he will be entitled to international protection.

181.   That question of whether there is a safe and reasonable internal relocation option, is a difficult and complex one in the Algerian context. Generally, there will be no real difficulty preventing relocation and there is no indication that disapproving family members have the means, inclination or reach to cause difficulties after relocation. But where such a person has established himself elsewhere in Algeria, as marriage is expected of all Algerian men, in pursuance of what is seen as an 'Islamic duty to procreate', it may well, sooner or later, become apparent that he has not adhered to the norms expected and that is likely to generate suspicion that he is a gay man.

182.   There is no real risk of gay men being subjected to violence or other persecutory ill-treatment outside the family home, either at the hands of

authorities or by members of the public with whom gay men have to engage. There is an absence of reliable evidence of that occurring.

183. Very few gay men live openly as such in Algeria. Gay Algerian men, as a consequence of cultural, religious and societal views, do not generally identify themselves as gay even if their sexual preferences lead them to prefer same sex relationships. Even Algerian men with settled sexual preferences for same sex relationships may well continue to entertain doubt about their sexuality. Second, gay men recognise the intense and deep rooted near universal disapproval of homosexuality that obtains in Algeria. Thus, Algerian gay men who have moved to France where, plainly, they face no obstacle to living openly as such, generally choose not to because they refuse to categorise themselves as gay, even though there is no persecutory disincentive to doing so.

184. The fact that there is very little evidence of gay men living openly in Algeria invites the conclusion that must be because the risk of persecutory ill-treatment likely to be attracted is such as to prevent that from happening. But the expert and other country evidence does not establish that, in fact, there is any real risk outside the family context of such persecutory ill-treatment being meted out to persons suspected as being gay. The expert evidence indicates that a gay man recognised as such is very likely to attract an adverse response from those by whom he is encountered as he goes about his daily business. But that adverse reaction is not reasonably likely to be such as to amount to persecution, being on a range of responses from simple expression of disapproval, mockery or name calling up to the possibility of physical attack. But there is simply no reliable evidence of the expression of disapproval being expressed in such circumstances generally being otherwise than at the lower end of that range of responses.

185. That gives rise to a conundrum. If there is no evidence of persecution of gay men who have escaped ill-treatment from family by relocating elsewhere, why is there no evidence of gay men feeling able to live openly? Alternatively, is the absence of evidence of physical ill-treatment of gay men due to the fact that there are no gay men living openly?

186. The answer, in our judgement, is as follows:

a.   The only risk of ill-treatment at a level to become persecution likely to be encountered by a gay man in Algeria is at the hands of his own family, after they have discovered that he is gay. There is no reliable evidence such as to establish that a gay man, identified as such, faces a real risk of persecutory ill-treatment from persons outside his own family.

b.   Where a gay man remains living with his family to whom he has disclosed his sexual orientation in circumstances where they are prepared to tolerate that, his decision to live discreetly and to conceal his homosexuality outside the family home is not taken to avoid persecution but to avoid shame or disrespect being brought upon his family. That means that he has chosen to live discreetly, not to avoid persecution but for reasons that do not give rise to a right to international protection.

c.   Where a gay man has to flee his family home to avoid persecution from family members, in his place of relocation he will attract no real risk of persecution because, generally, he will not live openly as a gay man. As the evidence does not establish that he will face a real risk of persecution if subsequently suspected to be a gay man, his decision to live discreetly and to conceal his sexual orientation is driven by respect for social mores and a desire to avoid attracting disapproval of a type that falls well below the threshold of persecution. Quite apart from that, an Algerian man who has a settled preference for same sex relationships may well continue to entertain doubts as to his sexuality and not regard himself as a gay man, in any event.

187.   Underpinning these conclusions is recognition that Algerian society is governed by strict Islamic values which all citizens, including gay men, in practice respect, even if only for pragmatic reasons.

188.   This gives rise to a compromise which in some senses in unsatisfactory but, as a matter of law, does not give rise to a right to be recognised as a refugee. Algerian society, including the state authorities, effectively tolerates private manifestations of homosexual conduct, both between young unmarried men and gay men who have established themselves away from the family home, provided there is no public display of it. Gay men choose to live discreetly not to avoid persecution, because there is no evidence that there is any, but because they recognise that the society they live in is a conservative one, subject to strict Islamic values, that is unable to openly embrace the existence of the practice of homosexuality, just as women are expected to submit to Islamic requirements such as being veiled and accepting other limitations upon their ability to act as they may wish to.

189.   The evidence before us indicates that as a result of societal views and conditioning, Algerian men with a preference for same-sex relationships generally do not in fact regard themselves as gay men and so have no reasons to identify themselves as such to others by conducting themselves in a manner that has come to be regarded as 'living openly' or discreetly. Therefore, choosing not to live openly as gay men is not due to a fear of persecution but other reasons to do with self-perception and how they wish to be perceived by others.

190.   For these reasons, a gay man from Algeria will be entitled to be recognised as a refugee only if he shows that, due to his personal circumstances, it would be unreasonable and unduly harsh to expect him to relocate within Algeria to avoid persecution from family members, or because he has particular characteristics that might, unusually and contrary to what is generally to be expected, give rise to a risk of attracting disapproval at the highest level of the possible range of adverse responses from those seeking to express their disapproval of the fact of his sexual orientation."

[41] An application for permission to appeal against the decision of the Upper Tribunal was refused at an oral hearing by Elias LJ. It is accepted that the appellant is entitled to challenge the decision of the Upper Tribunal in this case on the ground that it relied upon the decision in *OO (Algeria)* which is said to be

legally flawed. Equally it is accepted that this Court must accept the factual findings made the Upper Tribunal in *OO (Algeria)*.

The first part of Ground 1

[42] I turn then to the specific criticisms made of the decision in *OO (Algeria)* in written and oral submissions. There are essentially three. First it is said that the Upper Tribunal focussed solely on the question of whether gay men in Algeria would face a risk of physical violence and failed to consider other matters including the effects of stigma, hostility, discrimination, harassment or threats of violence and the fact that homosexual acts were criminalised. In so far as the Upper Tribunal did consider matters such as social stigma, it is submitted that the Upper Tribunal treated those as part of the social pressures that led gay men to conceal their orientation and as matters not capable of amounting to persecution.

[43] On any fair reading of the decision in *OO (Algeria)*, it is clear that the Upper Tribunal did not limit its consideration to the risk of physical violence. The review of the evidence covered criminalisation of homosexual acts, the risk of prosecution, the risk of physical attacks from the authorities, discrimination in the provision of services and employment and attitudes to homosexuality. Its conclusion dealt with those matters. It concluded that whilst homosexual acts were criminalised there was no real risk of gay men being prosecuted and Sharia law did not apply. There was a risk of violence within the family, but outside the family there was no real risk of gay men being subjected to violence. In relation to responses to homosexuality, the responses covered a range but would generally fall at the lower end of the range (see paragraphs 162 and 184). For that reason, it concluded at paragraph 182 that there is no real risk of gay men:

"being subjected to violence or other persecutory ill-treatment outside the family home, either at the hands of the authorities or by members of the public with whom gay men have to engage".

[44] Given the structure of the decision, the evidence it considered, and its conclusions, it is clear that the Upper Tribunal considered whether there was reliable evidence of physical violence and other forms of conduct in order to determine whether gay men in Algeria had a well-founded fear of persecution.

[45] Secondly, it is clear that in substance the Upper Tribunal did consider the cumulative effect of the treatment that it found occurred. It is correct that the Upper Tribunal dealt with different areas of conduct separately. It is correct that it does not use the word "cumulatively", or set out its findings in the way that the Upper Tribunal has in other cases (such as *TK (Gay man) St Lucia* [2019] UKUT 00092 (IAC)). I would accept that the Upper Tribunal in *OO (Algeria)* could have expressed its conclusions more fully in this respect. But the issue is one of substance rather than form. It is clear that the Upper Tribunal did look at each area of concern. Homosexual acts were criminalised but there no real risk of persecution, outside the family there was no real risk of violence, and other responses to adverse behaviour were at the lower end of the range. It drew all those matters together in paragraph 162 and, again, in paragraph 182 where it considered that there was no real risk of "violence or other persecutory ill-treatment outside the family". In substance, therefore, the Upper Tribunal did consider all matters cumulatively as well as individually.

[46] Thirdly, it is said that the Upper Tribunal in this case erred in law by failing to consider how a gay man living openly as such in Algeria would be treated and considered only how a man suspected or recognised as gay would be treated. I do not consider that there is any substance in this criticism. It expressly said at paragraph 11 of its judgment that any assessment had to be informed by the decision in *HJ (Iran)* and set out paragraph 82 of that judgment, separating out each aspect in turn and making it clear that, if it decided (as it did in this case) that the applicant was gay, the tribunal:

"must then ask itself whether it is satisfied on the available evidence that gay people who lived openly would be liable to persecution in the applicant's country of nationality".

[47] It therefore identified the relevant principle and applied that to the evidence before it. It sought to consider how openly gay men would be treated in Algeria. There were difficulties in doing that as the evidence was that most gay men in Algeria did not live as openly gay men and, indeed, many would not have identified themselves as gay for societal, cultural and religious reasons. But there is no doubt that the Upper Tribunal was seeking to determine how gay men who lived openly would be treated. By way of example only, it considered how the authorities would act when a person's homosexual behaviour was drawn to the attention of the authorities or members of the public (see paragraphs 23 and 69). Again, by way of example, it looked at how service providers and employers would react to homosexuals (see for example paragraphs 86 to 87 and 89 to 90). At paragraph 168, it specifically considered how a gay man who did live openly as such in Algeria would be likely to be treated and concluded that he would attract upsetting comments, his relationship with friends and work colleagues would be damaged and he would suffer discriminatory experiences not amounting to persecution. The Upper Tribunal had difficulty in assessing how gay men who lived openly would be treated as there were very few men who did so. But there is no doubt that it identified and asked the correct question, and sought, so far as it was able to do so, to consider how an openly gay man would be treated in Algeria. Furthermore, it also considered if the fact that there was little evidence of gay men living openly in Algeria was itself evidence that that was because of the risk of persecutory ill-treatment if they did so. The Upper Tribunal concluded on the evidence, however, that was not the case. Gay men did not live openly because of the cultural, religious and societal views prevalent in a conservative society subject to strict Islamic values. The Upper Tribunal did not therefore fail to ask the correct question.

[48] For completeness, I note that Mr Husain took us to a number of authorities dealing with criminalisation of homosexuality. They included the judgment of Sachs J in the *Constitutional Court of South Africa in National Council for Gay and Lesbian Equality and others v Minister for Justice and others* [1998] ZAAC 15 explaining how laws criminalising homosexual behaviour violated basic concepts of privacy, dignity and equality and were contrary to the South African constitution. Mr Husain referred to the judgments in the Supreme Court of India in *Johar and others v Union of India and others* (2018) SCC 781 and the inferences and conclusions it reached as to how laws criminalising homosexual behaviour implicitly sanction discrimination and the denial of equal participation in society and criminalised in truth not an act but a specific set of identities. He emphasised,

and referred to authorities, in which social stigma, discrimination, and harassment could amount to a denial of human dignity.

[49] Any court in this country would readily understand the importance of equality before the law for all, irrespective of factors such as a person's race, religion, gender or sexual orientation. The values underpinning the laws in this country reflect the importance of concepts of dignity, privacy and of personal autonomy. Courts in this country would readily understand and agree with the decisions of superior courts in other countries recognising the importance of such concepts.

[50] That, however, is not the issue. Different societies at different times have taken different views as to homosexuality. The Refugee Convention is intended to provide protection in the circumstances agreed by the contracting parties. See the observations of Lord Hope in *HJ (Iran)* [2011] AC 596 at paragraphs 2–3. The question is whether an applicant has a well-founded fear of persecution if returned to his country of nationality for a reason falling within Article 1A(2) of the Refugee Convention. The fact that homosexual acts are criminalised in a particular country is not, of itself, recognised as giving rise to a well-founded fear of persecution as was recognised by the Court of Justice of the European Union in Joined Cases C-199/12 to C-201/12 *Minister voor Immigratie en Asiel v X (United Nations High Commissioner for Refugees (Intervening)*. For the reasons given, the Upper Tribunal in this case, and in *OO (Algeria)*, correctly understood the question that it had to consider and reached findings of fact which this Court must respect. On that basis, the Upper Tribunal was entitled to conclude that, outside the family home, a gay man in Algeria would not have a well-founded fear of persecution by reason of his sexual orientation.

Ground 1B

[51] Mr Husain submitted that it is possible that the very fact of being forced to conceal or suppress one's sexual orientation will give rise to harm which reaches the threshold of persecution. He referred to paragraph 33 of the UNCHR Guidelines on International Protection which states that being compelled to conceal one's sexual orientation may result in significant psychological and other harm.

[52] This submission needs to be set in context. The fact is that the country guidance is that gay men do not live as openly gay men in Algeria because of social, cultural and religious norms in a conservative society subject to strict Islamic values. References to the "suppression" or "concealment" of sexual orientation should be understood in that context. The Upper Tribunal did not err in considering that the fact that a gay man would not live openly in Algeria for social, cultural and religious reasons was not sufficient to amount to persecution.

[53] First, that conclusion is consistent with the decision in *HJ (Iran)*. If it were the case that the fact that a gay man concealed his sexual orientation was sufficient to establish persecution, that would have been the basis of the decision of the Supreme Court in *HJ (Iran)*. Instead, as Lord Rodger recognises in paragraph 82 of his judgment, there are in essence three questions: is the applicant gay, would a gay man who lived openly be liable to persecution in the country of nationality, and what would the person do on return? If he would not live openly, a tribunal would have to ask why he did not do so. If that were the result of social pressures, then his application for refugee status would fail. That reasoning is inconsistent with the submission that the simple fact that a gay man in Algeria would conceal his sexual orientation amounts to persecution.

[54] Secondly, and separately, the fact of concealment results from societal pressures, not from the actions of the state. It is not realistic to suggest that the state is under a duty to protect an individual from the societal attitudes prevalent in that state. Mr Husain points out that the state is responsible for the enactment of legislation criminalising homosexual behaviour and its conduct cannot be severed from society generally. That is to amalgamate different issues. The state has criminalised homosexual acts but, for the reasons discussed, that does not amount here to persecution. The pressures to conceal one's identity, on the evidence considered by the Upper Tribunal in *OO (Algeria)*, result from a combination of cultural, religious and societal views, and the deep-rooted hostility on the part of the population of Algeria to homosexuality. A state is not under an obligation in the context of the Refugee Convention to take steps within the state to change or alter the religious, cultural or social values prevalent in that state. If those attitudes manifest themselves in action which did amount to persecution – for example, killings, violent attacks, or other ill-treatment amounting to persecution – the state would be under a duty to provide protection. Thus, in Algeria, family members do pose a real risk of violence to a family member whose homosexual orientation they discover and the state is under a duty to protect. That is why the combination of violence by family members, and the lack of protection by the Algerian authorities in those circumstances, leads to the conclusion that there is a well-founded fear of persecution in those circumstances. But that does not indicate that, absent such factors, the state is under a duty to protect a gay man from societal, cultural or religious values which are hostile to homosexuality but do not manifest themselves in ill-treatment of the kind to amount to persecution.

[55] Finally, on the facts of this case, it is appropriate to note that there was no evidence, and no suggestion before the First-tier Tribunal, that concealment by the appellant of his sexual orientation would result in psychological harm. His evidence on this matter was that he felt good about himself in the United Kingdom and did not feel ashamed about his sexuality. He considered that he would be judged and treated badly and would not be accepted in Algeria. He said that people in the United Kingdom were very open-minded and he did not worry about his behaviour or how people would view him but the situation would be different in Algeria. The First-tier Tribunal found that if he returned to Algeria he would not live openly as a gay person because of social norms and traditions. The evidence, and the findings, fall far short of any indication that the fact that the appellant would not live openly as a gay man if returned to Algeria gives rise, of itself, to a well-founded fear of persecution.

[56] For those reasons, the first ground of appeal fails.

THE SECOND ISSUE – INTERNAL RELOCATION

[57] Mr Husain submitted that the Upper Tribunal in this case, and in *OO (Algeria)*, erred in concluding that it would not be unduly harsh for the appellant to relocate within Algeria. It had found in this case that there was a well-founded fear of persecution if he returned to his home area because of the threat from his uncle and Anis' parents. The Upper Tribunal, he submitted, erred in failing to consider whether the need to conceal his sexual orientation was capable of, or contributed to, rendering relocation unduly harsh. That was a different, and lower,

test from whether concealment amounted to persecution. He relied upon the decision in *R (Hysi) v Secretary of State for the Home Department* [2005] INLR 602 where the Court of Appeal held that a tribunal erred by failing to consider the difficulties arising from the fact that a person of mixed Albanian and Roma ethnic origin would have to conceal his mixed-race origins if he were to relocate within Kosovo.

[58] Ms Demetriou for the Commissioner submitted that whether relocation would be unduly harsh required an assessment of all the circumstances of the individual. That was a fact-specific question dependent on the particular circumstances of the case. The test was a different and less demanding test than the test for determining whether the applicant had a well-founded fear of persecution.

[59] Mr Singh submitted that there was no error here. The First-tier Tribunal was entitled on the facts to conclude that relocation would not be unduly harsh. Further, the fact that the appellant would not live as an openly gay man if he relocated within Algeria because of social, cultural or religious pressures would not render relocation unduly harsh. To make that finding would simply be a means of enlarging the scope of the protection conferred by the Refugee Convention in circumstances where the concealment of one's sexual orientation did not give rise to a well-founded fear of persecution sufficient to attract the obligation of protection.

Discussion

[60] An individual may have a well-founded fear of persecution in the place where he lived in his country of nationality. He may not, however, have a well-founded fear of persecution in other places within the country. In such circumstances, if it were reasonable for him to relocate within his country of nationality he would not qualify as a refugee under the Refugee Convention: see *Januzi v Secretary of State for the Home Department* [2006] 2 AC 426 at paragraph 7.

[61] The appropriate test is well-established. It is that:

"The decision-maker, taking account of all relevant circumstances pertaining to the claimant and his country of origin, must decide whether it is reasonable to expect the claimant to relocate or whether it would be unduly harsh to expect him to do so ... There is ... a spectrum of cases. The decision-maker must do his best to decide, on such material as is available, where on the spectrum the particular case falls ... All must depend on a fair assessment of the relevant facts."

See paragraph 21 of the speech of Lord Bingham in Januzi, with which the other members of the House agreed, and paragraph 5 of his speech in *AH (Sudan) v Secretary of State for the Home Department (United Nations High Commissioner for Refugees intervening)* [2008] 1 AC 678, with whom the other members of the House agreed. Further, the test is different from that for determining whether a person has a well-founded fear of persecution. The issue of internal relocation presupposes that there is some place within the country to which he could be returned without a well-founded fear of persecution. The question then is whether it would be reasonable for him to relocate: see the explanation given by Baroness Hale in *AH (Sudan)* at paragraph 21.

[62] In the present case, it is important to bear in mind again the context and the facts. The appellant had a well-founded fear of persecution in relation to his home area in Algeria because he feared that his uncle would kill or harm him because of his homosexuality and the state was unwilling or unable to protect him from that risk. In terms of relocation within Algeria, the appellant's case was that he would be in danger and would be killed wherever he went in Algeria and that his uncle would be able to ill-treat him wherever he was.

[63] First, the First-tier Tribunal found that the appellant would not be at risk from his uncle (or Anis' parents) if he were to relocate within Algeria. Secondly, it found that he was not at risk of persecution elsewhere in Algeria and that he would not be in danger if he returned to Algeria. Thirdly, there was no evidence, and no suggestion, that the appellant would suffer any significant psychological harm if he returned to Algeria and concealed his sexuality. Fourthly, the First-tier Tribunal found that he had a way of life which would enable him to adapt to any place he decided to relocate to. As the Upper Tribunal noted at paragraph 20 of its judgment, that was said against a background where the appellant had been born and brought up in Algeria and had not left the country until he was 15. Since arriving in Britain, he had completed a hairdressing course and obtained work experience demonstrating self-reliance and initiative. Those circumstances well indicated how he could adapt back to life in Algeria and why relocation in Algeria would not be unduly harsh.

[64] The one other factor is that, as the First-tier Tribunal found, the appellant would not live as an openly gay person in Algeria. That was not because of persecution but because of respect for social norms and tradition and religion: see paragraph 29 of the judgment of the First-tier Tribunal, cited at paragraph 10 above. Care needs to be taken not to take parts of that paragraph out of context. Although it refers to the appellant not expressing himself as a gay person "not necessarily out of persecution, but also [out of respect for] social norms and traditions and religion" it is clear, reading the judgment as a whole, that the First-tier Tribunal was not suggesting or finding that the appellant would not live openly because, in part, of a fear of persecution. It had already found that there would be no real risk of ill-treatment amounting to persecution outside the treatment from his own family.

[65] The sole question, therefore, is whether it would be unduly harsh to require the appellant to relocate within Algeria where he would choose not to live openly as a gay man. That question cannot be avoided by saying (as did all the advocates before us) that the issue is fact-specific and dependent on all the circumstances. In the present case (and I would imagine in many cases involving gay men from Algeria seeking asylum), the stage has been reached where that is the only relevant circumstance. The fact is that the appellant would be choosing to conceal his sexual orientation because of social, cultural and religious pressures. Life would clearly be different, and probably immeasurably better, for him if he were able to live in a country where the society, and social, cultural and religious pressures, did not compel him to decide to conceal his sexual orientation. The Refugee Convention is not, however, intended to guard or protect an individual from such pressures. In those circumstances, I consider that the Upper Tribunal (and the First-tier Tribunal) were entitled to conclude that it would not be unduly harsh for the appellant to relocate within Algeria.

[66] Furthermore, I do not consider that the observations of the Upper Tribunal in *OO (Algeria)* on this question were flawed. The Upper Tribunal was dealing with a situation where it found that gay men would not live openly in Algeria not because of a fear of persecution but due to other reasons. As indicated above, the fact that a gay Algerian man would conceal his sexual orientation for those reasons would not alone, and of itself, make it unduly harsh for him to relocate within Algeria. In those circumstances, there would need to be something arising from the individual's personal circumstances which would make it unreasonable and unduly harsh to expect him to relocate within Algeria to avoid the risk of persecution from his family (see paragraph 190 of the judgment in *OO (Algeria)*). There is nothing inconsistent in that summary with the test expressed in Januzi and *AH (Sudan)* provided that the tribunal bears in mind the need to consider all the relevant circumstances of the applicant and his country of origin.

THE THIRD GROUND OF APPEAL – SIGNIFICANT OBSTACLES TO INTEGRATION

Submissions

[67] Mr Husain submitted that the Upper Tribunal erred in its assessment of whether return would be a proportionate means of pursuing a legitimate aim and so compatible with Article 8 of the Convention. In that regard, he submitted that the tribunal erred in considering that there were no significant obstacles in terms of paragraph 276ADE of the Immigration Rules to the Appellant re-integrating into Algeria. He submitted that there is ample authority that the question of significant obstacles under that rule is also relevant to the question of proportionality under Article 8 of the Convention. He submitted that the need for the appellant to conceal his sexual orientation was a significant obstacle to integration. He relied upon the observations of Sales LJ, as he then was, in *Kamara v Secretary of State for the Home Department* [2016] 4 W.L.R. 152 at paragraph 14, where he indicated that the concept of integration required a broad evaluative judgment of whether the individual would be able to participate in society and have a reasonable opportunity to be accepted there and be able to operate and build up human relationships. That opportunity would, Mr Husain submitted, be denied to the appellant who would be forced to conceal a fundamental aspect of his identity, namely his sexual orientation, and would be severely limited as a result in the extent to which he could function in society and build up relationships there.

[68] Mr Singh submitted that the Upper Tribunal considered these issues at paragraphs 19 and 20 of its decision and considered, as it was entitled to do on the evidence before it, that there were no very significant obstacles to integration.

Discussion

[69] I assume that the existence of very significant obstacles to integration would be relevant to an assessment of the proportionality of the interference to the appellant's right to respect for his private life recognised by Article 8 of the Convention. In substance, however, the position is similar to that already discussed above. As the Upper Tribunal noted, the appellant was born and lived in Algeria until he was 15, he had acquired skills and experience in the United

Kingdom and demonstrated self-reliance and initiative. In those circumstances, it was entitled to conclude that the appellant would be capable of adapting to life in Algeria.

[70] In terms of his sexual orientation, the appellant would not live an openly gay life because of the societal, cultural and religious mores of the society. That will be a severely limiting feature on aspects of his life in Algeria but it does not provide a very significant obstacle to his reintegration into Algeria.

[71] In relation to the decision in *Kamara*, it is, as always, important to bear in mind the facts of that case which provided the context in which Sales LJ made his observations. There, the appellant, Mr Kamara, was a national of Sierra Leone. He was a foreign national criminal whom the Secretary of State wished to deport. He had come to the United Kingdom at the age of 6 with his sister and half-sister. He had indefinite leave to remain. He was at the time of the judgment aged almost 29. He had no ties with Sierra Leone and did not speak any of the local languages. He was completely integrated into society in the United Kingdom. It was in that context that Sales LJ referred to the question of whether Mr Kamara would be "enough of an insider" in terms of understanding how life in Sierra Leone would be carried on and have a capacity to participate in it and a reasonable opportunity to be accepted, to function on a day-to-day basis and to build up human relationships. The facts are very different from the present case where the appellant is a person who lived in Algeria until the age of 15, speaks the language, and as the tribunals found, is resourceful and able to adapt in Algeria.

CONCLUSION

[72] The Upper Tribunal did not err in relying on the earlier country guidance case of *OO (Algeria)*. That case did properly consider whether gay men in Algeria had a well-founded fear of persecution. It addressed itself to the correct question of how an openly gay man would be treated in Algeria; it did not restrict the definition of persecution to acts of violence and did consider all the relevant evidence and circumstances. It was entitled to find on the evidence that, outside the family, a gay man in Algeria would not face a real risk of persecution. The fact that the Appellant would not live openly as a gay man if he returned because of social, cultural and religious norms in Algeria did not amount to persecution. Nor would it be unduly harsh on the facts of this case for the appellant to relocate within Algeria to avoid the risk of ill-treatment at the hands of his family. The Upper Tribunal was entitled to find that there were no significant obstacles to his reintegration into Algeria. For those reasons, this appeal is dismissed.

ROBINSON v SECRETARY OF STATE FOR THE HOME DEPARTMENT

SUPREME COURT

Lady Black, Lord Lloyd-Jones, Lord Sales, Lord Burrows and Lord Stephens

[2020] UKSC 53
16 December 2020

European Union law – expulsion – derivative right of residence – foreign criminal – third-country national – parent of dependent EU citizen child – Article 20 of the Treaty on the Functioning of the European Union – Zambrano *principle – no additional hurdle of 'exceptional circumstances' – human rights – Article 8 of the ECHR – private and family life – proportionality – best interests of the child – public policy*

The Claimant, a citizen of Jamaica, entered the United Kingdom as a visitor in 2002. She married a person present and settled in the United Kingdom in 2003 and was granted indefinite leave to remain in March 2006. In October 2006 the Claimant was convicted of supplying cocaine and sentenced to two and a half years of imprisonment. The Secretary of State for the Home Department ordered the Claimant's deportation in 2007. The Claimant was detained in September 2008, but her removal was deferred as she was pregnant. In December 2008 she gave birth to a son, D, who was a United Kingdom national and EU citizen. The Claimant challenged the deportation order culminating in an unsuccessful judicial review application in January 2009, following which she failed to co-operate with the authorities. In February 2012 the Claimant applied for leave to remain outside the Immigration Rules HC 395 (as amended). The Secretary of State refused that application having treated it as an application to revoke the deportation order. The Claimant appealed that decision.

The First-tier Tribunal dismissed the Claimant's appeal. Before the Upper Tribunal ("UT") the Claimant relied on *Zambrano v Office national de l'emploi* (Case C-34/09) in addition to Article 8 of the ECHR. In *Zambrano* the Court of Justice of the EU ("CJEU") held that a third-country national ("TCN") parent of a Union citizen child resident in Union territory, who was dependent on the TCN parent, was entitled to a right of residence if expulsion of the TCN parent would require the child to leave the territory of the Union, thereby depriving the child of the genuine enjoyment of the substance of the child's Union citizenship rights. The UT allowed the Claimant's appeal having proceeded on the basis that the *Zambrano* right of residence was unqualified, so that there was an absolute prohibition against deportation of the TCN parent without any consideration of proportionality even if that parent had committed serious crimes.

The Secretary of State appealed to the Court of Appeal. The appeal was stayed to await the judgments of the CJEU in *Secretary of State for the Home Department v CS* (Case C-304/14) and *Rendón Marín v Administración del Estado* (Case C-165/14), in which the CJEU held that there was a limitation on the *Zambrano* derivative right of residence so that the right was not absolute. The Secretary of State submitted that the Claimant's case should be remitted to the UT for redetermination. The Claimant argued that any error of law was not material as the decision of the UT would inevitably have been the same. She submitted that the test that should be applied in the light of the decisions of the CJEU in *Rendón Marín* and *CS* included a requirement of "exceptional circumstances" to justify her deportation. The Court of Appeal held that the phrase "exceptional circumstances" at paragraph 50 of *CS* simply referred to an exception to the general rule that a person who enjoyed the fundamental rights of an EU citizen could not be compelled to leave the EU, and that it did not, where other relevant criteria were satisfied, impose an additional hurdle. The Court of Appeal remitted the case for the UT to carry out the proportionality exercise required by the decisions of the CJEU in *CS* and *Rendón Marín.*[*] The Claimant appealed to the Supreme Court.

Held, dismissing the appeal:

(1) The first question to be addressed in determining whether there was a *Zambrano* derived right of residence was whether there was a relationship of dependency of such a nature that it would lead to the Union citizen being compelled to accompany the TCN concerned and to leave the territory of the Union as a whole: *KA v Belgium* (Case C-82/16) followed. Secondly, the national court had the task of examining what, in the TCN's conduct or in the offence that she committed, constituted a genuine, present and sufficiently serious threat affecting one of the fundamental interests of society or of the host Member State, which might justify, on the ground of protecting the requirements of public policy or public security, an order deporting her from the United Kingdom: *CS* followed. The existence of such a threat could not be drawn automatically on the basis solely of the criminal record of the person concerned. Furthermore, Article 20 of the Treaty on the Functioning of the European Union had to be interpreted as precluding national legislation which required a TCN parent of minor children who were Union citizens in her sole care to be automatically refused the grant of a residence permit on the sole ground that she had a criminal record, where that refusal had the consequence of requiring those children to leave the territory of the EU. Rather it was incumbent upon the national court to assess the extent to which the TCN parent's criminal conduct was a danger to society and any consequences which such conduct might have for the requirements of public policy or public security of the Member State concerned. Finally, if there was such a threat, then the national court should carry out an exercise balancing, on the one hand, the nature and degree of that threat which led to the legitimate aim of safeguarding public order or public security. On the other hand, the national court had to take account of the fundamental rights whose observance the CJEU ensured, in particular the right to respect for private and family life, as laid down in Article 7 of the Charter of Fundamental Rights of the European Union, and to ensure that the principle of proportionality was observed. In a case involving children, account was to be taken of the child's best interests when weighing up the interests involved. Particular attention had to be paid to his age, his situation in the Member State concerned and the extent to which he was dependent on the parent: *CS* and *Rendón Marín* followed (*paras 44 – 46*).

---

[*] *Secretary of State for the Home Department v Robinson (Jamaica)* [2018] EWCA Civ 85

(2) The CJEU did not hold in *CS* that *Zambrano* carers enjoyed enhanced protection from deportation such that they could only be deported in "exceptional circumstances". It had noted that conduct which was potentially contrary to public policy and security was capable, in principle, of justifying an "exception" to the ordinary general rule that a *Zambrano* carer could not be expelled where that would lead to the departure of the dependent EU citizen from the EU's territory. The CJEU had set out the test of whether the expulsion decision was founded on the existence of a genuine, present and sufficiently serious threat and then set out in detail the particular factors to be considered when deciding whether that test was satisfied. Paragraph 50 of *CS* provided a summary of what was contained in the preceding paragraphs so that the reference to "exceptional circumstances" could only sensibly be read in the context of what came before. The CJEU did not add any additional criterion through the use of the words "exceptional circumstances". On the contrary, and as the Court of Appeal correctly decided, it was simply explaining that, in the prescribed circumstances, an exception could be made to the general rule that a *Zambrano* carer could not be compelled to leave the territory of the Union. It was not stating that certain undefined "exceptional circumstances" had first to be demonstrated (*paras 51 – 57*).

(3) In *Rendón Marín* the CJEU carried out the same analysis as in *CS* as to the exception to the *Zambrano* derived right of residence, specifying the test to be applied and the factors to be taken into account. In that respect the analysis of the CJEU in *Rendón Marín* was identical to the analysis in *CS*. The CJEU also took the same approach in *KA*. On three occasions, the CJEU had set out what must be taken into account when the deportation of a *Zambrano* carer was being considered. Not once had it stated that an imperative grounds test applied, nor had it stated that there was an additional hurdle that there must also be exceptional circumstances. It was inconceivable that the CJEU would have omitted to mention that on three occasions if such a test applied: *Zambrano*, *Rendón Marín*, *CS* and *KA* considered (*paras 58 – 60*).

(4) The Court of Appeal's clearly reasoned conclusions could not be faulted. The phrase "exceptional circumstances" simply meant that it was an exception to the general rule that a person who enjoyed the fundamental rights of an EU citizen could not be compelled to leave the territory of the EU. The phrase did not import an additional hurdle. The appeal would be dismissed and as a consequence the order of the Court of Appeal would be maintained remitting the case to the UT for determination on the merits (*para 61*).

Cases referred to:

B (a Child), In the matter of [2013] UKSC 33; [2013] 1 WLR 1911; [2013] 3 All ER 929

Chavez-Vilchez and Others v Raad van bestuur van de Sociale verzekeringsbank and Others (Case C-133/15); [2017] 3 WLR 1326; [2018] QB 103; [2017] Imm AR 1387; [2017] INLR 708

Dereci and Others v Bundesministerium für Inneres (Case C-256/11); [2012] All ER (EC) 373; [2012] 1 CMLR 45; [2012] Imm AR 230; [2012] INLR 151

Hesham Ali (Iraq) v Secretary of State for the Home Department [2016] UKSC 60; [2016] 1 WLR 4799; [2017] 3 All ER 20; [2017] Imm AR 484; [2017] INLR 109

KA v Belgium (Case C-82/16); [2018] 3 CMLR 28

Marleasing SA v La Comercial Internacional de Alimentacion SA (Case C-106/89); [1990] ECR I-4135; [1992] 1 CMLR 305
McCarthy v Secretary of State for the Home Department (Case C-434/09); [2011] ECR I-3375; [2011] All ER (EC) 729; [2011] 3 CMLR 10; [2011] Imm AR 586; [2011] INLR 450
OH (Serbia) v Secretary of State for the Home Department [2008] EWCA Civ 694; [2009] INLR 109
Pfeiffer, Roith, Süß, Winter, Nestvogel, Zeller and Döbele v Deutsches Rotes Kreuz, Kreisverband Waldshut eV (Cases C-397/01 to C-403/01); [2004] ECR 8835; [2004] ECR I-8835; [2005] IRLR 137
R v Bouchereau (Case C-30/77); [1977] ECR 1999; [1978] QB 732; [1978] 2 WLR 250; [1981] 2 All ER 924; [1977] 2 CMLR 800
Rendón Marín v Administración del Estado (Case C-165/14); [2017] QB 495; [2017] 2 WLR 117; [2017] 1 CMLR 29; [2017] Imm AR 205; [2017] INLR 338
Secretary of State for the Home Department v CS (Case C-304/14); [2017] QB 558; [2017] 2 WLR 180; [2017] 1 CMLR 31; [2017] Imm AR 429; [2017] INLR 400
Secretary of State for the Home Department v Robinson (Jamaica) [2018] EWCA Civ 85; [2018] 4 WLR 81; [2018] Imm AR 892
Zambrano v Office national de l'emploi (Case C-34/09); [2012] QB 265; [2012] 2 WLR 886; [2011] All ER (EC) 491; [2011] 2 CMLR 46; [2011] Imm AR 521; [2011] INLR 481

Legislation and international instruments judicially considered:

Charter of Fundamental Rights of the European Union, Articles 7 & 24(2)
Directive 2004/38/EC ("the Citizens Directive"), Articles 3(1), 27, 28 & 32
European Communities Act 1972, section 2(1)
European Convention on Human Rights, Article 8
Treaty on the Functioning of the European Union, Articles 20 & 21
UK Borders Act 2007, section 32(5)

Representation

Mr H Southey QC and *Mr I Palmer* instructed by Barnes Harrild & Dyer (Croydon), for the Claimant;
Mr D Blundell QC and *Ms J Smyth* instructed by the Government Legal Department, for the Secretary of State.

Judgment

LORD STEPHENS: (with whom Lady Black, Lord Lloyd-Jones, Lord Sales and Lord Burrows agree)

I   Introduction

[1] This appeal raises the issue as to whether a third-country (ie non-member state) national ("TCN") otherwise benefiting from the derivative right to reside within the territory of the European Union pursuant to the principle in *Ruiz Zambrano v Office national de l'emploi* (Case C-34/09) EU:C:2011:124; [2012]

QB 265 ("*Zambrano*") enjoys enhanced protection against deportation, such that she can be deported in "exceptional circumstances" only. In *Zambrano*, the Court of Justice of the European Union ("the CJEU") held that a TCN parent of a Union citizen child resident in Union territory who was dependent on the TCN parent, was entitled to a right of residence if expulsion of the TCN parent would require the child to leave the territory of the Union, thereby depriving the child of the genuine enjoyment of the substance of the child's Union citizenship rights. The principle extends to dependants who are not children, and applies even though the Union citizen has not exercised their right of free movement. The right of residence of the TCN is a derivative right, that is, one derived from the dependent Union citizen. It flows from article 20 of the Treaty on the Functioning of the European Union ("article 20FEU") and was expressed in unqualified terms in *Zambrano* so as to be thought to prevent expulsion of the TCN parent in all circumstances.

[2] The Upper Tribunal ("the UT") in its decision promulgated on 23 August 2013 proceeded on the basis that the *Zambrano* right of residence was unqualified, so that there was an absolute prohibition preventing deportation of the TCN parent without any consideration of proportionality even if that parent had committed serious crimes.

[3] The Secretary of State for the Home Department ("the Secretary of State") appealed to the Court of Appeal against the determination of the UT which appeal was stayed to await the judgments of the CJEU in *S v Secretary of State for the Home Department* (Case C-304/14) EU:C:2016:674; [2017] QB 558 ("*CS*") and *Rendón Marín v Administración del Estado* (Case C-165/14) EU:C:2016:675; [2017] QB 495 ("*Marín*"). These judgments were delivered on 13 September 2016.

[4] By its judgments in *CS* and *Marín* the CJEU held that there was a limitation on the *Zambrano* derivative right of residence so that the right was not absolute. In *CS* at para 36 it stated that "article 20FEU does not affect the possibility of member states relying on an exception linked, in particular, to upholding the requirements of public policy and safeguarding public security." In the same judgment at para 50 it stated "However, in *exceptional circumstances* a member state may adopt an expulsion measure provided that it is founded on the personal conduct of that third-country national, which must constitute a genuine, present and sufficiently serious threat adversely affecting one of the fundamental interests of the society of that member state, and that it is based on consideration of the various interests involved, matters which are for the national court to determine" [emphasis added].

[5] Following the delivery of the judgments in *CS* and *Marín* the issues on appeal narrowed. The appellant accepted that the UT had erred in law in that it had wrongly concluded that protection against removal was absolute and there was no need to consider proportionality if it concluded that the deportation of a TCN parent would require a child who was a Union citizen to depart from the territory of the Union with the person being deported. On behalf of the Secretary of State it was submitted and the Court of Appeal [2018] EWCA Civ 85; [2018] WLR 81 held at para 67, that "exceptional circumstances" in para 50 of *CS* "simply means that it is an exception to the general rule" which general rule was "that a person who enjoys the fundamental rights of an EU citizen cannot be compelled to leave the EU". The Court of Appeal added that "It does not mean that, where the criteria set out in the proviso are satisfied, there is an additional hurdle that there must also

be exceptional circumstances." The Court of Appeal remitted the case to the UT in order to carry out the proportionality exercise required by the decisions of the CJEU in *CS* and *Marín*.

[6] The appellant applied for permission to appeal to the Supreme Court on three grounds:

a.　　Ground one: Whether the Court of Appeal was wrong to conclude that there was no need for exceptional circumstances to be established before a person relying on *Zambrano* could be deported.

b.　　Ground two: Whether there was a sufficient evidential basis for finding that the deportation of the appellant was potentially lawful.

c.　　Ground three: Whether the Court of Appeal erred by remitting rather than determining proportionality directly.

On 4 July 2019 permission to appeal was granted on ground one only (whether exceptional circumstances need to be established before a *Zambrano* carer could be deported). That is the only question to be determined in this appeal.

[7] After the Court of Appeal delivered its judgment on 2 February 2018 the CJEU on 8 May 2018 delivered judgment in *KA v Belgische Staat* (Case C-82/16) EU:C:2018:308; [2018] 3 CMLR 28 ("*KA*") which again addressed the test that should be applied as an exception to the *Zambrano* principle. This means that there are now three CJEU decisions addressing the sole issue in this appeal.

[8] It is a feature of this appeal that the decisions in *Zambrano*, *Marín*, *CS* and *KA* were all decisions of the CJEU (Grand Chamber). In this judgment I will refer to these decisions as the decisions of the CJEU to avoid repeating Grand Chamber on each occasion.

II　Factual background

[9] The appellant is a national of Jamaica who was born on 13 March 1975. She is now aged 45. Initially she entered the United Kingdom as a visitor on 2 August 2002 and was granted leave to enter until 23 August 2002. Further extensions were made permitting her to remain as a student until 28 February 2004.

[10] On 11 November 2003 the appellant married Marlon MacPherson, a person present and settled in the United Kingdom. Following her marriage and on 24 February 2004, she applied for leave to remain as the spouse of a person present and settled in the United Kingdom. She was granted leave until 2 March 2006. On 28 February 2006 she applied for indefinite leave to remain which was granted on 22 March 2006.

[11] The appellant committed a serious criminal offence, of supplying a class A drug (cocaine). On 5 October 2006, at Wood Green Crown Court the appellant was convicted of this offence and was sentenced to a period of imprisonment of two years and six months. The appellant's evidence to the First-tier Tribunal was that she decided to sell drugs as she needed additional funds because her grandmother had fallen seriously ill in Jamaica with heart failure, arthritis, and high blood pressure.

[12] On 20 November 2007 a deportation order in respect of the appellant was signed by the Secretary of State.

[13] On 24 September 2008 the appellant was detained, pending removal but her removal was subsequently deferred as she was pregnant.

[14] On 29 December 2008, the appellant gave birth to a boy, whom I will call D, who is now almost 12 years old. His father is Mr MacPherson. D is a British national and a citizen of the Union. The appellant's evidence is that D has lived in the United Kingdom with her throughout his life.

[15] There was a history of unsuccessful challenges to the deportation order culminating on 7 January 2009 with an unsuccessful judicial review application following which the appellant failed to co-operate with the authorities between 2009 and 2012, being listed as an absconder on 6 May 2009.

[16] On 20 February 2012, the appellant submitted an application for leave to remain outside the Immigration Rules. This was treated by the Secretary of State as an application to revoke her deportation order. On 29 August 2012, the Secretary of State refused the application. It is that decision which gave rise to a further right of appeal to the First-tier Tribunal and is the subject of these proceedings.

III   The judgments of the tribunals and the Court of Appeal

(a) The First-tier Tribunal

[17] On appeal to the First-tier Tribunal before Judge Mitchell the appellant contended that her deportation would violate rights under Article 8 of the European Convention on Human Rights ("ECHR"). The judgment of the CJEU in *Zambrano* which had been delivered on 8 March 2011 was referred to in the determination of Judge Mitchell promulgated on 7 December 2012. However, the appeal before Judge Mitchell proceeded purely on the basis that deportation would violate the Article 8 ECHR rights of the appellant, D and of Mr MacPherson. In summary the evidence before Judge Mitchell was that by 22 February 2012 the appellant and her husband were living separately but had prior to the hearing reconciled so that they were back together again. The appellant stated that her husband played an important role in D's life and that the deportation order requiring the appellant to leave the United Kingdom would also require D to leave with her so as to separate the appellant and her son from her husband who would remain in the United Kingdom. Judge Mitchell carried out an Article 8 ECHR proportionality exercise stating at para 74 that

> "the appellant was convicted of extremely serious offences. She is a foreign criminal. The scourge of drugs on society has been held many times to be utterly reprehensible. ... The decision of the Secretary of State to deport a foreign criminal who has received such a significant sentence for drugs offences is proportionate even taking into account the circumstances of the appellant's family and herself."

The judge dismissed the appellant's appeal finding that deportation would not violate Article 8 ECHR.

(b) The Upper Tribunal

[18] The appeal before the UT proceeded not only on the basis that deportation would violate Article 8 ECHR but also on the basis of the appellant's derived right of residence under the *Zambrano* principle. The UT (which comprised UT Judges

Jordan and Pitt) allowed the appeal with the determination being given by UT Judge Jordan. He held that the effective care of D was in the hands of the appellant so it followed that the appellant's removal would be the effective cause of D's removal to Jamaica. At para 19 he stated that

"... the rights of Union citizens arising from *Ruiz Zambrano* are not derived from rights arising under the Citizens [Parliament and Council Directive 2004/38/EC] or the Immigration (European Economic Area) Regulations 2006 (2006 No 1003) transposing them into domestic law. They are a principle of European Union citizenship law developed by the Court of Justice in [Luxembourg]. Importantly, they are not a principle of European human rights law operated on principles of proportionality. In other words, the court or tribunal is not deciding whether it [is] proportionate to remove the British child so that his best interests (as a primary consideration) are weighed against the public interest in favour of removing those who commit serious crimes. *The prohibition against removal is absolute and prevents removal, notwithstanding the seriousness of the offence.*" [Emphasis added]

On this basis the UT held that no question of proportionality arose as a matter of EU law and that the removal of the appellant was not permitted under the *Zambrano* principle. The UT then remade the decision and allowed the appeal against the Secretary of State. This meant that it was not necessary to consider proportionality, but "for the sake of completeness" the judge proceeded to do so in the context of Article 8 ECHR. He stated at para 28:

"The appellant was sentenced to 30 months imprisonment. Whilst this is at the low end of sentences for supplying cocaine, this was nevertheless serious offending and the canker caused by the spread of drugs – particularly those recognised as Class A – creates a substantial public interest in removing those who are involved, if their removal is permissible. D's best interests (those of a single individual) have to be weighed against the interests of society in its entirety."

That interest includes, UT Judge Jordan held, following Wilson LJ in *OH (Serbia) v Secretary of State for the Home Department* [2008] EWCA Civ 694 "the role of a deportation order as an expression of society's revulsion at serious crimes and in building public confidence in the treatment of foreign citizens who have committed serious crimes". On this basis UT Judge Jordan held that he was not persuaded that the appellant's removal together with D would be disproportionate, notwithstanding that the best interests of D was a primary consideration.

[19] I would add as a footnote to the quotation from *OH (Serbia) v Secretary of State for the Home Department* that in *Ali v Secretary of State for the Home Department* [2016] UKSC 60; [2016] 1 WLR 4799, at para 70 Lord Wilson regretted his reference to society's revulsion at serious crimes as being "too emotive a concept to figure in this analysis". However, he maintained the substance of the point made by stating that "Laws serve society more effectively if they carry public support." He continued that "Unless it lacks rational foundation (in which case the courts should not pander to it), the very fact of public concern about an area of the law, subjective though that is, can in my view add to a court's objective analysis of where the public interest lies: in this context it can strengthen

the case for concluding that interference with a person's rights under Article 8 by reason of his deportation is justified by a pressing social need."

(c) The Court of Appeal
[20] The issues before the Court of Appeal (which comprised Underhill, Lindblom, Singh LJJ) had become narrower because of the CJEU's determination in *CS* and *Marín* that the prohibition against removal was not absolute so that it was conceded by the appellant that there were errors of law made by the UT. The Secretary of State submitted that the case should be remitted to the UT for redetermination, after considering any further evidence that might be necessary. The appellant submitted that the errors of law were not material as the decision of the UT would inevitably have been the same so that the appeal should be dismissed. The appellant's submission raised the issue as to whether the test that should be applied in the light of the decisions of the CJEU in *Marín* and *CS* included a requirement of "exceptional circumstances" to justify the appellant's deportation.
[21] At para 47 Singh LJ giving the judgment of the court, identified all the remaining issues before the Court of Appeal as being:

"(1) Should this court perform the proportionality exercise itself or should it remit the case to the UT?

(2) What is the correct test that should be applied in the light of the decisions of the CJEU in *Rendón Marín* and (*CS*)?

(3) What is the current status and effect of the decision in *R v Bouchereau* (Case C-30/77) EU:C:1977:172; [1978] QB 732?

(4) What is the relevance, if any, of the Rehabilitation of Offenders Act 1974?"

[22] Singh LJ having referred to *In re B (A Child) (Care Proceedings: Threshold Criteria)* [2013] UKSC 33; [2013] 1 WLR 1911, rejected the appellant's submission that the Court of Appeal should perform the proportionality exercise itself. At paras 50–52 Singh LJ identified three difficulties with the appellant's submission, none of which could be subject to any sensible challenge particularly given that at no previous stage had the threat which the appellant posed to the United Kingdom's public policy or public security been considered in accordance with the proportionality test set out by the CJEU in *Marín* and *CS*. It is sufficient to refer solely to the third difficulty which Singh LJ identified. At para 52 he stated:

"This leads me to my third point. It is that the question of proportionality should be addressed in the present case only after full consideration has been given to the issues of fact and, in particular, up-to-date information should be placed before the UT. One reason for this in the present case is that it concerns the potential impact of deportation on a young child, D. Since the best interests of a child must always be a primary consideration for the court, it is important that the UT should have available to it the most up-to-date information about the likely impact of D's mother's deportation on him."

Singh LJ held that the case should be remitted to the UT for redetermination, but proceeded to address the remaining issues to provide guidance to the UT as to how it should approach the case on remittal.

[23] In relation to the correct test which should be applied in the light of the decisions of the CJEU in *Marín* and *CS* Singh LJ conducted a careful and comprehensive analysis of both of those judgments together with the joint opinion of the Advocate General (M Szpunar) in *CS* and *Marín* (p 500). The Advocate General made the following recommendation to the CJEU in the case of *CS* (at point 177 of his opinion):

"..., I propose that the court's answer should be that it is, in principle, contrary to article 20FEU for a member state to expel from its territory to a non-member state a third country national who is the parent of a child who is a national of that member state and of whom the parent has sole care and custody, when to do so would deprive the child who is a citizen of the Union of genuine enjoyment of a substance of his or her rights as a citizen of the Union. Nevertheless, in *exceptional circumstances*, a member state may adopt such a measure, provided that it: observes the principle of proportionality and is based on the personal conduct of the foreign national, which must constitute a genuine, present and sufficiently serious threat affecting one of the fundamental interests of society, and *is based on an imperative reason relating to public security*." [Emphasis added]

As is apparent from the words to which I have added emphasis, the Advocate General's recommendation included the phrase "exceptional circumstances" and a requirement of "an imperative reason" confined solely "to public security" so as to exclude an imperative reason relating "to public policy".

[24] Relying on that recommendation and the CJEU's reference to exceptional circumstances in para 50 of its judgment in *CS*, Mr Southey QC on behalf of the appellant sought to establish an enhanced level of protection for carers by restricting the exception to the *Zambrano* principle. Singh LJ's conclusions at paras 66–67 were as follows:

"66. Mr Blundell [on behalf of the Secretary of State] invites this court to attach significance to the fact that the last phrase in that passage ('and is based on an imperative reason relating to public security') did not find its way into the judgments of the CJEU. He submits that the CJEU did not adopt that part of the recommendation made by the Advocate General. He also points out that the language used by the Advocate General is the language of (Directive 2004/38/EC), in particular article 28(3). He submits that it imposes a higher test than the test that was eventually adopted by the CJEU in the context of articles 20–21FEU. I agree with those submissions by Mr Blundell.

67. Mr Southey emphasises the use of the phrase 'exceptional circumstances' in the opinion of the Advocate General, at para 177, and in the judgment of the CJEU in (*CS*), at para 50. I do not attach the significance to that phrase which Mr Southey submits it has. In my view, it does not import an *additional* requirement which the state must satisfy on top of what follows; rather the phrase is a helpful *summary* of what follows ('provided ...'). In other words 'exceptional circumstances' simply means that it is an exception to the general

rule, which is that a person who enjoys the fundamental rights of an EU citizen cannot be compelled to leave the EU. It does not mean that, where the criteria set out in the proviso are satisfied, there is an additional hurdle that there must also be exceptional circumstances."

Accordingly, the Court of Appeal held that the correct test that should be applied did not require "exceptional circumstances" to be established before someone in the appellant's position could be deported. Rather the reference to "exceptional circumstances" in the relevant case law of the CJEU was merely a reference to the fact that deportation of someone in the appellant's position is a departure from the general rule that a person who enjoys the fundamental rights of an EU citizen cannot be compelled to leave the territory of the EU.

[25] Singh LJ then addressed at paras 68–86 the current status and effect of the decision of the European Court of Justice in *R v Bouchereau*. That decision envisages that past conduct alone which has caused public revulsion and is therefore a threat to the requirements of public policy may be sufficient to justify deportation without there necessarily being any clear propensity on behalf of the individual to act in the same way in the future. Singh LJ concluded that, subject to various limitations this remained "good law". That conclusion has not been appealed to this court.

[26] In relation to the final issue as to the relevance of the Rehabilitation of Offenders Act 1974 Mr Southey conceded, and for the reasons set out at paras 8790 Singh LJ held, that the Act had no direct application in the present context.

[27] The outcome in the Court of Appeal was that the Secretary of State's appeal was allowed and the case was remitted to the UT for redetermination on the merits.

IV The impact on this appeal of the United Kingdom's withdrawal from the EU

[28] Section 2(1) of the European Communities Act 1972 ("the 1972 Act") provides:

"All such rights, powers, liabilities, obligations and restrictions from time to time created or arising by or under the Treaties, and all such remedies and procedures from time to time provided for by or under the Treaties, as in accordance with the Treaties are without further enactment to be given legal effect or used in the United Kingdom shall be recognised and available in law, and be enforced, allowed and followed accordingly; and the expression 'enforceable EU right' and similar expressions shall be read as referring to one to which this subsection applies."

Section 1 of the European Union (Withdrawal) Act 2018 ("the 2018 Act") repealed the 1972 Act on "exit day" which is defined by section 20 as 11pm on 31 January 2020. However, exit day is followed by an implementation period ("IP") which ends on the "IP completion day" defined in section 39 of the European Union (Withdrawal Agreement) Act 2020 ("the 2020 Act") as 31 December 2020 at 11pm. During this period the 1972 Act continues to have effect pursuant to section 1A of the 2018 Act, as amended by the 2020 Act. The Charter of Fundamental Rights of the European Union ("the Charter") also continues to have effect during this period: see Part Four of the Agreement on the Withdrawal of the United Kingdom of Great Britain and Northern Ireland from the European Union and the European Atomic Energy Community (OJ 2019, C384 l, p 1) and section 1A(3) of the 2018 Act.

[29] As to the position after "IP completion day" the current position is that the Immigration (European Economic Area) Regulation 2016, and relevant provisions of the FEU Treaty to the extent that they are not implemented in domestic law, would continue to have effect as retained EU law pursuant to sections 2 and 4 of the 2018 Act. However, this is subject to the Immigration and Social Security Coordination (EU Withdrawal) Act 2020 as well as secondary legislation made under it. This Act provides for repeal of the main retained EU law relating to free movement.

[30] The present position is that the United Kingdom's withdrawal from the EU has no impact on this appeal but the legal principles to be applied may change after 31 December 2020 at 11pm.

V Legal landscape

(a) Union citizenship and the right to move and reside freely

[31] Article 20(1)FEU establishes Union citizenship and provides that "Every person holding the nationality of a member state" is a citizen of the Union. Under article 20(2)(a)FEU, citizens of the Union have "the right to move and reside freely within the territory of the member states". Article 21(1)FEU also provides that "Every citizen of the Union shall have the right to move and reside freely within the territory of the member states". This right is not absolute but is "subject to the limitations and conditions laid down in the Treaties and by the measures adopted to give them effect". The significance of citizenship of the Union is apparent from *Zambrano* at para 41 and *KA* at para 47 in that "citizenship of the European Union is intended to be the fundamental status of nationals of the member states". The CJEU confirmed at para 48 of *KA* that Union citizenship conferred "a primary and individual right to move and reside freely within the territory of the member states" but continued that this was not absolute as it was "subject to the limitations and restrictions laid down by the Treaty and the measures adopted for their implementation".

(b) Parliament and Council Directive 2004/38/EC

[32] On 29 April 2004 the Parliament and Council of the European Union adopted Parliament and Council Directive 2004/38/EC of 29 April 2004 on the right of citizens of the Union and their family members to move and reside freely within the territory of member states (OJ 2004 L158, p 77) ("the Directive"). The Directive lays down the conditions surrounding the exercise of the right of free movement and residence within EU territory, the right of permanent residence and the limits placed on those rights. Under the rubric of "Beneficiaries" article 3(1) provides that the Directive applies to all Union citizens who move to or reside in a member state (the host member state) other than that of which they are a national and to their family members who accompany or join them. Accordingly, the Directive does not apply in this case as the only Union citizen is D and he has not moved to or resided in a member state other than that of which he is a national, see *Zambrano* at para 39, *CS* at para 22 and *Marín* at para 40. In so far as D is not covered by the concept of "beneficiary" for the purposes of article 3(1) of the

Directive, a member of his family is not covered by that concept either, given that the rights conferred by that Directive on the family members of a beneficiary of the Directive are not autonomous rights of those family members, but derived rights, acquired through their status as members of the beneficiary's family: see *McCarthy v Secretary of State for the Home Department* (Case C-434/09) EU:C:2011:277; [2011] ECR I-3375; [2011] All ER (EC) 729, para 42. However, both articles 27 and 28 of the Directive are relevant as the CJEU has used some but not all of the language in those articles in relation to the limitation on the *Zambrano* derived right of residence under article 20FEU.

[33] Articles 27 and 28 are in Chapter VI of the Directive under the rubric "Restrictions on the right of entry and the right of residence on grounds of public policy, public security or public health".

[34] Article 27 of the Directive under the rubric "General principles" and in so far as relevant provides:

"1. Subject to the provisions of this Chapter, member states may restrict the freedom of movement and residence of Union citizens and their family members, irrespective of nationality, *on grounds of public policy, public security* or public health. These grounds shall not be invoked to serve economic ends.

2. Measures taken on grounds of public policy or public security shall comply with *the principle of proportionality* and shall be based exclusively on the personal conduct of the individual concerned. Previous criminal convictions shall not in themselves constitute grounds for taking such measures.

The personal conduct of the individual concerned must represent *a genuine, present and sufficiently serious threat affecting one of the fundamental interests of society*. Justifications that are isolated from the particulars of the case or that rely on considerations of general prevention shall not be accepted." [Emphasis added]

The CJEU has incorporated into the limitation on the *Zambrano* derived right of residence many parts of article 27, including those parts to which I have added emphasis. In relation to the grounds of "public policy" and "public security" see *Marín* at para 81, *CS* at para 36 and *KA* at para 90. In relation to the requirement to comply with the principle of proportionality see *Marín* at para 85, *CS* at para 41 and *KA* at paras 93 and 97. In relation to the requirement that the conduct must represent "a genuine, present and sufficiently serious threat affecting one of the fundamental interests of society" see *Marín* at para 84, *CS* at para 40 and *KA* at para 92.

[35] Article 28(1) of the Directive under the rubric "Protection against expulsion" provides:

"Before taking an expulsion decision on grounds of public policy or public security, the host member state shall take account of considerations such as how long the individual concerned has resided on its territory, his/her age, state of health, family and economic situation, social and cultural integration into the host member state and the extent of his/her links with the country of origin."

Again, the CJEU has incorporated into the limitation on the *Zambrano* derived right of residence the language of article 28(1). In relation to the requirement to take into account "considerations such as how long the individual concerned has resided on its territory, his/her age, state of health" (etc) see *Marín* at para 86, *CS* at para 42 and *KA* at para 94. As expected given the context of both a crime committed by the TCN parent and the interests of children, the list of factors identified by the CJEU as "in particular" to be taken into account include factors not mentioned in article 28(1), such as the nature and gravity of the offence committed, the extent to which the person concerned is currently a danger to society, the age of the children at issue and their state of health, as well as their economic and family situation. The CJEU also referred to the legality of the residence of the TCN parent as a relevant factor, which is not specifically mentioned in article 28(1).

[36] Article 28(2) and (3) provides:

"2. The host member state may not take an expulsion decision against Union citizens or their family members, irrespective of nationality, who have the right of permanent residence on its territory, except on *serious grounds* of public policy or public security.

3.   An expulsion decision may not be taken against Union citizens, except if the decision is based *on imperative grounds of public security*, as defined by member states, if they:

(a)   have resided in the host member state for the previous ten years; or

(b)   are a minor, except if the expulsion is necessary for the best interests of the child, as provided for in the United Nations Convention on the Rights of the Child of 20 November 1989 ['the UNCRC']."

The CJEU has not incorporated into the limitation on the *Zambrano* derived right of residence the parts of article 28(2) and (3) to which I have added emphasis. However, in relation to the UNCRC the *Zambrano* derived right of residence is within the ambit of EU law so that article 24(2) of the Charter applies which provides that "In all actions relating to children, whether taken by public authorities or private institutions, the child's best interests must be a primary consideration". Furthermore, article 7 of the Charter which provides for the right to respect for private and family life must be read in conjunction with the obligation to take into consideration the child's best interests, recognised in article 24(2) of the Charter, see *Marín* at paras 66 and 81.

[37] In considering article 28(3) it should be recalled that the Directive does not apply in this case. However even if the Directive did apply D is not the individual subject to the expulsion decision so that article 28(3) would not be engaged. It is correct that the effective result of the expulsion of D's *Zambrano* carer is that D also is expelled. However, the consequences are different as between D and a minor expelled under article 28(3). D is entitled to return to the territory of the Union at any time whilst a minor expelled under article 28(3) is restricted to submitting an application under article 32 after a reasonable period, depending on the circumstances, and in any event after three years from enforcement of the final exclusion order by putting forward arguments to establish that there has been a

material change in the circumstances which justified the decision ordering their exclusion. It is then for the member state concerned to reach a decision on this application. Furthermore, a minor expelled under article 28(3) has no right of entry to the territory of the member state concerned while their application under article 32 is being considered.

(c) Implementation of the Directive into domestic law

[38] The Directive was implemented into domestic law by the Immigration (European Economic Area) Regulations 2006 (SI 2006/1003) ("the 2006 Regulations"). Those Regulations were amended on 16 July 2012 to give effect to a number of derivative rights of residence in EU law and to include an associated power of removal for persons enjoying such rights, where removal would be "conducive to the public good". The 2006 Regulations were further amended on 8 November 2012 to make wider provision reflecting CJEU case law, as then embodied in the *Zambrano* decision, based, as it was, on article 20FEU and to apply the "conducive to the public good" removal provision to such persons. The 2006 Regulations have since been replaced by new Regulations made in 2016 ("the 2016 Regulations"). However, it was the 2006 Regulations that applied at the time of the impugned decision (see paragraph 5 of Schedule 6 to the 2016 Regulations). The 2006 Regulations must, to the extent possible, be interpreted to ensure conformity with article 20FEU. If, in its case law since the *Zambrano* decision, the CJEU has interpreted article 20FEU as requiring "exceptional circumstances" as an additional requirement, then national courts must strive to interpret the 2006 Regulations on that basis in accordance with the *Marleasing* principle, see *Marleasing SA v La Comercial Internacional de Alimentación SA* (Case C-106/89) EU:C:1990:395; [1990] ECR I-4135; [1992] 1 CMLR 305, para 13 and *Pfeiffer v Deutsches Rotes Kreuz Kreisverband Waldshut eV* (Joined Cases C-397/01 and C-403/01) EU:C:2004:584; [2005] ICR 1307; [2004] ECR I-8835; [2005] 1 CMLR 44, para 115. So, the focus of this appeal returns to the decisions of the CJEU in order to determine what test is to be applied in order to accord with CJEU's case law.

(d) The Zambrano right of residence

[39] The CJEU's ruling in *Zambrano* is the landmark decision. Mr Ruiz Zambrano and his wife, Mrs Moreno Lopez, were both nationals of Colombia. While they were living in Belgium Mrs Moreno Lopez gave birth to two children, who acquired Belgian nationality by operation of Belgian law. Accordingly, both children were also citizens of the EU and their parents were TCN parents. The two children did not at any stage exercise their right to move freely within the EU but remained in Belgium with their parents. Mr Zambrano applied for unemployment benefit. That application was rejected on the ground that, since he had never held a work permit in Belgium, he did not have the requisite qualifying period as required by national legislation governing the residence and employment of foreign workers. The Employment Tribunal in Belgium made a reference to the CJEU which held that article 20FEU is to be interpreted as precluding a member state from refusing a TCN on whom his minor children, who are European Union citizens, are dependent, a right of residence in the member state of residence and nationality of those children, and from refusing to grant a work permit to that

TCN, in so far as such decisions deprive those children of the genuine enjoyment of the substance of the rights attaching to the status of European Union citizen.

(e) The Zambrano right of residence is a derivative right

[40] As is apparent from para 50 of *KA* the Treaty provisions on citizenship do "not confer any autonomous right on third-country nationals. Any rights conferred on third-country nationals are not autonomous rights of those nationals but rights derived from those enjoyed by a Union citizen. The purpose and justification of those derived rights are based on the fact that a refusal to allow them would be such as to interfere, in particular, with a Union citizen's freedom of movement": see also *CS* at para 28.

(f) The consideration of a Zambrano right of residence falls within the ambit of European Union law

[41] Consideration of whether there is a *Zambrano* derived right of residence falls within the ambit of EU law. Accordingly, account must be taken of the right to respect for private and family life, as laid down in article 7 of the Charter, an article which, must be read in conjunction with the obligation to take into consideration the child's best interests, recognised in article 24(2) of the Charter, see *Marín* at para 81.

(g) The very specific situations giving rise to the Zambrano derived right of residence

[42] The "very specific situations" giving rise to this derived right of residence are set out in *Zambrano* at paras 43 and 44, in *Chavez-Vilchez v Raad van bestuur van de Sociale verzekeringsbank* (Case C-133/15) EU:C:2017:354; [2018] QB 103; [2017] 3 CMLR 35 at para 63 and most recently in *KA* at paras 51 and 52 as follows:

"51. ..., a right of residence must nevertheless be granted to a third-country national who is a family member of that Union citizen, since the effectiveness of Union citizenship would otherwise be undermined, if, as a consequence of refusal of such a right, that citizen would be obliged in practice to leave the territory of the EU as a whole, thus depriving him of the genuine enjoyment of the substance of the rights conferred by that status ...

52. However, a refusal to grant a right of residence to a third-country national is liable to undermine the effectiveness of Union citizenship only if there exists, between that third-country national and the Union citizen who is a family member, a relationship of dependency of such a nature that it would lead to the Union citizen being compelled to accompany the third-country national concerned and to leave the territory of the EU as a whole ..."

[43] The requirement of being compelled to leave the territory of the EU as a whole as opposed to being compelled to leave the territory of the member state was specifically referred to in the decision of the CJEU in *Dereci v Bundesministerium für Inneres* (Case C-256/11) EU:C:2011:734; [2011] ECR I-11315; [2012] All ER (EC) 373; [2012] 1 CMLR 45. The CJEU stated at para 66 of its judgment that the criterion "refers to situations in which the Union citizen has, in fact to leave not only the territory of the member state of which he is a national but also the territory of the Union as a whole".

(h) The first question to be addressed by the national court

[44] On this basis the first question to be addressed in determining whether there is a *Zambrano* derived right of residence is whether there is a relationship of dependency of such a nature that it would lead to the Union citizen being compelled to accompany the TCN concerned and to leave the territory of the Union as a whole. In determining that question the CJEU set out at para 71 of *KA* the factors to be taken into account. The CJEU stated:

> "More particularly, in order to assess the risk that a particular child, who is a Union citizen, might be compelled to leave the territory of the EU and thereby be deprived of the genuine enjoyment of the substance of the rights conferred on him by article 20 TFEU if the child's third-country national parent were to be refused a right of residence in the member state concerned, it is important to determine, in each case at issue in the main proceedings, which parent is the primary carer of the child and whether there is in fact a relationship of dependency between the child and the third-country national parent. As part of that assessment, the competent authorities must take account of the right to respect for family life, as stated in article 7 of the Charter, that article requiring to be read in conjunction with the obligation to take into consideration the best interests of the child, recognised in article 24(2) of the Charter (*Chavez Vilchez* [2017] 3 CMLR 35, para 70)."

(i) The second question to be addressed by the national court

[45] In *CS* at para 40 the CJEU stated that an expulsion decision founded on the existence of a genuine, present and sufficiently serious threat to the requirements of public policy or of public security, in view of the criminal offences committed by a TCN who is the sole carer of children who are Union citizens, could be consistent with EU law. At para 46 it stated that the national court has the task of examining what, in the TCN's conduct or in the offence that she committed, "constitutes a genuine, present and sufficiently serious threat affecting one of the fundamental interests of society or of the host member state, which may justify, on the ground of protecting the requirements of public policy or public security, an order deporting her from the United Kingdom". Accordingly, the second question to be addressed is whether there is such a threat. It is clear from *CS* at para 41 and *Marín* at para 85 that the existence of such a threat cannot be drawn automatically on the basis solely of the criminal record of the person concerned. Furthermore, article 20FEU must be interpreted as precluding national legislation which requires a TCN parent of minor children who are Union citizens in his sole care to be automatically refused the grant of a residence permit on the sole ground that he has a criminal record, where that refusal has the consequence of requiring those children to leave the territory of the European Union. Rather it "is incumbent" upon the national court to assess (i) the extent to which the TCN parent's criminal conducts is a danger to society and (ii) any consequences which such conduct might have for the requirements of public policy or public security of the member state concerned, see *Marín* at para 87 and *CS* at para 47.

(j) The third question to be addressed by the national court

[46] If there is such a threat then the national court carries out an exercise balancing, on the one hand, the nature and degree of that threat which leads to the legitimate aim of safeguarding public order or public security. On the other hand, the national court has to take account of the fundamental rights whose observance the CJEU ensures, in particular the right to respect for private and family life, as laid down in article 7 of the Charter and to ensure that the principle of proportionality is observed. In a case involving children account is to be taken of the child's best interests when weighing up the interests involved. Particular attention must be paid to his age, his situation in the member state concerned and the extent to which he is dependent on the parent: see *CS* at paras 48–49.

VI Whether exceptional circumstances need to be established before a Zambrano carer can be deported

(a) The parties' submissions

[47] On behalf of the appellant Mr Southey submitted that "the use of the phrase 'exceptional circumstances' demonstrates the weight to be attached to the interests of the *Zambrano* child when conducting a proportionality balancing exercise." He also submitted that "the use of the phrase 'exceptional circumstances' in *CS* at para 50 cannot merely connote a departure from the norm" but rather that "it implies that the interests of the *Zambrano* child must carry great weight that can only be outweighed by particularly compelling reasons."

[48] On behalf of the Secretary of State Mr Blundell relied on the CJEU decisions in *CS, Marín* and *KA* in order to submit that the "imperative grounds" test does not apply, and nor does any broader "exceptional circumstances" test. He submitted that on a proper textual analysis of the judgment in *CS* the single use of the phrase "exceptional circumstances" was to be read as an exception to the usual application of the *Zambrano* principle.

(b) Rejection by the CJEU of "imperative grounds of public security"

[49] Advocate General M Szpunar in his opinion in *CS* proposed the adoption of enhanced protection based on "imperative grounds relating to public security". At point 168 he stated that

"In the present case, given that the minor child who is a citizen of the Union might, as a consequence of the expulsion of his mother, temporarily have to leave the territory of the European Union altogether, it is appropriate, to my mind, that he should be accorded *the enhanced protection implied by the term 'imperative grounds of public security'*. Accordingly, *only imperative grounds of public security are capable of justifying the adoption of an expulsion order against (CS) if, as a consequence, her child would have to follow her.*" [Emphasis added]

In this paragraph he did not propose the adoption of the phrase "exceptional circumstances".

[50] At point 177 Advocate General M Szpunar proposed that the court's answer in *CS* should be

"that it is, in principle, contrary to article 20FEU for a member state to expel from its territory to a non-member state a third-country national who is the parent of a child who is a national of that member state and of whom the parent has sole care and custody, when to do so would deprive the child who is a citizen of the Union of genuine enjoyment of the substance of his or her rights as a citizen of the Union."

He went on to define a proposed limitation on the derived right of residence in terms that used the phrases "exceptional circumstances" and "based on an imperative reason relating to public security". He proposed that

"Nevertheless, in *exceptional circumstances*, a member state may adopt such a measure, provided that it: observes the principle of proportionality and is based on the personal conduct of the foreign national, which must constitute a genuine, present and sufficiently serious threat affecting one of the fundamental interests of society, and is *based on an imperative reason relating to public security*." [Emphasis added]

[51] At para 36 of the judgment in *CS* the CJEU recognised "an exception" to the *Zambrano* principle "linked, in particular, to upholding the requirements of public policy and safeguarding public security". That is entirely inconsistent with the test of imperative grounds in article 28(3) of the Directive which is only linked to public security. The rejection of the test of imperative grounds is also apparent from para 40 which requires the expulsion decision to be "founded on the existence of a genuine, present and sufficiently serious threat". That is not a test of "imperative grounds". Again, in that paragraph it is made clear that this is a threat to either "the requirements of public policy or of public security". I consider that it is clear that the CJEU rejected the proposal of enhanced protection based on imperative grounds of public security. Two questions remain. The first is whether by using the phrase "exceptional circumstances" Advocate General M Szpunar was proposing that a *Zambrano* carer should enjoy enhanced protection against deportation, such that she can be deported in "exceptional circumstances" only. In view of his associated proposal that there should be "an imperative reason relating to public security" I am prepared to proceed, without deciding the point, on the basis that he was proposing an additional requirement of "exceptional circumstances". On the basis of that assumed answer to the first question the second remaining question is whether the CJEU adopted Advocate General M Szpunar's proposal of "exceptional circumstances".

(c) Textual analysis of the judgment in CS

[52] I consider that a textual analysis of the judgment in *CS* makes it clear that the CJEU did not adopt the proposal in relation to "exceptional circumstances".

[53] In *CS* the applicant, a TCN, married a British national and was granted indefinite leave to remain in the United Kingdom where she had a child for whom she was the sole carer. She was convicted of a criminal offence in the United Kingdom and sentenced to a term of imprisonment whilst her child was still very young. The Secretary of State rejected the applicant's asylum application and ordered her deportation after she had been released from prison, in reliance on, *inter alia*, section 32(5) of the UK Borders Act 2007 under which deportation would always be ordered in respect of a TCN who was convicted of an offence of a certain gravity, unless that order breached the offender's rights under, *inter alia*, the European Union treaties. The applicant's appeal was allowed by the First-tier Tribunal on the ground that her deportation would lead to, *inter alia*, a breach of her child's right as a Union citizen to move and reside within the European Union under article 20FEU in that, if the applicant were deported, her child would also have to leave the European Union. On the Secretary of State's appeal, the UT referred to the CJEU for a preliminary ruling the question whether article 20FEU precluded the national legislation. The CJEU held that a decision to expel a TCN who was the sole carer of a Union citizen child on the ground of public policy or public security could not be made automatically on the sole basis of the criminal record of the person concerned. The CJEU went on to consider the basis upon which such an expulsion decision could be made.

[54] In paras 34–50 of the judgment and under the heading "The possibility of limiting a derived right of residence flowing from article 20FEU" the CJEU set out its analysis of the limitation on the *Zambrano* right of residence.

[55] At para 36 the CJEU stated as follows:

"It should be pointed out that article 20FEU does not affect the possibility of member states relying on *an exception* linked, in particular, to upholding the requirements of public policy and safeguarding public security." [Emphasis added]

In other words, conduct which is potentially contrary to the interests of public policy and public security – in most cases, the commission of a criminal offence – was capable, in principle, of justifying an "exception" to the ordinary general rule (namely, that a *Zambrano* carer cannot be expelled where to do so would lead to the departure of the dependent EU citizen from the territory of the Union). As I have emphasised the CJEU specifically referred to reliance on "an exception", rather than the existence of "exceptional circumstances".

[56] At para 37 in relation to the exception the CJEU relying on its case law stated that the concepts of "public policy" and "public security" must be "interpreted strictly". At para 38 the CJEU considered the exception as linked to upholding the requirements of "public policy" identifying that in addition to "the disturbance of the social order which any infringement of the law involves" there must exist "a genuine, present and sufficiently serious threat affecting one of the fundamental interests of society". At para 39 the CJEU analysed its case law in relation to the public security exception. At para 40 the CJEU set out the test as being whether the expulsion decision is founded on the existence of "a genuine, present and sufficiently serious threat to the requirements of public policy or of public security". Then at paras 41–42 and 46–49, the CJEU set out in detail the particular factors which have to be considered when deciding whether that test was satisfied.

[57] I consider that para 50 provides a summary of what is contained in the preceding paragraphs so that the reference to "exceptional circumstances" can only sensibly be read in the context of what comes before. When seen against the background of the analysis beginning at para 34, it is clear that the CJEU did not add any additional criterion through the use of the words "exceptional

circumstances". On the contrary, and as the Court of Appeal correctly decided, it was simply explaining that, in the prescribed circumstances, an exception could be made to the general rule that a *Zambrano* carer could not be compelled to leave the territory of the Union. It was not stating that certain undefined "exceptional circumstances" had first to be demonstrated.

(d) The judgments in Marín *and* KA

[58] In *Marín* under the same heading as used in *CS* ("The possibility of limiting a derived right of residence flowing from article 20FEU") the CJEU at paras 81–88 carried out the same analysis as in *CS* as to the exception to the *Zambrano* derived right of residence, specifying the test to be applied and the factors to be taken into account. In that respect the analysis of the CJEU in *Marín* is identical to the analysis in *CS*. Furthermore, the test in para 84 of *Marín* is in the same terms as the test in para 40 of *CS*. In paras 85 and 86 in *Marín* the CJEU set out the matters to be taken into account. There is no reference in *Marín* to the phrase "exceptional circumstances".

[59] The CJEU also took the same approach in *KA*, at paras 85–97. In that case, the Belgian authorities refused to consider applications for residence permits from the TCN parents of Belgian children on the grounds that the applicant was subject to an entry ban. Having dealt with the circumstances in which a *Zambrano* right could come into being at paras 63–76, the CJEU repeated at para 90 that article 20 TFEU did "not affect the possibility of member states relying on an exception linked ... to upholding the requirements of public policy and safeguarding public security". The CJEU went on, at paras 90–97, to repeat the factors set out in *CS* and *Marín* which should be taken into account when that test is being applied. At para 92 it stated:

> "..., it must be held that, where the refusal of a right of residence is founded on the existence of a genuine, present and sufficiently serious threat to the requirements of public policy or public security, in view of, *inter alia*, criminal offences committed by a third-country national, such a refusal is compatible with EU law even if its effect is that the Union citizen who is a family member of that third-country national is compelled to leave the territory of the EU ..."

Again, this is a repetition of the test in para 84 of *Marín* and in para 40 of *CS*. Nowhere in its detailed analysis in *KA* does the CJEU state or even imply that there is an additional hurdle that there must also be exceptional circumstances.

[60] On three occasions, the CJEU has set out what must be taken into account when the deportation of a *Zambrano* carer is being considered. Not once has it stated that an imperative grounds test applies, nor has it stated that there is an additional hurdle that there must also be exceptional circumstances. I consider that it is inconceivable that the CJEU would have omitted to mention this on three occasions if such a test applied.

VII Disposal of the appeal

[61] For my part I consider that the Court of Appeal's clearly reasoned conclusion cannot be faulted and was plainly right. The phrase "exceptional circumstances" simply means that it is an exception to the general rule that a

person who enjoys the fundamental rights of an EU citizen cannot be compelled to leave the territory of the EU. The phrase does not import an additional hurdle. I would dismiss the appeal and would, as a consequence maintain the order of the Court of Appeal remitting the case to the UT for redetermination on the merits.

QC (VERIFICATION OF DOCUMENTS; *MIBANGA* DUTY) CHINA

UPPER TRIBUNAL (IMMIGRATION AND ASYLUM CHAMBER)

Lane J (President) and Mr CMG Ockelton (Vice President)

[2021] UKUT 33 (IAC)
12 January 2021

Evidence – credibility of the claimants – consideration "in the round" – Mibanga duty – documentary evidence – verification of documents – Tanveer Ahmed* [2002] UKIAT 0439 affirmed

The Claimant, a citizen of China, arrived in the United Kingdom in February 2014 but did not claim asylum until October 2018, following his arrest on immigration matters. In March 2019, the Secretary of State for the Home Department refused the Claimant's protection claim. The Claimant appealed to the First-tier Tribunal ("FtT"). He advanced two discrete reasons to be in need of international protection. First, his family home had been demolished in 2009 by the Chinese authorities, in order to build a new road. He sought compensation from the authorities but was beaten by them and his collar bone broken. Secondly, while living in another area of China, he was introduced to Tibetan Buddhism and became aware of the injustice meted out to the Tibetan people by the Chinese authorities. When those authorities raided the premises in which the Claimant was living, they arrested his friend but the Claimant managed to hide himself. He said that the Chinese authorities were now aware that he was a Tibetan Buddhist. He fled China because he feared what might happen to him as a Tibetan Buddhist who supported Tibetan independence.

The FtT dismissed the Claimant's appeal. The FtT Judge did not find that the Claimant's account of being involved in a land dispute with the Chinese authorities was credible. Regarding the second claim, the Judge noted that, at his screening interview in October 2018, the Claimant made no reference to his involvement with Tibetan Buddhism or support for Tibetan independence. The Judge also noted that, in his asylum interview in March 2019, the Claimant was unable to demonstrate a fundamental knowledge of the tenets of Tibetan Buddhism. Moreover, the Claimant had given inconsistent accounts of his worship at a Tibetan Buddhist centre in Glasgow in his asylum interview and witness statement. The Claimant's failure to establish that he was a Tibetan Buddhist undermined his claim that he was wanted by the authorities because he was a Tibetan Buddhist. The Judge also considered an arrest warrant issued in March 2014 and submitted to the FtT the day before the hearing in July 2019. In the light of the finding that the Claimant was not involved with Tibetan Buddhism, the FtT Judge found that the arrest warrant was "evidentially neutral".

Before the Upper Tribunal, the Claimant submitted first that, as the Secretary of State had not carried out any verification checks on the arrest warrant, it was not open to her, or the FtT, to impugn such a document. Secondly, the FtT Judge had allowed his adverse credibility findings to sway the assessment of the arrest warrant. Thirdly, the Judge had erred by failing to be slow to draw adverse inferences from omissions/inconsistencies arising from the screening interview. The Upper Tribunal considered in what circumstances the Secretary of State had an obligation to make enquiry in order to verify the authenticity and reliability of a document, and the consequences of her not doing so; and the nature of the obligation on judicial fact-finders to consider the evidence before them "in the round".

Held, dismissing the appeal:

(1) The decision of the Immigration Appeal Tribunal in *Tanveer Ahmed (Documents unreliable and forged) Pakistan** [2002] UKIAT 0439 remained good law as regards the correct approach to documents adduced in immigration appeals. The overarching question for the judicial fact-finder would be whether the document in question could be regarded as reliable. An obligation on the Secretary of State to take steps to verify the authenticity of the document relied on by a claimant would arise only exceptionally (in the sense of rarely). That would be where the document was central to the claim; could easily be authenticated; and where, as in *Singh v Belgium* 2012 ECHR 33210/11, authentication was unlikely to leave any "live" issue as to the reliability of its contents. It was for the Tribunal to decide, in all the circumstances of the case, whether the obligation arose. If the Secretary of State did not fulfil the obligation, the Secretary of State could not challenge the authenticity of the document in the proceedings; but that did not necessarily mean the Secretary of State could not question the reliability of what the document said. In all cases, it remained the task of the judicial fact-finder to assess the document's relevance to the claim in the light of, and by reference to, the rest of the evidence (*paras 13 – 37*).

(2) Credibility was not necessarily an essential component of a successful claim to be in need of international protection. Where credibility had a role to play, its relevance to the overall outcome would vary, depending on the nature of the case. What that relevance was to a particular claim needed to be established with some care by the judicial fact-finder. It was only once that was done that the practical application of the "*Mibanga* duty" to consider credibility "in the round" could be understood: *Francois Mibanga v Secretary of State for the Home Department* [2005] EWCA Civ 367 applied. The significance of a piece of evidence that emanated from a third-party source might well depend upon what was at stake in terms of the individual's credibility. What the case law revealed was that the judicial fact-finder had a duty to make his or her decision by reference to all the relevant evidence and needed to show in their decision that they had done so. The actual way in which the fact-finder went about that task was a matter for them. As had been pointed out, one had to start somewhere. At the end of the day, what mattered was whether the decision contained legally adequate reasons for the outcome. The greater the apparent cogency and relevance of a particular piece of evidence, the greater was the need for the judicial fact-finder to show that they had had due regard to that evidence; and, if the fact-finder's overall conclusion was contrary to the apparent thrust of that evidence, the greater was the need to explain why that evidence had not brought about a different outcome (*paras 38 – 57*).

(3) In the instant case, the arrest warrant was first sent to the FtT the day before the hearing. If the duty of verification arose, it would place the Secretary of State in an immensely difficult position. Either the Presenting Officer would have to

seek an adjournment, in order for attempts at verification to take place; or he or she would be precluded from challenging the authenticity of the document before the FtT. Where the duty of verification was a live issue, the timing of the production of the document was, plainly, one of the fact-sensitive matters to which regard must be had in deciding, in all the circumstances, whether the duty arose on the facts of the case. The arrest warrant document was very far from having the attributes needed to make the verification duty a live issue. On the contrary, leaving aside its egregiously late production, the fundamental reason why the duty did not arise in respect of the arrest warrant was because it was merely an unremarkable example of the kind of document encountered by judges of the FtT on a daily basis in protection appeals. If every such document were required to be verified by the Secretary of State, the appellate process would be severely impaired. Such an exercise would be entirely disproportionate: *Tanveer Ahmed* and *PJ (Sri Lanka) v Secretary of State for the Home Department* [2014] EWCA Civ 1011 applied. Accordingly, the first ground of appeal failed (*paras 58 – 63*).

(4) The Claimant's assertion that the FtT Judge had allowed his adverse credibility findings to sway the assessment of the arrest warrant was rejected. The Judge did not treat the arrest warrant as another example of the Claimant giving deceitful evidence: *TF v Secretary of State for the Home Department* [2018] CSIH 58 considered. Nor did the Judge fall into the related error, identified in *TF*, of treating all evidence supportive of the Claimant's case as merely further examples of him manufacturing a false claim. The FtT Judge came to the conclusion that the arrest warrant was neutral in its significance. That was very different from the mischief which the Inner House sought to identify in *TF*. The Judge was entitled to conclude on the evidence that the Claimant was not a Tibetan Buddhist and to treat the arrest warrant as evidentially neutral: *AR v Secretary of State for the Home Department* [2017] CSIH 52 considered. It had no relevance to the question as to whether the Claimant actually was a practitioner of Tibetan Buddhism, which was the proposition upon which his claim to international protection was based. For those reasons, the second ground of appeal failed (*paras 64 – 68*).

(5) It was trite that a person claiming international protection was not expected in his screening interview to set out every detail of his claim. Notwithstanding that the Claimant in the instant case was claiming asylum following an event, his arrest, over the timing of which he had no control, the FtT Judge was entitled to have some regard to the fact that Tibet and Tibetan issues did not feature in the reasons given by the Claimant for claiming asylum. In any event, however, reading the decision as a whole, it was manifest that the basis for the FtT Judge's adverse credibility findings arose not from the screening interview but from the detailed asylum interview. Accordingly, the third ground of appeal failed (*paras 69 – 73*).

Cases referred to:

AM (Afghanistan) v Secretary of State for the Home Department [2017] EWCA Civ 1123; [2018] 4 WLR 78; [2018] 2 All ER 350; [2017] Imm AR 1508; [2017] INLR 839
AR v Secretary of State for the Home Department [2017] CSIH 52
Francois Mibanga v Secretary of State for the Home Department [2005] EWCA Civ 367; [2005] INLR 377
HH (medical evidence; effect of Mibanga*) Ethiopia* [2005] UKAIT 164

*MJ (*Singh v Belgium*:* Tanveer Ahmed *unaffected) Afghanistan* [2013] UKUT 253 (IAC); [2013] Imm AR 799
MN v Secretary of State for the Home Department; IXU v Secretary of State for the Home Department [2020] EWCA Civ 1746
PJ (Sri Lanka) v Secretary of State for the Home Department [2014] EWCA Civ 1011; [2015] 1 WLR 1322; [2015] Imm AR 68
R v Secretary of State for the Home Department ex parte Ravichandran [1995] EWCA Civ 16; [1996] Imm AR 97
S v Secretary of State for the Home Department [2006] EWCA Civ 1153; [2007] Imm AR 7; [2007] INLR 60
Singh v Belgium 2012 ECHR 33210/11
TF and MA v Secretary of State for the Home Department [2018] CSIH 58; 2019 SC 81; 2018 SLT 1225
Tanveer Ahmed (Documents unreliable and forged) Pakistan* [2002] UKIAT 439; [2002] Imm AR 318; [2002] INLR 345

Representation

Mr S Winter instructed by Katani & Co Solicitors, for the Claimant;
Mr D Clarke, Senior Home Office Presenting Officer, for the Secretary of State.

Decision and reasons

THE HON. MR JUSTICE LANE:

A. The issues

[1] This case concerns two related issues. The first is about the circumstances in which the Secretary of State may have an obligation to make enquiry in order to verify the authenticity and reliability of a document; and the consequences of her not doing so. The second issue is the nature of the obligation on judicial fact-finders to consider the evidence before them "in the round".

B. The appellant and his claim

[2] The appellant is a citizen of China, born in 1979. He arrived in the United Kingdom in February 2014 but did not claim asylum until October 2018, following his arrest. On 19 March 2019, the respondent refused the appellant's protection claim. The appellant exercised his right of appeal to the First-tier Tribunal and his appeal was heard in Glasgow on 17 July 2019 by First-tier Tribunal Judge Doyle.
[3] Before the First-tier Tribunal Judge, the appellant advanced two discrete reasons to be in need of international protection. His family home had been demolished in 2009 by the Chinese authorities, in order to build a new road. The appellant and his father were beaten when they sought to resist the acquisition of their property. The father suffered a heart attack and died, following which the appellant's mother committed suicide. The appellant sought compensation from the authorities but was beaten by them and his collar bone broken.
[4] In April 2010, the appellant was living in another area of China. There he said he was introduced to Tibetan Buddhism. He attended public events

recounting the cruel treatment and injustice meted out to the Tibetan people by the Chinese authorities. When those authorities raided the premises in which the appellant was living, they arrested his friend but the appellant managed to hide himself. The appellant said that the Chinese authorities were now aware that he is a Tibetan Buddhist. He fled China because he feared what might happen to him as a Tibetan Buddhist who supports Tibetan independence.

C. The First-Tier Tribunal's decision

[5] Having set out the background evidence, so far as it related to these two claims, the First-tier Tribunal Judge's decision noted the appellant's oral evidence. The judge also had regard to a medical report, which described a healed fracture to the appellant's left clavicle. Whilst the doctor concluded that the appellant's injuries were consistent with the explanation given for them, it was not possible to exclude other injury mechanisms. The appellant's account of receiving twenty days' hospital treatment was regarded by the doctor as "excessive for this type of injury", were the appellant to have been treated in the United Kingdom.

[6] At his screening interview in October 2018, the appellant was asked about his religion, to which he replied "Just with Balai [*sic*] organisation". Asked why he had come to the United Kingdom, the appellant replied "House in China taken down. Chinese government are going to kill me". There was no reference made in this interview to the appellant's involvement with Tibetan Buddhism or support for Tibetan independence.

[7] In his witness statement of 25 January 2019, the appellant stated "I am a Tibetan Buddhist". Shortly thereafter, the appellant underwent a substantive asylum interview. At Q 109, the appellant was unable to answer questions about Tibetan prayer flags, confusing a central Tibetan Buddhism method of meditation with the colours of the Tibetan flag. In answer to Q 116, the appellant said he did not use water but prayed to the flag. According to the judge, this provided "No knowledge at all about the spiritual significance of water in Tibetan Buddhism". Furthermore, taking the appellant's answers together, the judge considered that the appellant demonstrated that he "does not recognise Tibetan prayer flags, but prays to a symbol of Tibetan nationality. The appellant demonstrates an inability to distinguish the spiritual from the temporal".

[8] Paragraph 12 of the First-tier Tribunal Judge's decision continues as follows:

"(h)   The appellant arrived in the UK in 2014. On his own evidence, he has not practised Tibetan Buddhism in the UK. In answer to question 104, the appellant says that there is no Buddhism in the UK. The appellant could not be more wrong. The appellant has lived in Glasgow for years. Glasgow has a Tibetan Buddhist meditation centre. If the appellant was truly a Tibetan Buddhist, then the practice of his faith would had driven him to find his local Tibetan Buddhist meditation centre. The appellant claims that he is a renowned Tibetan Buddhist in China, yet he is not even known to the Tibetan Buddhists in Glasgow, where he has lived for the last 5 years.

(i)   The appellant's third inventory of productions contains photographs intended to demonstrate that the appellant worships at a Buddhist Centre in Glasgow. At paragraph 43 of his witness statement, the appellant claims to have started his search for an [*sic*] Buddhist Centre in 2017 – but it took him until April 2019 to find a Tibetan Buddhist centre in Glasgow. His evidence must be viewed against the appellant's answer to question 14 of the asylum interview (which took place in March 2019). In March 2019 the appellant said that there is no Buddhism in the UK. He can't have it both ways. He cannot have been worshipping at a Buddhist Centre since 2017 when he says in asylum interview in March 2019 that such a place does not exist.

(j)   The appellant was asked to identify the photographs now produced. He said that they were taken earlier this year, but he could only name one person in the photographs. He said that none of the people depicted in the photographs could come to give evidence to support him because none of them have identification documents in the UK. The appellant was unable to specify the address of the Buddhist centre that he claims he goes to every week.

(k)   Because of the inconsistent account that the appellant gives & because the appellant is not able to demonstrate a fundamental knowledge of the tenets of Tibetan Buddhism, I find that the appellant fails to establish that he is a Tibetan Buddhist. That finding wholly undermines the appellant's claim to have concealed himself in a flat whilst his friend he was arrested; it wholly undermined the appellant's claim that he is wanted by the authorities because he is a Tibetan Buddhist.

(l)   The second inventory of productions for the appellant contains a number of translated documents, including an item which bears to be an arrest warrant issued in March 2014. The second inventory also contains a statement from Liwen Zhang which speaks to an arrest warrant being issued and provides details of the political movement the appellant claims he became involved in. I remind myself of *Tanveer Ahmed** 2002 UKIAT 00439 when considering the documentary evidence. The arrest warrant is clearly designed to corroborate the appellant's account. As I find that his account is so fundamentally flawed (because I find he was not involved with Tibetan Buddhism) I find that there is the arrest warrant is evidentially neutral."

[9] At paragraph 12(m), the judge said that, although the appellant said he was involved in the movement for an independent Tibet,

"the fulcrum of this aspect of the appellant's asylum claim is that he became involved in a religion and the practice of that religion led towards advocating independence for Tibet. The dearth of evidence of the practice of religion undermines the appellant's claim to have been politically involved in an independence movement. On the facts as I find them to be, the appellant fails to demonstrate that he has had any involvement with Tibetan Buddhism. As the appellant claims … that it was Tibetan Buddhism that led him to his political opinion and advocating an independent nation, then, by analogy, I find that the appellant was not involved with publicly advocating independence for Tibet."

[10] At paragraph 12(n) to (s), the judge gave his reasons why he did not find that the appellant's account of being involved in a land dispute with the Chinese authorities was credible. At paragraph 12(f), the judge noted that the appellant had waited four and a half years before claiming asylum. He had also travelled through Germany, without claiming asylum there. This conduct damaged the appellant's overall credibility.

[11] In the light of these findings, at paragraph 13 the First-tier Tribunal Judge stated that the appellant had not discharged the burden of proof to establish that he was a refugee. At paragraphs 15 to 17, the judge gave his reasons why the appellant was not entitled to humanitarian protection. At paragraphs 18 to 23, the judge considered the appellant's position by reference to Articles 2 and 3 of the Human Rights Convention. The judge found that those articles were not engaged, given the findings he had made. The judge ended his decision by giving his reasons why the appellant's removal would not breach the latter's right to respect for private and family life under Article 8 of the ECHR.

D. The grounds of appeal

[12] The grounds of appeal reads as follows:

"Ground 1 – errors of law in relation to the documentary evidence

2.   The FTT erred in law when assessing the documentary evidence, at paragraph 12(l), for the following reasons:

(i)   By misapplying the law and failing to recognise that as the respondent had not carried out any verification checks on the arrest warrant, it was not open to the respondent, or the FTT, to impugn such a document. The document was central to the claim and it was not said it was not easily verifiable (*PJ (Sri Lanka) v Secretary of State for the Home Department* [2015] 1 WLR 1322 at paragraphs 30 and 31; *AR* [2017] CSIH 52 at paragraph 35). *Separatim* the FTT erred where the respondent had failed to consider routes which the document could be verified. Although the document is an arrest warrant, that does not prohibit discrete investigation. In *AR, supra* the respondent was able to carry out verification checks on the FIR at a police station in Pakistan. Such errors are material where if the document can be relied upon, the adverse credibility findings are otiose;

(ii)   further the FTT has allowed the adverse credibility findings to sway the assessment of the arrest warrant. As such this is a misapplication of the law and is a material error of law (*TF & MA* 2019 SC 81 at paragraph 49 *per* Lord Glennie);

(iii)   *separatim* the FTT erred by failing to be slow, at paragraph 12(e), to draw adverse inferences from omissions/inconsistencies arising from the screening interview (*Kavungu* [2002] UKIAT 00243; *YL (rely on SEF) China* [2004] UKIAT 00145 at paragraph 19)."

E. Verification of documents

[13] The leading Tribunal authority on the proper approach to documents of the kind with which we are concerned is *Ahmed (Documents unreliable and forged) Pakistan** [2002] UKIAT 00439 (hereafter "*Tanveer Ahmed*"). In that case, a senior panel of the Immigration Appeal Tribunal gave authoritative guidance on the approach to such documents. It is instructive to return to the actual terms of the Tribunal's decision in *Tanveer Ahmed*, approved as it has been on numerous subsequent occasions in the higher courts.

[14] At paragraph 31, the Tribunal said:

"31.   It is trite immigration and asylum law that we must not judge what is or is not likely to happen in other countries by reference to our perception of what is normal within the United Kingdom. The principle applies as much to documents as to any other form of evidence. We know from experience and country information that there are countries where it is easy and often relatively inexpensive to obtain 'forged' documents. Some of them are false in that they are not made by whoever purports to be the author and the information they contain is wholly or partially untrue. Some are 'genuine' to the extent that they emanate from a proper source, in the proper form, on the proper paper, with the proper seals, but the information they contain is wholly or partially untrue. Examples are birth, death and marriage certificates from certain countries, which can be obtained from the proper source for a 'fee', but contain information which is wholly or partially untrue. The permutations of truth, untruth, validity and 'genuineness' are enormous. At its simplest we need to differentiate between form and content; that is whether a document is properly issued by the purported author and whether the contents are true. They are separate questions. It is a dangerous oversimplification merely to ask whether a document is 'forged' or even 'not genuine'. It is necessary to shake off any preconception that official looking documents are genuine, based on experience of documents in the United Kingdom, and to approach them with an open mind."

[15] In light of the more recent decisions of the Court of Appeal and the Court of Session, to which we shall turn, what the Tribunal said in paragraph 31 is instructive. What appears to be an official document, emanating from some authority abroad, may not, in truth, emanate from that authority. But, even if it does, what the document says (for example, about the person seeking international protection) may not be reliable. Unlike the position in the United Kingdom where, happily, instances of corrupt officialdom are relatively rare, it is possible that the foreign official who produced the document may have been suborned. This explains the Tribunal's exhortation that one should approach such documents "with an open mind".

[16] At paragraphs 34 to 36, the Tribunal in *Tanveer Ahmed* addressed the issue of the respondent's obligations in respect of such documents:

"34. It is sometimes argued before Adjudicators or the Tribunal that if the Home Office alleges that a document relied on by an individual claimant is a forgery and the Home Office fails to establish this on the balance of probabilities, or even to the higher criminal standard, then the individual claimant has established the validity and truth of the document and its contents. There is no legal justification for such an argument, which is manifestly incorrect, given that whether the document is a forgery is not the question at issue. The only question is whether the document is one upon which reliance should properly be placed.

35. In almost all cases it would be an error to concentrate on whether a document is a forgery. In most cases where forgery is alleged it will be of no great importance whether this is or is not made out to the required higher civil standard. In all cases where there is a material document it should be assessed in the same way as any other piece of evidence A document should not be viewed in isolation. The decision maker should look at the evidence as a whole or in the round (which is the same thing).

36. There is no obligation on the Home Office to make detailed enquiries about documents produced by individual claimants. Doubtless there are cost and logistical difficulties in the light of the number of documents submitted by many asylum claimants. In the absence of a particular reason on the facts of an individual case a decision by the Home Office not to make inquiries, produce in-country evidence relating to a particular document or scientific evidence should not give rise to any presumption in favour of an individual claimant or against the Home Office."

[17] The leading Court of Appeal case on the nature of the respondent's "verification" obligations is *PJ (Sri Lanka) v Secretary of State for the Home Department* [2014] EWCA Civ 1011. The facts of this case are important for a proper understanding of what the court held. As appears from the headnote in [2015] 1 WLR 1322, PJ contended that he would face serious harm if returned to Sri Lanka because of perception of the authorities there as to his political opinion. In support of his asylum application, PJ submitted certified copies of court documents which had been obtained on his behalf by a Sri Lankan lawyer. These included a police report, which revealed that PJ was to be arrested on arrival in Sri Lanka in connection with a bombing; and also a warrant for his arrest. The respondent refused PJ's claim, finding that, given the ease with which it was possible to obtain forged documents in Sri Lanka, the respondent could not be satisfied that the documents were genuine. PJ's solicitors then instructed a second Sri Lankan lawyer who, through his junior, obtained a complete certified copy of the documents, which matched those produced by the first lawyer.

[18] The First-tier Tribunal dismissed PJ's appeal, concluding that no weight could be placed on the documents. The Upper Tribunal dismissed PJ's further appeal. PJ appealed, contending that where court documents were obtained and provided by foreign lawyers, they were to be presumed to be genuine unless the respondent proved otherwise; and that the respondent bore the responsibility of investigating the reliability of such documents unless such an investigation was not feasible.

[19] One of the tasks undertaken by the Court of Appeal in *PJ* was to consider *Tanveer Ahmed* in the light of the decision of the European Court of Human Rights in *Singh v Belgium* (Application No. 33210/11), given on 2 October 2012. In *Singh*, Sikhs who had fled Afghanistan claimed refugee status in Belgium. Their claim was rejected because they had failed to prove their Afghan nationality.

On appeal, they provided new documents, comprising emails between their lawyer and a representative of the Belgium Committee for the Support of Refugees. This committee was a partner of the High Commission of the United Nations for Refugees ("UNHCR"). A UNHCR representative in India had furnished, by way of attachments to the emails, "attestations" which indicated that the petitioners had been recorded as refugees under the UNHCR mandate and that one of them had requested naturalisation in India. Notwithstanding this documentation, it was held on appeal that the petitioners had failed to prove their Afghan nationality and that the documents were of no convincing value, since they were of a type that was easy to falsify and the petitioners had failed to produce the original copies of the documents.

[20] The ECtHR held that, since the possible consequences for the petitioners were significant, there was an obligation on the state to show that it had been as rigorous as possible and had carried out a careful "examination" (in fact, a "review") of the grounds of appeal. Since the documents were at the heart of the request for protection, rejecting them without checking their authenticity fell short of the careful and rigorous investigation that was expected of national authorities in order to protect individuals from treatment contrary to Article 3 of the ECHR, when a simple process of enquiry would have resolved conclusively whether the documents were authentic and reliable.

[21] In M.J v *Secretary of State for the Home Department* [2013] Imm AR 799, the Upper Tribunal considered whether *Singh* was compatible with *Tanveer Ahmed*. The panel concluded that it was:

"50. It is relevant, however, to consider (the decision in Ahmed's case) in the context of what was said in *Singh v Belgium*. On consideration we do not think that what was said in *Singh*'s case is inconsistent with the quotation we have set out above from para 35 of *Ahmed*'s case. *Ahmed*'s case does not entirely preclude the existence of an obligation on the Home Office to make enquiries. It envisages, as can be seen, the existence of particular cases where it may be appropriate for inquiries to be made. Clearly on its facts *Singh*'s case can properly be regarded as such a particular case. The documentation in that case was clearly of a nature where verification would be easy, and the documentation came from an unimpeachable source. We do not think that (counsel) has entirely correctly characterised what was said in *Singh*'s case in suggesting that in any case where evidence was verifiable there was an obligation on the decision maker to seek to verify. What is said at paragraph 104 is rather in terms of a case where documents are at the heart of the request for protection where it would have been easy to check their authenticity as in that case with the UNHCR. ... We do not think that what is said in *Singh v Belgium* in any sense justifies or requires any departure from the guidance in Ahmed's case which is binding on us and which we consider to remain entirely sound."

[22] We can now return to *PJ*. Giving the judgment of the court, Fulford LJ held:

"29. In my judgement, there is no basis in domestic or European Court of Human Rights jurisprudence for the general approach that Mr Martin submitted ought to be adopted whenever local lawyers obtain relevant documents from a domestic court, and thereafter transmit them directly to lawyers in the United

Kingdom. The involvement of lawyers does not create the rebuttable presumption that the documents they produce in this situation are reliable. Instead, the jurisprudence referred to above does no more than indicate that the circumstances of particular cases may exceptionally necessitate an element of investigation by the national authorities, in order to provide effective protection against mistreatment under Article 3 Convention. It is important to stress, however, that this step will frequently not be feasible or it may be unjustified or disproportionate. In *Ahmed*'s case [2002] Imm AR 318 the court highlighted the cost and logistical difficulties that may be involved, for instance because of the number of documents submitted by some asylum claimants. The inquiries may put the applicant or his family at risk, they may be impossible to undertake because of the prevailing local situation or they may place the United Kingdom authorities in the difficult position of making covert local enquiries without the permission of the relevant authorities. Furthermore, given the uncertainties that frequently remain following attempts to establish the reliability of documents, if the outcome of any enquiry is likely to be inconclusive this is a highly relevant factor. As the court in *Ahmed*'s case observed, documents should not be viewed in isolation and the evidence needs to be considered in its entirety.

30. Therefore, simply because a relevant document is potentially capable of being verified does not mean that the national authorities have an obligation to take this step. Instead, it may be necessary to make an inquiry in order to verify the authenticity and reliability of a document – depending always on the particular facts of the case – when it is at the centre of the request for protection, and when a simple process of inquiry will conclusively resolve its authenticity and reliability: see *Singh v Belgium* given 2 October 2012, paras 101 – 105. I do not consider that there is any material difference in approach between the decisions in *Ahmed*'s case and *Singh v Belgium*, in that in the latter case the Strasbourg court simply addressed one of the exceptional situations when national authorities should undertake a process of verification.

31. In my view, the consequence of a decision that the national authorities are in breach of their obligations to undertake a proper process of verification is that the Secretary of State is unable thereafter to mount an argument challenging the authenticity of the relevant documents unless and until the breach is rectified by a proper inquiry. It follows that if a decision of the Secretary of State is overturned on appeal on this basis, absent a suitable investigation it will not open to her to suggest that the document or documents are forged or otherwise are not authentic.

32. Finally, in this context it is to be emphasised that the courts are not required to order the Secretary of State to investigate particular areas of evidence or otherwise to direct her inquiries. Instead, on an appeal from a decision of the Secretary of State it is for the court to decide whether there was an obligation on her to undertake particular inquiries, and if the court concludes this requirement existed, it will resolve whether the Secretary of State sustainably discharged her obligation: see *NA v Secretary of State for the Home Department* [2014] UKUT 205 (IAC). If court finds there was such an obligation and that it was not discharged, it must assess the consequences for the case."

[23] Several matters arising from paragraphs 29 to 32 of *PJ* need to be emphasised. First, the fact that lawyers have been involved does not mean the documents they produce are for that reason reliable. Secondly, the sort of exercise required by the ECtHR in *Singh v Belgium* will only arise exceptionally (treating that word as an indicator of frequency, rather than as a legal test). Thirdly, *Tanveer Ahmed* was clearly regarded by Fulford LJ as being compatible with *Singh v Belgium*, as the Upper Tribunal had found in *MJ*. In particular, Fulford LJ stressed the point made in *Tanveer Ahmed*, that issues of cost and logistical difficulty, owing to the sheer number of documents submitted in asylum claims, will be a relevant consideration in determining whether, in the particular circumstances, an obligation on the respondent arises. The point made in *Tanveer Ahmed* that documents should not be viewed in isolation but considered in their entirety in connection with the rest of the evidence, was also approved.

[24] As we can see from paragraph 30, in order to engage the obligation, the document in question needs to be at the centre of the request for protection. Even then, there should be a simple process of inquiry that will conclusively resolve both authenticity and reliability. Given the status of the body that had produced the documents in *Singh v Belgium*, there could be little doubt that, if authentic, what the documents said could also be assumed to be reliable. But, as the Tribunal pointed out in *Tanveer Ahmed*, in other cases involving foreign documentation, the discovery that the document emanates from a genuine official source may have little or nothing to say about the reliability of its contents.

[25] This is relevant to an understanding of paragraph 31 of *PJ*, where Fulford LJ addressed the consequence of the respondent not undertaking a proper process of verification, where the obligation is found to exist. Fulford LJ held that, in such a scenario, the respondent would be "unable thereafter to mount an argument challenging the authenticity of the relevant documents unless and until the breach is rectified by a proper enquiry". It would, in other words, not be open to the respondent "to suggest that the document or documents are forged or otherwise are not authentic". It is apparent that, in paragraph 31, Fulford LJ was deliberately restricting his description of the effects of failing to discharge the obligation, so as to preclude the respondent from challenging the authenticity, as opposed to the reliability, of a document.

[26] Paragraph 32 makes it evident that courts and tribunals cannot require the respondent to investigate particular areas of evidence. It will be for the court or tribunal to decide whether the obligation to undertake particular enquiries arises, with the consequences for the respondent that Fulford LJ had described.

[27] The final sentence of paragraph 32 is of particular significance. If a tribunal concludes that the respondent has, exceptionally, become subject to an obligation to verify, but has not done so, the consequence for her will be that she is unable to contend that the document is not authentic. It will, nevertheless, be for the judicial fact-finder to decide, in all the circumstances of the case, and by reference to the totality of the evidence, whether the document is "reliable" as to both its provenance and contents. If the judicial fact-finder is so satisfied, this may, of course, prove to be determinative of the claim to international protection. But such a result will not necessarily follow. It all depends on the nature of the case being advanced and the fact-finder's conclusions on the entirety of the evidence.

[28] It is instructive to see how the court in *PJ* reached its conclusion to allow the appeal and remit the matter to the Upper Tribunal. At paragraph 41, Fulford LJ found that the First-tier Tribunal Judge had doubted the validity of the documents

disclosed by the lawyers "on a significantly false basis". The fact that two independent lawyers had turned up the same material from the Magistrates' Court clearly struck Fulford LJ as very significant. Once it had been established that the documents originated from a Sri Lankan court, "a sufficient justification was required for the conclusion that the claimant does not have a well-founded fear of persecution". It was, furthermore, "difficult to understand how the claimant could have falsified a letter from the Magistrate of the relevant court to the Controller of Immigration and Emigration ordering the claimant's arrest which he then placed in the court record so it could later be retrieved by two separate lawyers". Fulford LJ held that, at the very least, this evidence required "detailed analysis and explanation".

[29] At the end of the day, therefore, the issue of the respondent's duty in reality played little or no part in the court's reasoning in *PJ*. Both the First-tier Tribunal and the Upper Tribunal had, in effect, failed to give legally sufficient reasons for concluding that PJ was not at real risk on return to Sri Lanka, in the light of all the evidence.

[30] In *AR v the Secretary of State for the Home Department* [2017] CSIH 52, the Inner House was concerned with an appeal from the Upper Tribunal against a decision to dismiss AR's appeal against the First-tier Tribunal, which had dismissed his appeal against the respondent's decision that AR was not at real risk in Pakistan as a gay man. The First-tier Tribunal had before it a copy First Information Report, which narrated that the father of the individual with whom AR was said to have committed an act of sodomy had reported the matter to the police. The Tribunal also had a newspaper article of 31 March 2003, in which the father was reported as saying that his son's friend had taken the son from his house and sodomised him against his will. Although it is unclear, it appears that a second "official" document before the judge was a record of the police notifying local police stations of the appellant's escape from custody.

[31] At paragraph 30, the Inner House (*per* Lord Malcolm) noted that:

"the evidence consists of the petitioner's account, which in its essential elements is supported by a number of documents, two of them of an official nature, and all easily verifiable. To our eyes at least, they have the hallmarks of valid documents, albeit no doubt there is at least a possibility that they were fabricated, although, if they were, why would there be internal inconsistencies on points of detail?"

[32] Beginning at paragraph 33, Lord Malcolm has this to say:

"33. The appeal in this court focussed on two matters, namely (a) the treatment of the documents and (b) the evidence of the supporting witness. So far as the documents are concerned, we have mentioned that, on their face, they appear to be valid and authentic, for example, where applicable, being duly stamped and signed. They are supportive of the essentials of the petitioner's account of the events which led him to leave his family and homeland. Judge Macleman ruled that the authorities were under no obligation to verify the documents. Be that as it may, in our view it does not address the logically prior question, namely, did the First-tier Tribunal have and explain a sound basis for their rejection? If the answer to that question is no – the test set out in *PJ (Sri Lanka)* does not arise.

34. The submission is that the First-tier Tribunal Judge did not set out any good reasons for dismissing the documents as unreliable. We agree with that submission. We have studied the terms of the decision, but can find no proper support for the terms of paragraph 34. For example, what was the reason for placing the FIR in the unreliable category? While no doubt there is 'a high incidence of false "official" documents', there must also be some genuine documents. One cannot simply rely on doubts as to the veracity of the account given by the claimant as a reason for rejecting the documents when on their face, they support his asylum claim. The 'holistic' approach endorsed by Judge Macleman would require the overall assessment to be made after all of the evidence has been considered and assessed. In other words, and by way of example, one might ask – do the documents support the claim? If yes, is there any reason arising from the documents themselves to reject their authenticity? If no, how does this affect, if it does affect, doubts that have arisen as to the claimant's account? In our view, if those doubts are used as *a priori* reason to undermine and reject the documents, there is an obvious risk that supportive evidence is being wrongly excluded from the overall assessment.

35. We remind ourselves of the need to examine the facts with care (sometimes referred to as 'anxious scrutiny'), and of the low standard of proof applicable in cases of this nature. We are persuaded that these factors have been given insufficient weight and attention in the more recent decisions. We recognise that there may be cases where the concerns over the veracity of a claimant's account may be so clear-cut that the decision-maker is driven to rejection of supporting documents, even though on their face they appear to be authentic; but even then, given what is at stake, we would expect some consideration to be given to easily available routes to check authenticity. There is no question that these documents are at the centre of a request for international protection. The decision-maker should stand back and view all of the evidence in the round before deciding which evidence to accept and which to reject, and on the proper disposal of the appeal."

[33] As with *PJ*, it is necessary to consider this passage of the opinion of the Inner House in detail. An immediately notable feature of *AR* is that, at paragraph 30, the Inner House made its own assessment of the "official" documents, holding that these had "the hallmarks of valid documents" and that, at paragraph 33 "they appear to be valid and authentic, for example, where applicable, being duly stamped and signed".

[34] It is evident that the Inner House did not find that the FIR and the other document apparently emanating from the Pakistan police required to be verified by the respondent. In paragraph 33, Lord Malcolm did not dissent from the finding of the Upper Tribunal Judge that the respondent was, in this case, under no obligation to verify the documents. The basis upon which the Inner House reached its conclusion was that the Upper Tribunal had not addressed "the logically prior question, namely, did the First-tier Tribunal have and explain a sound basis for their rejection?" The First-tier Tribunal had erred by relying on doubts regarding the veracity of the account given by the claimant as a reason for rejecting the documents when, on their face, they supported his claim. The fact that the Inner House had formed its own view about the validity and authenticity of the documents affected the nature of the requirement imposed on the judge to give

legally adequate reasons for his overall conclusion that the appellant was not entitled to international protection.

[35] At paragraph 35, the Inner House nevertheless recognised that there may be cases where the concerns over the veracity of an account "may be so clear-cut that the decision-maker is driven to rejection of supporting documents, even though on their face they appear to be authentic". Although paragraph 35 goes on to say that, even then, one would expect some consideration to be given to easily available routes to check authenticity, it is apparent that the Inner House was not expressing any disagreement with the limitations identified by Fulford LJ in *PJ* on the respondent's obligations in this area.

[36] We have already observed how the Tribunal in *Tanveer Ahmed* was at pains to avoid falling into the trap of assuming that, just because an official-looking document emanating from abroad may have been issued by the authority whose name appears on the document, the contents of the document must be reliable. This is of particular relevance in the case of FIRs, the purpose of which is to record an accusation made by an individual about another person or persons. Even if the compiler of the FIR has not been suborned, it can readily be seen that the fact the accusation has been made is in no sense probative of the fact that the relevant authority believes the accusation, let alone of its veracity.

[37] It is, we consider, possible to summarise the law on this issue as follows. The IAT's decision in *Tanveer Ahmed* remains good law. The overarching question for the judicial fact-finder will be whether the document in question can be regarded as reliable. An obligation on the respondent to take steps to verify the authenticity of the document will arise only exceptionally (in the sense of rarely). This will be where the document is central to the claim; can easily be authenticated; and where (as in *Singh v Belgium*) authentication is unlikely to leave any "live" issue as to the reliability of its contents. It is for the Tribunal to decide, in all the circumstances of the case, whether the obligation arises. If it does, the respondent cannot challenge the authenticity of the document in the proceedings; but that does not necessarily mean the respondent cannot question the reliability of what the document says. In all cases, it remains the task of the judicial fact-finder to assess the document's relevance to the claim in the light of, and by reference to, the rest of the evidence.

F. The "*Mibanga*" duty

[38] That last observation brings us to the cases on the second, related issue described in paragraph 1 above; namely, the assessment of the case "in the round".

[39] In *Francois Mibanga v Secretary of State for the Home Department* [2005] EWCA Civ 367, the claim for asylum was based on the appellant's account that he had been captured in the Democratic Republic of Congo by Rwandan-backed rebels, who had tortured him. The appellant produced a medical report on his injuries, together with a report by a country expert. The Court of Appeal held that the adjudicator who dismissed the appellant's appeal had disregarded both expert reports in concluding that the appellant's case lacked credibility. She had only turned to the reports after making that adverse credibility finding. Both reports were regarded by the Court of Appeal as detailed and impressive documents.

[40] In his judgment, Wilson J said:

"23. In the light of my view as to the proper despatch of this appeal, it would be wise for me to keep my own views about the effect of the evidence to a minimum. The basis of the appeal is not that the weight of the appellant's evidence, coupled with that of the two experts, should have driven every reasonable fact-finding body to accept his account and to uphold his appeal but that he has been the victim of a flawed fact-finding exercise on the part of the adjudicator and that the tribunal fell into legal error in failing to recognise it and to remit the appeal for redetermination. In this regard Miss Braganza relies heavily upon the way in which the adjudicator folded the doctor's report into her enquiry only at a point after she had reached her conclusions and upon the way in which she jettisoned the focussed comments of the professor.

24. It seems to me to be axiomatic that a fact-finder must not reach his or her conclusion before surveying all the evidence relevant thereto. Just as, if I may take a banal if alliterative example, one cannot make a cake with only one ingredient, so also frequently one cannot make a case, in the sense of establishing its truth, otherwise than by combination of a number of pieces of evidence. Mr Tam, on behalf of the Secretary of State, argues that decisions as to the credibility of an account are to be taken by the judicial fact-finder and that, in their reports, experts, whether in relation to medical matters or in relation to in-country circumstances, cannot usurp the fact-finder's function in assessing credibility. I agree. What, however, they can offer, is a factual context in which it may be necessary for the fact-finder to survey the allegations placed before him; and such context may prove a crucial aid to the decision whether or not to accept the truth of them. What the fact-finder does at his peril is to reach a conclusion by reference only to the appellant's evidence and then, if it be negative, to ask whether the conclusion should be shifted by the expert evidence. Mr Tam has drawn the court's attention to a decision of the tribunal dated 5 November 2004, namely *HE (DRC – Credibility and Psychiatric Reports)* [2004] UKIAT 00321 in which, in paragraph 22, it said:

'Where the report is specifically relied on as a factor relevant to credibility, the Adjudicator should deal with it as an integral part of the findings on credibility rather than just as an add-on, which does not undermine the conclusions to which he would otherwise come.'"

[41] Buxton LJ agreed:

"30. … The adjudicator's failing was that she artificially separated the medical evidence from the rest of the evidence and reached conclusions as to credibility without reference to that medical evidence; and then, no doubt inevitably on that premise, found that the medical evidence was of no assistance to her. That was a structural failing, not just an error of appreciation, and demonstrated that the adjudicator's method of approaching the evidence diverted from the procedure advised in paragraph 22 of *HE*, set out by my Lord.

31. Further, though perhaps less obviously, I agree that if an expert's view is to be rejected in the conclusive terms adopted by the adjudicator in this case, then

proper procedure requires that at least some explanation is given of the terms and reasons for that rejection."

[42] Following *Mibanga*, there were many challenges to Tribunal decisions, on the asserted basis that a judge had failed to treat (usually) a medical report in the way the Court of Appeal had held it should be treated in that case. Dealing with such a challenge, the AIT in *HH (medical evidence; effect of* Mibanga) *Ethiopia* [2005] UKAIT 00164 attempted to dispel some of the misconceptions that had grown up around *Mibanga*:

"19. Finally, the grounds assert that the Immigration Judge erred in law in failing to treat the medical report as part of the overall evidence in this case, to be considered "in the round" before coming to any conclusion as to the appellant's credibility. Reference is made to the Court of Appeal judgments in *Mibanga* [2005] EWCA Civ 367, in particular paragraph 24 of the judgment of Wilson J:

'It seems to me to be axiomatic that a fact-finder must not reach his or her conclusion before surveying all the evidence relevant thereto. Just as, if I may take a banal if alliterative example, one cannot make a cake with only one ingredient, so also frequently one cannot make a case, in the sense of establishing its truth, otherwise than by combination of a number of pieces of evidence.'

...

21. The Tribunal considers that there is a danger of *Mibanga* being misunderstood. The judgments in that case are not intended to place judicial fact-finders in a form of forensic straight-jacket. In particular, the Court of Appeal is not to be regarded as laying down any rule of law as to the order in which judicial fact-finders are to approach the evidential materials before them. To take Wilson J's "cake" analogy, all its ingredients cannot be thrown together into the bowl simultaneously. One has to start somewhere. There was nothing illogical about the process by which the Immigration Judge in the present case chose to approach his analytical task."

[43] In *S v Secretary of State for the Home Department* [2006] EWCA Civ 1153, the Court of Appeal, faced with a similar submission, emphasised the exceptional nature of the factual matrix in *Mibanga*. Rix LJ said:

"21. ... The injuries described in the medical report in *Mibanga* were extraordinary in their severity and in their nature. There was a mass of scars of different kinds all over Mibanga's body, described in detail, for instance, at paragraph 11 and 12 of Wilson J's judgment in that case. Some of them were consistent with beatings with a belt. Many of them were consistent with bites from leeches, which reflected Mibanga's allegation that he had been thrown by way of punishment into a barrel of leeches. In particular (and when I say in particular, I reflect the use of that expression found repeatedly throughout Wilson J's judgment in referring to this aspect of the evidence in that case) there were two injuries, one at the tip and one at the base of Mibanga's penis, which were consistent with the application of electrodes to his genitals. Indeed, Dr Norman in that case had referred in her report to a book on the medical documentation of torture which provided the basis, or one of the bases, upon which she concluded that those injuries were consistent with the application of electrodes; see paragraph 25 of the judgment in that case.

22. It is against that background that although Wilson J, at paragraph 23 and elsewhere in his judgment, stated that he wished to be cautious about what he said about the facts of the case in the light of the consequence that the matter would have to be remitted for reconsideration at a new hearing, it is nevertheless clear from that paragraph 23 and elsewhere that he, and this court, had the very gravest doubts about the fact finding process which had been conducted by the adjudicator in that case. That, therefore, was the context in which Wilson J stated that the adjudicator had fallen into legal error by addressing the medical evidence only after she had conclusively rejected central features in the appellant's case as incredible. One only has to recite the facts of that case to see why the approach of the adjudicator there should have led to such concern.

23. In a concurring judgment, Buxton LJ referred to the error of law as being one in which there had been an artificial separation amounting to a structural failing, and not just an error of appreciation, in dealing with credibility entirely separately from the medical evidence.

24. It seems to me that the logic of *Mibanga* does not apply to this case, essentially for two separate reasons. One is that the structure of the immigration judge's reasoning here does not fall foul of that artificial separation and structural failure which were found to exist in *Mibanga*, and the other is that the medical evidence in *Mibanga* was so powerful and so extraordinary as to take that case into an exceptional area."

[44] Rix LJ went onto distinguish the striking facts of *Mibanga* from the medical report of Dr Steadman in *S*, which "was not consistent with direct assault of any kind at all. It was merely consistent with debris falling from above, in itself an essentially lacklustre gloss of what the appellant had really relied upon, which was shrapnel from a bullet or flying debris caused by ricocheting bullets" (paragraph 27).

[45] At paragraph 32, Rix LJ approved the comments of the AIT in *HH*, regarding the danger of *Mibanga* being misunderstood.

[46] In *TF v Secretary of State for the Home Department* [2018] CSIH 58, the Inner House was concerned with appeals by asylum seekers from Iran, who feared persecution if returned to that country, by reason of their conversion in Scotland to Christianity. The appellants adduced evidence from members of a particular church, testifying to the genuineness, in the eyes of the witnesses, of the religious conversions. The appellants' appeals were unsuccessful in the First-tier Tribunal and the Upper Tribunal.

[47] At paragraph 4, Lord Glennie, delivering the opinion of the court, was at pains to explain the nature of the appellants' case to be in need of international protection. The genuineness of the claim to have converted to Christianity whilst

in Scotland lay at the heart of the case. It was not disputed that a genuine Christian convert faced a real risk of persecution if returned to Iran:

> "They would be regarded as apostates. They could not be expected to conceal their religious beliefs so as to avoid persecution…Hence the importance of the question whether their conversion to Christianity was genuine; if it was not genuine they would be unlikely in Iran to act in a way which attracted attention and invited persecution. There was no suggestion in these appeals that the claim for asylum could succeed on the basis that, even if the *sur place* conversions were not genuine, the appellants would nonetheless be perceived as Christians because of their attendance at church in the United Kingdom and would, if returned to Iran, be persecuted as if they were Christians."

[48] At paragraph 37, Lord Glennie found that what the First-tier Tribunal Judge had done in one of the appeals was to take his assessment of the appellant, which was adverse:

> "and apply it to all the evidence which could, on one view, be in favour of MA's claim to be a genuine convert to Christianity, so that that evidence simply becomes a further example of MA manufacturing evidence in bad faith in order to support his appeal."

[49] At paragraph 37, Lord Glennie considered that it was, to some extent, justified for the First-tier Tribunal to treat with scepticism the views of third parties as to the genuineness of the conversion to Christianity of an asylum seeker. There were, however, "limits to this approach" (paragraph 38). Just as juries in criminal trials are commonly directed that the fact an individual may have lied about one point does not necessarily mean he is lying about other matters, "The same words of caution should be taken to heart by tribunal judges hearing evidence in immigration and asylum appeals. People have different reasons for not telling the truth, or the whole truth, about particular matters". They may, for example, be anxious not to get others into trouble. Nor was it necessarily suggestive of dishonesty to fail to give every detail on the first occasion they were asked about it, but only to come out with the full story on a second or subsequent occasion.

[50] At paragraph 39, Lord Glennie emphasised that the appellant's case "has to be considered in the round, not only on the basis of the appellant's own evidence, which may or may not be accepted as credible, but also on the basis of other evidence that may be available". Much would depend on what that other evidence is. "If, for example, that other evidence comes from some wholly-independent source and is, on the face of it, impartial and objective, it is difficult to see how a finding that the appellant himself is dishonest can materially affect the weight to be attached to it". By contrast, if the third party evidence "simply comprises information based entirely upon what the appellant has previously told the witness", then it may well be legitimate for the tribunal to take account of its findings about the credibility of the appellant, "on the basis that it has found the appellant to be a liar and capable of making up a story, fabricating an account and spreading that account amongst others as part of a web of deception". Much would depend upon the time and circumstances that the third party witness was given the information.

[51] It is also relevant at this point to remind ourselves of what the Inner House said at paragraph 35 of *AR* (see paragraph 32 above). There may be cases where concerns over the veracity of a claim and its account may be so clear-cut that the judicial fact-finder is driven to rejection of other evidence, such as supporting documents, even though these appear to be authentic.

[52] Since this decision began to be drafted, the Court of Appeal has had occasion to consider the *Mibanga* line of cases in *MN and others v Secretary of State for the Home Department* [2020] EWCA Civ 1746. At paragraph 108 of its judgment, the court held that the basic principle established by *Mibanga* was summarised by Sir Ernest Ryder in *AM (Afghanistan) v Secretary of State for the Home Department* [2017] EWCA Civ 1123, when he said at paragraph 19(a) that:

"It is an error of approach to come to a negative assessment of credibility and then ask whether that assessment is displaced by other material."

[53] It is often the case that a person's claim to be in need of international protection turns on whether or not that person is adjudged to be credible. Credibility, however, is not necessarily an essential component of a successful claim. On the contrary, as Simon Brown LJ held in *R (Ravichandran) v Secretary of State for the Home Department* [1995] EWCA Civ 16:

"... the question whether someone is at risk of persecution for a Convention reason should be looked at in the round and all the relevant circumstances brought into account. I know of no authority inconsistent with such an approach and, to my mind, it clearly accords both with paragraph 51 of the UNHCR handbook and with the spirit of the Convention."

[54] In some cases, credibility will have no role to play in the *Ravichandran* exercise. For example, a person may have told lies about everything involving their past life in a particular country and yet be entitled to international protection because there is evidence that shows there is a real risk of serious harm if the person is returned; for instance, because the authorities of that country persecute all returnees from abroad who have sought international protection.

[55] An example of the protean nature of credibility as a determinant of entitlement to international protection can be seen from *TF*. The evidence of the church witnesses, who deposed to the genuineness of the appellants' conversions, went to the issue of whether the appellants had genuinely converted. Had their cases been that they would be perceived as apostates and persecuted for having undergone baptism or some other form of initiation, whether or not they intended to behave as Christians in Iran, the evidence of the church witnesses would have assumed a very different significance.

[56] The relevance of an individual's credibility to their particular claim accordingly needs to be established with some care by the judicial fact-finder. It is only once this is done that the practical application of the *Mibanga* duty can be understood. The significance of a piece of evidence that emanates or purports to emanate from a third party source may well depend upon what is at stake in terms of the individual's credibility. An arrest warrant from Afghanistan that states an individual was arrested on 1 April 2020 in Afghanistan may not advance that individual's claim if there is reliable EURODAC evidence that the individual was fingerprinted whilst in detention in Germany on that very date. In such a scenario, the judge still has a duty to explain why (assuming he or she so finds) the arrest warrant does not assist the individual's case; but the reasons are likely to be relatively straightforward. In the absence of the EURODAC evidence, the requirement of what will constitute legally adequate reasons for rejecting the individual's claim may well be more onerous.

[57] To sum up, the judicial fact-finder has a duty to make his or her decision by reference to all the relevant evidence and needs to show in their decision that they have done so. The actual way in which the fact-finder goes about this task is a matter for them. As has been pointed out, one has to start somewhere. At the end of the day, what matters is whether the decision contains legally adequate reasons for the outcome. The greater the apparent cogency and relevance of a particular piece of evidence, the greater is the need for the judicial fact-finder to show that they have had due regard to that evidence; and, if the fact-finder's overall conclusion is contrary to the apparent thrust of that evidence, the greater is the need to explain why that evidence has not brought about a different outcome.

G. Deciding the appeal

[58] We can now return to the facts of the present appellant's case. As we have seen, the first ground of challenge to the First-tier Tribunal Judge's decision proceeds on the assumption that, on the facts of this case, the respondent had an obligation to carry out verification of the arrest warrant; and that it was not open to the respondent or, indeed, the First-tier Tribunal Judge "to impugn such a document". The arrest warrant is said to be "central to the claim and it was not said it was not easily verifiable". The First-tier Tribunal Judge "erred where the respondent had failed to consider routes which the document could be verified".

[59] In his asylum interview, the appellant made no reference to there being an arrest warrant in his name in China. When asked at Q 151 why the Chinese authorities would still be interested in the appellant after several years, the appellant replied that they were interested in arresting those who support Tibet's independence. At Q 152, the appellant said he had friends who went back to China and he had asked them to find out what had happened back home. They had confirmed that he was still wanted.

[60] The asylum interview took place on 4 March 2019. The respondent's decision, refusing the appellant's claim, is dated 19 March 2019. There is no suggestion that, at the time the refusal letter was prepared, the appellant had sent a copy of the arrest warrant to the respondent. Nor is there any suggestion that it had accompanied the appellant's notice of appeal against the respondent's decision, which was received by the First-tier Tribunal on 2 April 2019.

[61] In fact, the document in question was only sent to the First-tier Tribunal under cover of a letter from Katani & Co dated 16 July 2019, the day before the hearing, as part of the second inventory of productions. A copy of what itself appears to be a photocopy, purporting to be the warrant, occurs at page 15 of this inventory. It bears a stamp in the name of Global Language Services Ltd, indicating that it was translated into English on 16 July 2019. The English translation, at page 14, carries an identical stamp. After describing the appellant as suspected of participation in activities of Tibetan separatist organisations and attendance at illegal gatherings, etc, the warrant requests all local public security authorities to take all possible measures to search for the "suspect" after receiving this warrant. The public is urged to call the police "on 110" to report; and the

bureau is said to be offering a high-value reward to anyone who provides useful information or who captures the suspect and sends him to the local public security authority.

[62] In the light of this chronology, it can readily be seen that the appellant can derive no assistance whatsoever from the judgments in *PJ* or *AR*. The respondent's Presenting Officer, like the First-tier Tribunal Judge, would have seen the arrest warrant and its translation only upon receipt of the second inventory of productions, which would appear to have been on the very day of the hearing. Mr Winter valiantly submitted that, even so, the duty of verification arose. If correct, that would, of course, place the respondent in an immensely difficult position. Either the Presenting Officer would have to seek an adjournment, in order for attempts at verification to take place; or he or she would be precluded from challenging the authenticity of the document before the First-tier Tribunal. Where the duty of verification is a live issue, the timing of the production of the document is, plainly, one of the fact-sensitive matters to which regard must be had in deciding, in all the circumstances, whether the duty arises on the facts of the case.

[63] In the present case, however, the arrest warrant document is very far from having the attributes described in paragraph 37 above as being needed to make the verification duty a live issue. On the contrary, leaving aside its egregiously late production, the fundamental reason why the duty does not arise in respect of the arrest warrant is because it is merely an unremarkable example of the kind of document encountered by judges of the First-tier Tribunal on a daily basis in protection appeals. If every document of this kind were required to be verified by the respondent, the appellate process would be severely impaired. We remind ourselves of what the Tribunal said at paragraph 36 of *Tanveer Ahmed* and what Fulford LJ said at paragraph 29 of *PJ*. Such an exercise would be entirely disproportionate. The appellant's ground (i), accordingly, fails.

[64] We turn to item (ii) of the grounds. This contends that the First-tier Tribunal Judge allowed his adverse credibility findings to sway the assessment made of the arrest warrant. Reference is made to *TF*. However, we approach the matter in the light of the wider caselaw analysed above, regarding the treatment of evidence "in the round".

[65] So far as *TF* is concerned, we have already seen that the opinion of Lord Glennie was much more nuanced than the present appellant appears to suggest. At paragraph 38, Lord Glennie identified the need for caution before deciding that, because an individual may have lied about one point, that meant that he must be lying about other matters.

[66] As is plain from the decision of the First-tier Tribunal in the present case, the judge did not take this approach to the arrest warrant. He did not treat it as another example of the appellant giving deceitful evidence. Nor did the First-tier Tribunal Judge fall into the related error, identified at paragraph 32 of *TF*, of treating all evidence supportive of the appellant's case as merely further examples of him manufacturing a false claim. The First-tier Tribunal Judge came to the conclusion that the arrest warrant was neutral in its significance. That is very different from the mischief which the Inner House sought to identify in *TF*.

[67] We have seen that, in paragraph 35 of *AR*, the Inner House recognised that there may be cases where concerns over the veracity of a claimant's account may be so clear-cut and decisive that the decision-maker is driven to a rejection of supporting documents. It is plain that this was the approach taken by the First-tier

Tribunal Judge in the present case. The appellant had asserted that he was a Tibetan Buddhist. He had, however, demonstrated a remarkable ignorance of the tenets of that faith, as can be seen from the Asylum Interview Record. At Q 114 (the reference in paragraph 12(h) of the decision to Q 104 is plainly a misprint), the appellant said that he prayed to "the flag" because "here there is no Buddhism". As someone who was supposed to be a Tibetan Buddhist, who had by his own account fled China in part for that reason, the First-tier Tribunal Judge was perfectly entitled to treat this answer as destructive of the appellant's case to be a Tibetan Buddhist. That was reinforced by the findings in paragraph 12(i).

[68] Against that background, the First-tier Tribunal Judge was entitled to treat the arrest warrant as evidentially neutral. It had no relevance to the question whether the appellant actually was a practitioner of Tibetan Buddhism, which was the proposition upon which his claim to international protection was based. For these reasons, the ground advanced in sub-paragraph (ii) fails.

[69] Ground (iii) contends that the First-tier Tribunal Judge "erred by failing to be slow, at paragraph 12(e), to draw adverse inferences from admissions/inconsistencies arising from the screening interview". At paragraph 12(e) the First-tier Tribunal Judge referred to the screening interview of 5 October 2018. The judge noted that nowhere in that interview did the appellant say anything about his belief in Tibetan Buddhism or support for Tibetan independence. Although the written answer to the question about religion – "just with Balai organisation"- might have been a misprint for the Dalai (Lama), it is nevertheless true that the appellant did not mention Tibetan Buddhism or Tibet at his screening interview.

[70] It is trite that a person claiming international protection is not expected in his screening interview to set out every detail of his claim. What might be reasonably expected to be found in a person's answers at an asylum screening interview will depend on the facts of the particular case. A person who volunteers themselves to the respondent, in order to make a claim for asylum, after having lived in the United Kingdom for a significant period of time, might, as a general matter, be expected to provide somewhat more detail than, say, a person who is screened immediately after an arduous journey to this country, concealed in the back of a lorry.

[71] In the present case, the appellant had been in the United Kingdom for several years before he was arrested in connection with immigration matters. That was when he claimed asylum. Notwithstanding that the appellant was claiming following an event (his arrest) over the timing of which he had no control, we nevertheless consider that the First-tier Tribunal Judge was entitled to have some regard to the fact that Tibet and Tibetan issues did not feature in the reasons given by the appellant for claiming asylum.

[72] In any event, however, reading the decision of the First-tier Tribunal as a whole, it is manifest that the basis for the First-tier Tribunal Judge's adverse credibility findings arose not from the screening interview but from the detailed asylum interview. It was in that interview that the appellant made the remarkable assertion that there was no Buddhism in the country in which he was claiming asylum.

[73] For these reasons, ground (iii) is not made out.

H. Decision

The decision of the First-tier Tribunal Judge does not contain an error on a point of law. The appellant's appeal is accordingly dismissed.

Direction Regarding Anonymity – Rule 14 of the Tribunal Procedure (Upper Tribunal) Rules 2008

Unless and until a Tribunal or court directs otherwise, the appellant is granted anonymity. No report of these proceedings shall directly or indirectly identify him or any member of their family. This direction applies both to the appellant and to the respondent. Failure to comply with this direction could lead to contempt of court proceedings.

BINAKU (S.11 TCEA; S.117C NIAA; PARA 399D)

UPPER TRIBUNAL (IMMIGRATION AND ASYLUM CHAMBER)

Lane J (President) and Norton-Taylor UTJ

[2021] UKUT 34 (IAC)
27 January 2021

Procedure and process – deportation – foreign criminal – section 117C of the 2002 Act determinative of appeal – re-entry in breach of deportation order – paragraph 399D of the Rules not relevant to statutory criteria – rights of appeal – section 11 of the TCEA – no right of appeal where exact outcome achieved

The Claimant, a citizen of Kosovo, entered the United Kingdom in June 1998 and applied for asylum. The application was refused and his appeal against that decision was dismissed in April 2009. In the interim, the Claimant had been convicted in November 2008 of theft and possession of a weapon and was sentenced to 12 months' imprisonment. As a result, the Secretary of State for the Home Department made a deportation order in September 2009. The Claimant married his wife, a naturalised British citizen, in June 2010. In October 2011 he accrued further convictions, this time for supplying Class A drugs, and was sentenced to three years' imprisonment. His appeal against a decision to deport him was dismissed in April 2012. He was deported to Kosovo in July 2012. The Claimant re-entered the United Kingdom in 2014 in breach of the deportation order. His presence in the country was only detected when he was arrested in June 2018. He then requested that the deportation order be revoked based on his family life with this wife and the couple's two children, born in November 2014 and July 2017, both of whom were British citizens. He asserted that he and his wife suffered from significant mental health problems and that the family unit could neither relocate to Kosovo, nor be split up. The Secretary of State reconsidered the Claimant's case but refused his human rights claim in June 2019. The Claimant appealed.

The First-tier Tribunal ("FtT") Judge concluded that it would be unduly harsh on the children to have to live in Kosovo or to be separated from their father. The effect of that conclusion was that the Claimant had satisfied the family life exception under section 117C(5) of the Nationality, Immigration and Asylum Act 2002 ("the 2002 Act"). As the Claimant had re-entered the United Kingdom in breach of a deportation order, the Judge also directed herself to paragraph 399D of the Immigration Rules HC 395 (as amended), noting that the threshold in that provision was an "extremely demanding one". The Judge regarded her conclusion that relocation or separation was unduly harsh as "one factor in the 399D balancing exercise" and ultimately concluded that the very high threshold established by paragraph 399D had not been met and thus the Claimant's appeal fell to be dismissed.

On appeal, the Upper Tribunal considered two issues, one procedural in nature, and the other substantive. The procedural issue was whether a party who had succeeded on all available grounds in an appeal before the FtT, and who might therefore be described as "the winner", could then appeal to the Upper Tribunal on a point of law. The Claimant argued that the winning party could appeal and therefore must comply with the applicable procedural steps. The Secretary of State submitted that the only appropriate vehicle for that party to raise such a ground was by way of a response under rule 24 of the Tribunal Procedure (Upper Tribunal) Rules 2008 (a "rule 24 response") when the losing party had applied for, and been granted, permission to appeal. The answer to the procedural question was entirely academic in the instant case and the observations made on the issue did not form part of the *ratio* of the decision. The substantive issue was whether the satisfaction by an individual of the relevant criteria under section 117C(4), (5), and (6) of the 2002 Act was determinative of an appeal, notwithstanding the provisions of the Immigration Rules. The parties agreed that the ability to meet either of the two exceptions or to show very compelling circumstances over and above those described in the exceptions would be determinative of an appeal. Although the Secretary of State initially challenged the FtT Judge's findings on the undue harshness issue under section 117C(5) of the 2002 Act in her rule 24 response, she later withdrew reliance on the rule 24 response. That had the effect of leaving the Judge's findings on the undue harshness issue unchallenged.

Held, allowing the Claimant's appeal:

(1) The appellate regime established by the 2002 Act, as amended, was concerned with outcomes comprising the determination of available grounds of appeal. A party who had achieved the exact outcome(s) sought by way of an appeal to the FtT being allowed on all available grounds relied on (in respect of an individual) or because it had been dismissed on all grounds (in respect of the Secretary of State) could not appeal to the Upper Tribunal under section 11(2) of the Tribunals, Courts and Enforcement Act 2007 against particular findings and/or reasons stated by the judge. In order to ensure that the outcome(s) could be clearly identified, and in turn the extent to which one party or the other was "the winner", judges should set out fully the precise basis, or bases, of their decision, whether favourable to the appellant or otherwise. It followed that an appellant who was able to, and did, rely on a number of grounds *would* have a right of appeal in respect of those upon which they were unsuccessful. *Secretary of State for the Home Department v Devani* [2020] EWCA Civ 612 represented binding authority from the Court of Appeal to that effect: *Anwar v Secretary of State for the Home Department* [2017] EWCA Civ 2134 distinguished. Parties were not encouraged to instigate appeals against decisions of the FtT in circumstances where they had succeeded in respect of certain grounds and as a result achieved in substance what they might have sought all along, namely a grant of leave flowing from the favourable outcome (*paras 20 – 64*).

(2) The substantive issue concerned the relationship between Part 5A of the 2002 Act and the Immigration Rules. By virtue of section 117A(1) of the 2002 Act, a tribunal was bound to apply the provisions of primary legislation, as set out in sections 117B and 117C, when determining an appeal concerning Article 8. In cases concerning the deportation of foreign criminals, as defined, it was clear from section 117A(2)(b) that the core legislative provisions were those set out in section 117C. It was now well-established that those provisions provided a structured approach to the application of Article 8 which would produce in all cases a final result compatible with protected rights. It was the structured approach set out in

section 117C which governed the task to be undertaken by the Tribunal, not the provisions of the Rules. A foreign criminal who had re-entered the United Kingdom in breach of an extant deportation order was subject to the same deportation regime as those who had yet to be removed or who had been removed and were seeking a revocation of a deportation order from abroad. The phrases "cases concerning the deportation of foreign criminals" in section 117A(2) and "a decision to deport a foreign criminal" in section 117C(7) were to be interpreted accordingly. Paragraph 399D of the Rules had no relevance to the application of the statutory criteria set out in section 117C(4), (5) and (6). It followed that the structured approach to be undertaken by a Tribunal considering an Article 8 appeal in the context of deportation began and ended with Part 5A of the 2002 Act (*paras 69 – 97*).

(3) The FtT Judge had erred in law by treating the satisfaction of Exception 2 under section 117C(5) of the 2002 Act as constituting simply one factor to be considered in the light of paragraph 399D of the Rules, and, as a consequence, failing to treat the satisfaction of the exception as being determinative of the Claimant's appeal. The FtT's decision was accordingly set aside. The Secretary of State had accepted that the FtT Judge was entitled to find that it would be unduly harsh for the family unit to relocate to Kosovo and for the children to be separated from the Claimant. The Claimant satisfied Exception 2 under section 117C(5) of the 2002 Act. That was determinative of the appeal and entitled the Claimant to succeed on Article 8 grounds (*paras 98 – 100*).

Cases referred to:

Anwar v Secretary of State for the Home Department [2017] EWCA Civ 2134; [2018] 1 WLR 2591; [2018] Imm AR 660; [2018] INLR 127

CI (Nigeria) v Secretary of State for the Home Department [2019] EWCA Civ 2027; [2020] Imm AR 503; [2020] INLR 191

IT (Jamaica) v Secretary of State for the Home Department [2016] EWCA Civ 932; [2017] 1 WLR 240; [2017] Imm AR 414

KO (Nigeria) v Secretary of State for the Home Department; IT (Jamaica) v Secretary of State for the Home Department; NS (Sri Lanka and Others) v Secretary of State for the Home Department; Pereira v Secretary of State for the Home Department [2018] UKSC 53; [2018] 1 WLR 5273; [2019] 1 All ER 675; [2019] Imm AR 400; [2019] INLR 41

Katsonga ("Slip Rule"; FtT's general powers) [2016] UKUT 228 (IAC)

MH (review; slip rule; church witnesses) Iran [2020] UKUT 125 (IAC); [2020] Imm AR 983

NE-A (Nigeria) v Secretary of State for the Home Department; Secretary of State for the Home Department v HM (Uganda) [2017] EWCA Civ 239; [2017] Imm AR 1077; [2018] INLR 88

OH (Algeria) v Secretary of State for the Home Department [2019] EWCA Civ 1763; [2020] Imm AR 350

R (on the application of Mansoor) v Secretary of State for the Home Department *(Balajigari – effect of judge's decision)* [2020] UKUT 126 (IAC); [2020] Imm AR 956

Rexha (S.117C – earlier offences) [2016] UKUT 335 (IAC); [2016] Imm AR 1426; [2017] INLR 412

Secretary of State for the Home Department v Devani [2020] EWCA Civ 612; [2020] 1 WLR 2613; [2020] Imm AR 1183
Secretary of State for the Home Department v SU [2017] EWCA Civ 1069; [2017] 4 WLR 175
Smith (appealable decisions; PTA requirements; anonymity) [2019] UKUT 216 (IAC); [2019] Imm AR 1325; [2019] INLR 788
Williams (scope of "liable to deportation") [2018] UKUT 116 (IAC); [2018] INLR 668

Legislation and international instruments judicially considered:

European Convention on Human Rights, Articles 3 & 8
Human Rights Act 1998, section 6
Immigration Rules HC 395 (as amended), paragraphs 322(3) & 399D,
Nationality, Immigration and Asylum Act 2002, sections 82(1), 84 & 117A–D
Tribunals, Courts and Enforcement Act 2007, sections 11 & 13
Tribunal Procedure (Upper Tribunal) Rules 2008, rule 24

Representation

Mr Z Malik instructed by SMA Solicitors, for the Claimant;
Mr I Jarvis, Senior Home Office Presenting Officer, for the Secretary of State.

Decision and reasons

UPPER TRIBUNAL JUDGE NORTON-TAYLOR:

Introduction

[1] This is an appeal against the decision of First-tier Tribunal Judge Bunting ("the judge"), promulgated on 25 February 2020, by which she dismissed the appellant's appeal against the respondent's decision to refuse his human rights claim, which in turn had been made in the context of the appellant having re-entered the United Kingdom in breach of a deportation order.

[2] This case raises two issues; one procedural in nature, the other substantive. In respect of the former, we can state the question as follows: can a party who has succeeded on all available grounds in an appeal before the First-tier Tribunal and who may therefore be described as "the winner", then appeal to the Upper Tribunal on a point of law?

[3] On this the parties are divided. The appellant argues that the winning party can appeal and therefore must comply with the applicable procedural steps. The respondent submits that the only appropriate vehicle for that party to raise such a ground is by way of a response under rule 24 of the Tribunal Procedure (Upper Tribunal) Rules 2008 (SI 2008/2698) (a "rule 24 response") when the losing party has applied for, and been granted, permission to appeal.

[4] We have concluded that the respondent's position is broadly correct, but, for reasons set out in due course, the answer to the procedural question is entirely academic in this case and the observations we make on the issue do not form part of the *ratio* of our decision.

[5] The substantive issue concerns the relationship between the Immigration Rules ("the Rules") relating to deportation and the statutory framework set out in

Part 5A of the Nationality, Immigration and Asylum Act 2002, as amended ("the 2002 Act"), with a particular focus on section 117C. At its heart, the question is whether the satisfaction by an individual of the relevant criteria under section 117C(4), (5), and (6) of the 2002 Act is determinative of an appeal, notwithstanding the provisions of the Rules.

[6] In contrast to the position regarding the procedural question, the parties are in agreement as to the correct answer: the ability to meet either of the two exceptions or to show very compelling circumstances over and above those described in the exceptions will be determinative of an appeal. That view accords with our own and provides the basis upon which we have concluded that the First-tier Tribunal erred in law and that the decision in this appeal should be re-made in the appellant's favour.

[7] Before moving on, we wish to express our gratitude to both representatives for the skill with which they presented their respective cases, both in writing and orally.

Background

[8] The appellant is a citizen of Kosovo, born in 1979. He first arrived in the United Kingdom in June 1998, whereupon he made an asylum claim. This was refused in July 2005 and an appeal dismissed in April 2009. In the interim, the appellant had been convicted in November 2008 of theft and possession of a weapon and was sentenced to 12 months' imprisonment. This resulted in a deportation order being made on 21 September 2009. The appellant married his wife, a naturalised British citizen, in June 2010. In October 2011 the appellant accrued further convictions, this time for supplying Class A drugs, and was sentenced to 3 years' imprisonment. An appeal against a decision to deport him was dismissed in April 2012. Having signed a disclaimer, the appellant was deported to Kosovo on 3 July 2012.

[9] The appellant then re-entered the United Kingdom on an unspecified date in 2014, in breach of the deportation order. His presence in this country was only detected when he was arrested in June 2018. Representations were submitted in January 2019 requesting that the deportation order be revoked. These were predicated on the appellant's family life in the United Kingdom with his wife and the couple's two children, born in November 2014 and July 2017, both of whom are British citizens. It was said that the appellant and his wife suffered from significant mental health problems and that the family unit could neither relocate to Kosovo, nor be split up.

[10] Following an initial rejection of the representations and the instigation of judicial review proceedings, the respondent agreed to reconsider the appellant's case and consequently refused his human rights claim by a decision dated 7 June 2019.

The decision of the First-tier Tribunal

[11] The judge recorded that the appellant was not pursuing a claim that his appeal should succeed on the basis of his mental health problems alone. She subsequently concluded that the appellant could not meet the private life exception under section 117C(4) of the 2002 Act.

[12] The primary focus of the judge's attention was on the position of the two children. Having accepted in full all of the evidence presented by the appellant, including a significant body of medical evidence and the report of an independent social worker, the judge concluded that it would be unduly harsh on the children to have to go to live in Kosovo or to be separated from their father. The effect of that conclusion was that the appellant had satisfied the family life exception under section 117C(5) of the 2002 Act.

[13] Importantly, the judge's consideration of the appellant's case did not end there. As the appellant had re-entered the United Kingdom in breach of a deportation order, the judge directed herself to paragraph 399D of the Rules. She noted that the threshold in that provision was an "extremely demanding one", as made clear by the Court of Appeal in *SSHD v SU* [2017] EWCA Civ 1069; [2017] 4 WLR 175. The judge regarded her conclusion that relocation or separation was unduly harsh as "one factor in the 399D balancing exercise." Having considered other surrounding circumstances resting on both sides of the balance sheet, the judge ultimately concluded that the very high threshold established by paragraph 399D had not been met and thus the appellant's appeal fell to be dismissed.

The grounds of appeal and grant of permission

[14] The grounds of appeal took aim at the judge's consideration of a number of factors weighed up in the proportionality exercise. Nothing was specifically raised in respect of the interaction between the conclusion that the exception under section 117C(5) had been met and the failure to have satisfied the test under paragraph 399D.

[15] In granting permission, Upper Tribunal Judge Norton-Taylor deemed it appropriate to state an additional issue in relation to which the judge may have erred in law. This was put in the following terms:

"[W]as the judge entitled to conclude that the appellant had to meet the test under paragraph 399D of the Immigration Rules in order to succeed, notwithstanding the fact that exception 2 under section 117C [of the 2002 Act] applied, or was satisfaction of that exception determinative of the appeal?"

[16] In the event, it is the answer to this question which has provided the basis on which we have ultimately decided this appeal.

The procedural issue: relevant legal framework

[17] The two core legislative provisions relevant to the procedural issue are sections 11 and 13 of the Tribunals, Courts and Enforcement Act 2007 ("the 2007 Act"). Subsections (1) and (2) of section 11 provide:

"(1)   For the purposes of subsection (2), the reference to a right of appeal is to a right to appeal to the Upper Tribunal on any point of law arising from a decision made by the First-tier Tribunal other than an excluded decision.

(2)   Any party to a case has a right of appeal, subject to subsection (8)."

[18] Subsections (1) and (2) of section 13 provide:

"(1)   For the purposes of subsection (2), the reference to a right of appeal is to a right to appeal to the relevant appellate court on any point of law arising from a decision made by the Upper Tribunal other than an excluded decision.

(2)   Any party to a case has a right of appeal, subject to subsection (14)."

[19] Subsections (8) of section 11 and (14) of section 13 have no bearing on our consideration of this case.

The procedural issue: discussion

[20] The procedural issue in this case arose because, following the grant of permission, the respondent provided a rule 24 response. This purported to challenge the judge's findings on the undue harshness issue under section 117C(5) of the 2002 Act.

[21] This attempted challenge was refuted in the appellant's first skeleton argument, wherein it was asserted that the respondent had not sought to appeal to the Upper Tribunal on the issue in question and therefore was precluded from mounting an attack at this stage. The rule 24 response could not cure this jurisdictional defect.

[22] It is this initial dispute which put in train the considerable amount of thought applied by the parties to what we are describing as the procedural issue in this case, as set out in paragraph 2, above.

[23] Before turning to address the respective arguments, we record the respondent's decision (contained in Mr Jarvis' skeleton argument dated 4 November 2020) to withdraw reliance on the rule 24 response. That had the effect of leaving the judge's findings on the undue harshness issue unchallenged, whatever our conclusions on the procedural issue. The decision to resile from the response was of course entirely a matter for the respondent. For what it is worth, we regard it as wholly justified. The judge clearly took relevant evidence into account and made eminently sustainable findings thereon in accordance with sound legal self-directions.

[24] Rather than setting out the parties' submissions on the proceeded issue in detail here, we will endeavour to address their substance as we progress through the discussion. Suffice it to say at this stage that the disputed territory is said to be occupied by two judgments of the Court of Appeal: *Devani* [2020] EWCA Civ 612; [2020] 1 WLR 2613 and *Anwar* [2017] EWCA Civ 2134. Mr Malik relies on *Anwar* as authority for the proposition that the winning party before the First-tier Tribunal can appeal to the Upper Tribunal on a point of law. He submits that *Devani* should be read consistently with that judgment and, if it cannot, is wrong and was decided *per incuriam*. Mr Jarvis argues that *Devani* expressly decides the procedural issue against the appellant's position and can be readily distinguished from *Anwar*.

[25] The *Devani* case concerned a Kenyan businessman facing extradition to his own country in order to face prosecution for alleged fraud. Mr Devani sought to resist this on the ground that he would be detained in prison conditions which violated Article 3 ECHR. The Divisional Court rejected this claim on the basis of assurances provided by the Kenyan government. Mr Devani then made a protection claim to the Secretary of State, still relying on the prison conditions issue. The claim was refused. On appeal, the First-tier Tribunal purported to reject all grounds put forward, namely that the refusal was contrary to the United Kingdom's obligations under the Refugee Convention and that it breached Mr Devani's rights under the ECHR, specifically Articles 3 and 8. However, the substance of the judge's reasoning was to the effect that she in fact intended to allow the appeal on Article 3 grounds only. Believing that he could not rely on the so-called "slip rule" in order to correct this error, Mr Devani appealed to the Upper Tribunal on the basis that it should substitute that aspect of the judge's decision (or "order") relating to Article 3. The Secretary of State was unhappy with the judge's reasoning on Article 3, but neither lodged an appeal nor provided a response under rule 24. Her position was that she could not pursue an appeal as the ostensible "winner" before the First-tier Tribunal. Instead, there was an attempt to challenge the judge's reasoning at the hearing before the Upper Tribunal. The Deputy Upper Tribunal Judge declined to consider this challenge. Having first concluded at paragraphs 23–24 that the case of *Katsonga ("Slip Rule"; FtT's general powers)* [2016] UKUT 228 (IAC) was wrongly decided (see also *MH (review; slip rule; church witnesses) Iran* [2020] UKUT 125 (IAC)), Underhill LJ (with whom Nicola Davies and Males LJJ agreed) turned to the matter with which we are presently concerned. The scene is set in paragraph 26, with paragraph 27 containing the relevant conclusions:

"26. I turn to the substantive issue under this head, namely whether the Judge erred in law in declining to consider the Secretary of State's challenge to paras. 48–49 of the FTT's Reasons. His reason for taking that course was that she had failed to raise that challenge in accordance with "the relevant procedure rules": specifically, he referred to her failure (a) to appeal or (b) to provide a rule 24 response or (c) to serve a skeleton argument. Mr Chapman submitted that that was a misdirection: there was no obligation on the Secretary of State to take any of those steps.

27. I start with the alleged failure by the Secretary of State herself to appeal. I agree with Mr Chapman that there was no such failure. In my view Mr Tufan was quite right in his submission to DUTJ Latter (see para. 16 above) that that course was not open to her because she was (ostensibly) the winning party. As appears from para. 17 of his decision, the Judge acknowledged that that had once been the law, but he said that the position was changed by section 11 (2) of the Tribunals, Courts and Enforcement Act 2007, which reads "Any party has a right of appeal, subject to subsection (8)3." Subsection (1) defines a right of appeal, so far as relevant, as a right of appeal to the UT on a point of law. I accept that on a literal reading subsection (2) could be construed as giving a right of appeal not only to a party against whom an order has been made but also to a party who has obtained, as regards that order, the exact outcome that they sought: although usually the winning party would have no wish to appeal, occasionally they may be dissatisfied with particular findings made by the Court or with aspects of its reasoning (the present case, if the slip rule were unavailable, would be an example albeit of a very specific kind). But for the winning party to have a right of appeal in such a case would be contrary to well-established case-law governing the position in the common law courts, which

reflects important policy considerations; the authorities are well-known, and I need only refer to the commentary in para. 9A-59.3 of the White Book. It was not suggested to us that there was any reason why Parliament should have intended a different approach in the case of appeals to the Upper Tribunal. Ms Broadfoot sought to support DUTJ Latter's conclusion by reference to the decision of the UT in *EG and NG (Ethiopia)* [2013] UKUT 000143 (IAC), but that was not concerned with the present point at all. I am sure that section 11 (2) of the 2007 Act is intended to confer a right of appeal only against some aspect of the actual order of the FTT, and that the phrase "any party" must be read as referring only to a party who has in that sense lost."

[26] We are satisfied that the Court's attention was not drawn to *Anwar.*

[27] The essential facts of *Anwar* were as follows. Mr Anwar, a citizen of Pakistan, had been in the United Kingdom with leave to remain as a student. In 2013 he made an application for further leave in the same category. The refusal of that application was in part based on the conclusion that Mr Anwar had breached a condition of his leave, namely a prohibition on switching between different educational institutions without first making a new application to the respondent. It was said that paragraph 322(3) of the Rules applied. The appeal against the decision was dismissed by the First-tier Tribunal. The Upper Tribunal allowed Mr Anwar's onward appeal on the limited basis that the respondent had failed to exercise a discretion and that the resulting decision was not otherwise in accordance with the law (in order for the Upper Tribunal to have reached that stage it must also have been the case that the First-tier Tribunal had failed to address this issue or had done so erroneously). However, the finding by the First-tier Tribunal that Mr Anwar had breached a condition of his leave was expressly upheld. Mr Anwar appealed to the Court of Appeal against this aspect of the Upper Tribunal's decision.

[28] The relevant part of the judgment of Singh LJ (with whom Peter Jackson LJ agreed) is relatively brief and it is best to set it out in full:

"Is the Present Appeal Academic?

14. When permission to appeal in the present case was first refused on the papers by Simon LJ, it was on the ground that the case had become academic because the Appellant's appeal had succeeded in front of the UT. As I have already mentioned, the outcome of the appeal was that the UT remitted the case to the Secretary of State for reconsideration.

15. In granting permission at the oral hearing on 5 May 2016 Lewison LJ noted that the normal rule in ordinary litigation is that appeals are made against orders rather than against the reasons for making those orders. That was decided in *Lake v Lake* [1955] P 336, although, as Lewison LJ observed, where the appellant does not get all the relief from the lower court that he is entitled to, the court nevertheless has the power to entertain an appeal: see *Curtis v London Rent Assessment Committee* [1999] QB 92.

16. Lewison LJ also noted that the right of appeal to this Court in cases of the present kind is conferred by section 13 of the Tribunals, Courts and Enforcement Act 2007. Subsection (1) of that section provides:

'For the purposes of subsection (2), the reference to a right of appeal is to a right to appeal to the relevant appellate court on any point of law arising from a decision by the Upper Tribunal other than an excluded decision.'

17. Lewison LJ said that 'any point of law arising from a decision' is wider than the normal rule for appeals. He said:

'I am satisfied that this Court does have jurisdiction to entertain the appeal, and that if the appeal were to succeed it would significantly affect any future decision which the Secretary of State were to make in relation to the appellant's application for an extension of leave to remain.'

18. I respectfully agree with those observations.

19. There is one further point which should be mentioned at this stage, because it too goes to the question of whether this appeal has become academic.

20. Since the UT decision, on 13 August 2015, the Secretary of State made a fresh decision, again refusing the application for leave to remain as a Tier 4 (General) Student. However, the Secretary of State did not cite the breach by the Appellant of an immigration condition as a reason for this decision. Nevertheless, the Appellant submits that this appeal has not become academic. The Secretary of State has not suggested that it has become academic; indeed she maintains that the Appellant was in breach of a condition which was attached to his leave to remain in 2011.

21. In my view, it is appropriate for this Court to consider the points of law which are raised, because the Appellant continues to have an interest in the matter. As things stand, it has been held by a judicial body that he was in breach of an immigration condition. As will become apparent later, that could, at least in principle, render him liable for a criminal offence. In any event, that is something which is on his record and may affect future applications he may make, perhaps if he wishes to go to another country elsewhere in the world."

[29] The Court ultimately concluded that the condition of leave in question had not been lawfully imposed and thus Mr Anwar was not in breach. His appeal fell to be allowed on that ground.

[30] In the first instance, and for the reasons set out below, we conclude that *Anwar* can be distinguished from *Devani*.

[31] It is self-evidently the case that *Anwar* was concerned with section 13 of the 2007 Act, not, as in *Devani*, section 11. Section 13 specifically addresses the Court of Appeal's jurisdiction to hear appeals brought against decisions of the Upper Tribunal. Whilst set out within the statutory framework of the 2007 Act, it is apparent from the observations of Lewison LJ when granting permission in *Anwar* that the Court's long-established common law tradition formed an element of the backdrop against which the issue in hand was being considered.

[32] More importantly, there is an important distinction between the specific issues being considered by the Court in the two cases: *Anwar* was, as is apparent from paragraphs 16 and 17 of the judgment, concerned with subsection (1) of

section 13; whereas paragraphs 26 and 27 of *Devani* make it clear that it was the jurisdictional scope of subsection (2) of section 11 which arose as a material issue and as such the conclusions reached constituted an aspect of the *ratio* of the Court's decision on the appeal.

[33] In our view, the purpose underlying subsection (1) of sections 13 and 11 is to clarify that the right of appeal exercisable under subsection (2) of either section must be founded upon "any point of law arising from a decision" of the Upper Tribunal or First-tier Tribunal (as the case may be) other than an excluded decision. *Anwar* is a decision on the scope of that statutory phrase, at least in so far as procedure and jurisdiction is concerned. What it does not purport to do is address the questions of who has the right of appeal in the first place: that is the domain of subsection (2) of sections 13 and 11. The phrase in subsection (2) "any party to a case" does not carry with it the implicit meaning that a successful party has, *in all circumstances*, a right of appeal. All it does is to confirm that an appellant and respondent in the proceedings below, together with any other party which may have been joined, has the right of appeal, subject to any provisions made by the Lord Chancellor.

[34] Thus, the Court in *Anwar* was concerned with a statutory provision (subsection (1) of section 13 of the 2007 Act) which was not only different from that arising for specific consideration in *Devani*, but one which cannot have a decisive bearing on the question of whether "the winner" below has a right of appeal under subsection (2) of sections 11 and 13.

[35] Further and in any event, cognisant of the marked similarity in the wording of subsections (1) and (2) of sections 11 and 13 of the 2007 Act, it is appropriate to offer additional analysis of *Anwar* and *Devani* were it to be said that we are wrong in seeking to distinguish these cases on the basis set out above.

[36] A proper understanding of the two judgments, and indeed the entire appellate regime under the 2007 Act, comes down to the question of outcomes. By "outcomes" we mean the decision of the First-tier Tribunal or Upper Tribunal (in respect of a re-making decision undertaken) on the ground(s) relied on by an appellant under section 84 of the 2002 Act in an appeal. This may be described as constituting the "order" of the First-tier Tribunal or the Upper Tribunal.

[37] Following the wholesale changes to Part 5 of the 2002 Act by virtue of the Immigration Act 2014, the number of appealable decisions under section 82(1) was very significantly reduced, as were the corresponding grounds of appeal available to an appellant. Where, as occurred in *Devani*, an individual makes a protection and a human rights claim, and both are refused by the respondent, a challenge against the decisions will result in two appeals running in parallel.

[38] The limited grounds of appeal available in respect of a protection appeal are set out in section 84(1):

"(1) An appeal under section 82(1)(a) (refusal of protection claim) must be brought on one or more of the following grounds –

    (a)   that removal of the appellant from the United Kingdom would breach the United Kingdom's obligations under the Refugee Convention;

(b)　　that removal of the appellant from the United Kingdom would breach the United Kingdom's obligations in relation to persons eligible for a grant of humanitarian protection;

(c)　　that removal of the appellant from the United Kingdom would be unlawful under section 6 of the Human Rights Act 1998 (public authority not to act contrary to Human Rights Convention)."

[39] It is to be noted that the ground under section 84(1)(c) covers Article 3 in the context of a protection appeal.

[40] In an appeal against the refusal of a human rights claim, the only available ground is that under section 84(2):

"(2)　　An appeal under section 82(1)(b) (refusal of human rights claim) must be brought on the ground that the decision is unlawful under section 6 of the Human Rights Act 1998."

[41] The outcomes (as we have defined that term) in any appeal are in effect constituted by the success or otherwise of the specific ground(s) of appeal relied on. If, for example, an individual pursuing an appeal against a refusal of a protection claim asserts that they are a refugee and the ground of appeal under section 84(1)(a) is made out, they will have obtained the "exact outcome" sought, namely a recognition of their status and a binding decision that their removal would breach this country's international obligations. The same is true for an individual who successfully relies on a claimed entitlement to humanitarian protection in reliance on the ground of appeal under section 84(1)(b). Notwithstanding the legislative oddity that a protection claim cannot be based on the assertion that removal would violate Article 3, in an appeal against a refusal of such a claim an individual can, pursuant to the ground of appeal under section 84(1)(c), assert that removal would expose them to, for example, the real risk of being detained in prison conditions contrary to that absolute right. In respect of an appeal against a refusal of a human rights claim, the position is somewhat more nuanced. It is possible for an individual to rely on Articles 3 and 8 where, for example, it is asserted that their removal in consequence of the decision would give rise to a sufficiently high risk of suicide and that they additionally enjoy family life in the United Kingdom. Whilst the only ground of appeal available is that contained within section 84(2), with a favourable decision being that the respondent's refusal of the human rights claim is unlawful under section 6 of the Human Rights Act 1998, a tribunal should in our view state its decision in respect of the different protected rights expressly relied on; in the example given, Articles 3 and 8. The issues in respect of each provision will often be sufficiently distinct to justify a differentiation in terms of the decision(s) made. In any event, and more importantly, an appellant who expressly relies on different articles of the ECHR is entitled to an outcome decision in respect of each. There is, however, no scope for a legally effective delineation between success on the basis of private life or in respect of family life within Article 8: success on this basis amounts to a composite outcome.

[42] We re-emphasise here the fact that the respondent can also be the "winner" as the result of a decision by the First-tier Tribunal dismissing an appellant's appeal on all grounds. Indeed, that is the scenario considered by the Court in

Devani itself, albeit that the judge had intended to allow the appeal on a single ground.

[43] As a matter of common practice, the outcome of an appeal is usually stated under a subheading entitled "Decision" or "Notice of Decision" within the decision and reasons document produced by judges in the Immigration and Asylum Chamber of both Tribunals. By way of example, one may see the following form of words employed:

"I dismiss the appeal against the respondent's refusal of the protection claim in respect of the Refugee Convention and humanitarian protection.

I allow the appeal against the respondent's refusal of the protection claim on Article 3 ECHR grounds.

I dismiss the appeal against the respondent's refusal of the human rights claim in respect of Article 8 ECHR."

[44] In order to ensure that the outcome(s) can be clearly identified, and in turn the extent to which one party or the other is "the winner", judges should set out fully the precise basis (or bases) of their decision, whether favourable to the appellant or otherwise.

[45] The outcomes-based approach is reflected in the conclusion of Underhill LJ in paragraph 27 of *Devani* that the right of appeal under section 11(2) of the 2007 Act lies only against an aspect of the "order" (or, as we have previously explained, the determination of the specific ground(s) relied on, including, where applicable, different articles of the ECHR) and that a party who has obtained "the exact outcome" sought cannot, as the "winning party", mount an appeal. It follows that an appellant who is able to, and does, rely on a number of grounds *will* have a right of appeal in respect of those upon which they are unsuccessful. This is simply because they have not, in effect, obtained the "exact outcome" sought, a point implicitly recognised by Underhill LJ in footnote 4 of his judgment: the "winner" can appeal under section 11 of the 2007 Act because their success has been partial and one or more additional outcomes may ultimately be achieved.

[46] What is set out in the preceding paragraph represents, in our respectful view, a correct analysis of the current appellate regime and we regard *Devani* as binding authority on the point.

[47] We return to *Anwar*. This too is a case concerned with outcomes. Mr Anwar succeeded on a narrow basis (the decision of the respondent under appeal was found to be not otherwise in accordance with the law and was sent back for it to be retaken on a lawful basis). This was not the outcome hoped for, or, to put it in the terms of the common law cases, he did not get all the "relief" he believed he was entitled to.

[48] What is important to note is that Mr Anwar's appeal to the First-tier Tribunal and then to the Upper Tribunal was pursued under the statutory regime in place prior to the changes brought about by the Immigration Act 2014. As a consequence, he had at his disposal a variety of grounds of appeal under the unamended section 84 of the 2002 Act on which to rely, including the contentions that the respondent's decision was not in accordance with the Rules (section 84(1)(a)) and that it was not otherwise in accordance with the law (section 84(1)(e)). Thus, it had been open to him on appeal to the First-tier Tribunal and (in respect of the re-making of the decision) the Upper Tribunal to argue that paragraph 322(3) of the Rules did not apply to him and that he had satisfied all other requirements of the Rules relating to students. If this ground of appeal had succeeded, it appears to us clear that his appeal would have been allowed outright by the Upper Tribunal and he would have been granted leave in line with it, as opposed to the more circumscribed basis of success afforded by the conclusion that the respondent's decision was not otherwise in accordance with the law. In other words, Mr Anwar succeeded in respect of one ground of appeal, but failed on another which would have provided a more beneficial result for him.

[49] The Court's reference to the potential success of Mr Anwar's appeal having a significant effect on future decisions taken by the respondent sits happily with our analysis. If the ground upon which Mr Anwar had been unsuccessful before the Upper Tribunal was ultimately upheld, it would have been as a consequence of a finding that he had not in fact breached a condition of his leave, and in turn his immigration record would have remained impeccable. This consideration can also be seen as the question of materiality going to the Court's willingness to consider the appeal notwithstanding Mr Anwar's success before the Upper Tribunal on another ground.

[50] Seen in this way, the Court's conclusion that it had jurisdiction to entertain Mr Anwar's appeal, despite him being, in respect of one ground of appeal only, "the winner", is consistent with what is said in *Devani*.

[51] It follows from the *ratio* of *Devani* and our reading of *Anwar* that a winning party does not have a right of appeal against particular findings or reasons made by a tribunal in circumstances where these have not resulted in a negative determination of the relevant ground of appeal. This category is what in our view Underhill LJ was referring to in paragraph 27 when concluding that to provide a right of appeal in "such a case" would be contrary to well-established case-law (as discussed in paragraph 9A-59.3 of the White Book).

[52] If this were not the case, the Upper Tribunal and Court of Appeal would be faced with the distinct possibility of successful parties seeking to appeal against a plethora of findings and/or reasons regarded as undesirable or problematic. Quite apart from the likelihood of a very substantial increase in the number of appeals brought, in our judgement it would result in an unprincipled state of affairs which would run contrary to the statutory scheme in which outcomes play the pivotal part.

[53] Mr Malik has put forward the submission that to preclude a winner before the First-tier Tribunal from appealing to the Upper Tribunal would result in "extraordinary consequences." In support, he gives two examples. An individual who has been found to have acted dishonestly in the context of the obtaining of a TOEIC certificate or discrepancies in tax returns, but nonetheless succeeds in an appeal on the only available ground relating to Article 8, will be unable to challenge that finding in an onward appeal. The finding would be likely to cause the individual significant difficulties in respect of any future applications for indefinite leave to remain or naturalisation as a British citizen. Conversely, the respondent will be unable to challenge a potentially legally flawed finding that an individual is innocent of any dishonesty if an appeal is dismissed. The respondent would therefore be "stuck" with that finding and may be required to grant a future application to an undeserving individual.

[54] Mr Malik's solution to these scenarios is to suggest the adoption of a "material benefit" test attaching to the availability of a right of appeal for a

winning party: such a party will be able to appeal to the Upper Tribunal (and presumably to the Court of Appeal in light of the similarity in wording of subsections (1) and (2) of sections 11 and 13 of the 2007 Act) if success of the appeal would provide a "material benefit" to the appealing party, with an example being that it would "significantly affect any future decision." This approach is said to be consistent with *Anwar* and the decision in *Smith (appealable decisions; PTA requirements; anonymity)* [2019] UKUT 216 (IAC).

[55] Whilst attractively put, the submission is unsustainable for a number of interconnected reasons.

[56] First, if we are correct in distinguishing *Anwar* from *Devani*, reliance on the former takes Mr Malik's argument no further.

[57] Second, in any event it is contrary to what we regard as the binding authority of *Devani* on the meaning of section 11(2) of the 2007 Act and the central importance of outcomes in the appellate regime established by Parliament.

[58] Third, we see nothing extraordinary, absurd, or perverse, arising from the conclusions drawn in *Devani*. The individual found to be dishonest but successful in their appeal on the only available ground will not be able to challenge that finding to the Upper Tribunal through the appellate route, but would be able to seek a remedy through judicial review proceedings if a future application was refused by the respondent in reliance on that finding. That was the situation in *Mansoor (*Balajigari – *effect of judge's decision)* [2020] UKUT 126 (IAC), a decision which we regard as consistent with *Devani* and unsupportive of Mr Malik's current position. The applicant in that case had been found to have practised deception, but his appeal to the First-tier Tribunal was allowed on the basis of additional matters relevant to Article 8. There had been no attempted appeal to the Upper Tribunal in respect of the adverse finding. The judicial review proceedings arose following the respondent's refusal of a subsequent application for indefinite leave to remain based on the finding of deception. It is incorrect to assert that *Mansoor* implicitly adopted Mr Malik's interpretation of the approach in *Anwar*, and in any event, the Upper Tribunal was clearly not concerned with section 11 of the 2007 Act.

[59] Alternatively, if the respondent appealed against the allowing of the appeal and was granted permission, the individual would then be able to argue that the finding on deception was wrong, pursuant to rule 24 response.

[60] As regards the respondent's position where an allegation of deception may have been erroneously rejected by the First-tier Tribunal, but the appeal dismissed in any event, the respondent would be able to challenge the particular finding by way of a rule 24 response if the individual were to appeal to the Upper Tribunal and be granted permission.

[61] Even if the potential avenues for challenge set out above were not available in any given case, it would in our view simply be a consequence of the statutory regime, which may, on occasion, give rise to hard-edged results for one party or another.

[62] Fourth, reliance on the decision in *Smith* takes Mr Malik's argument no further. *Smith* concerned the situation in which an appellant had succeeded before the First-tier Tribunal on one ground of appeal, but the judge had declined to determine the ground relating to Article 8. The conclusion of the Upper Tribunal that this failure constituted a "decision" which could be appealed under section 11 of the 2007 Act is clearly consistent with *Devani*: the individual in *Smith* had "won" in respect of one ground, but effectively "lost" on the other and thus had

not achieved all the outcomes sought. In addition, the central issue in *Smith* was whether a partially successful party must bring an appeal against a decision of the First-tier Tribunal; or whether they are entitled to await a challenge by the other party and then seek to argue those grounds on which they were initially unsuccessful by way of a rule 24 response. It is plain that this does not address the prior question of whether a party can bring an appeal in the first place.

[63] Nothing in what we have set out in our analysis on the procedural issue should be taken as an encouragement to parties to instigate appeals against decisions of the First-tier Tribunal in circumstances where they have succeeded in respect of certain grounds and as a result achieved in substance what they may have sought all along, namely a grant of leave flowing from the favourable outcome.

The procedural issue: summary of conclusions

[64] In answer to the question posed in paragraph 2 of this decision, our *obiter* conclusions are as follows:

(a) The appellate regime established by the Nationality, Immigration and Asylum Act 2002, as amended, is concerned with outcomes comprising the determination of available grounds of appeal;

(b) A party who has achieved the exact outcome(s) sought by way of an appeal to the First-tier Tribunal being allowed on all available grounds relied on (in respect of an individual) or because it has been dismissed on all grounds (in respect of the Secretary of State) cannot appeal to the Upper Tribunal under section 11(2) of the Tribunals, Courts and Enforcement Act 2007 against particular findings and/or reasons stated by the judge;

(c) *Devani* represents binding authority from the Court of Appeal to this effect.

The substantive issue: relevant legal framework

[65] Section 117A of the 2002 Act provides as follows:

"117A Application of this Part

(1) This Part applies where a court or tribunal is required to determine whether a decision made under the Immigration Acts –

(a) breaches a person's right to respect for private and family life under Article 8, and

(b) as a result would be unlawful under section 6 of the Human Rights Act 1998.

(2)   In considering the public interest question, the court or tribunal must (in particular) have regard –

(a)   in all cases, to the considerations listed in section 117B, and

(b)   in cases concerning the deportation of foreign criminals, to the considerations listed in section 117C.

(3)   In subsection (2), 'the public interest question' means the question of whether an interference with a person's right to respect for private and family life is justified under Article 8(2)."

[66] Section 117C is very familiar to all and provides:

"117C Article 8: additional considerations in cases involving foreign criminals

(1)   The deportation of foreign criminals is in the public interest.

(2)   The more serious the offence committed by a foreign criminal, the greater is the public interest in deportation of the criminal.

(3)   In the case of a foreign criminal ('C') who has not been sentenced to a period of imprisonment of four years or more, the public interest requires C's deportation unless Exception 1 or Exception 2 applies.

(4)   Exception 1 applies where –

(a)   C has been lawfully resident in the United Kingdom for most of C's life,

(b)   C is socially and culturally integrated in the United Kingdom, and

(c)   there would be very significant obstacles to C's integration into the country to which C is proposed to be deported.

(5)   Exception 2 applies where C has a genuine and subsisting relationship with a qualifying partner, or a genuine and subsisting parental relationship with a qualifying child, and the effect of C's deportation on the partner or child would be unduly harsh.

(6)   In the case of a foreign criminal who has been sentenced to a period of imprisonment of at least four years, the public interest requires deportation unless there are very compelling circumstances, over and above those described in Exceptions 1 and 2.

(7)   The considerations in subsections (1) to (6) are to be taken into account where a court or tribunal is considering a decision to deport a foreign criminal only to the extent that the reason for the decision was the offence or offences for which the criminal has been convicted."

[67] Section 117D defines the term "foreign criminal":

"(2)   In this Part, 'foreign criminal' means a person –

    (a)   who is not a British citizen,

    (b)   who has been convicted in the United Kingdom of an offence, and

    (c)   who –

        (i)   has been sentenced to a period of imprisonment of at least 12 months,

        (ii)   has been convicted of an offence that has caused serious harm, or

        (iii)   is a persistent offender."

[68] Paragraphs 398–399A of the Rules will also be familiar to the reader and do not, for the purposes of this appeal, require setting out. Paragraph 399D is of greater relevance and it provides as follows:

"399D. Where a foreign criminal has been deported and enters the United Kingdom in breach of a deportation order enforcement of the deportation order is in the public interest and will be implemented unless there are very exceptional circumstances."

The substantive issue: discussion

[69] In his skeleton argument prepared for the hearing on 5 November 2020, Mr Jarvis made the following essential submissions:

    (a)   When a Tribunal is considering an appeal based on Article 8 ECHR in a deportation context, it should first apply section 117C of the 2002 Act, this being consistent with the "normal approach" that primary legislation is the starting point and in line with what is said in *CI (Nigeria)* [2019] EWCA Civ 2027;

    (b)   There is no difference in approach whether a tribunal is considering a pre-deportation scenario (i.e. where the individual has not yet been removed from the United Kingdom) or a refusal on the respondent's part to revoke a deportation order, whether the individual is abroad or they have re-entered this country in breach of an order;

    (c)   In *SU* [2017] EWCA Civ 1069, the Court of Appeal did not address the question of the interaction between the 2002 Act and the Rules;

    (d)   That the test of undue harshness under section 117C(5) of the 2002 Act bore the meaning attributed to it by the Supreme Court in *KO (Nigeria)* [2018] UKSC 53; [2018] 1 WLR 5273;

(e) That once the judge in the present case had reached her conclusions under section 117C(5), she should not then have gone on to consider paragraph 399D of the Rules;

(f) As the findings on the unduly harsh issue had been open to the judge, her decision should be set aside and the decision be re-made in the appellant's favour.

[70] Unsurprisingly, in his first skeleton argument Mr Malik endorsed the respondent's analysis.

[71] At the remote hearing on 5 November 2020, we raised a concern as to the respondent's concessions, as set out in (b) and (e), above. It was not immediately apparent to us why paragraph 399D of the Rules added nothing to the equation. On one possible reading of section 117C(7), it might be said that the mandatory considerations set out in subsections (1) to (6) did not cover all of the ground in a case concerning an individual who re-entered the United Kingdom in breach of a deportation order and that they might legitimately face an even stronger public interest counterweight to their Article 8 claim than would be the case in a pre-deportation or post-deportation scenario. In turn, where it was not simply the fact of previous convictions which underpinned the decision under appeal, the elevated threshold under paragraph 399D of the Rules may play a part, with the effect that the satisfaction of either of the exceptions under section 117C(4) and (5), or indeed the wider exercise under (6), might not in fact be determinative of an appeal.

[72] As this particular angle on the substantive issue had not been considered by the parties, an adjournment was granted in order for further submissions to be provided. This was done through additional skeleton arguments from Mr Jarvis and Mr Malik, together with their concise oral submissions at the resumed hearing.

[73] On behalf of the respondent, Mr Jarvis maintained the concession previously made and provided the following refined submissions:

(a) One of the purposes of section 117C(7) of the 2002 Act is to ensure that the mandatory considerations set out in subsections (1) to (6) are applied by tribunals only in so far as the decision under appeal is predicated upon a conviction or convictions and not other factors such as offending which did not lead to a conviction;

(b) The provision also has the effect of ensuring that all convictions may in principle be relevant to an assessment under section 117C;

(c) That "a decision to deport a foreign criminal" in section 117C(7) should be read together with the phrase "cases concerning the deportation of foreign criminals" in section 117A(2)(b): both should be construed as covering all aspects of the respondent's efforts to carry out and maintain deportation action, whether that involves deporting an individual in the first instance, preventing them from re-entering in breach of deportation order, or seeking to deport those who have managed to re-enter;

(d)   In the case of an individual who is able to rely on either of the two exceptions under section 117C(4) and (5) and in fact satisfies one or both thereof, the effect of section 117C(3) is that the public interest does not require deportation and the appeal would fall to be allowed;

(e)   The Rules play no part in the assessment of undue harshness under section 117C(5) and are only of relevance where a tribunal is considering section 117C(6) in so far as they provide "further insight into the character of the public interest". Even then, it is the very compelling circumstances test which must be applied rather than the very exceptional circumstances threshold under paragraph 399D of the Rules.

[74] Mr Malik again agreed with Mr Jarvis' position. Relying on *CI (Nigeria)*, he submitted that the provisions of Part 5A of the 2002 Act established a structured approach which would produce in all cases a final result compatible with Article 8. This approach, it is said, applies to all foreign criminals, including those who re-enter the United Kingdom in breach of a deportation order. He then posited two solutions to the question posed by the substantive issue:

(a)   For the purpose of paragraph 399D of the Rules, "very exceptional circumstances" will exist in a case where either of the two exceptions in section 117C(5) and (6) of the 2002 Act applies; or

(b)   Where either of the two exceptions in section 117C(5) and (6) of the 2002 Act apply, the appeal will succeed even if there are no "very exceptional circumstances" for the purposes of paragraph 399D of the Rules.

[75] Strictly speaking, the two exceptions arise under subsections (4) and (5), not (6), although the point being made by Mr Malik is clear enough: an ability to satisfy any of the criteria in these subsections will be determinative of an appeal without needing to have recourse to the provisions of the Rules.

[76] In our judgement, the collective position of the parties on the substantive issue in this appeal is essentially correct and our initial concern (set out in paragraph 71, above) falls away. Our reasons for reaching this conclusion are as follows.

[77] By virtue of section 117A(1) of the 2002 Act a tribunal is bound to apply the provisions of primary legislation, as set out in sections 117B and 117C, when determining an appeal concerning Article 8. In cases concerning the deportation of a foreign criminal (as defined), it is clear from section 117A(2)(b) of the 2002 Act that the core legislative provisions are those set out in section 117C. It is now well-established that these provisions provide a structured approach to the application of Article 8 which will produce in all cases a final result compatible with protected rights (see for example *NE-A (Nigeria)* [2017] EWCA Civ 239, at paragraph 14, and *CI (Nigeria)*, at paragraph 20).

[78] By contrast, the relevant Rules are not legislation, but a statement of the practice to be followed by the respondent's officials when assessing a claim by an individual seeking to resist deportation and a reflection of her view as to where the public interest lies. On this basis, Leggatt LJ (as he then was) concluded at paragraph 21 of *CI (Nigeria)* that:

"In these circumstances it seems to me that it is generally unnecessary for a tribunal or court in a case in which a decision to deport a 'foreign criminal' is challenged on Article 8 grounds to refer to paragraphs 398–399A of the Immigration Rules, as they have no additional part to play in the analysis."

[79] We respectfully agree. It is the structured approach set out in section 117C of the 2002 Act which governs the task to be undertaken by a tribunal, not the provisions of the Rules.

[80] We recognise that the Court in *CI (Nigeria)* was not concerned with an individual who had re-entered the United Kingdom in breach of a deportation order and thus paragraph 399D of the Rules did not arise. This factual difference with the present case does not, however, undermine our view as to the general correctness of the respondent's considered position, as put forward by Mr Jarvis.

[81] In the context of construing and applying Part 5A of the 2002 Act we see no reason in principle as to why the re-entry scenario should not be considered as much a part of what was described in *Williams (scope of "liable to deportation")* [2018] UKUT 00116 (IAC) as the "deportation regime" as removal action and exclusion from this country during the currency of a deportation order, and that the phrases "cases concerning the deportation of foreign criminals" in section 117A(2) and "a decision to deport a foreign criminal" in section 117C(7) should be interpreted accordingly. The fact that an individual has endeavoured to circumvent the banishment consequent to being deported does not thereby take them outside of the schematic framework in place to give effect to the public interest.

[82] We find support for our view in the case-law. In *Williams*, the Upper Tribunal was dealing with an individual who had been deported and was seeking to have a deportation order revoked whilst still outside of the United Kingdom. It concluded that section 117C applied to those against whom there was an extant deportation order, whether or not they had yet to be deported (see paragraph 27 and 28). The Tribunal considered itself to be bound by the Court of Appeal's judgment in *IT (Jamaica)* [2016] EWCA Civ 932 (although it stated that the same conclusion would have been reached in the absence of such authority).

[83] Paragraph 52 of *IT (Jamaica)* is instructive for present purposes:

"The function of section 117C is to set out the weight to be given to the public interest to be taken into account in the proportionality exercise to be carried out under Article 8 of the Convention in the case of a foreign criminal. Section 117C(1) states that the deportation of foreign criminals is in the public interest. In this context, and indeed in the other uses of the word 'deportation' in this section, the word 'deportation' is being used to convey not just the act of removing someone from the jurisdiction but also the maintaining of the banishment for a given period of time: if this were not so, section 117C(1) would achieve little."

[84] We of course acknowledge that the specific conclusions stated at paragraphs 55 and 64 of *IT (Jamaica)* (which effectively equated the undue harshness test with that of very compelling reasons) were subsequently disapproved by the Supreme Court in *KO (Nigeria)*. However, the point made in the passage quoted above was not the subject of criticism and it holds good.

[85] In *SU*, the Court of Appeal was faced with a factual scenario similar to that with which we are concerned. The novelty of this was stated at the outset of the judgment of David Richards LJ (with whom the Chancellor of the High Court and Asplin J (as she then was) agreed):

> "2. We were told that this is the first occasion on which this court has been concerned with the correct approach to the revocation of a deportation order where it has been implemented but the deportee has, in breach of the deportation order, returned to the UK and has established a private and family life during the following period of unlawful presence here."

[86] The Court acknowledged that the provisions of Part 5A of the 2002 Act had applied to the appellant's appeal before the First-tier Tribunal. However, the focus of attention rested squarely with the Rules relating to deportation and in particular whether there was a material difference between the very compelling circumstances test under paragraph 398 and that of very exceptional circumstances under paragraph 399D. In rejecting the appellant's argument and concluding that there was, Stephen Richards LJ concluded at paragraph 45 that:

> "45. I am unable to accept this submission. The difference in the language of paragraphs 398 and 399D, suggesting a more stringent requirement under paragraph 399D, reflects a real difference in the circumstances covered by each paragraph. Paragraph 398 addresses the question whether a deportation order should be made, or an existing order maintained, against a person who has yet to be deported, whereas paragraph 399D addresses the very different case of a person who has been deported and then re-enters illegally and in breach of the order. In the latter case, any Article 8 claim that was raised by the deportee before his original deportation will, *ex hypothesi*, have been decided against him. It is readily understandable that in the cases covered by paragraph 399D the Secretary of State should have formed the view that there is a particularly strong public interest in maintaining the integrity of the deportation system as it applies to foreign criminals."

[87] For whatever reason, no consideration was given to the application of the structured approach under Part 5A of the 2002 Act and, in particular, the import of section 117C and its relationship with the Rules. As such, we do not regard *SU* as constituting binding authority to the effect that paragraph 399D of the Rules imports an additional threshold to be met over and above what is contained in section 117C.

[88] Nor are we persuaded that the reasoning in *SU* should otherwise lead us to depart from the view set out at paragraph 81, above, namely that section 117C applies equally to all three aspects of the deportation regime: pre-removal; exclusion from the United Kingdom once an individual has been removed; and efforts to remove an individual who has re-entered this country in breach of a deportation order.

[89] That the respondent herself has expressly accepted that we should not do so is clearly significant. So too is the fact of what has not been provided for in section 117C. If Parliament had intended to impose a higher threshold in respect of those individuals re-entering United Kingdom in breach of a deportation order, it could have said so in express terms. For example, that class of persons could have been treated as though they had received a sentence of four years or more, and were thus precluded from relying on either of the two exceptions under section 117C(4) and (5) and that in addition they would have to show very exceptional circumstances in order to succeed on appeal rather than the very compelling circumstances stated in section 117C(6). Finally, there is the plain wording of section 117C itself. We look to subsections (3) and (6), which provide:

"(3) In the case of a foreign criminal ("C") who has not been sentenced to a period of imprisonment of four years or more, the public interest requires C's deportation unless Exception 1 or Exception 2 applies.

…

(6) In the case of a foreign criminal who has been sentenced to a period of imprisonment of at least four years, the public interest requires deportation unless there are very compelling circumstances, over and above those described in Exceptions 1 and 2."

[italics added]

[90] The effect of the use of the term "unless" is inescapable: if the medium offender can satisfy either of the two exceptions, or if they cannot or are precluded from doing so due to the length of a custodial sentence, but yet can show that very compelling circumstances exist, the public interest will *not* require their deportation and the appeal will be allowed. Nothing in the Rules can be treated as modifying the statutory criteria and outcomes provided for.

[91] It follows from the foregoing that the structured approach to be undertaken by a tribunal considering an Article 8 appeal in the context of deportation begins and ends with Part 5A of the 2002 Act. Paragraph 399D of the Rules has no part to play in the application of section 117C(5), or for that matter section 117C(4) (although we find it hard, if not impossible, to conceive of a situation in which an individual who had re-entered the United Kingdom in breach of a deportation order would be able to rely on the private life exception). Nor can paragraph 399D constitute a relevant factor when a tribunal is considering section 117C(6) and we reject this particular aspect of Mr Jarvis' submissions to the contrary. If, as we have concluded it does, the "deportation regime" established under Part 5A applies equally to those individuals within the three categories identified in paragraph 89, above, it must follow that the criterion under subsection (6) should be applied consistently as between each. The significance attached by the respondent to a re-entry in breach of a deportation order, as represented by paragraph 399D, is in the first instance a matter for her officials to assess when making decisions on human rights claims.

[92] It will be recalled that Mr Malik proposed two possible means by which paragraph 399D could be incorporated into our conclusions: the very exceptional circumstances threshold will be met where an individual can satisfy the criteria in section 117C(5) or section 117C(6); alternatively, that where the statutory criteria have been met, the appeal must succeed even if no very exceptional circumstances exist. In light of what we have said, it is unnecessary to come down in favour of one or the other. The provisions of section 117C speak for themselves and do not need to be reconciled with paragraph 399D of the Rules. For the sake of

completeness, either proposition offered by Mr Malik will suffice and a judge will not have materially erred in law by stating a preference if she/he is minded to do so.

[93] We turn to the other two submissions made by Mr Jarvis as to the interpretation of section 117C(7) of the 2002 Act, both of which we agree with. In support of his position that the provision in principle permits a tribunal to take account of all convictions acquired by a foreign criminal, *Rexha (S.117C – earlier offences)* [2016] UKUT 335 (IAC) is cited. At paragraph 15, the Upper Tribunal concluded as follows:

> "15. We see no reason for construing Section 117C(7) as limiting the considerations relevant to sub-Sections (1) to (6) to solely the most recent offence or offences for which the person has been convicted. Firstly, that is not what the Section expressly says. It does not say in Section 117C(7) that only the offence or offences immediately prior to the deportation decision are the be taken into account. Secondly, the use of the phrase 'only to the extent that the reason for the decision was the offence or offences for which the criminal has been convicted" expressly requires an examination of the decision to identify which parts of the criminal's antecedent history provide the basis for the decision. It will be a matter for the respondent to decide in each case which parts of a candidate for deportation's criminal past is to be relied upon in support of the making of a deportation order. It may well be that in the vast majority of cases the criminal offending will provide the reason for the decision. Equally, there may be cases where some of the person's criminal past could not properly be relied upon. This could occur, for instance, because of their youth at the time of the offending or because of the passage of a significant period of time, or because the offending was rooted in beliefs or circumstances now quite irrelevant to the justification for a deportation order being made. Thus, in our view what is required is careful scrutiny pursuant to Section 117C(7) of those offences which are on the person's criminal record which have provided a reason for the decision to deport. All of those convictions are then relevant to undertaking the exercise required by Section 117C(1) to (6)."

[94] Whilst this passage does indeed confirm that the totality of an individual's criminal history can be relevant, it also highlights the important caveat imposed by section 117C(7) to the effect that the mandatory considerations under subsections (1) to (6) are only to be applied to the conviction(s) actually relied on in the decision.

[95] The reasoning in *Rexha* was approved by the Court of Appeal in *OH (Algeria)* [2019] EWCA Civ 1763, implicitly at paragraph 46 and expressly at paragraph 48.

[96] Mr Jarvis' final point is that the wording of section 117C(7) requires a nexus between the taking into account of the mandatory considerations in subsections (1) to (6) and the existence of a conviction or convictions relied on in the decision under appeal. In other words, the mandatory considerations are not to be taken into account in respect of any aspect of a decision which is not based on a conviction or convictions. By way of example, the considerations will not apply to that part of a decision based on information from the police relating to associations and suspected criminality, but in respect of which there have been no

convictions. This is consistent with what is said in *Rexha* and *OH (Algeria)* and we agree with Mr Jarvis' position.

Summary of conclusions

[97] Our central conclusions on the substantive issue in this appeal can be summarised as follows:

(a)   By virtue of section 117A(1) of the 2002 Act, a tribunal is bound to apply the provisions of primary legislation, as set out in sections 117B and 117C, when determining an appeal concerning Article 8.

(b)   In cases concerning the deportation of foreign criminals (as defined), it is clear from section 117A(2)(b) of the 2002 Act that the core legislative provisions are those set out in section 117C. It is now well-established that these provisions provide a structured approach to the application of Article 8 which will produce in all cases a final result compatible with protected rights.

(c)   It is the structured approach set out in section 117C of the 2002 Act which governs the task to be undertaken by the tribunal, not the provisions of the Rules.

(d)   A foreign criminal who has re-entered the United Kingdom in breach of an extant deportation order is subject to the same deportation regime as those who have yet to be removed or who have been removed and are seeking a revocation of a deportation order from abroad. The phrases "cases concerning the deportation of foreign criminals" in section 117A(2) and "a decision to deport a foreign criminal" in section 117C(7) are to be interpreted accordingly.

(e)   Paragraph 399D of the Rules has no relevance to the application of the statutory criteria set out in section 117C(4), (5) and (6);

(f)   It follows that the structured approach to be undertaken by a tribunal considering an Article 8 appeal in the context of deportation begins and ends with Part 5A of the 2002 Act.

Decision on error of law

[98] In light of the respondent's concession on the substantive issue, with which, for the reasons set out above, we agree, the judge erred in law by treating the satisfaction of Exception 2 under section 117C(5) of the 2002 Act as constituting simply one factor to be considered in light of paragraph 399D of the Rules, and, as a consequence, failing to treat the satisfaction of the exception as being determinative of the appellant's appeal.

[99] On this basis, we set the judge's decision aside. It is unnecessary to address the remaining grounds of appeal.

Re-making the decision

[100] The re-making of the decision in this appeal can be stated briefly. It is now accepted by the respondent that the judge was entitled to find that it would be unduly harsh for the family unit to relocate to Kosovo and for the children to be separated from the appellant. The appellant satisfies Exception 2 under section 117C(5) of the 2002 Act and, given our conclusions on the substantive issue, this is determinative of the appeal and entitles the appellant to succeed on Article 8 grounds.

Anonymity

[101] The First-tier Tribunal made an anonymity direction in this case, although no reasons for doing so were provided.

[102] We had reservations as to whether the anonymity direction should be maintained and gave the parties an opportunity to provide written submissions on this issue. In light of their responses and for the reasons set out below, we have concluded that it is not appropriate to maintain the anonymity direction.

[103] First, a concern raised by the appellant was that details of the mental health difficulties suffered by both he and his wife, together with information relating to the latter's past experiences, might be set out in our decision. As is apparent, no such disclosure has occurred.

[104] Second, this case does not fall within any of the categories requiring anonymity (see Upper Tribunal Immigration and Asylum Chamber Guidance Note 2013 No.1).

[105] Third, no protection-based issues arise.

[106] Fourth, the general principle that open justice is a fundamental tenet of our legal system is not displaced by any other features in this case. Indeed, as rightly pointed out by the respondent, there is a significant public interest in disclosing the appellant's identity in light of his offending history and re-entry to this country in breach of a deportation order.

Notice of decision

[107] **The making of the decision of the First-tier Tribunal involved the making of an error on a point of law.**

[108] **We set aside the decision of the First-tier Tribunal.**

[109] **We re-make the decision by allowing the appeal on Article 8 ECHR grounds.**